HOMER · THE BIBLE · AESCHYLUS · DANTE · SOPHOCLES · EURIPIDES · RABELAIS · CERVANTES · MILTON · GOETHE · SHAKESPEARE · MONTAIGNE · NIETZSCHE · WORDSWORTH · ARNOLD · WHITMAN · DOSTOIEVSKY · MELVILLE · POE

ENJOYMENT
OF LITERATURE

John Cowper Powys

SIMON AND SCHUSTER
New York · 1938

Manufactured in the United States of America

Affectionately dedicated
to

MAX SCHUSTER AND RICHARD SIMON

Table of Contents

Illustrations

Introduction

MAGICIANS have never been able to control their angels or their demons until they discovered their names. The origin of all literature lies here. A word is a magic incantation by which the self exercises power—first over itself and then over other selves and then, for all we know, over the powers of nature.

After commanding and creating life, the next thing that words have to do is to criticize it. Many attempts have been made to codify, to catalogue, to differentiate the various forms taken by the vast mass of literature now accessible through our recent progress in printing and publication. We hear of the literature of knowledge and the literature of power; we hear of the literature of interpretation and the literature of escape; but when the whole thing is reduced to its essence it is hard to see how Matthew Arnold's dictum that good literature of any kind must be a criticism of life can be improved on.

In a very definite sense even a book like Grimm's *Fairy Tales* is such a criticism, playing upon the fantastic mysteries of luck; while on the other horizon you get Hegel's *Logic*, playing upon the fantastic mysteries of reason. Not the airiest lyric, not the most humorous comedy, not the most thrilling tale of adventure, but on its own particular level and in its own peculiar vein, offers some commentary, creates some mood, stirs up some speculation, emphasizes some significant fact, or theory, or feeling, which in its special connection, and in its own tone, accent, and measure, criticizes our life upon earth.

And, when you come down to bed-rock in the matter, how impossible it is to separate in its entirety one kind of writing from another!

All literature is "literature of power." All literature is "literature of knowledge." All literature is "literature of escape." A single remark of Spinoza's, for instance, is power, knowledge, and escape, in one sentence!

A human ego, confronted by the shifting facts, the ambiguous laws, the evasive feelings of the experience of being alive, collects data, invents theories, utters oracles, yields to inspiration, exposes illusions, creates myths, tells a story, suggests a reform, agitates for revolution, advocates reaction, confesses its weaknesses, exhibits its peculiarities, boasts of its insight, weeps over its ignorance, pours forth its learning, declares its loves, its hates, its admirations, its hopes, its despairs, suggests, asserts, denies, discriminates; and, through it all, cries out to its fellows, "Consider these facts of mine! Have regard to this theory of mine! Let me dominate you with my magic, let me liberate you with my imagination, let me seduce you with my subtle impressions, let me take you out of your dull self with my whimsies, my fancies, my humours!"

The expression "belles lettres" seems to me quite as fatuous as the expression "art for art's sake." There is much more "art" in some of the seductive systems of philosophy than in all the *Arabian Nights*, and much more "belles lettres" between the black covers of any Bible than in the daintiest bindings of the bibliophiles.

But one thing is certain. Though books, as Milton says, may be the embalming of mighty spirits, they are also the resurrection of rebellious, reactionary, fantastical, and wicked spirits! In books dwell all the demons and all the angels of the human mind. It is for this reason that a bookshop—especially a second-hand bookshop—is an arsenal of explosives, an armoury of revolutions, an opium den of reactions.

And just because books are the repository of all the redemptions and damnations, all the sanities and insanities, of the divine anarchy of the soul, they are still, as they have always been, an object of suspicion to every kind of ruling authority.

In a second-hand bookshop are the horns of the altar where all the outlawed thoughts of humanity can take refuge! Here, like desperate bandits, hide all the reckless progeny of our wild, dark, self-lacerating hearts. A bookshop is a powder-magazine, a dynamite-shed, a drug-store of poisons, a bar of intoxicants, a den of opiates, an island of sirens.

Of all the "houses of ill fame" which a tyrant, a bureaucrat, a propagandist, a moralist, a champion of law and order, an advocate of keeping people ignorant for their own good, hurries past with averted eyes or threatens with his minions, a bookshop is the most flagrant.

Plato, that poetical enemy of poets, would certainly recommend his philosopher-kings to abolish second-hand bookshops. A second-hand bookshop can blow sky-high the machinations of centuries of first-hand politicians. It sets the prophet against the priest, the prisoner against society, the has-nothing against the has-all, the individual against the universe! It is as heavily charged with the sweet mischiefs of sex as the privy-walls of a railway station, or the imagination of St. Anthony.

Here are the poisons to kill, the drugs to soothe, the fire-water to madden, the ichor to inflame, the nectar to imparadise! The infinite pathos of all the generations lies here, their beatings against the wall, their desperate escapes, their triumphant reconciliations. In the Beginning

was the Word; and the Word was with God—and the
Devil stole the Word out of the cradle. The everlasting
contrariety, whereby creation is stirred into movement,
seethes and ferments in books, in *all* books; and from
the cold glaciers of books plunge down the death-avalanches
of ultimate negation that whirl us into the gulf.

It is true that in certain moods we turn away in weariness
and disgust—even as Solomon did—from all the books
under the sun, finding in them nothing but vanity and
vexation of spirit. When we are in a mood like this the
weight of so much printed matter, piled up ceiling-high in a
second-hand shop, strikes us as Odysseus was struck by the
hollow gibbering of the thin wraiths in Hades as something
almost unbearable, as something from which it is a comfort
to escape.

And so we escape from it into the architectural spaces
of the public library of our town, where matriarchy prevails,
and where the mad reasonings of the sons of men are kept in
complete control by the aid of catalogues and dusters.

But after all one has only to think of those old, great,
heroic bookworms of the early times, with their voracious,
insatiable maw for everything written, only to think of
Rabelais for instance, who certainly would have been
caught invading those forbidden shelves, to be led back
to our second-hand bookshop.

But alas! all is not as it should be even here, for the
most amiable of shopmen is often inclined to look askance
at a "browser" who with no more than a "dime" in his
pocket is for ransacking all the spoils of Byzantium. For
the truth must out. In the world of books, as in the world
of other precious and lovely delights, poverty is a bitter
handicap. Not only does it take from us the leisure, and
often the heart to read, but it takes from us—unless we
have incredible tenacity of purpose—the power of accumu-
lating more than a shelf or two of our favourite books.

And it can never be quite the same to read a great author in a library book, as in one bought and paid for out of our own pocket. Fiction I think *is* a little different in this respect. Most book-lovers, I fancy, wouldn't object to reading *The Possessed*, or *Cousin Bette*, or *War and Peace*, or *Jude the Obscure* in a library edition; but to read *Urn Burial* or *Thus Spake Zarathustra*, or *Leaves of Grass*, or the *Oxford Book of Ballads*, or Rabelais himself, in a book with a public stamp on it, would give them the feeling that they were entertaining the Muse at a social tea, rather than laying the lovely immortal, as Burns would put it, between them "and the wa'."

What I would like to do in these pages is just this very thing. I would like to play pander between many sensitive and erotic souls and these immortal, invisible, and evasive odalisques.

And what I want to concentrate upon in this work—and here and now I kiss upon both cheeks whoever it may be that picks up *this* book from one of those pavement counters to which all literary flesh must come—is not so much the general objective value of any particular volume as being of supreme influence in the making of human history or of capital importance in the technique of human art, as the emotional, realistic, and entirely personal effect it may have upon our individual nerves, upon our secret pleasures and pains, upon our furtive psychological reactions, upon our physical sensitivities, upon the hidden vices in us, as well as upon our attitude to those "fallings from us, vanishings, blank misgivings of a creature, moving about in worlds not realized," which startle us all at certain moments of our lives.

A book about books must obviously be addressed to people who love reading; and the question naturally crosses one's mind as to how big a percentage among us can be called lovers of reading. Would *one*, in every family, be too large a guess?

Well! granting *one to a family* to be a fair though a rough average, what I want to hold before my mind as I write this book is an average day in such a book-lover's life; so that it may be possible to indicate what particular favourite books of mine will probably be *his* favourites too, and how our imagination, our endurance, our insight, our pity, our genius for escape, can thereby be artfully increased, while our miseries are in some measure abated. I would like to prove myself such a master abstracter of the quintessential relationships between books and reality that these same isolated persons may see that I know what the crises in life are likely to be, when we cry to the spirit of Dostoievsky or Dante or Homer or Shakespeare or Walt Whitman for spiritual insight and planetary cunning! I would like to summon up the particular kinds of psychological and emotional experiences—some gross, some spiritual, some touched by love, some touched by hate, some life-destroying, some life-giving, but all of a symbolic character, to which the reading of certain great books can suggest a clue, and over which they can give us a certain measure of imaginative control.

What I would like to do would be to bring these books, however ancient and primitive, into direct touch with the most realistic shocks of life and all its worst levels of monotony.

I would like—as in the mingling of chemicals in a laboratory—to note what would happen were the spirit of Gogol brought into contact with one kind of crisis, of Goethe with another, of Rabelais with another, of Homer with another, and then of Proust, let us say, and with yet another!

Of course the essence of my own experiences must inevitably saturate a book like this. Only so can it get pungency and poignancy. But by using my imagination I can well visualize how this same average book-lover—one from every family—could get grist for his mill out of the *Odyssey*, out of the "Inferno," out of the *Mabinogion*, just as well as out of Hardy, or Theodore Dreiser, or Thomas Mann.

If such a thing were possible I would like to suggest the most stimulating and sustaining mental food for each epoch, in natural succession, of all the normal "seven ages" of man; but neither shall I feel quite satisfied if I do not dig a little deeper than I have ever done before into the life-springs of my own favourite writers. Our sophisticated epicures of literary flavours are for ever comparing one nuance of taste with another, testing them with their aesthetic proboscis-tongues like humming-bird moths.

This method has its place, but it is not mine. I cannot rest till I have connected the most intimate peculiarities of a writer's style with the very centre of his soul's circumference and the widest parabola of its circling flight.

I doubt whether many readers among us realize how the profoundest motions of our minds are affected by particular words and by words in particular combinations. We all make secret mental gestures whose value is mysteriously enhanced when we give them names and think of them in connection with the long history of man's endurance of life.

And this, I think, is the reason why the *logoi* of those primitive *soothsayers* who were half-poets and half-prophets, are psychologically more valuable to us than the elaborate systems of technical philosophy that seek to round off what refuses to be rounded off, and to eliminate contradiction and paradox from what seems made up of these "knots of contrariety."

Books are more than a second nature. They are an under-nature and an over-nature. They are nature in her appalling universality, strained through the divine-diabolic sieves of every type of human imagination.

Books are the ideas of things before things begin. Books create worlds and destroy worlds. Books are the mirrors of light and the mirrors of darkness in which the universe sees its own face.

People who say, "I can get on without books; I live by experience; my ideas are my own," are themselves no more than very simple and very well-worn books, letting the wind turn their pages; pages that have been turned millions of times before!

The conceit of the most drugged and dazed of doddering bookworms is nearer the Eternal Spirit that builds the world than the mock-modesty of these book-despisers.

Neither the one nor the other can escape the impact of the visible world. Who of the children of men *can* escape it? But the book-lovers possess two worlds. They are the bilinguists of human destiny. They have to live; but they deal, pedantically enough very often but still they deal, with the ideas *from* which and *towards* which all life moves. Of course literature is art; but it is much more than art! That is where it is greater than music or painting or sculpture. Dancing alone precedes it. But dancing, with its accompanying gestures, is a kind of literature. As De Casseres well says, the essence of all writing, even the transcription of the gravest knowledge, is "exhibitionism."

One writer exhibits himself in statistics, another in mathematics, another in politics, another in ethics, another in some curious history of courtesans. The primal art-urge lies behind the baldest scientific statement, as it lies behind Homer and Shakespeare.

We catch the ear of another and hold it, by some trick, by some device, by some measure of charm, of clarity, of plausibility, of emphasis, of personal persuasion, whether what we want to convey to this other is our vision of a tiny segment of reality, or our vision of what the whole of reality *ought* to be.

In the beginning was dancing; and dancing implied everything: then came speech, then came song, and then the story. The magic dance included incantation and invocation. It was the cosmic goat-song to life-death and to death-life; and the nearer literature approaches to the dance, the more hypnotic is its effect.

All literature reeks of magic. Religion came soon after, and all literature smells of incense. The positive must appear before the negative. The oracle must be uttered before it can be gainsaid. Literature must taste first of holy smoke: afterwards it may smell as pungently as you please of all your unholy disinfectants!

What a history of human excesses a second-hand book-shop is! As you "browse" there—personally I can't abide that word, for to my mind book-lovers are more like hawks and vultures than sheep, but of course if its use encourages poor devils to glance through books that they have no hope of buying, long may the word remain!—you seem to grow aware what a miracle it was when second-hand bookshops were first invented. Women prefer libraries, free or otherwise, but it too often happens that the books an ordinary man wants are on the "forbidden shelves." But there is no censorship in a second-hand bookshop. Every good bookseller is a multiple personality, containing all the extremes of human feeling. He is an ascetic hermit, he is an erotic immoralist, he is a papist, he is a Quaker, he is a communist, he is an anarchist, he is a savage icono-clast, he is a passionate worshipper of idols.

I believe from any carefully made census of the patrons of second-hand bookshops, and especially of those boxes on the pavement outside, it would be proved that by far the majority of visitors to these places are men, and not only men but poor men.

Women who are not rich, and a great many who are and who ought to go to the bookshops instead, make wonderful use of libraries! Nothing they bring home is more precious to them than these well-worn "containers" of life, and of the opium to forget life.

And yet you hear certain conceited virtuosos of literature sneering and scoffing, and making no bones about holding dirt-cheap the favourite story-tellers of women. God bless my soul! When do we find these contemptuous gentlemen lost to the world in the reading of Homer in his Greek or even of the bawdy Petronius in his Latin?

Not at all! We find them amusing themselves with bagatelles compared with which . . .

But turning from bibliophiles to "browsers," you have only to watch the faces of the men who hover round those pavement counters of books to catch a strange light upon the psychology of readers. Heads of priests, heads of prophets, heads of every kind of mystic, heads of every type of human eccentricity, perversity, fantasy, reaction, and revolt, are gathered there; and yet this is only one side of the shield! In how many hidden chambers all over the world, in how many railway carriages, subways, buses, cabins at sea, huts in the desert, hospital wards, prisons, madhouses, pot-houses, cloisters, brothels, would be found, if some Martian sociologist turned a super-X-ray upon this troubled earth, human faces looking up, dazed, bemused, entranced, imparadised, from the Lethean comfort of the devil knows what queer fragment of print!

It seems as if there must be darkness and light, evil and good, in any great human work; yes, and clarity and obscurity, too. Sometimes I am tempted to think that a supreme work of fiction cannot exist without an element of appalling obscenity. Even the most idealistic of great books often dips deep down into the mud, deep down into that abysmal silt at the bottom of the ocean without which reality would not be reality.

The oversweetness of pious optimism comes at last to smack of death, till the bitter antidote of desperate pessimism galvanizes it back into life.

The "yea" of the white magician cloys the palate, till the "nay" of the black magician bites that sweet tongue. Nevertheless, for all their tragedy and for all their terrible reality, there rises from these books, a mood, an atmosphere, an aftertaste—but this is a mystery not lightly to be spoken of—that reveals something impossible to be put into words, something too tenuous to be called hope, and yet something utterly different from despair.

The great books are the books that create a world, a world to which, with its atmosphere, its situations, its characters, you can compare the haphazard chances and casual impressions of real life as they cross your path.

Such is the world of Dostoievsky, of Balzac, of Henry James, of Dickens, of Proust, of Theodore Dreiser. Life, as Goethe says, is always fumbling towards the very thing that the great artists create.

The highest honour you can do to a fragment of reality is to call it Biblical, or Homeric, or Dantesque, or Shakespearean, or Dickensian, or Rabelaisian. The toughminded or hard-boiled individual who despises books, but enjoys what he calls "life," carries his experience on the horn of a rhinoceros, on the hump of a camel, between the teeth of a shark! The "something that infects the world" doesn't trouble him, the "something far more deeply interfused" doesn't touch him. He is a slave of the transitory. The recurrent symbols of the permanent in nature and human nature, of which books are the everlasting mirrors, are to a man like this of less importance than the "ads" in his newspaper.

A person can be "successful" without books, he can grow rich without books, he can tyrannize over his fellows without books, but he cannot "see God," he cannot live in a present that is charged with the past and pregnant of the future without a knowledge of the diary of our race.

A man may tell you he can think for himself, and thus has no need for books; but you have not to be long in his company without discovering that these native reactions, these original thoughts, this mother wit of which he is so proud, are nothing but the tags and commonplaces of old folk-shrewdness dropped from ancient books into the crowded market-places of long ago.

The gathered wisdom of the old times was handed down in custom, in tradition, in ritual, in the sayings and proverbs and oracles of a still remoter past, but all this was, as it were, a mass of books, only of unwritten books; so that *even then* the originator, the prophet, the magician drew his inspiration from what had gone before— All progress in ideas is spiral, for ever returning upon itself.

Every revolution is a reaction, every leap forward a renaissance, every new thought a returning to a spring that has been choked up. Second-hand bookshops are the oases where these old fountains of living water can still flow. Each age has its originators; but the prophets of each age petrify into the priests of the next, and the creators of each age wither into the scholars of the next.

It is all in books; only it is necessary to scrape away the rubble of scholarship and release the living stream that has flowed down the ages since the beginning.

The greatest miracle of evolution is man's moral sense, his pity, his justice, his gentleness—but these are the very things that we touch in rumours and legends of a remote paradisic past.

The millennium is a reversion to the golden age. The kingdom of Christ is a renewal of the reign of Saturn. And in books alone is this occult continuity between our lost Eden and our New Jerusalem kept unbroken through the generations.

No one thoroughly enjoys what does not satisfy his spirit, what does not release his imagination, what does not heighten his life. There is a time for drunkenness in this region, a time for drugs, and a time for the unspeakable relief of opium.

But for a more lasting pleasure, for a pleasure that can mitigate our labours and transform our monotonies, we need books that support, deepen, and thicken out our profoundest life-illusion.

All the same it is nonsense to think that we can appropriate to our especial purpose *all* great books. Among books, as among people and events, our character is our fate. We can extend the boundaries of ourselves, we can enrich our native roots; but it is waste of time to struggle to enjoy what we are not destined to enjoy!

Thus the choice of books becomes, like the choice of a mate, or of a life-friend, a series of cross-roads of appalling significance. All readers with any consciousness of their mental growth will recall the actual spot, the actual physical surroundings, where they first read the books that have affected them the most.

Youth is obviously the time for bold and drastic experiments. In middle life we find ourselves narrowing our margins, straightening our boundaries, digging in and banking up. The lively advocates of modernity are liable to forget that the essentials of life upon earth remain the same, and our common human nature remains the same, below all the external changes; and they forget too that each of these old works is the culminating creation of many centuries and has survived the sifting and winnowing of many generations, whereas, on the face of it, it is unlikely that our own brief lifetime should witness the emergence of *many* books

of so supreme a value to the human spirit. Justice, tolerance, and pity are, it is true, a little more prevalent than
they were, for in these things lies the only real progress, the
only real path of evolution; but the inspiration of these
things is to be found in the most ancient books equally with
the most modern, for the spirit that works in man drove him
upon this difficult way from the beginning. This is still, and
ever will be, the "oversoul" in all books; for in books, as in
the rising waters of a great tidal wave that mounts higher
and higher as it rolls down the centuries, the burden from
the beginning until this hour has been the same—by
justice, by tolerance, and by pity is the real evolution
known!

Yes, all constituted authorities from the dawn of literature have been suspicious of books, for it is in books that the
unconquerable spirit of man moves forward into new justice
and new tolerance, moves backward into old justice and
old tolerance, breaking up the fatal hypnosis of the prejudices of the day. The tables of the old law, written on stone,
are for ever being broken to make room for the tables of the
new law, written on flesh and blood; but these also in their
turn are erased, as the fire and the water of the spirit work
upon them.

And yet there is no stone fragment, there is no human
hieroglyph without secrets to which the heart of man must
for ever be returning, lest in its struggle towards new points
in the circumference it loses touch with the centre. The
present is not enough; and the present and the future together are not enough. The past also hath its absolute; for
the timeless underlies at every point the flowing of the
mystery of time.

Sometimes in our testy moods we are tempted to draw
back in disgust from the torrent of printed matter that
rushes past us to-day, but this is a morbid feeling.

Our culture must be a poor thing if it undermines our philosophical tolerance and turns our sympathetic understanding into pharisaic contempt. A real book-lover looks with infinite indulgence upon the simplest person's choice of books. He has the wit to know that this flood of second-rate invention upon which so many feed their fancy and by which so many endure the monotony of their lives is something quite different from what it seems to the person who just glances at it as he passes by. He has the wit to know that every page of these second-rate books as it impresses the mind of the living reader is transmuted by the alchemy of the imagination into something beyond the literal meaning of the words. All readers are imaginative readers. They wouldn't be readers at all otherwise. And the sneerers at popular books must remember how it is with children; how children turn the most banal and ridiculous and vulgar words into Eldorados of mysterious delight.

Goethe says that good literature lifts you up to its own level while bad literature develops your faults. This may be true enough as long as you remember that "good" and "bad" are relative terms. Every reader has his own "good" and his own "bad" in the world of books, and if you are more sophisticated than I am, my "good" in literature, that which lifts me up and refines me, may very easily be your "bad" and carry with it loads of fertilizing manure for your most unpleasant faults.

Fanatics of the modern school love to point out that it is use and wont and reverent piety and liturgical repetition that give half their glamour to the old writers; but Croce's admirable doctrine that every creation *needs* its completion by the minds of the generations before it can be really mature, is the answer to this disparagement.

The great passages in Homer and the Bible and Shakespeare and Dante and Rabelais and Cervantes and Goethe and Dostoievsky are actually *greater*—i.e. more full of spiritual and imaginative power to stir us—by reason of the number of human souls who have been moved by them, and whose own experiences have added something to them as they were carried down the stream.

There are as many varieties of book-readers as there are diversities of human character; and in almost all of them *some* doubtful impulses play a part. It is better not to be too nice or meticulous with regard to our motives in reading. Snobbishness of some sort is almost sure to be present; and as in the composing, so in the enjoying of books, the desire to assert ourselves, to feel superior, to gratify our pride, is bound to enter. If there is the snobbishness of forcing ourselves to read "high-brow" books, there is also the snobbishness of being so curiously and exquisitely sophisticated that we prefer "low-brow" books.

It is just as possible for a scholar to read the greatest classics in a frivolous and trifling manner, fussing over unessentials, as it is for an ignorant person to skip everything but the excitement of an engrossing plot. The urge to read is like charity. It covers a multitude of sins.

And all reading—even from the lowest motives—brings us in touch with the vast flowing tide of humanity's *second thoughts* upon its fate under the sun.

That is the whole thing. Below the formless chaos of chance and accident and blind occasion, below the senseless bludgeonings, the meaningless jolts, the brutal shocks, the infinite disgusts, the unspeakable loathings, below the intolerable monotonies and the barren wastelands, flows ever, large and free and deathless, refusing none, welcoming all, the boundless ocean of books!

Here are our human purposes fulfilled, our human efforts grandly, heroically, gloriously defeated. Here, blending, mingling, shifting, rising and sinking, like waves and ripples of one huge sea, all philosophies, all redemptions, all hopes against hope, that our race has ever had roll forward together, bearing *the thoughts of man* into the unknown cosmic future. The poorest, the grossest, the shallowest, the most melodramatic of books carry with them *something*, some tincture, some essence, some suggestion, of the wisdom of the ages that has melted into this vast flood.

Books are man's rational protest against the irrational, man's pitiful protest against the implacable, man's ideal against the world's real, man's word against the cosmic dumbness, man's life against the planetary death, man's revelation of the God within him, man's repartee to the God without him. Whoever touches a book touches not only "a man" but Man. Man is the animal who weeps and laughs—*and writes*. If the first Prometheus brought fire from heaven in a fennel-stalk, the last will take it back—*in a book*.

ENJOYMENT OF
LITERATURE

The Bible as Literature:
The Old Testament

THE APPEARANCE of *The Bible Designed to Be Read As Living Literature*, with Ernest Sutherland Bates as the editor, has been a final proof—considering the huge response this edition has found on both sides of the Atlantic—of the truth of Matthew Arnold's words about the eternal value to humanity of what he called *Hebraism*.

The great critic's declaration that the two fountain-heads of all that is most precious in our Western civilization are the genius of the Hebrews and the genius of the Greeks, was one of those simple sayings that dive to the very bottom of the tossing and wavering ocean of ethnological values.

But it was Matthew Arnold who went on to add the more questionable remark that since three-fourths of human life are conduct, and since the Hebrew Scriptures deal preeminently with conduct, their influence, at any rate on the English-speaking portion of our Western civilization, is three times as important as the influence of the Greeks.

This latter remark of Matthew Arnold's is of course calculated to arouse the most angry controversy; it being exactly the sort of airy generalization that stings our Western temperament as if with the flick of a whip, but the very turmoil it excites in us all—some of us stirred to one reaction, some of us to another—is proof that our British Socrates, whether we agree with him or not, touched the quick of one of the most jumpy of our human nerves.

It appears that few of the Reformed Dutch, or the Lutheran Germans either, went to the lengths of Bible-worship to which our English and American Puritans went; nor can it I think be disputed that of all the Western literatures it is our own that has been most deeply influenced by the Bible.

But not only in "conduct"! For although both our English and our American ancestors *were* affected in that practical sense—and their Bible-inspired "conduct" was by no means always charitable or desirable—an equally powerful influence was exerted over their emotions, over their imagination, over their most secret feelings.

Mr. Bates' *Bible as Literature* has certainly appeared at the right moment in our English-speaking countries; for I am old enough to have seen in the last half-century a tremendous change in the reading of the Hebrew Scriptures. I cannot tell whether the same change has passed over the habits of the less orthodox Hebrews themselves, but certainly when I was a child all my Gentile elders were saturated with Bible-reading; and their imagination as well as their conduct both for good and evil showed Biblical influence at every turn.

But now, after fifty years, it is not so any more. Neither in England nor in America do people read the Bible as they used to do. In fact, I would go further than that and say that apart from educational compulsion, the professional studies of ministers and school-teachers and the devotion of a few religious eccentrics and men of letters, it is unusual for a young modern person to read the Bible at all. Think of the working-men you know; do any of *them* read the Bible? Think of the doctors, lawyers, manufacturers, and gentlemen of leisure you know; do any of *them* read the Bible? When I was a child, from almshouse pensioners to admirals of the fleet, from bargemen and engine-drivers to great merchants of the City, all elderly people read the Bible.

When I was young it was only the most extreme of free-thinkers who dared to express disbelief in this book; whereas to-day some of the most sensitive and spiritual-minded among my friends actually detest it, and do so on moral, aesthetic, and psychological grounds, quite apart from questions of science and philosophy!

The African population of the United States still, I fancy, read the Bible; but the great Middle West, which is the part of the country I know best and the part of the country least affected by European influence, has completely given up the custom; and I confess, though I so obstinately indulge in the habit myself I would take a malicious pleasure in assuring Matthew Arnold that though the great American Middle West no longer reads the Bible, no region in the world, in all the essential human charities, has a more *naturally Christian soul.*

But though the post-war generation may not read the Bible as its ancestors did, none of us can escape its influence. The thing has gone too deep. Humanity cannot saturate itself for centuries with a book like the Old Testament, and throw off the spell in a couple of generations. Writers of our race, on both sides of the water, especially the more pro-phetic ones, have always used the Scriptures to noble account; and now with this new tendency, encouraged by Mr. Bates' excellent version, to treat these books in a new, fresh, and secular manner, it seems likely enough that this underlying influence inherited from our fathers may take on a new and living meaning.

Undoubtedly such a revival of interest in the Bible cannot restore all the good that our ancestors got out of it. And let us hope it will not restore the evil! But we have to pay for our enjoyment of it in this new, fresh, secular spirit by the loss of something that, both for good and evil, can never return.

I am thinking of those who come back to it after a real lapse of the habit. There are, of course, many of my own generation who, like their fathers in the time of Matthew Arnold, have gone on reading the book, though with minds free of the old gloomy and illiberal temper, and such have lost nothing. But when there *has* been this break in the atmospheric continuity those who return to it are apt to find that just in proportion as they have got rid of the old, evil, Puritan sanctimoniousness and sinister gloom, so also they have lost and can never quite get back that mysterious continuity of emotional atmosphere which, like those "happy pieties" spoken of by Keats, carries with it such magical and indefinable power.

And it is to the Puritans that we owe, both in Great Britain and America, this powerful *Biblical tradition*, from which, as I have hinted, so many individual free spirits from the time of Wycliffe down to the time of William Blake have drawn human inspiration.

For though plenty of evangelical gospel-men, both within and without the Church, have "preached Christ and Him crucified," it has been on the strength of the less amiable, less peaceable, less mystical, but not less poetical Old Testament that so many men of the old breed on both sides of the Atlantic have sustained in perils of land and in perils of water, in the face of tyrants and in the teeth of penury and disaster, their indomitable endurance.

And it is from the stern spirits of these stout soldiers of fortune that a protest must always rise when our mystical interpreters would fain expurgate, prune, soften, and allegorize away, for the sake of "purer" conceptions, the human wisdom, the human sensuality, the human anger, the human justice, the human magnanimity, the human triumph, of this old shameless *literature of the Old Testament*.

What both the sacerdotal and the evangelical churches are apt to forget, in their apologies for the Christian hope, is the innumerable company—for if the magical Christ is the God of youth, Jehovah is the God of old age—of old shepherds, old herdsmen, old hedgers and ditchers, old stonemasons, old carpenters, old sailors, old soldiers, old miners, old pioneers, old fishermen, together with their old wives, who have managed to dispense with all such airy expectations, whether Christian or otherwise, in the stoical consciousness of an "Eternal, not themselves, who makes for righteousness," but whose ways, alas, are not their ways nor His thoughts their thoughts!

But whether forgotten or not by the livelier and more sociable children of the mystery, it is these isolated and taciturn "stoics of the Scriptures" who alone, save for a few old-fashioned Miltonic scholars, do real justice to the Old Testament. These are they who take life for that troubled and brief thing that the wisdom of the Lord declares it to be.

> Man that is born of a woman is of few days and full of trouble. He cometh forth like a flower, and is cut down; he fleeth also as a shadow, and continueth not. . . . For there is hope of a tree, if it be cut down that it will sprout again and that the tender branch thereof will not cease. Though the root thereof wax old in the earth and the stock thereof die in the ground; yet through the scent of water it will bud and bring forth boughs like a plant. But man dieth and wasteth away; yea, man giveth up the ghost, and where is he?

The Gospels are radiant with youthful joy and with fresh hope; and although Jesus frequently threatens His Father's enemies with "wailing and gnashing of teeth" the general feeling of the New Testament, though it is too serious to be called buoyant, is certainly the opposite of pessimistic.

The Old Testament has a beautiful and poetic light shining from it, but it is the light of a sunset that is streaked with human blood; whereas the light that shines from the New Testament is the light of the dawn; and though it also is streaked with blood, it is the blood of a god, not the blood of men. The whole atmosphere of the New Testament is completely different from that of the Old, and our English translators have observed this difference, giving to the English words a correspondent tone, so that, in comparison with the Old, the style of the New resembles a picture in water-colours as compared with one in oils.

In spite of a few desperate ejaculations, the general drift of the Old Testament is against any life after death.

> Wilt thou shew wonders to the dead? Shall the dead arise and praise thee? Shall thy loving kindness be declared in the grave? or thy faithfulness in destruction?

And save for a certain vein in the Prophet Ezekiel which must have influenced William Blake, and an apocalyptic tone in Daniel that must have influenced the author of the Book of Revelation, the Old Testament is singularly free from what we usually call mysticism.

To speak plainly, the Old Testament is anything but a spiritual book; but on the other hand it is a profoundly religious one, and although the Hebraic attitude to the Creator, whether under His name Elohim, or El Shaddai, or Yahweh, or the Lord of Hosts, is the propitiation of a jealous, revengeful, and cruel deity, yet so passionately emotional towards the Unseen, so furiously faithful to the God of Abraham, Isaac, and Jacob, of Sarah, Rebekah, and Rachel, was the Hebrew spirit that by the sheer intensity of its poetic imagination it transformed this tribal Demiurge, first into the Creator of heaven and earth, and then into the High and Holy One who inhabiteth Eternity —in other words, into the Nameless Tao or indefinable Absolute.

Spinoza's sublime conception of God—though he was excommunicated for holding it—was really implicit in the Old Testament from the start; not philosophically implicit, for the ancient Hebrews and the modern English resemble each other in their suspicion of philosophy, but emotionally, dramatically, and imaginatively so.

As one reads the story of Jacob in the first book of the Bible, and is forced against one's will to respect and more than respect this tenacious thief of blessings, one feels that as he gathered together one of his "heaps" of desert stones, under those far-off stars, he would not have been *emotionally* staggered or surprised, though he would have certainly been puzzled, had one of his "angels of the Lord," anticipating history, instructed him in the philosophy of Spinoza.

But what we discover in reading the King James Bible, when once by the help of our modern English commentary edited by Dr. Peake and the *Bible As Literature* edited by Mr. Bates we use the book as we use Homer, is the surprising fact that instead of finding our religious awe in the presence of life undermined—that awe which Goethe said was the highest privilege of man—we find it intensified a hundred-fold!

Liberated in this manner from that sinister, gloomy, morbid, and wicked-pious atmosphere which the hypocrisy of human fraility has thrown over this work we get a new and fresh inspiration; an inspiration not only from its literary beauty but from its real religious significance. One comes to feel as one gets older that intellectual persons make too much of the philosophic distinctions at which they arrive with so much pains, whereas the value of the literary or poetic approach is that we realize with more and more clearness that, in this matter of reverence for the mystery of life, "feeling is all in all," while the precise philosophic groove through which this feeling expresses itself is of relatively small importance.

Thus our response to the Bible as poetry rather than as doctrine does not imply less emotional and imaginative feeling but more; because it is by great literature rather than by great doctrine that we save our souls alive.

For Catholics the miracle of the Mass is greater than all theological doctrine *about* the Mass; and in the same way for us, as devoted Lollards, the poetry of the Bible is beyond all doctrines *about* the Bible.

And in truth the Bible, as we enjoy it to-day in this astounding translation, in which all that is deepest in the Hebrew nature mingles with all that is deepest in our Anglo-Celtic nature, is not a book for one, but a book for all. Never was such a melting pot of all those beautiful, natural inevitable *contradictions*, with which, from its "missing-link" ancestors down to this day, humanity has contradicted itself!

Whatever this dubious entity "truth" is *not*, we know one thing that it certainly *is*, namely, a monstrous container of insoluble contradictions.

And what proves the Bible to be a greater book than any other in the world except Homer and Shakespeare is the huge gamut of contradictory moods that mount up in its cresting tide.

In King James' Authorized Version we have a beautiful proof of the power of both the Hebrew race and the Anglo-Celtic race to "contain," as Walt Whitman said he himself did, "multitudes." In fact, in this unique book can be found the *literary equivalent* to that power of adapting themselves to so many various *climates* which is the mark of both your wandering Jew and your wandering Englishman.

It seems incredible that the same blending of old Hebrew and old British scholarship could pass from narration as perfect as that when Joseph in Egypt first sees Benjamin among their brothers:

And he lifted up his eyes and saw his brother Benjamin, his mother's son, and said, "Is this your younger brother of whom he spake unto me?" And he said, "God be gracious unto thee, my son."

And Joseph made haste; for his bowels did yearn upon his brother: and he sought where to weep; and he entered into his chamber, and wept there.

—could pass, I say, from narration like that to poetry like this:

O that thou wert as my brother, that sucked the breasts of my mother! when I should find thee without, I would kiss thee yea, I should not be despised, I would lead thee, and bring thee unto my mother's house, who would instruct me, I would cause thee to drink of spiced wine of the juice of my pomegranate. His left hand should be under my head and his right hand should embrace me. . . .

Set me as a seal upon thine heart, as a seal upon thine arm; for love is strong as death; jealousy is cruel as the grave; the coals thereof are coals of fire, which hath a most vehement flame. Many waters cannot quench love, neither can the floods drown it; if a man would give all the substance of his house for love, it would utterly be contemned.

No! the power of the Bible does not lie in its doctrine, does not lie in its spirituality, does not even lie in its righteousness. It lies in its supreme emotional contradictions, each carried to its uttermost extreme, and each representing, finally and for all time, some unchanging aspect of human life upon earth.

What an individual needs so as to deepen the poetry of his life, what a race needs so as to deepen the poetry of its life, are various ritualistic and traditional *sets of words* in its own tongue, but in a heightened and dignified example of its own tongue, like some noble old piece of domestic furniture, a thousand years old, smooth with the touches of generations.

Up-to-date editions of the Bible may be examples of lively cleverness and sincere piety. But what I personally feel about them is that they are simply *not the Bible*. They have their place. They belong to the category of pious experiments and revivalistic movements; whereas *the Bible*, our Authorized Jewish-British classic, is part of our normal daily life. We taste it with our bread. We drink it with our beer. We smoke it—as John Milton used to do—with our tobacco. To the tune of its words we are born and die. To the tune of its homely grossness we enjoy the pleasures of bed and board. It blesses the spade with which our garden is dug, the plough that ploughs our fields, the keel of the boat from which our fish are caught.

Nor is there a natural and normal *sin*—among those which we all of us commit every day—that cannot be sinned, and punished, and repented of, to the accompaniment of these ancient words!

The Bible is to us what Homer was to the Greeks. Its words have become more than words. They have become a magic touch that throws across the passing details of each individual life the undying beauty of the life of humanity. And into the actual words themselves of the Authorized Version the life of humanity has now passed; so that when we hear the Revised Version translate that clue-word of the secret of Jesus—the word *agapé*—as "love" in place of the familiar "charity" we get an uncomfortable shock. Nor does "love" mean the same thing. Technically it may. Actually it *does not!*

The Bible, as we read it now in the Authorized Version, has for its main theme the ways of man to the Eternal and the ways of the Eternal to man. Man's ways to man, and man's feeling for Nature, are the warp and the woof between which this dominant thread moves. It is as illogical to say that there is no God because Jehovah acts in an arbitrary and immoral manner, as to say that there is no civilization because man used to dress in skins and fight with weapons of flint.

Jehovah was the name that the old Hebrews applied to the Nameless Power behind our astronomical universe; and when the Hebrews describe their Jehovah as at once infinitely merciful and infinitely cruel I cannot for my own part see that in this He differs very much from the Ultimate Mystery before whom we must all bow.

Too well do we know that the laws of the Nameless for human life upon earth are like its laws for the lives of beasts and birds and reptiles and fishes—dark and strange and utterly inscrutable! We must needs trust in Him, for He is all there is. He is life. He is death. He is pleasure. He is pain. He is the Whole; and He is beyond the whole. He is the Great Tao of whom to say nothing is the best wisdom. He is Being. He is Not-Being. He is Matter and He is Mind. He is the One and He is the Many. We mortal creatures of a day, conceived in darkness and acquainted with tribulation, born to trouble as the sparks fly upward, who are we to do more than dodge His thunder and enjoy His sunshine, until our dust returns to the earth as it was, and our spirit unto Him who gave it?

And the strange thing about the Old Testament is that it is so easy, I might say so *inevitable*, to feel in this tribal God of Israel, this Lord of Hosts, this Yahweh, this Jehovah, this Elohim, the deeper, more mysterious presence of the nameless Sustainer and Absorber of all things.

This is the gist of the whole business; this is the sum and meaning of all. We feel awe in the presence of *that* which we cannot name, of *that* which, judging by the cruelty and indifference of nature, seems to us—as It did to Job—no more good than It is evil; and yet with this very awe, and in proportion as we experience this awe, there rises in us the feeling that what we have come to call *goodness* is the one thing alone that in the last resort really matters.

That is the point. "Feeling is all in all. The name is sound and smoke, obscuring Heaven's clear glow." Names are nothing and everything. They are nothing, because their sounded syllables are but breath and air and custom. They are everything, because behind this breath, behind this custom, is the *feeling of awe*, the awe that points to simple goodness as the needle points to the north! Our ship goes down; we are gathered to our fathers; but "the word of the Lord"—that is to say the goodness that survives us— "endureth from generation to generation."

The Nameless Power that excites this awe, seems Itself, judging by the ways of Its universe, to be no whit less wayward than Yahweh or Elohim, but the awe It excites in us is an atmosphere, say what you will, that suits the good better than it suits the evil.

What we call "morality" changes with epoch and place. It is a thing of custom and convention, and is often both cowardly and wicked; but the spirit of goodness is the same "yesterday, to-day, and for ever."

And it is this awe excited by the Nameless, that is to say by what the prophets of Israel called "God," that the merciful man—in spite of the ways of Nature—feels to be *with* him, while the unmerciful man feels it to be *against* him.

The Old Testament is the inspiration of the race which, of all races, has felt the *awe of the Nameless* most powerfully; and when some unsophisticated Uncle Tom, or some simple-minded John Bunyan broods over this book, it doesn't matter how "anthropomorphic," as we call it, his own image of the Nameless is, or how immoral the ways of Jehovah were. What matters is that he feels the "awe of God" and the "presence of God" and comforts and sustains his soul amid the flow of the things that pass away by the feeling of being in touch—and what right have we to call such a feeling an illusion?—with That which was, and is, and is to come.

The Old Testament gives us no assurance about life after death, no commands to be spiritual or chaste. It conveys to us no delicate scruples about lying and fighting and eating and drinking and being revenged on our enemies. It suggests no ascetic suspicion that the accumulation of riches is wrong, no implication that the pleasures of sex are unlawful.

Jacob, or Israel, the father of the Twelve Tribes, is fully as crafty and tricky as the Homeric Odysseus, and bargains and argues and pleads with his jealous God, just as Odysseus does with Athene.

Wherein then, it may be asked, lies the greatness of this Patriarch's character? Wherein, for all the patient and humble and much-enduring men and women who have learnt by heart this tale "of our Father Jacob," is to be found the secret of the attraction that holds them? Does it not lie, as in all exciting stories from the beginning, in the protagonist's intense *awareness of his destiny*, his intense self-consciousness in everything he does, the unconquerable tenacity of his purpose? Isn't the whole secret of the Old Testament's attraction for egoists like ourselves to be found in that remark of Goethe's, "Earnestness alone makes life eternity"? The crafty, amorous, patient, unswerving, unwarlike Jacob takes his life with a gravity, with an awareness, with a sense of responsibility that is overwhelming, that is sublime, that is something before which all obstacles melt, as if by a slow, resistless magic!

Think of what the man must have felt when he awoke that morning after that tricky marriage—"*and behold it was Leah*"! But to serve another seven years for the woman he loved was as inevitable to his incorrigible tenacity as it was to steal Esau's birthright. Every sunrise that smote red into his tent found him, metaphorically speaking, wrestling with his angel, found him with his obstinate head on some sacred stone.

"How mysterious, how memorable," he is always thinking, "is this godlike spot, this godlike dawn, this godlike
hour!" And with his "ladder" always ascending from time
and space into the Nameless, Jacob naturally, inevitably,
becomes Israel, the father of multitudes!

The most stirring and dramatic part of the four books
that follow this patriarchal Genesis, namely Exodus, Leviti-
cus, Numbers, and Deuteronomy, which are by far the
least inspiring and the least interesting books in the whole
Bible, have to do with the extraordinary personality of
Moses, furious leader and far-sighted lawgiver, who must
have been a sort of inspired Hebraic Merlin with his
neurotic moods of "meekness," his fits of blind wrath, his
black magic, and his terrifying intimacies with Jehovah.

Certain stories we are told about Moses carry upon their
face, casually though they are related, the very seal of psychological truth. Such is the story, for instance, of how
Aaron and Miriam, his brother and sister, revolted against
him, because he, the great eugenic medicine man, took to
wife an Ethiopian woman.

But do we not get the whole secret of the magnetic
ascendancy of Moses in the effect of his appeal to his divine
friend against these jeering purists, this high priest and this
priest-loving lady; an appeal that was so effective that the
great soothsaying Miriam had to flee from the face of that
Ethiopian, and from the face of the whole camp, literally
sick with terror!

In this single sentence it can be seen why it is that the
English, the most individualistic of all races, had until
yesterday such a mania for this Hebrew book.

And the Lord came down in the pillar of the cloud and
stood in the door of the tabernacle, and called Aaron
and Miriam and they both came forth. And he said, "Hear
now my words: if there be a prophet among you I the Lord
will make myself known unto him in a vision and will

speak unto him in a dream. My servant Moses is not so, who is faithful in all my house. With him will I speak mouth to mouth, even apparently, and not in dark speeches; and the similitude of the Lord he shall behold; wherefore then were ye not afraid to speak against my servant Moses?"

From the disappearance of Moses—for none knoweth his sepulchre unto this day—to the establishment of the kingdom under Saul and David the Old Testament intensifies its awe-inspiring drama.

The main theme of this great accumulative symphony is still the relation between man and the Nameless; and still does the Nameless, as in the stories of Samson and of Saul, find in Jehovah exactly what Jehovah found in Moses, an erratic, wayward, cantankerous, but faithful mouthpiece of its mysterious will.

And after all, as we know from bitter experience neither Milton's pure and eternal Spirit, who "Dove-like sats't brooding on the vast abyss and mads't it pregnant," nor the "loving Father" of Jesus, fills up or completes altogether the characteristics of the Power that governs the cosmos.

There has always been found, in its ways to men, and to animals and birds and fishes too, an element that is different from both these qualities, an element neither spiritual nor loving, an element indeed that has not only cruelty in it but an unmistakable touch of satanic malice.

It was St. Paul who made of Jesus—"but we have the mind of Christ"—what Aeschylus lacked the penetration to make of Prometheus, that is to say a God of *pure goodness*, to stand between us and this devilish element in the Nameless; for it was no more concealed from St. Paul than it was concealed from Dostoievsky how impossible it is to justify "the ways of God to man."

Certain figures in the Old Testament stand forth with dramatic outlines as distinct and with intensity of feeling as tragic as any figures in classic or Nordic literature. Such

are the figures of Samson the Nazarite and Elijah the Tish-
bite. Both these gigantic personalities were peculiarly dear
to the heart of the Nameless, who, as we read, inspired
them with something of Its own cruel violence as well as
with Its own creative spirit.

How often must the Hebrew race, and many another
race, too, in their hour of subjection, have pondered, as
Milton under the "barbarous dissonance" of the Restoration, upon the death of this hero of the Eternal!

The description of the death of Samson, as our King
James Version translates it, is indeed a perfect example of
how when we treat the Bible "as literature" we neither
lessen its grandeur nor diminish its inspiration.

Treated as "the word of God," as our fathers treated it,
how easily by taking it all for granted in one monotonous
level of consecrated gloom can we lose altogether that
poetry which is the highest "word" of all, and which is
without any question the very inspiration of the Nameless!

> And it came to pass, when their hearts were merry,
> that they said, "Call for Samson, that he may make us sport."
> And they called for Samson out of the prison house; and he
> made them sport: and they set him between the pillars. And
> Samson said unto the lad that held him by the hand, "Suffer
> me that I may feel the pillars whereupon the house standeth
> that I may lean upon them. . . ." And Samson called upon
> the Lord and said, "O Lord God, remember me, I pray
> thee, and strengthen me, I pray thee, only this once, O
> God, that I may be avenged of the Philistines for my two
> eyes. . . ." And Samson said, "Let me die with the Philistines."
>
> And he bowed himself with all his might; and the house
> fell upon the lords and upon all the people that were therein.
> So the dead which he slew at his death were more than
> they which he slew in his life.

But that Elijah its prophet made an even deeper impression on the Hebrew mind than Samson its champion is proved by the words of Jesus himself who hesitates not to declare that His great herald, John the Baptist, was actually a reincarnation of Elijah.

But unquestionably the favourite book of the Old Testament with average philosophistic Nordics is the Book of Job. And how significant it is of the manner in which Jehovah so effectively represents the Nameless, that God's only reply to our outraged indictment of his extraordinary ways should be a thundering description of our weakness compared with His strength!

It would be difficult to find anything more different from the tender and desperate piety of the Psalms than the sly worldly wisdom of the Proverbs; and how characteristic it is of the particular genius of our English translators that just as they can respond to the revolutionary spirit of these old writings, so they can convey in their version of the Proverbs that particular tone of what might be called *moderation in virtue*, which is the chief characteristic of our English Prayer Book!

"Be not over-righteous, nor take upon thyself to be too wise. Why should'st thou destroy thyself?" And certainly in their power of catching the poetic cynicism of *Ecclesiastes* side by side with the desperate humilities of the Psalms the King James scholars were not less than inspired. My own favourite book in the Bible is the Psalms, and it gives me a peculiar satisfaction to know that this was the feeling of our most sophisticated of all secular critics, Walter Pater. And what a book for the lonely and the unhappy the Psalms is!

Rationalist opponents of religion speak sometimes as if the organized churches were responsible for the Bible's hold over people. Nothing could be more untrue! The Old Testament, as cannot be repeated too often, remains the grand revolutionary arsenal for the individual's weapons against all constituted authority; and if, as William Blake says,

Jesus Christ was the greatest revolutionary of all time, was indeed the supreme anarchist, who—

His seventy disciples sent
Against Religion and Government!

it is from the prophetic books of the Old Testament that Jesus drew, as so many others have done, the spirit of divine revolt against "the Powers of this World."

The *Biography* of our English Bible is, as Mr. Bates so admirably sums it up, the story of the resistless demand of the masses of the people, *against the will of constituted authority*, to possess this dangerous book.

We have, however, as the editor of *The Bible As Literature* willingly admits, to give the credit for our unequalled Authorized Version to one of our most eccentric rulers, namely to "the wisest fool in Christendom," King James the First! Making use of the earlier labours of William Tyndale and Miles Coverdale, this learned monarch's committee of scholars, headed by Dr. Reynolds of Corpus Christi, Oxford, and Dr. Lancelot Andrewes, dean of Westminster, brought out this work—the greatest translation ever made— in the year 1611. Ardent as he was in this noble undertaking and assiduously pushing his churchmen on, James, Mr. Bates reminds us, insisted that no return should be made to the Tyndale-Coverdale translation of the Greek word *ecclesia* in the proper, classical, democratic sense of an "assembly" or "congregation," but that the sacerdotal expression "church," used in the so-called "Bishops' Bible," should be the word employed.

But never has the peculiar genius of English scholars, and never has, one must add, the peculiar genius of the English language, been displayed to grander effect than in this book, the actual words of which, even in the case of sundry expressions that cleverer and smarter revisions have "improved upon," have sunk so deeply into our popular consciousness that they have become for many of us the inveterate form through which our love, our hate, our happiness, our lust, our greed, our pity, our pride, our humility, our despair, our ecstasy, yea! and even our cursing of life, must be expressed, if they are to be expressed from the bowels of our soul!

And the curious thing is that, while for those who instinctively respond to the prelatical translation of *ecclesia* as "church," our English Prayer-Book offers its unequalled counterpart to the Latin of authority, of tradition, of order, of *organization*, King James's Bible has remained to this day the inexhaustible inspiration of heretics, outlaws, and rebels!

From the time of the Lollards this book has been the book of those who, like Walt Whitman, are critical of institutions, critical of priesthoods, critical of states and governments. The culmination of the Old Testament is in the spirit of prophecy; and the prophet, from the beginning of time unto this day, has been the despised of the rich, the trouble of the priests, and the mad terror of the ruler.

If any unwearied reader of the Bible were asked why after racing through this book from cover to cover he proceeds to repeat this singular performance, his answer would in essence be the same as that of Uncle Tom, the same as that of Tom o' Bedlam, the same as that of a vast anonymous multitude of Toms and Johns; namely, that it gives him the will, the tenacity, the cunning, even if it cannot give him the strength or the courage, *to put the world's values in their place!*

The greatest literary works of our Western world, and I cannot help suspecting of the whole round earth, are three in number. They are the Hebrew Scriptures, Homer, and Shakespeare. It was the greatest of Germans who said, "How can I hate the French when I owe to them my intellectual culture?" and it is hard not to feel that this Goethean idea of the power of literature to destroy race-prejudice is destined to outlive all that an inhuman and illiterate science can do in its eager desire to put weapons of destruction into the hands of oppressors.

And how ironical it is that any bold free-thinker among us with any real imaginative response to life should, out of his "intolerance of intolerance," give up enjoying this shameless, passionate, poetical, earth-loving Old Testament, in which there is no illusion about personal immortality, no illusion about ethical idealism, no illusion about the friendliness of the universe, no false hopes about this "thinking reed" so preposterously made in the image of God!

How ironical that such persons should say in their hearts: "The Bible is so obscure, so inconsistent, so full of sweet mirages and pleasant lies; let us therefore put in its place the simple, indubitable utterances of speculative psychology and the profound never-to-be-changed revelations of experimental physics!"

Many attempts have been made to explain the secret of the peculiar beauty of this great translation. One feels at once that the essential quality both of its prose and its poetry is at the opposite pole from the prevailing stylistic manner of modern writers.

The form of the ancient Hebrew poetry, as the Authorized Version catches its spirit, depends chiefly upon two elements—imaginative exaggeration and musical repetition.

It is in its subject-matter, however, that its power chiefly lies and this consists in the inter-blending of three dominant motifs—the glory and shame of man, the beauty and terror of nature, and the sometimes appalling and sometimes consoling mystery of the First Cause. Each of these recurrent motifs is constantly appearing and disappearing, as the wild music of the ocean of life flows forward; while it is always with this life, and never with any attempt to attain another life, that the Old Testament is concerned. Nor does the ancient prose style of the Hebrews, as King James's scholars render it, differ very much from that of their poetry, save that the rhythmic repetition is less pronounced, and the majestic realism of the simple narration holds the subject even yet closer to the earth.

The Eternal must help us, *at least by the feeling of His Presence*, in this actual life; for it is unlikely—so runs the constant refrain of the Old Testament—that we shall hear His voice out of the dust.

It is impossible, for persons who love reading the Bible from beginning to end, not to feel thankful that the *canonical order* of the books it contains, so artfully different from the chronological conclusions of scientific research, has been allowed, by the deep dramatic sense of those who arranged it and those who translated it, to mount up, exactly as we have it to-day, from Genesis to Malachi.

The Book of Genesis contains, as it should contain, the simplest narrations of all; monumental vignettes of human pathos and drama, only equalled by Homer.

> And Isaac his father said unto him, "Who art thou?" And he said, "I am thy son, thy first-born Esau." And Isaac trembled very exceedingly, and said, "Who? where is he that hath taken venison, and brought it to me, and I have eaten of all before thou camest, and have blessed him? yea and he shall be blessed."
>
> And when Esau heard the words of his father, he cried with a great and exceeding bitter cry, and said unto his father, "Bless me, even me also, Oh my father."

But then, as we read on, following this totally unscientific but surely inspired canon, though it be but the canon of a multitude of anonymous Hebrew scholars, and pass from Moses to the Judges, and from the Judges to Saul and David and the Kings, the tone of the writing grows steadily more subjective, more lyrical, more cosmic.

And he came thither unto a cave, and lodged, there; and behold, the word of the Lord came to him and he said unto him, "What doest thou here, Elijah?" And he said, "I have been very jealous for the Lord God of hosts; for the children of Israel have forsaken thy covenant, thrown down thine altars, and slain thy prophets with the sword; and I, even I only, am left; and they seek my life to take it away."

And he said, "Go forth, and stand upon the mount before the Lord." And behold, the Lord passed by, and a great and strong wind rent the mountains, and brake in pieces the rocks before the Lord; but the Lord was not in the wind; and after the wind an earthquake; but the Lord was not in the earthquake; and after the earthquake a fire; but the Lord was not in the fire; and after the fire a still small voice . . . "yet have I left me seven thousand in Israel, all the knees which have not bowed unto Baal, and every mouth which hath not kissed him."

Still following the canonical order handed down to us from these old nameless Jewish sages, an order charged with the *amor fati* of the most fate-conscious of all races, we arrive at the Book of Job, where, *de profundis* indeed, the soul of man turns upon the Manager of his World-Show, and, as Ivan Karamazov says, "returns Him the ticket."

And Job spake and said, "Let the day perish wherein I was born, and the night in which it was said, 'There is a man child conceived.' Let that day be darkness; let not God regard it from above, neither let the light shine upon it. Let darkness and the shadow of death stain it; let a cloud dwell upon it; let the blackness of the day terrify it. . . . Lo, let that night be solitary, let no joyful voice come therein. . . . Let it look for light, but have none; neither let it see the dawning of the day: because it shut not up the doors of my mother's womb, nor hid sorrow from mine eyes. . . . For now should I have lain still and been quiet, I should have slept; then had I been at rest . . . as an hidden untimely birth, I had not been; as infants which never saw light. There the wicked cease from troubling; and there the weary be at rest. There the prisoners rest together; they hear not the voice of the oppressor.

"The small and great are there; and the servant is free from his master.

"Wherefore is light given to him that is in misery, and life unto the bitter in soul . . . which rejoice exceedingly, and are glad when they can find the grave?"

And thus having reached the uttermost depths, and peradventure like Job, finding ourselves still alive, still going to and fro upon the earth, what chord, in this great ancient world-tragedy, will be struck after the second act, struck as the orchestra plays for the intermission?

Which of us who have lasted it out to middle age and tested the nature of the world cannot respond to the voice of the Preacher, that low-pitched paean of the second-best, whose disillusionment no Horace, no Voltaire, no Anatole France can surpass, but which by some dramatic instinct in humanity has fallen into its place in the very centre of the Bible?

For to him that is joined to all the living there is hope: for a living dog is better than a dead lion. For the living know that they shall die: but the dead know not any thing, neither have they any more a reward; for the memory of them is forgotten. . . . Whatsoever thy hand findeth to do, do it with thy might; for there is no work, nor device, nor knowledge, nor wisdom, in the grave, whither thou goest.

I returned, and saw under the sun, that the race is not to the swift, nor the battle to the strong, neither yet bread to the wise, nor yet riches to men of understanding, nor yet favour to men of skill; but time and chance happeneth to them all.

Thus we hear the voice of the Preacher—"And behold! all is vanity and vexation of spirit."

"All," as the greatest of the Greek philosophers said, "all flows away and nothing abides."

Nothing? Faint and low, as if upon the wind of space, outside all our egoistic cravings, outside all our inevitable frustrations, comes still the voice of the Psalmist, that voice from "the God," as Emily Brontë says, "within our breast," the God within us and yet beyond us, that is our real "being and breath."

> My days are like a shadow that declineth; and I am withered like grass. . . . Of old hast thou laid the foundations of the earth; and the heavens are the work of thy hands. They shall perish, but thou shalt endure; yea, all of them shall wax old like a garment, as a vesture shalt thou change them, and they shall be changed: But thou art the same, and thy years shall have no end.

When Matthew Arnold said that the power of the Bible lay in its appeal to mercy and justice, in its appeal to what we call "righteousness," he was not wrong; but there is more in it than that.

The culmination of the Old Testament is in the Prophets. All leads up to the Prophets. Prose and poetry, lamentations and exultations, despairs and resignations, to the Prophets it mounts up, and with the Prophets it ends.

The poetry of the Psalms washes, like a cleansing air, over the bitterness of every personal life; and its lyrical burden, soothing away our personal griefs, is always the same. We as individuals are and are not; but the Power by which we live, the Power into whose hands we sink when we die, *That*, and *That* alone, abideth for ever; and in *That*, and not in the self that perishes, is immortal life.

> Lord, thou hast been our dwelling-place in all generations. Before the mountains were brought forth, or ever thou hadst formed the earth and the world, even from everlasting to everlasting thou art God.

Thou turnest man to destruction; and sayest, "Return, ye children of men." For a thousand years in thy sight are but as yesterday when it is past, and as a watch in the night. Thou carriest them away as with a flood; they are as a sleep: in the morning they are like grass which groweth up. In the morning it flourisheth and groweth up; in the evening it is cut down and withereth. . . .

The days of our years are three-score years and ten; and if by reason of strength they be fourscore years, yet is their strength labour and sorrow; for it is soon cut off, and we fly away.

Some will say, "What comfort is it to the individual who perishes that God, that the Nameless, should live for ever?" I think the answer is that for all its tragic finality there remains a strange beauty, a deep feeling of peace and calm and infinite escape, in the thought of the death of the individual self and the eternity of something that is not individual.

The greatest of modern American poets, Edgar Lee Masters, has expressed this feeling, the feeling that comes over us again and again as we give ourselves up to the ebb and flow of this Psalm-music, a music like a sad and tender night-wind passing over the roofs of the world and over the "window'd raggedness" of the outcasts of the world, giving us not hope but peace.

> Ice cannot shiver in the cold,
> Nor stones shrink from the lapping flame.
> Eyes that are sealed no more have tears;
> Ears that are stopped hear nothing ill;
> Hearts turned to silt are strange to pain;
> Tongues that are dumb report no loss;
> Hands stiffened, well may idle be;
>
> .   .   .   .
>
> Work is, but folded hands need work not;
> Nothing to say is for dumb tongues.

The rolling earth rolls on and on
With trees and stones and winding streams—
My dream is what the hill-side dreams!

Yes, there is a strange satisfaction, mysterious as death, a satisfaction that the music of poetry alone can give in this feeling of the troubles of time being over, and the timeless "hill-side" of the Eternal alone continuing.

The individual passes; but there come moments when we are content that it should be so; for we feel that the thoughts of the most abject among us are not altogether lost. In the Eternal they still live—those thoughts and the labours of those hands.

> Let thy work appear unto thy servants, and thy glory unto their children. And let the beauty of the Lord our God be upon us, and establish thou the work of our hands upon us, yea the work of our hands establish thou it.

It is easy enough—alas, we all know that!—to lay so much stress upon the loss of our personal identity—this Jack and Tom and Bob and Bill, this Bess and Nell and Sue and Kate which is all we feel ourselves to be—that such talk as this about our "thoughts," or our "work," or some unearthly de-personalized "essence" surviving in the Eternal, sounds like a mockery of wordy rhetoric.

But living men are we, lively particles of dust and vapour, not algebraic equations, and if in everything else we get comfort from faint, vague, dim, flickering chances, and intimations of chances, such as when you press too hard upon them flit away like smoke, surely it is no mere priestly trick but a natural motion of the soul, as inevitable as the clutch of an embryo's fingers, that we should make the most of these old dim paleolithic hints of immortality.

But if the poetry of the Psalms is like the music of a long-drawn wind in the night, in the beauty of which we accept the passing of that which most certainly passes and the abiding of that which we may hope abides, when we come to the Prophets a different note is heard.

It is obscurer, it is wilder, it is more irrational. There is that in it that struggles to find an utterance for an inspiration that rolls away the great stone that all our reasonable and all our natural, and all our logical conclusions have placed upon the wishing-well of the heart's desire, the well of "our father Jacob," in the great desert.

In a new and unpredictable direction does this prophetic cry carry us. Hitherto, in the books of the Old Testament, it has been by tenacity of purpose, by heroic endurance, by strength and courage and faith, by the proud fulfilling of the Law, by the magnanimous practice of benevolence and righteousness, that the will of the Eternal was obeyed.

But in the Prophets the mystery of the universe is approached from a totally different direction. It is in fact not "approached" at all. *It is found within ourselves.* Yes, this great thundering and undying Eternal, whose only answer to Job was to shout him down, is now discovered to be a living part, the only living part, of the individual soul that perishes!

"For my thoughts are not your thoughts, neither are your ways my ways," saith the Lord. . . . "Can a woman forget her sucking child, that she should not have compassion on the son of her womb? Yea, they may forget, yet will I not forget thee. . . ." For thus saith the high and lofty One that inhabiteth eternity. . . .

"I dwell in the high and holy place with him also that is of a contrite and humble spirit, to revive the spirit of the humble, and to revive the heart of the contrite."

It is as though the poetry of the Psalms had brought an echo out of infinite space.

For what is the "high and lofty One" doing here except answering the cry of that familiar Psalm that quivers through the chords of man's betrayed nerves like the wind through telegraph-wires?

> Create in me a clean heart, O God, and renew a right spirit within me. . . .
> For thou desirest not sacrifice, else would I give it; thou delightest not in burnt offering. The sacrifices of God are a broken spirit; a broken and a contrite heart, O God, thou wilt not despise. . . .

There is certainly nothing like this in Homer, and not very much resembling it in Shakespeare; nor, to confess the truth, is it very common in the Old Testament. It belongs rather to that particular aspect of the New Testament whereof Dostoievsky is the greatest modern exponent.

But rare though it be, it is the climax towards which the whole of the Old Testament moves, since Cain, the firstborn went forth a wanderer over the face of the earth. It is nothing less than that psychological emptiness in the heart's abyss, which, when it is filled by the spirit of the Nameless, becomes what Emily Brontë calls "the God within my breast."

The difference, between this Hebrew emptiness in the soul that can only be filled by the Spirit beyond all worlds— dark and strange though that Nameless be—and the metaphysical selflessness advocated by Buddhism, is that the former treats the Nameless as a Person.

It was none other than Goethe who said, "and there is room for this also"; and for myself, as a sworn irrationalist, I can only say that I am proud to follow William Blake in placing this Semitic Book above all our Aryan metaphysic.

After all, the only thing I know *for certain* is my own personal mind; and *that* I know to be a Being that loves and hates and feels pleasure and pain. Why then must I interpret the Eternal in terms of mathematical symbols of which I know nothing and of chemical forces which I only know from the outside, while I reject as a childish analogy the living identity which I know so intimately *and from the inside?*

It is true that these subtle intellectual systems in dealing with the Self and "the escape from the self" call upon us to enter upon a cold-blooded scientific "process of salvation" in which by a premeditated method we craftily drop the part of the self that anyway is doomed, in order to hitch some evasive fragment of what is left, as securely as we can, to the slippery spirals of the Absolute.

But the reason why the Jewish Bible has so completely beaten off the field—at any rate as far as our Anglo-Celtic soul is concerned—all this Aryan metaphysic, is because it interprets the world in terms of the heart rather than in terms of the head; and because it finds, as indeed the great Kant himself found, that the secret of things lies in the inspiration of the human conscience rather than in the cunning decrees of the human intellect.

And here again I cannot see why humility *before* the Eternal, and an escape from ourselves *into* the Eternal in the simple emotional manner of the Psalms and the Prophets, should not lift us into the Timeless quite as effectively as any mental concentration.

Jesus was only carrying the Psalms and Prophets a "fathom and a half" further when he used his famous expression about losing your life to save it; and the mere fact that the imaginative tone in the Psalms and the Prophets turns the relations |between the temporal and the eternal into a poetic one rather than a chemical or a mathematical one is from my point of view all to its advantage.

Few impassioned readers of the Bible have been dutiful adherents of organized sacerdotal religion; for the spirit of both Old and New Testament is a spirit of revolt against organization of every kind.

Certainly in Great Britain, from the time of the Lollards to the present hour, the strongest Bible-lovers have been anything but meek adherents of either Church or State. Very often, as with the old independents, they have been fierce opponents of them both. This is where the spirit of the Bible differs from the spirit of the Prayer-Book; and I am tempted to think that whereas the more docile and more feminine piety in these islands cleaves to the Prayer-Book the Bible is still the inspirer of the greater number of solitary souls who prefer to worship in the "House not made with Hands."

For myself I lean to the view that if our survival after death depends, as some maintain, upon the measure of our detachment from self-absorption, there is a stronger liberating magic in the psychological humility of the Semitic method than in the metaphysical humility of the Aryan method, the former being spontaneous and imaginative, the latter premeditated and scientific.

In any case I am sure that the growing prejudice which so large a segment of our younger generation feels against the Bible is due to the fact that they link it with the disgusting hypocrisy, the sly maliciousness, the half-suppressed goatishness, of so many among its official champions.

But to hate the Bible because many of its adherents are repulsive is as absurd as to hate Homer because you had an unpleasant teacher at school. Herein lies the advantage of coming fresh to this book as if it were heathen literature. It puts back the heart into it, the heart that has been destroyed by the repulsive hypocrisies and odious cruelties of the past.

Written in the East, and made the supreme Sacred Book in the West, this living projection of the soul of Israel will no doubt have its rebirths and its revaluations to the end of time.

And we have to face the fact that our Anglo-Celtic race has come to find its *individual religion* in Jewish emotion and in Jewish imagination as nowhere else. This when you come to think of it is a very strange thing. I doubt if even the practical Romans allowed themselves to be dominated by the genius of the poetical Greeks to such a tune as this!

How has this come about? For it is clear that in the Latin of the Catholic Church the Hebrew element is not preserved to anything like the extent it is in our English Bible. Is it because we are the most unphilosophic and individualistic of all races and the race above all others to exalt the prophet at the expense of the thinker and the priest? Or was there, perhaps, in the ancient Iberian aboriginals of these islands a pre-Celtic strain that was not Aryan at all, and that is stirred in its atavistic depths by this Semitic book?

It is at any rate significant that just as the Irish were strengthened in the struggle to retain their racial identity by the Roman Church, so have the Welsh been strengthened in a similar struggle by the Welsh Bible.

Anyway, the whole of this Authorized Version, wherein the religious spirit of England is wedded to the religious spirit of the Jews, is inspired by what we call the *religious idea*, namely, the idea, defined by Goethe at the end of *Faust*, that all transitory things are symbols of what is beyond time.

"The great globe itself," as Shakespeare says, "yea! all which it inherit, shall dissolve and . . . leave not a rack behind."

But how can there be this flowing away without some hidden permanence whereby in reality we measure the speed of the flow? But the existence of this permanence, beyond and beneath the universal flux, is rather an intimation that comes to us in moments of deep feeling than a scientific conclusion.

And its presence, the presence of something beyond the laws of cause and effect, not unfrequently presents itself—at least it did to the ancient Hebrews and old-fashioned Englishmen—in the form of what we now call the "miraculous."

Thus Matthew Arnold's contention that the Bible will survive by its "morality touched by emotion" does not cover the whole field. What the Bible lives by is its undying protest in imperishable poetry against a world wherein "miracles" cannot happen!

The Biblical attitude is that creation *implies* the "miraculous"; and when one thinks of the fantastic shifts to which science has been put to get life going without the miraculous ever since Democritus had to supply his atoms with fish-hooks it seems that the Biblical attitude still holds good.

The Bible is great literature; but it is literature that "has the peculiarity," as the ancient Welsh books would put it, of giving our earth-wisdom a wholesome shock; the sort of shock that Hercules gave Antaeus when he lifted him into the air. But "this kind goeth not forth" without inspiration; and is the prerogative of the prophet rather than of the philosopher.

The hand of the Lord was upon me and carried me out in the spirit of the Lord, and set me down in the midst of the valley which was full of bones. And caused me to pass by them, round about; and behold, there were very many in the open valley; and lo, they were very dry.

And he said unto me, "Son of man, can these bones live?"

And I answered, "O Lord God, Thou knowest."

The Bible as Literature:
The New Testament

I BELIEVE that most of us feel in our hearts that it is easier to "enjoy," as we say, "simply as literature" the Old Testament than the New.

The Old Testament contains the grandest mass of poetry, history, drama, jurisprudence, ever collected in one human volume; and the comfort of it is that we can throw ourselves into it, as poetry and mythology and religious and irreligious soothsaying, without being any more committed to its varied ways of taking life than we are in the case of Homer or of Shakespeare.

But it is a very different story when we open the New Testament! Here we are confronted, sentence by sentence, verse by verse, with words that have become the mystic and ritualistic background, the moral and aesthetic atmosphere, of our whole life. We may have long ago given up "going to church" but few of us with any sensitiveness or imagination or curiosity about existence have been able to dodge the familiar scenes and familiar sayings in the Gospels.

With what a mixture of shyness, of awe, of *Temps retrouvé*, of heathen resistance, of uneasy conscience do we turn these pages! That disconcerting, disarming, disturbing *personal appeal* of our Man-God's divine narcissism, majestically, magnetically drawing us towards Him—"I am the Way, the Truth and the Life" . . . "Come unto Me all ye that are weary and heavy-laden" . . . "I am the light of the World. He that followeth me shall not walk in darkness but shall have the light of life"—is certainly a thing, whether we consciously resist it or passionately yield to it, or, as most of us do, dodge it with uneasy respect, so startling in our individual experience, that it seems outside what we hear scientific scholarship so coolly entitle the history of comparative religion.

Alas! There are few modern philosophers as liberated from both rationalistic and religious prejudice as the late incomparable William James; and yet what we want, we humble, patient, and Pyrrhonian free spirits in the presence of this fatal Lover, whose irresistible magnetism begins to trouble our little skiff, even when still leagues away from its in-sucking whirlpool, is a protective psychology of the imperilled conscience.

A capricious bookworm is hardly the person to supply this need; but I have myself found it a protection against the sorcery of the Man-God of my childhood to realize the fact that the mere possession of human consciousness gives us perforce such an *interior sensation of spiritual space* that it is hard not to surround this "interlunar cave" within ourselves with an aerial atmosphere of *divine* consciousness frighteningly aware of everything we think and feel! This interior landscape, this far-stretching mental space within us with its Watchful Warden, is the scene of a constant painful drama, with the compass-needle of our free-will, that delicate instrument, as Nietzsche so beautifully says, *of torture*, wavering and shivering between the South Pole of "I want" and the North Pole of "I ought," while the Man-God, "who died on tree," watches gravely and sadly its distressing jerks backward and forward.

Now when once we have become thoroughly aware of the teasing necessity of "having the feeling" of this interior mental space, so easily invaded by the flickering needle of free-will and by the insatiable "divine eye" and "sacred heart," we have in a curious way protected ourselves, protected our natural timid bookworm selves, from this formidable "Lovest thou me?" with its fatal mystic attraction and its appalling corollary that if you *don't* respond you will lose your immortal soul. I think that to a cautious earthbound mind this implicit threat, mingled with sweet love, this threat almost feminine in its fury of love rejected—"I know ye not! Depart from me into everlasting fire!"—is alone a considerable protection.

Approaching the New Testament, therefore, in an irrationalistic but at the same time a cautious spirit, perhaps more in the spirit of "the devils who believe and tremble" than of Herbert Spencer with cotton-wool in his ears, the first thing that must strike us is that the writings of St. Paul are much closer to our modern nervous troubles than the magical story told by St. Luke or the metaphysical love-rhapsodies of St. John. And he is this because St. Paul is the *psychologist* of the Revelation; and it is of the nature of psychology to dive into the ocean of life and to move through that ocean at a deeper level than either magic or metaphysic. By metaphysic we scan the horizons and find where water ends and air begins; by magic we make fish fly and birds float, but in the "Nautilus" named "Psyche" we swim through the very heart of the element itself.

Modern criticism takes the view that the Fourth Gospel —the metaphysical one—is of much later date than the rest, is indeed, perhaps, the last human addition made to the Bible; but it surmises the existence of two earlier documents used by all the first three Evangelists, one of which they visualize as an original sketch or skeleton of the events filled in later by the three writers, and the other as an anonymous collection of the sayings of Christ.

More in harmony with our present purpose is a comparison between the Gospels in the light of what we can gather as to the particular treatment of Jesus of Nazareth in each of them; and certainly from this angle of investigation the most arresting discovery we make is the superiority over the others in the pure art of biography of the Gospel according to St. Luke. St. Luke's personality, with its method, its style, its predilections, its culture, its taste, its unique genius, is a thing we can grasp, a thing we can understand in the most natural and human sense.

Across the crimes and manias and blunders of nearly twenty centuries the voice of this great poet-physician is still personally audible, with its almost Shakespearean tenderness and its balladlike grace.

You have only to hurry through Matthew and Mark—reading them as if you had never read them before—and plunge into St. Luke, to find yourself at once under the spell of a really great biographer, and one of a peculiarly winning and endearing charm.

Like Shakespeare this great healer of souls, whom I suspect to have saved the "Russian" nerves of St. Paul, the subject of his second masterpiece, by a wisdom as godlike as any of the miracles he records, was in a special sense a champion and interpreter of that sex towards which his excitable friend was so perversely hostile.

We come upon this peculiarity at the very start, in relation to the birth of both Jesus and John the Baptist. In sentence after sentence, full of a magic like that of the pictures of the Old Masters, and full, too, of a homely beauty like that of the anonymous ballads, he sketches the figures of the women whose sons are to change the world.

Nothing is more appealing in art, as Pater so well said, speaking of the early Renaissance, than the mingling of different "cultures" when each has behind it a deep and rich tradition; and St. Luke did through the medium of poetry what St. Paul did through the medium of psychology. He fused the humane intelligence of the Greek mind with the passionate poetry of the Hebrew soul. And, beyond both of these things, St. Luke anticipates the romantic feeling of the Middle Ages. Poet and physician in equal measure, it is as if he reverted on one hand to the healing science of the great classical Galen while on the other he stretched forward to the Celtic enchantments of Malory and the Holy Sangreal.

St. Luke and St. Paul are indeed the two writers to whom the New Testament owes what is most precious and memorable in its pages, and while the latter's epistles are the earliest of our Christian documents St. Luke's two amazing biographies dedicated to his friend Theophilus—and what would not we book-lovers give to possess translations in English of all the manuscripts in the library of this excellent bibliophile!—make up together what we might call the Record of the Case for the Defence in the Trial of God before the Court of Man.

St. Luke's biography of Paul of Tarsus, commonly called the Acts of the Apostles, certainly does much to increase our confidence in him as the biographer of Jesus. It is true his use of the pronoun "we" in the apostles' adventures evokes a realistic assurance to which the poetic spell he casts over the more momentous story carries no counterpart; but this is compensated for by the world-importance of the events. There have been rationalists who held the view—there may be some still—that Jesus of Nazareth never existed; but since it is impossible to question the existence of St. Paul, and since both in his own letters and in St. Luke's chronicle of his "excursions and alarums" St. Paul is for ever reverting to the recent death of his Man-God and hesitates not to dispute about Him with St. Peter, it is very hard to take this view. It becomes still harder to take it, when, in reading St. Luke's Gospel, the actual personality of Jesus with His ways, His paradoxes, His tenderness, His furious bursts of anger, His frustrations, His miraculous life-illusion, gathers body and blood before us.

Had St. Luke done with Him as we can conceive some crafty Simon Magus doing with some Hebraic Mithras, in order to obtain an occult background for his own sorceries, St. Luke would be a genius as much greater than Cervantes as Christ was greater than Don Quixote.

If the Jesus of St. Luke never lived, all one can say is that it is St. Luke and none other who is responsible for inaugurating that magic fairy Christ of the Middle Ages whom it is hard not to regard as humanity's most poetic creation, as much more aesthetically beautiful as he is less *verifiable*, than the "Christ" in our own deep, dark hearts, revealed to us by St. Paul!

But the point is if it hadn't been for the Jesus whose biography St. Luke writes St. Paul would never have discovered that there was what he calls "the mind of Christ" in all human souls, that "mind of Christ" which is the best hope of our blasted civilization.

Indeed one can say that if it hadn't been for the existence of Jesus St. Paul himself would never have existed, though no doubt there would have been in the annals of Tarsus a truculent and very learned Jew, proud of having been born at once a Pharisee of the Pharisees and a citizen of Rome; while the greatest step forward in evolution, where alone evolution matters, that is to say in the *humanizing of individuals*, would have been indefinitely postponed.

St. Luke makes it clear what an instinctive dramatist he is and no vulgar special pleader for the "Kingdom" by the prominence he gives to John the Baptist as the herald of this transvaluation of all values. The Baptist's own moral teaching was certainly sound and simple from the specimens St. Luke gives of it, and like Jesus himself this voice crying in the wilderness seems to have been an implacable

enemy to the crafty hypocrisies of church and state. And
yet with what dramatic feeling for the subtle differences between the great rebels does St. Luke indicate the touching
confidence the Baptist shows in the superiority of his rival.
And St. Luke with the most delicate art elucidates this superiority. He makes it consist entirely in the nature of the
"Kingdom," a kingdom revealed by Jesus as already present "among us" as well as "within us," but its *recognition* by
our hard hearts and clever brains "hidden," as St. Paul
would put it, "from the foundation of the world"!

And let us pretend for a moment, reader, that we are
literally and not merely metaphorically a bookworm, a
bookworm endowed with superhuman curiosity, who, in
some huge terrestrial *Bodleian*, has nibbled at the *logoi* of
Lao-tse and Kwang-tse, at the *logoi* of Heraclitus and Pythagoras, at the *logoi* of Buddha and Zoroaster—a real bookworm, more innocent of the actual world than the greatest
scholar. What would such a devourer of great men make of
this biography of Jesus as the artful poet-doctor rounds it
off for the benefit of Theophilus?

He would be quite ignorant, let us remember, of the dis-
putes of Catholics and Protestants, of Rationalists and Religionists. He would not "even so much as have heard" that
there was an Archbishop of Canterbury. All he would know
about Jesus, and about this "Kingdom" of his, would be
what St. Luke tells him—no more and no less. It would be
the King James Version he should be devouring; and as he
moved from page to page of that strange itinerary, with
Jerusalem ever growing always nearer, and the place called
Golgotha, "which is, being interpreted, the place of a skull,"
growing always nearer, and the as-yet-untenanted tomb of
the Arimathean growing always nearer, he would I think
cry out that he had found a drama equal to all the Greek
plays put together. Ignorant of so much as he would have
been he would at least, in his vermicular progress through

the library of Theophilus, know what physical pain meant and what necessity meant, and what the "insolence of office" meant, and what shame and remorse and humiliation meant, and what pride and hypocrisy and self-righteousness meant. Above all, he would know what every worm knows whether born in the leaves of a Bible or in the wood of a Gallows, that there's some illness, some sickness, some curse upon life, that makes cheerful endurance rather than thrilling happiness the prevailing temper of organic creation.

And our vermicular pilgrim would be surprised to discover that the *phenomenon of pain,* whether physical or mental, was *not* here, as it was with Buddha, the crux, pivot, and chief motive force of all philosophizing.

He would soon become aware that pain for the children of the "Kingdom" was incidental to life, was a means to life; and instead of "Nirvana," or escape from the Great Wheel, what "My Father's Kingdom" offered was simply "more life," life more abundant than ear has heard, or eye seen, or heart dared to imagine!

And he would further discover—with less of a shock perhaps *being what he was* than if he'd been the body-louse of a lama—that to be the lowest rather than the highest, the slave rather than the master, the fool rather than the wise, the last rather than the first, the tramp rather than the statesman, the harlot rather than the matriarch, the failure rather than the success, the abject rather than the distinguished, the desperate rather than the competent, was, though no more than pain and suffering an end in itself, in fuller harmony with the spirit of the "Kingdom" and offering a better chance of the "life everlasting."

Our bookworm would also be amazed, and even perhaps, if he were a very scholarly worm, a little horrified, at the part played by women in St. Luke's life of Jesus. Unused as he may be to *quite* such an *equality of all souls*, our little friend would find the "tempo" of this biography to savour more of the cheaper daily papers than of *The Education of Henry Adams*. Women and marvels, love and marvels, wedding-feasts and marvels, madmen and marvels, obstruction of traffic and marvels, faith-healing and marvels, riots in temples and marvels, disturbances at funerals and marvels, contempt of court and marvels, damage to property and marvels, interference with justice and marvels; and always women and love, women and death, and always the difference between the "haves" and the "have-nots"!

With women and the opening of the womb this artful doctor begins his story; and with women and the opening of the tomb he ends it.

And certainly it is not only scientists who have cause to be disturbed by this healing of the sick, this curing of the lame, the blind, the deaf, the dumb, without recourse to vivisection. The consistent moralist has every reason to be offended. "He that is not with me is against me." "He that is not against me is with me." What are we to make of such contradictions? And the unhappy fig-tree? And the drowned swine? And the unfair treatment of the hard-working elder son who got no "fatted-calf," and the laborious workers who had "borne the burden and heat of the day" compared with the lucky rogues who slipped in at the eleventh hour? And the subtle, complicated, mysterious ironies, as puzzling to us as to the simple disciples, about making friends with Mammon, and agreeing with our adversary quickly, and paying tribute to Caesar and letting the dead bury their dead? Well, there it is! Had these Gospel-writers been the tricky priests our rationalists call them, would they not have smoothed out these enigmatical creases in the coat without seam?

Apparently the great Baptist was completely satisfied before that fatal "strip-tease dance" took place in the palace; but modern critics want, it appears, quite other credentials from a Man-God than the lame walking, and the deaf hearing, and the poor being told they are nearer the "Kingdom" than the rich. And so the burden of that reiterated question still runs on, sighed, moaned, wailed, by a multitude of articulate and inarticulate voices, "Is this He we look for, or do we wait for another?"

Certainly upon one modern trouble of ours St. Luke's Jesus is strangely silent. What about the question, "Is it all worth it? Is it better to be alive than to be dead?" Or, again, is it perhaps all equal, all the same, one event or the other event, something or nothing, to be or not to be, all the same, all equal, the good and the evil, the just and the unjust, the merciful and the unmerciful, all equal, all a weariness and a folly?

But read as we may in this biography of Jesus, it does not appear that for one single moment did this ultimate doubt *as to the worth of life* present itself to the mind of the "Son of Man." And why was this? Why—so our worm might inquire—did the Devil, in his temptation in the wilderness, confine himself to such obvious human weaknesses as greed and power-lust and pride, and not suggest to the mind of the Saviour a Mephistophelean doubt as to the value of God's having meddled at all with the original and most blessed *nothingness*?

I fancy myself that our vermicular critic will have to wait for any bookish answer to this terrific question, this question as to why St. Luke didn't make a craving for nothingness, a longing for annihilation Our Lord's final temptation, till he arrives, in his nibbling progress, at Spengler's *Decline of the West*. Here he will discover that our Four Gospels represent the "springtime of Magian culture"; and that it is the characteristic of the "springtime" of every "culture" not only to take an optimistic view of the value of life, but to be *incapable of imagining any other view*.

We ourselves may be permitted to ask: "Is it the Semitic instinct as against the Hindu instinct, this upward-moving, dawn-growing, sap-rising *life-love* in St. Luke's Jesus? One can hardly say so, in face of the abysmal world-weariness in certain places in the Old Testament, particularly in the Book of Ecclesiastes. And if "nothingness" and its familiar-spirit death-longing are absent from the thoughts of Jesus, it is certain also that Carlyle was wrong when he called Christianity a "worship of sorrow."

Pain and grief, tears and mourning, privation, beggary, humiliations, insults, injuries—all these things are *only the way* to more natural happiness, to fuller natural life. They are a means to an end. They are *not* the end. Carlyle made the grand mistake of all perverted puritans.

I suspect that the poetical St. Luke in his medical attendance upon Paul of Tarsus reached an intimate knowledge of the fatal Manichaean twist that *could* be given to such sayings as, "He who looketh at a woman to lust after her hath committed adultery already with her in his heart," which is after all only what Shakespeare makes King Lear remark of the beadle and the whore. One has only to contemplate the life-tempo of the majority of the physically comfortable people one knows; and how dull, how stupid, how weary, stale, flat, and unprofitable they have allowed their response to life to grow!

The truth is you can much more justly accuse the Jesus of St. Luke of an immoral refusal to make *virtue its own reward* than you can accuse him of worshipping pain or calling upon any one else to worship pain. The *tribulations* of those who accept the "Kingdom of Heaven" are certainly one great way of overcoming the world, but St. Luke's Jesus never implies they are the *only* way. One feels sure that St. Luke did in the end get it into the head even of his self-tormenting patient, the neurotic St. Paul, that the great thing is not to worship the tribulations, but to *overcome the world*!

And St. Luke makes it quite clear that initiates of the "Kingdom of Heaven" fight with the world and with the powers of the world, and with the conventions and brutalities of the world, not for morbid or masochistic motives, but simply because, by reason of some profound cosmic law that Jesus discovered it is actually possible "to die to live" and that by "taking the lowest place" and diffusing one's self-assertion, and sacrificing one's pride, yes! by the actual endurance of pain itself, you sensitize your nature to subtleties unguessed at, and throw open, as it were, the pores of your psyche to magnetic waves of happiness from unknown depths!

But I would myself suggest that the problem of why Satan didn't tempt Jesus with the futility of creation and with the escape of nothingness, is best answered in a most simple way. All the feelings attributed by St. Luke to Jesus are natural feelings, natural and actual and human, though by no means always moral. May it not be therefore that St. Luke's Jesus does not struggle with a craving for nothingness and a weariness of Creation for the simple reason that this "nothingness" about which we moderns are so fond of talking, this "nihilism" with which we satisfy our cosmic sadism, has no *real existence*!

St. Luke's Jesus is a terrifying realist. He is so much a realist that he refuses, just as his heroic antagonist Nietzsche did, to dodge or to cover up with ideal phrases the ultimate contradiction between the will to power in us and the will to sacrifice. Neither of them compromised: for the one said, "Not my will but Thine be done!" and the other said, "Not I, but the Overman!" But we must confess the truth—the truth which as children, learning our "gentle-Jesus" rigmaroles, we longed to cry out!—the truth that St. Luke's Jesus is startlingly, shockingly, violently *arbitrary*. Inconsistency is the life-breath of realism. It is not our instinct, it is our reason that is consistent—"and that way madness lies." Had

St. Luke's Jesus displayed the "sweet reasonableness" with which Matthew Arnold credited him humanity would never have been brought to worship him as a God. Nietzsche has described some of the qualities of his Overman; but a far more interesting problem is, "What are the qualities necessary to a Man-God?"

And this problem has been solved once for all by St. Luke. This great biographer emphasizes in his magical picture of Jesus just exactly those qualities that lend themselves most to the desire, to the desperate *determination* of the anonymous generations of humanity that some particular "Son of Man" should be also the "Son of God." And is it necessary to repeat, what our vermicular pilgrim through the library of Theophilus has already discovered, that among these essential qualities in the making of a God it is not justice, not morality, not self-control, not stoicism, not reason, not consistency, that supply the necessary chemistry? And this is natural enough; for all these are qualities adapted rather to *disciples* of the "Kingdom" than to its "King."

Majestic lovableness and a magnetic passion for being loved, these are the chief characteristics that our Gospels, for it is not wily priests but imaginative poets who are the god-makers, give to their creations. Wherein lies the superiority, in this theandric art, of Christ over Buddha? Well, for the chief thing, Buddha never had a Semitic Greek like St. Luke to paint his picture!

It is the poetical scenes—Christ washing his disciples' feet, Mary Magdalen washing His feet, His encounter with the polyandrous woman at the well, His raising of Lazarus, His blessing the children, His turning water into wine, His encounter with the beautiful and rich young man, His riding into Jerusalem, His fondness for the young St. John, His praying in the garden, His denial by Peter, His shattering cry in His pain that His Father had left Him—much more than His blessings or His cursings or His parables, that make us call out as we read, like the remorseful Centurion at the end of the crucifixion, "Surely this *must* be the Son of God!"

No, it is the poetic realism of St. Luke's Jesus that saves him from our modern conception of *nothingness*. And, as I tried to hint just now to my imaginary bookworm, it *may* be that such nothingness doesn't exist but is a mere invention of our generation. Man invents devils and hells, why shouldn't he invent "nothingness"? Of course, as a matter of fact, no one has ever *experienced* this "nothingness" or, in the nature of things, ever *can* experience it. Even in sleep we do not know it, for we always dream, whether we remember our dreams or not. The hell that Jesus believed in, and to which he consigned His Father's enemies, so that the sound of their wailing and the gnashing of their teeth and their screams for one single drop of water might reach the glorified ears of all the Lazaruses in the bosom of Abraham, is a very different thing from *nothingness*.

I cannot tell how far Spengler would regard a belief in an everlasting hell for the hypocritical rich and for those who do not see in "the least of these little ones" the lineaments of God, as a healthy optimistic sign, a sign of a "springtime culture." But in any case it seems to me that, after once worshipping Christ, humanity will never be able to go back to Dionysus and his Vine-leaves, and will be extremely dubious about all Overmen.

The great question is, are there depths, I will not say in official Christianity (for *that* as we know has its "Faith Once for All Delivered" and had better stick to it), but in following Jesus, as we catch a clue here and a light there in the *New Testament as Literature*, that are still unfathomed?

Spengler and others have suggested that such a new direction may be found in the metaphysical Gospel of St. John. I do not believe it! And if I may, at the last, identify myself with our Theophilistic worm, I would confess a wormlike hesitation in accepting even William Blake's "Everlasting Gospel."

Had he been Anti-Christ, creeping Jesus,
He'd have done anything to please us!

Well, I'm not quite sure about that. Of course, you can say that the proof of the pudding is in the eating and that there is something aesthetically unpleasing about the pale, bland, soft, unrugged, edgeless, unbedevilled look of certain types of Christians; and I dare say these were the gentry whose "creeping" souls Blake so heartily damned. But on the other hand what is sometimes called "muscular Christianity" is almost equally unpleasant; and most of us Theophilus-worms have been bothered in our time by types that managed to blend together *both* these disagreeable elements. But to the devil with all this ungenerous un-Rabelaisian carping! God made them, these unengaging ones; and I dare say we, their heathen critics, don't always appear as beautiful as Shelley or as witty as Voltaire.

I cannot all the same help thinking that there *are* yet left deep veins of psychological secrets in the art of handling life and getting happiness out of life to be found in the literature of the New Testament that have scarcely been tapped at all. And for myself I would look for these new underground mole-runs in the direction I will now try to indicate, a direction not metaphysical but psychological.

As I have hinted, our Theophilus-worm after devouring pages of Lao-tse and Kwang-tse found the Semitic Saviour of the world a little too simple in his promises of life-happiness to those who loved him and suffered for his sake. But suppose we discount these promises as arguments *ad homines*. Isn't it possible that there are deep electric power-currents in the human *psyche* that can be tapped by exactly the same uncontending, uncompeting, un-self-assertive spirit, such as Jesus was to reward so liberally in "My Father's mansions," without any very vivid hope of ever reaching that "house, eternal in the heavens"?

And can one not imagine, too, a happy reversion to Rabelaisian Christianity, and even some subtle merging—hints of which I fancy I have found in Rabelais—of a cosmic beatitude and a delight in all sex-joys that "mean no harm" with the feeling of "being born again" into a selfless equality of all souls?

My San Francisco friend, Dr. Schott, has developed, on lines not unlike those followed by the famous Miss Weston in *From Ritual to Romance*, a theory about the birth of our Lord that gives it a ritualistic rather than a supernatural origin; but for my own purpose just here it is on the *Gospel itself* rather than the Gospel-Bringer that I want to concentrate.

Is it not sad how the unkind and spiteful piety of orthodox believers militates against the psychological evolution of Christ's Kingdom? How can we do justice to the divine anarchism that emanates from this Person until, as He suggests Himself, we prefer to blaspheme against Him rather than against the Spirit?

And the point that rationalists tend to forget is that if Western humanity *hadn't* worshipped Him as a God this terrific and shattering "message" would have only reached us as the sayings of Heraclitus or Pythagoras did, without *that weight*, as of "One who spoke with authority, and not as the scribes." Is it not possible that the evolutionary power, in, *and behind* our cosmos, did actually reveal in this Person's revolutionary attitude to human valuations a secret so important that the manner by which He reached it, whether by being a great Magician, or by being a great Prophet, or by being "the Christ, the Son of the Living God," is comparatively unimportant? Surely to any simple-hearted reader who tries to rule his thoughts—the one thing that does seem almost within our power!—by the godlike books

produced by inspired men, the problem as to the particular
relation between this one inspired Person and the power
behind the universe is a less important problem than the
intrinsic nature of His revelation?

What our Lord revealed as to the *best in life* was and remains something of such magnitude in the evolution of our
species that whether His view of Himself as "Son of Man"
and "Son of God" was, or was not, a scientifically correct
one, cannot, in comparison with the *content* of His revelation, trouble us very much. And if what Jesus thought about
Himself in relation to God is of minor importance, one may
certainly say that to any one who, while holding a magical
view of life, holds that in literature—in the New Testament
itself, for example!—rather than in organized religion, such
a view is found in its purest integrity, the question as to
what the churches decide to believe, or to disbelieve, is a
matter of no importance at all.

We are grateful, profoundly grateful, to Church and
State for keeping alive our interest in the Gospel according
to St. Luke; but we cannot but remember that the first
translators of this subversive Book, this portrait of the Jewish Anarchist "whose Kingdom was not of this World,"
were revolutionary scholars who were persecuted, tortured,
burnt, and their very bones desecrated, by organized government.

What St. Luke's Jesus did was to crack the heavy stone
rolled by the privileged and the powerful and the clever
and the scientific upon the spirit of man. The stone is there
still, with "the Children of this World" worshipping it, *but
the crack is there too;* and henceforth there must always come
moments in our lives when we doubt whether benevolence
and righteousness are quite enough, moments when, like
Dostoievsky's Alyosha accepting the fact that his hero's
corpse stank, we catch a breath of air through that crack,
a breath of air from outside, a breath of air that writes like

a finger in the dust. The world hums on and the cosmos hums on—and our last word is not St. Luke's; nor knoweth any man what it is. The world hums on and the cosmos hums on. . . . "But Jesus stooped down and with his finger wrote on the ground *as though he heard them not.*"

Homer

WERE THE Chinese the first among philosophers to indicate the magic power of the virtue of humility? The
ancient Taoists certainly perceived, not only the spiritual,
but the pragmatic efficacy of this subtle and—for most
men—this very difficult intellectual secret.

Nothing gets in the way of the culture of the young so
much as a certain self-confident conceit in their own
judgment, and not only in their own but in the equally
self-confident snap-verdicts of contemporary opinion.

Few things, it seems to me, are more important, in the
art of appropriating to our individual use the famous books
of the past, than a certain cautious suspension of judgment
where our personal reaction differs *negatively* from the long-
accumulated consensus of human feeling. As Goethe discovered, in one grand flash of illumination during his
Italian pilgrimage, it is better to give up once and for all
this vice of wasting our energy on the negative, on attacking
what we *don't* appreciate, instead of quietly and steadily
enlarging the sphere of what we *do*. The stultifying curse of
this kind of conceit works, of course, both ways. Many of us,
just because we don't understand and don't want to understand the creation of new forms and the subtlety of new
feelings, waste our strength in deriding what is to us
strange, obscure, repulsive. But I confess there seems more
excuse for this—for after all there must be *some* contempo-

53

rary fashions that will soon be buried in complete oblivion—
than for the same sort of negative arrogance applied to
books that the anonymous generations of our race have
sifted out from the rest as being of undying value.

The ideal thing as far as our personal culture is concerned is to have as few literary principles and convictions
as possible; and to "advance," if I may say so, forwards
and backwards at the same time, learning to overcome both
our natural distaste for the very new and our natural
distaste for the very old.

The easiest epoch to appreciate, among the writers
offered us, is the epoch just passing away. The further we
go back the harder it is, and we all know our difficulty with
an absolutely new genius, who has, as Coleridge so neatly
says, "to create the taste by which he is enjoyed."

The cultural "humility" I am advocating is after all
only the application to intellectual matters of the Taoistic
and, in a sense, the Christian secret as applied to more
mystical things.

Coming to Homer, then, in this unprincipled, unopin-
ionated, and fluid state of mind, we find ourselves confronted by a legend of grandeur that has gathered weight
for what I suppose must be nearly three thousand years.
Here is the origin of that wearisome word "epic," which,
like its exhausting relative, the word "saga," has become
a catchword of sounding hollowness and tinkling tedium.
There is something strangely symbolic in the fact that both
Homer and Shakespeare, the greatest poets among men up
to this hour, should have lost their identity as persons.

I do not say that in a corresponding manner we too must
lose our individual life-illusion in order to enjoy these great
mediums of the anonymous generations; but I do suggest
that there is a certain kind of personal conceit that sometimes hinders people from getting the full benefit from

Homer and Shakespeare as well as from more personal poets such as Dante and Milton and Goethe.

But the "humility" I have in mind is not at all the renouncing of our ego or the sacrifice of the inalienable "I, I, I" that urges us on, and by which we live. It is in fact the enlarging of this "I," and its unspeakable enrichment.

For when we read Homer the hard opaque stuff of our narrower selves melts into an element far more flowing, far less limited. Like water, like air we become; and in place of losing its identity the "I" in us slips out of its own brief transitoriness into the enduring continuity of endless generations of lives. In place of being a rock-bound pool of the ocean's flood, we become a living wave of its vast tide, rising and falling with it, and realizing our identity with it.

There are many reasons why a modern person finds it easier to read the *Odyssey* than the *Iliad*; and since up to the present I have shared this weakness—if weakness it be—and there does seem something hypocritical in advocating a virtue one has dodged oneself, I intend to confine my remarks to this easier work.

There are several reasons why the *Odyssey* is better adapted to modern minds than the austerer and more warlike poem. The first of these is the fact that women play a much more prominent part. Such a part indeed do they play—and not only women in person, whether mortal or immortal, but the things belonging to women's lives—that the more often we read the *Odyssey* the more indulgent we find ourselves to Samuel Butler's daring idea that a woman was its author!

Against this, however, must be set the passionate sympathy with minstrels that the poem displays, and with feudal servants, both masculine and feminine; and I sometimes feel as if it were more natural to attribute the *Odyssey* to the legendary blind Homer, leaving the advocates of the bardic school of oral reciters to apply their unappealing and to my mind unconvincing theory to the earlier poem.

At any rate, it is hard to resist the impression, as one reads, that the *Odyssey* is not only a later poem than the *Iliad*, but much more definitely the work of one hand.

It has, in fact—and that brings me to its second appeal to modern minds—an extremely marked *novelistic* interest. The "wrath of Achilles" is a larger, more complicated, more dramatic theme, and certainly our sympathy with that "sweet war-man" Hector supplies an "antagonist" lacking in the *Odyssey*, but for the simple and natural excitement—what is going to happen next?—the later work holds us more powerfully, holds us indeed as Odysseus himself held the crowd in the palace of Alcinous: "And they were all hushed in silence, and were spellbound throughout the shadowy halls."

But in addition to the emphatic feminine element, with so much space given to domestic life and to the feelings of servants, and in addition to the more intense interest of one single hero's adventures by land and sea, there is yet a third thing—and one much harder to define—that strikes us as more apparent in the *Odyssey* than the *Iliad*; I mean the romantic note. Here we get a touch, a tone, a feeling, especially in description, that comes very near to that peculiar Celtic quality so beautifully indicated by Matthew Arnold in his phrase "natural magic."

The essence of the Homeric attitude to life is the same in both poems, only a modern reader is, I think, seduced into an appreciation of this, and even—I would say—into an *acceptance* of this, more easily in the poem of adventure than in the poem of war.

Certain single episodes in the *Iliad* rise to grander, austerer, more rugged, more poignant, and, I admit, more overwhelming heights, heights unsurpassed in the Bible or in Shakespeare; but except for some of the speeches at the very beginning there is nothing tedious in the *Odyssey*.

It is the kind of tale that, from the neolithic age to our own, human beings have sat late by their fires to hear; whereas the everlasting killing and being killed in the *Iliad* does frequently grow very wearisome.

And what *is* this Homeric attitude that takes its place alongside of all the other abiding philosophies which our race has found for the endurance of life under the sun? It certainly comes nearer to the Nietzschean attitude than to any other. Can you not catch the a-moral aestheticism of Nietzsche's tone in this characteristic Homeric remark, "The gods spin the skein of ruin for men, that there might be a song for those yet to be born"?

But it is more massive, more earthy, and in a sense more tender and magnanimous than the desperate *sanctity reversed* of that misunderstood prophet of the spirit. And it is more pessimistic; for Nietzsche regarded death after the manner of all the great individual pagans from Catullus to Hardy, as an eternal sleep—*nox est perpetua una dormienda*— whereas in the Homeric system "the weary nations of the dead" survive in a pitiful half-life, in the dim Cimmerian underworld of Hades.

Some would say, "Why should we try to realize and to appropriate to our imaginations this Homeric view, if it be so dark and tragic?" Because it is *not* the tragedy of the general human fate that debases our spirit and lowers the temper of our lives; it is the burden of our private griefs, our private wrongs, and the weight of all the private ills "that flesh is heir to." It may be noted, in passing, how, in connexion with Homer's view of death, there occurs one of the most flagrant of all pietistic meddlings with a great passage. In Homer's Hades none other than Heracles himself speaks of his doom "although a son of God"; whereat some optimistic commentator hurries to interpolate a pious reminder that *this* Heracles is only an "eidolon" of the real one.

Granting that the Homeric view of the fate of the dead is the darkest—save for Dante's hell for the enemies of God—that has ever been accepted as life's background, it remains that it saves a man from that irrational fear of the vengeance of the Creator, which, while it has kept few cruel ones from their cruelty, has driven insane so many sensitive and gentle natures.

And what most of us suffer from is our absorption in our own cares and worries and afflictions, not any indignant spiritual protest against the general fate of the human race.

The value of "appropriating to our imagination" any intellectual or poetical view of death that has made a deep dent on the consciousness of the generations is that it shakes us out of the dull lethargy and sordid cares of the moment, and forces us to retort to the vision that shocks us, with a different vision, more congenial to our heart and our mind.

And what applies to this dark Homeric attitude to death—though it must be noted, in passing, that unlike the feeling of Catullus and Hardy and so many other noble heathen, the Homeric view allows for certain great exceptions to this sad half-life beneath the earth—applies also to the Homeric view of the primal importance of fame. To be had in honour among those who shall come after you—that is the grand wish-fulfilment, repeated over and over again, through the whole of the *Iliad* and *Odyssey*.

And we find exactly the same note in Dante and Milton. It is the one irresistible bribe that Dante's guide uses, all through the "Inferno," to make the lost souls reveal their identities: "This man I bring with me can give you fame upon earth."

And my point here is, not that we should accept this view of the importance of fame, which obviously can be of comfort only to the few, but that by being forced to substitute some subtler or more spiritual, or more philosophical

life-value for this emphasis on earthly renown, we are
pulled up in the midst of our meaner preoccupations to
establish some other life-illusion for ourselves, that shall
give dignity and meaning to our days.

Come, let the word be said! It does not matter much
what set of ultimate life-values we select, the Homeric, the
Mediaeval, the Shakespearean, the Christian. What is
important is that our consciousness should be continually
absorbing the magnetic ether of our race's subtler inspirations; and if they clash and contradict one another it matters
nothing. Indeed the clash between several noble ways of
life is the high tragedy of human existence, the everlasting
drama whereof the gods themselves are the audience!

If we are to be the true heirs of our immense heritage
we should aim at the power of passing from one to another of
these great ways of life, not merely picking out from them
something *here* or something *there*, for in eclecticism of such a
kind we tend to miss the deeper secrets of them all, but
actually throwing ourselves whole-heartedly first into one of
them *in its totality* and then into another! The richer our
own nature is, and the stronger our imagination, the deeper
we can go in fathoming the diverse secrets of these opposing
ways of life, all of which have their own magic, their own
mystery, their own illumination and their own eternal
values. The supreme sin, as Jesus would put it, "against
the Holy Ghost," is to allow ourselves to develop that
opaque encrustation of naïve modern conceit which renders
us blind to the high tragic drama that is being played out
every moment behind "the passing show," as the imperishable ideals of humanity meet and clash in the over-ether
of the spirit. Nothing in sacerdotal Christianity, nothing
in the less dogmatic moral Christianity of our time,
nothing in mediaeval romance, nothing in the Bible, nothing
in the great metaphysical systems of the Orient, can take

the place, in our actual day-to-day life, of what it is possible to draw from Homer.

The Homeric "secret," if I may use an expression applied to a very different way of life by Matthew Arnold, reduces itself in essence to a bold and drastic *selection* amid the chaos of fleeting impressions brought to us by our daily life.

Man is the valuing animal. His fellow creatures driven by instinct and necessity suffer and perish, even as he does; but one thing they lack—the glory and the pain of choice.

All men, even the most miserable, even those most driven by necessity, have innumerable occasions for making decisions. Such moments are often our most unhappy ones, for what we call "free will," whether an illusion or not from the point of view of rational logic, is man's supreme curse as well as his unique glory. It exists, for all our logic, as an intuitively felt fact. And it applies, not only to our outward actions but to our thoughts, to our emotional and sensuous responses to the life-stream round us. And this power of choice belongs to the deepest abysses of the soul. It is wilful, it is arbitrary, it is often insane; it is the assertion of the unique self within us against all reason, against all order, decency, duty, interest. The self within us, down in its unfathomable profundities, is the accomplice not only of life but of death, not only of creation but of destruction.

A man, as Dostoievsky explains in that story of his to which Hamlet might have given the title, "the fellow i' the cellarage," frequently wills his own hurt, his own injury, his own debasement, his own destruction.

But he can also will—even in the midst of the malice of circumstance—a certain *selection of things* upon which to concentrate, such as, set up in opposition to the venom of casualty, can give a grace, a dignity, a significance to the drift of his days.

Nor is that grouping of things, that isolation of things, that disentangling of certain things from certain other things, which the Homeric "secret" implies, out of the reach of any man or woman who is free from extreme physical pain.

Some heroic spirits among us can even practise this art when they *are* in great physical suffering, but this is so far beyond our average power that we need not consider it. In such extremity a man needs superhuman possession by the spirit, for at such times all normal philosophies, all systems, all methods, all "secrets" fail.

It is a question, *then*, of the spirit or nothing! The naked soul wrestles then with the adversary as best it may, and in a loneliness whereof few who have endured such things return to report. But the Homeric way of taking life is a perpetual process of mental and sensuous selection. It does not imply any idealization of life, or any enduring of this world on the strength of faith in another. It implies, above everything, an aroused and heightened consciousness of *the life-feeling in itself*. It implies a conscious pleasure in the feel of our limbs, feeble, ailing, or unathletic as these may be! It implies a conscious pleasure in movement as well as in rest, in getting up as well as in lying down, in the sweetness of falling asleep as well as in the sweetness of awakening to a new day.

By its continual process of selection, together with its parallel process of reducing to nonentity all the drift and rubble that it does not select, it enables us, *without idealizing anything*, to take each successive experience of the most normal day in a peculiar and special manner, and under a particular light.

Each of the experiences it selects, reducing the rest to automatic unconsciousness, is of a definite sort, of the sort that by natural necessity has been repeated in the lives of men for thousands of years.

The use of water is the first of these. Never in Homer is the act of washing the hands before a meal allowed to pass unrecorded. Then the meal itself is never partaken, according to Homeric ritual, without some kind of offering to the Immortals "from men who eat bread upon the earth."

And along with the gravest symbolic emphasis upon the simple act of the making of your bed, or the preparing of a bed for a guest—and all strangers at your gate, especially the destitute and poor, are under the peculiar and special protection of the Father of Gods and Men, the friend of supplicants—there is always placed a magical significance upon the mere act of crossing the threshold, either to enter or to go forth, of any, even the humblest abode of men. Nor can too much be made of a certain exquisite delicacy of feeling at these Homeric hearths, a feeling full of what one might call superdomestic refinement; such as when the king stops Demodocus in the middle of his lay because of the sobbing of their guest.

What I have presumed to call the "secret" of Homer is indeed the isolation of, *and the poetic deepening of our consciousness of*, those recurrent situations, necessities, significant human gestures, in the span of any ordinary life, that in the nature of the case have been repeated since the beginning. What the Homeric way of thought delivers us from is that accursed habit of taking the essentials of life for granted which cheapens, debases, and vulgarizes all, and steals the heart out of the very mystery of being alive.

The Homeric "secret" restores to the relation between man and wife, child and parent, chief and companion, comrade and fellow, that overtone of poetic dignity that in its essence is a religious acceptance of fate. It gives back to life, and it gives back to death as the inevitable rounder-off of life, that sense of a tragic and a pitiful grandeur, which our overbalanced concentration on absorbing realistic details takes away.

In our unphilosophical sophistication we pine for a thousand assuagements, demanding novelties, excitements, distractions, agreeable shocks, tributes to our vanity, and a thousand sweet morsels for the palate of our insatiable egoism such as the nature of things in the normal continuity of human life cannot supply. "If *only* it had been *so!*" we groan. "*If only* we had chosen *that* instead of this!" while all the while the large, majestical zodiac signs of the destiny that *is* ours look down in melancholy wonder upon our fussy petulance.

Hard and difficult was life for our fathers before us; hard and difficult is life for us. But, along with the endurance of this, there remains our consciousness of the historic dignity of the struggle itself and the preciousness of those recurrent compensations that of necessity come round in their hour to all but the most unhappy.

There are moments of terrible tragedy in these Homeric poems and there are moments of radiant exultation; but the deeper note that rises up from the accumulated weight of their oceanic flow is a note of solemn quiet, of fate accepted, of life not exuberantly commended but taken for what it is, grim and pitiful, with its own strange, sad beauty, and at least able to be justified—as an incredible tale.

In all the greatest poems of the world as they tell us this tale of fate, this struggle and this acceptance, there come moments, often near the end of it all, that convey an indescribable sense of peace. At such moments there rises from the very simplicity of the words a magic and a healing that totally evades definition. Under the touch of this magic a great quiet descends upon our spirit and we grow ashamed of our turbulence, our hurry, our ignoble self-pity, our insatiable discontent. It is not—as with the Christians—that we turn from defeat in this world to triumph in another. It is rather as though we heard the voice of our personal wrongs and private miseries caught or sinking down into the orchestral utterance of all the generations, into the tune of the ancient sorrow of the earth herself.

Shakespeare has a passage of this sort where Lear's madness is cured by Cordelia; and again where they go away to prison together. Dostoievsky has it between the Prince and Ragozin when they meet over the murdered corpse of Nastasia. And in the *Odyssey* we get it as early as the thirteenth book, when, long after he has had his final word with the daughter of the house whose love he has had to reject, after he has finished his tale and the sun has gone down, and the ship is ready for its silent voyage through the night, he prepares to cross for the last time that hospitable threshold.

> So he spoke . . . and they poured libations to the blessed gods, who hold broad heaven, from where they sat. But goodly Odysseus arose and placed in the hand of Arētē the two-handled cup, and spoke and addressed her with winged words:
> "Fare thee well, O queen, throughout all the years, till old age and death come, which are the lot of mortals. As for me, I go my way, but do thou in this house have joy of thy children and thy people and Alcinoüs the king."
> So the goodly Odysseus spake and passed over the threshold.

Now I am not unaware that to many among my readers these simple lines will convey no particular significance; but, as Plato might say in his tentative manner, "does it not seem" as if a certain magical end-of-the-day evocation, full of tender assuagement and an almost religious solemnity, gathers upon us as we read, not so much like the rich, harsh, mystic note from some Gothic bell-tower, as like the very sound of the river of life itself, deep and full-brimming, infinitely sad and yet infinitely healing?

No, the underlying secret of Homer's poetry, below all the stirring romance and below all the majestic primordial drama, is *a divine spirit of selection* by which the monumental facts of human existence, caught under a certain imperishable poetic light, stand forth in noble relief, freed from the vulgarity, the triviality, the litter and debris, of the transitory and the unessential.

Who that loves to read Homer can cross any human threshold either entering or leaving, without something of that momentous symbolic feeling that is so well summed up in the familiar Biblical expression, "Peace be upon this house!"?

And it is the same with the basic dignity of human beings themselves. Along with the thoughtless cruelties of that age of "pitiless brass," following perhaps only too closely upon a kindlier age, the legended "Saturnian age" of peace and the unbloody cult of the Great Mother, along with women sold for so many heads of cattle, along with the reckless sacking of cities, and all the slaughter and the blood, there does appear—stress the proud aristocratic note as much as you please!—a grand primeval natural democracy in these poems, wherein to be a man under the sun, or a woman under the sun, is a thing *in itself* of magical awe and reverence.

None who has read Homer can say that swords and spears and chariots and horses are the only poetry he knows. Not only are earth and sea and the revolving seasons and the stars in their courses treated as they have never been treated since, but the recurrent amenities of life within our gates, the preparation of fire and food, the mixing of wine, the pouring of water, and, above everything, the handiwork of women, their fabrics, appliances, and utensils, together with the exquisite crafts of divine artificers, all in fact that might be called the eternal poetry of man's domination of matter, play such a part in these cosmogonic ballads that those who read only for the excitement of the action will be fain to skip many long-drawn passages.

There is no poem in the world in which the dramatic significance of the revolving hours of the day plays so dominant a part. From the earliest rising of "rosy-fingered dawn" upon her twilit "dancing lawns," till the moment when "all the ways grow dark" we are made aware of the huge ethereal background against which we are fated to yield or endure, to perish or survive.

And although the abiding monotone of the whole is the long endurance of man amid his arduous days and his incessant tribulations, there come moments, again and again, when the ineffable dew of golden happiness, of large and liquid rest, descends to redeem all sorrows. To bear for a bitter space, to enjoy for a brief moment, is the Homeric norm; but beneath both the long endurances and the divine interludes there is always a thin film of inextinguishable exultation; exultation, if one may say so, in being permitted the double-edged experience at all, in being allowed the privilege of sharing the tragic human consciousness, before which and through which, the enchanting and abominable spectacle is unfolded.

Those who read Homer merely as beautiful poetry, or enjoy it with antiquarian zest as something old and naïve and quaint, miss entirely, in my view, the real Homeric spirit. The mistake of such readers is to put an impassable gulf between our life and the Homeric life, treating our gods, our cults, our ways of feeling as true to reason and common sense, while Homer's have a merely pedantic, a merely curious, a merely aesthetic interest.

Quite the reverse of this is the case. Much of our modern thought depends upon scientific dogmas that will only last a few brief years before they are superseded by others, doomed in their turn to be discarded; whereas in its essentials the Homeric secret pertains to the unperishable gestures and the eternally recurrent situations of life, which are as real and as true to-day as they were ten thousand years ago!

Another mistake these curious dalliers and dabblers fall into is to lay all the stress upon the warlike and athletic aspects of these poems, completely missing what the mere legend of Homer himself as a blind slave among the women and the minstrels should have led us to look for, and of which the poets who have most loved him, nervous sensitives like Cowper, cripples and invalids like Pope, imaginative city dwellers like Keats, are the best proof, namely that, as in the case of Walt Whitman and Rabelais and Shakespeare, there is a magical secret here which is dedicated, above everything else, to put new life into the feeble knees, new strength into the feeble hands, and a new world-feeling into the perverted senses of the depressed, the timid, the sickly, the degenerate.

Each of us who can say in his heart, "I am a man" or "I am a woman," and, "I still eat bread upon the earth," and "I am still among the living and have not yet gone down among the dead," when one of those four winds, of which Homer is always speaking, blows upon his face, or when one of these constellations, to which Homer is always pointing, rises above his head, or when that unique voice, of what Homer calls the "many-sounding" sea, comes surging to his ears, or the Master of Life, "who seeth all things and heareth all things," comforts him with his rays, and can once more gather up "his steadfast heart within him" to endure and enjoy, lives, whether he knows it or knows it not, in the spirit of the secret of Homer.

For there is a magic touch in these poems that arouses something in the deep soul of a man that accepts our hard fate beneath the sun though it never hinders him from relieving his soul in the sweet comfort of shameless weeping.

There is certainly no Nordic pride in Homer over the restraining of tears! In Homer we always feel that tears themselves are an essential part of the mystery of life, linking cradle to grave on the sobbing surge of a great salt sea of lamentation.

"So saying, he sat down, and Telemachus, flinging his arms about his father, wept and shed tears; and in the hearts of both arose a longing for crying. And they wailed aloud more vehemently than birds . . . sea-eagles . . . whose young the country-folk have taken from their nest before they were fledged; even so piteously did they let tears fall from beneath their brows."

And it must be remembered that all this unconquerable acceptance of the way life is has always as its infinitely pitiful background what must seem to many of us a sadder fate than absolute annihilation.

"So she spoke, and I pondered in heart, and was fain to clasp the spirit of my dead mother. Thrice I sprang towards her, and my heart bade me clasp her, and thrice she flitted from my arms like a shadow or a dream, and pain grew ever sharper at my heart. . . .

" 'My mother, why dost thou not stay for me, who am eager to clasp thee, that even in the house of Hades we two may cast our arms each about the other, and take our fill of chill lamenting?' "

But even this pitiful glimpse of the state of the dead is not totally unredeemed. The great pendulum between pleasure and pain can still swing a little, even in the final abyss!

Odysseus tells Achilles in that sad twilight the one piece of news that could really stir him.

"So I spoke, and the spirit of the son of Aeacus departed with long strides over the field of asphodel joyful in that I said that his son was pre-eminent."

One piece of advice I want especially to offer to all young people anxious to be initiated into the Homeric attitude to life. Avoid, like the devil, *all* poetical translations. Let the Homeric secret reach you through the simplest, barest, baldest prose translation! Let it be *your* business to throw the imaginative and the poetic glamour over what you read. Out of *your* mind, out of *your* sensibility must come the magical touch, what I might call *the Homeric Greek of the soul*. Something of this sort is necessary even if, in your youth, you have learnt the Greek letters; but if the literal Greek remains impossible to you, remember that no poetic rendering, except what springs from your own mind and imagination, is of the least avail.

Make the simplest prose version your text, and let your own spirit be the great original! All the supreme poets of the world can adapt their secrets somehow to our modern life, but none can do so as naturally, as easily, as inevitably as Homer.

Airplanes, sky-scrapers, automobiles, the wireless, the new ways of love, the new illusions, the new disillusions, all can be accepted, all can be disregarded, in the Homeric mood.

For the spirit of Homer is the spirit of man's contact with the elements, of his life in relation to the elements.

As long as air and water, as long as earth and fire remain, none else but these can be the real background of our struggle.

The dignifying, the simplifying, the heightening of our endurance depends still upon those large and significant moments wherein something corresponding to the Homeric secret blows like a fresh wind upon the turmoil of our days.

Still, as in the great king's prayer, in the third book of the *Iliad*, we instinctively fortify our weakness by calling upon these immortal spectators of our loyalties and treacheries, that they may strengthen our covenant. "O Sun," we cry still, "who beholdest all things and hearest all things! O rivers! O earth! O ye that in the world below have done with life! Be our witnesses this day that we keep faith with ourselves, and with one another, and with our fathers that were before us!"

Greek Tragedy

THE BEST *Introibo ad altare* for a person approaching
Greek tragedy for the first time or returning to it
after a lapse of years would be to read Walter Pater's
Greek Studies; but better still would it be, without any
such "grace," to plunge boldly into the dark waters.

Second only to Homer in their influence over our Western
nations, the three great tragic dramatists of Athens have
come to dominate not only the theatre, where even Shakespeare's magic has been unable to resist them, but the whole
field of what might be called the imaginative culture of
Europe.

In our own time this is still true. Greek tragedy, and not
Shakespeare, was in Hardy's mind when he wrote *The
Dynasts*. Greek tragedy, and not Shakespeare, looms up
as the main aesthetic influence behind the plays of Eugene
O'Neill; and when you turn from the modern stage to the
modern novel, this same tremendous tradition, austere,
sombre, ironic, naked and stripped, will be still found, like
a submerged spirit under the ship's keel of each powerful
new book, dominating the particular dark course it
ploughs.

It is not the influence of Shakespeare that we find in the
architectonics of their work in such opposite talents as
those of Ibsen and Strindberg, such different temperaments
as those of Edgar Lee Masters and Theodore Dreiser. In

such a strange, powerful, modern story as William Faulkner's *Absalom, Absalom!* the dark background, the underlying scaffolding of the subject is Sophoclean, not Shakespearean.

Nor is it without significance that the enormous tidal wave of psychoanalysis takes so much of its mysterious wine-dark pressure from this same source.

Listen to what Jocasta says to her husband-son in *Oedipus the King* :

> *Why should a mortal man, the sport of chance,*
> *With no assured foreknowledge, be afraid?*
> *But live a careless life, from hand to mouth.*
> *This wedlock with thy mother fear not thou.*
> *How oft it chances that in dreams a man*
> *Has wed his mother!*

The terrifying poetry of the American Jeffers, the terrifying stories of James Hanley, carry on the same lurid *frisson*, the same dark shudder, purging still, as Aristotle said, our grosser, feebler passions, by means of the sublime catharsis of pity and terror.

And the curious thing is that so many of us whose actual knowledge of Greek tragedy is extremely limited, in some cases *nil*, are found gravely making use of the House of Atreus, or the doom of Oedipus, or the fate of the prophetic Teiresias, in order to score some passing point in an aesthetic dispute, or to establish some dubious excellence in a favourite author.

To my mind the two supreme influences over our modern imagination in all ultimate *intellectual passions* are Dostoievsky and Nietzsche; and what could be more in the vein of Greek tragedy than the murder of the father in *The Brothers Karamazov* or more clairvoyant of the double-edged secret of their handling of life than Nietzsche's distinction between the Apollonian and the Dionysian, and his tremendous paradox that the horror of these old plays was the result of the overbrimming of a heroic happiness, that found relief in ritualistic atrocity, *not* a resentful pessimism, taking its revenge upon life?

The subject of the present volume being the enrichment of our pleasure in reading the great books of the world, a word at this point directed to such younger readers as have been, in Charles Lamb's phrase, "defrauded of the sweet food of academic institution" seems not out of place.

I would modestly suggest that any reader at present unacquainted, save from hearsay, with Greek tragedy, in place of reading academic books about them, and in place of reading brilliant poetical reproductions of them, should get hold of the baldest, plainest, simplest *literal prose translation*—one or two plays of each of the three—and note his immediate personal reaction, his reaction to Aeschylus, to Sophocles, to Euripides, with all the preferences, predilections, and comparative responses excited by such successive encounters.

When one is young—I am pretty sure I am not only speaking for myself—one has a tendency to read with eager passion every subtle and penetrating appreciation one can come at of these tremendous works, enjoying the fascinating impressions of literary scholars rather than undertaking the harder mental effort, with the text in our hands, of analysing our own individual reactions.

In certain rare instances, such as in the case of Walter Pater's *Greek Studies* and Nietzsche's *Birth of Tragedy Out of Music*, this method *has* its justification; but these two critics are unique. They not only think, feel, and see for us, they compel us to think, feel, and see for ourselves; whereas the many other charming, plausible, and erudite books on the subject inform us without inspiring us, enlighten us without transporting us, and thicken out our knowledge in place of giving us a living, growing, and organic experience of our own. There does remain, however, the quite legitimate pleasure of noting the favouritism shown by later poets for one or other of these three dramatists.

It would seem that both Milton and Goethe had a partiality for Euripides; while Matthew Arnold, on the other hand, is at pains to make clear his preference for Sophocles; and I like to think that the reference to Aeschylus at the end of his sacrifice of *Tess* may indicate the one among the three to whom Thomas Hardy most instinctively turned.

Homer was the inexhaustible quarry from which they all drew their inspiration; and coming to which of them you will, you cannot but be impressed by his inability to catch that incomparable chord of absolute human simplicity which that greatest of poets alone can strike.

Take these lines, for instance, describing the tears of Penelope while her husband, as yet unknown to her, gives her his unquestionable proof that he had really seen the lost hero:

> He spoke; and made the many falsehoods of his tale seem like the truth, and as she listened her tears flowed and her face melted as the snow melts on the lofty mountains, the snow which the East Wind thaws when the West Wind has strewn it, and as it melts the streams of the rivers flow full: so her fair cheeks melted as she wept and mourned for her husband, who even then was sitting by her side.

It is a tone like this that inevitably lifts the heightened simplicity of Homer, with its direct ballad-like poignance, into "an ampler ether, a diviner air" than can ever be attained by the more lurid tension of drama.

Let us begin by considering the greatest of all trilogies, the three closely-knit plays of Aeschylus dealing with the deaths of Agamemnon and Clytaemnestra and the hunting of Orestes by the Furies.

And, by the way, isn't it significant of the absolute predominance of these old Greek poets, that to-day, almost within a decade of the middle of the twentieth century, the highest ambition of a modern novelist should be to compose a "trilogy" reminiscent of this one, just as the highest praise a critic can give to any spiritual tale of adventure is to call it "epic"?

The "fragment from the Homeric feast" which Aeschylus expands into the greatest as it is the earliest trilogy of our human stage is still inferior to its fountain-source. Odysseus is telling them in the halls of Alcinous, how across his trench of blood at the mouth of Hades he spoke to the outraged spirit of the dead king:

"When then Holy Persephone had scattered this way and that the spirits of the women there came up the spirit of Agamemnon, son of Atreus, sorrowing. . . . He knew me straightway, when he had drunk the dark blood, and he wept aloud, and shed big tears, and stretched forth his hands toward me eager to reach me. But no longer had he aught of strength or might remaining such as of old was in his supple limbs . . . but he straightway made answer and said . . . 'Ere now thou hast been present at the slaying of many men . . . but in heart thou wouldst have felt most pity hadst thou seen that sight, how about the mixing bowl and the laden tables we lay in the hall and the floor swam with blood. And the most piteous cry that I heard was that of the daughter of Priam, Cassandra, whom the guileful Clytaemnestra slew by my side. And I sought to raise my hands and smite down the murderess, dying though I was, pierced through with the sword. But she, the shameless one, turned her back upon me, and even though I was going down to the house of Hades deigned neither to draw down my eyelids with her fingers nor to close my mouth.' "

What one notices especially—and no doubt it is of the essence of dramatic as against epic poetry—is that in every single point where horror can be increased by the particular twist given to the tale it *is* increased and where passion can be intensified to the breaking-point it *is* intensified; although in both cases something—that strange redeeming sense of the normal world going on when it is all over, that sense of an indescribable peace out of storm which Shakespeare, dramatist though he was, aims at giving us in *his* greatest plays—is of necessity lost.

Yes, dramatist though he was, Shakespeare made an obvious effort at the end of all his great tragedies to catch something of the redeeming peace of the monotone of normal life as the last wail of passion dies down and the last crimson bubbles sink. But consider the close of all the greatest plays of Aeschylus, Sophocles, and Euripides.

Oepidus at Colonus does indeed actually close with the words:

> *Wail no more, let sorrow rest,*
> *All is ordered for the best.*

And this tone is made possible by the nature of the protagonist's mysterious departure from the world. But the actual feeling with which we are left as the man's unhappy daughters depart for their besieged home is not so much expressed in this complacent tag as in those lines a little before, when the ill-starred Polyneices is about to make his unwanted appearance:

> *Not to be born at all*
> *Is best, far best that can befall,*
> *Next best, when born, with least delay*
> *To trace the backward way.*

In the same manner, by reason of its comparatively "happy ending," the *Eumenides* of Aeschylus closes on a serene tone. But this is something very different from that

Shakespearean feeling of calm produced by the flowing onwards of the long-drawn tide of normal human life.

The close of the *Prometheus Bound* as well as of the *Agamemnon* and the *Libation-Bearers* is upon the note of unrelieved disaster; and as for the manner in which Euripides ends his *Bacchanals* and his *Medea* one can only say that one hopes our grosser passions *are* purged by such piling up of frightfulness, for we have certainly no other comfort left!

Curiously enough, Euripides closes both the *Medea* and the *Bacchanals* with the same words, save that in the former the issue is attributed to the dooms of Zeus, *tamias Zeus*, and in the latter to the works of the gods, *morphai tōn daimoniōn*:

O the works of the Gods—in manifold wise they reveal them:
Manifold things unhoped-for the Gods to accomplish bring.
And the things that we looked for, the Gods deign not to fulfil them;
And the paths undiscerned of our eyes, the Gods unseal them.
So fell this marvellous thing.

To grasp what Greek tragedy really means, to grasp what of its mystic secret we can appropriate to ourselves in this modern age, what we can make our own for the benefit of that undertide of our life that remains unaffected by outward occasion, it is necessary to recall its ecstatic, orgiastic origin.

Whenever any human being among us feels that particular mystic rapture which brings spirit and sex together, and religion and sex together, and nature and sex together, and life and death together, he is in musical harmony with the essence of Greek tragedy!

Whether you are by the destiny of your character a worshipper of *Apollo*, that is to say of creative order, of reasonable beauty, of self-control, of intellectual light, or on the other hand a worshipper of *Dionysus*, that is to say of losing yourself in the delirious darkness of those wild, torn,

broken intimations that set beauty and reason and even
decency at defiance, you can find underlying the austere
traditional forms of Greek tragedy certain mysterious channels, dug down deep into the passion-rock of your life,
along which your strongest feelings can flow.

Few of us go through existence without being aware of
intermittent emotions which seem to belong neither to
what we call morality nor to what we call immorality,
seem in fact to spring directly from some supermoral or
submoral level of being, where *these* distinctions disappear,
but where others even deeper in their opposition rise up
and manifest themselves. Religion and irreligion, reverence
for Zeus and defiant fellowship with Prometheus, alternate
in these emotions like turn and counter-turn, strophe and
antistrophe, in an orgiastic dance of the opposing poles
of the life-force.

Against the proud sun-smitten lute-strings of Apollo you
will feel, rising and falling on the wind, the dark, ensorcerized flute-breathings of Dionysus. To each of them in
mystic alternation responds the heart-beat of a universe
at war with itself.

It is the ritual-dance of creation which is also the ritual-
dance of the destruction of creation. It is the sex-dance of
Destiny with Chance. "Om! Om! Om!" beat the tom-toms
of the one. "Konx! Om! Pax!" clash the cymbals of the other.
Greek tragedy may strike us to-day as something austere
and wooden, and yet something monstrous and superhuman like the galvanic gestures of vast cosmic dolls, who,
rising on the rim of our round world, nod and wail at one
another, bow and bend to one another, and hurl at one
another bleeding thunderbolts of meteoric malediction.

Out of spontaneous rural pantomime, out of fantastic
mumming and miming, out of the wild dances of satyrish
grotesques, out of what was half-ritual, half-orgy, out of
what must have been touched from the beginning by the

darker elements of this cult of the beautiful, cruel, womanish god, who was the perilous life-sap of creation, was moulded at last, by one of the strangest metamorphoses in the history of art, what we now know as Greek tragedy.

From ecstasy in the stirring of the sap, from ecstasy in the blood of the grape, and from ecstasy in the seminal pulse of sex rose ritual, and from ritual rose this mysterious and unique art, an art that could spiritualize and sublimate the wildest excesses of its phallic origin by the pity and terror of the Tragic Muse. It was the ritual of musical *orgia*—a Greek word that connoted much more than mere erotic excess—that led to the tragedies performed in the Dionysian festival; and running like a mystic undertone through all these plays is a sense of the undivulged mysteries of Eleusis wherein the cult of Dionysus was mingled with that of the Earth-Mother and with that of her daughter, the bride of Hades.

Thus it comes about that at the heart of Greek tragedy we recognize the abysmal contradictions of the world we know, the contradiction between Good and Evil, Mortality and Immortality, Fate and Free Will, and remotely and dimly discerned behind even these—with the presence of the Eleusinian Mysteries always in the background—yet stranger oppositions, and "knots of contrariety," in the very workshop of creation itself!

It is because these tragedies were linked from the start with the equivocal figure of Dionysus, that suffering and wounded and yet cruelly-avenging power, that so mystic an undertone slips again and again into their texts, culminating in Aeschylus with the pacifying of the Furies, in Sophocles with the "passing" of Oedipus, and in Euripides with the blood-lust of the fatal god himself.

Stiff and formal as they may seem—with only the death-cries of their victims reaching us from behind the stage—they never quite lose their original erotic and orgiastic tension, never quite lose a certain un-Achaean, un-Dorian, un-Apollonian element, an element that suggests Asia *and even Africa,* an element thaumaturgic, exotic, incestuous, barbaric.

It must always be something of a shock to come to one of these great tragedies, to *Agamemnon,* or *Oedipus Rex,* or *Medea,* after reading Homer.

It is in Homer we get the pure Greek tone, unaffected by the "sciences," as Taliessin would say, of "Asia and Africa"; and the curious thing is that in Homer we feel as though the very *physical stature* of the heroes were more human, more normal, more like ourselves.

Something has entered into the style of these plays from the enormity of the masks they put on, from the height of the buskins that supported them, perhaps even from the megaphonic contrivances within those masks that made it possible for their voices to reach that huge Dionysian audience, something that overpowers the lovely and natural humanity that we know in Homer. In Homer the very gods are humanized, while the sun that "beholdest all things and hearest all things" is the natural sun with which we are all familiar. The elements are *our* elements, those we struggle with and instinctively worship in our common human experience. The sea is *our* sea, into which our own sailors still "go down in ships." The furrows made by Homeric ploughs through the "grain-bearing earth" are the furrows we see round us in the fields of our own childhood.

And in spite of all the lurid and blood-curdling situations in these plays we are never touched—no! not when Euripides makes Medea speak of the rose-petal breath of the children she is going to slaughter—by the real pity of life, as we are in Homer when Andromache's child is scared by Hector's helmet, or when the dog Argus knows its master before it dies. Shakespeare is twenty times more Homeric than Aeschylus or Sophocles or Euripides.

How often our reviewers cry "like a Greek chorus"! But although this same chorus has grown to be, for our obsequious modern mind, the sharpest sting of dramatic contrast and the deepest bite of ironic emphasis, there is surely more real "irony" and far more human poignance in the crazy jesting of the nameless Fool in *Lear* than in any comment made by "Asian Bacchanals" or "Argive Elders" or "Ladies of Corinth."

"You are as good as a chorus, my lord," says Ophelia to Hamlet, and so he was; and indeed the whole method of Shakespeare compared with Sophocles is to bring this detached commentary upon the philosophy of events into the circle of a man's own consciousness.

"Duncan is in his grave: after life's fitful fever he sleeps well," might perhaps be murmured by a Sophoclean protagonist, but it would have to be left to a Sophoclean chorus to chant the words:

> *—Man must abide*
> *His going hence, even as his coming hither;*
> *Ripeness is all.*

But it is foolish to spend more than a moment in indicating what Greek tragedy is not! Enough to note that to be what it is, to be as great and unique as it is, something had to be sacrificed; and what was sacrificed—to leave Shakespeare out of it and return to Homer—was that lovely, magical, natural poetry of normal life that thrills us most when it brings down Zeus and Hera and Athene and Apollo and Priam and Helen and Penelope and Circe and Calypso and Achilles and Odysseus to our own human level.

Yes, in Homer the sun is the sun, and the earth the earth; and the gods are even as we ourselves are, save that death cannot touch them, whereas in the tragedians—due in part no doubt to that narrow stage and that great altar-space and those masks and buskins and megaphonic devices—every event, every person, seems surrounded by a cloud of mysterious ritual, seems to carry an aura of supernatural significance that recedes into invisible regions.

Compare the dialogue between Odysseus and Penelope in Homer over the matter of the *bedstead* with that between Agamemnon and Clytaemnestra over the matter of the *carpets*. Quite apart from the completely different situations you feel that in the one case the question concerns a real bedstead in a real court made from a real olive bush.

While you feel in the other that before some nebulous and windy portico to some vast royal Palace, "out of Space, out of Time," these imperial carpets, streaming blood-red in their blood-red extension, are unrolled before a chariot of vapour and a phantom king!

Take the Homeric scene first:

"—Nay come, nurse, strew me a couch that all alone I may lay me down, for verily the heart in her breast is of iron. . . ."

"Come, Eurycleia, strew for him the stout bedstead which he made himself . . . thither do ye bring it. . . ."

"Woman, truly this is a bitter word that thou hast spoken! Who has set my bed elsewhere? Hard would it be . . . for a long-leafed olive was growing within the court . . . and from this I hewed out my bed . . . but I know not, woman, whether my bedstead is still fast in its place or whether by now some man has cut from beneath it the olive stump and set the bedstead elsewhere."

So he spoke, and her knees were loosened where she sat, and her heart melted, as she knew the sure tokens which Odysseus told her. Then with a burst of tears she ran straight toward him and flung her arms about the neck of Odysseus and kissed his head and spoke saying:

"Be not vexed with me, Odysseus, for in all else thou wast ever the wisest of men. It is the gods that gave us sorrow, the gods who begrudged that we two should remain with each other and enjoy our youth and come to the threshold of old age. . . ."

And now would the rosy-fingered Dawn have arisen upon their weeping, had not the goddess glaucous-eyed Athene taken other counsel. The long night she held back at the end of its course, and likewise stayed the golden-throned Dawn at the streams of Oceanus and would not suffer her to yoke her swift-footed horses that bring light to men, Lampus and Phaethon, who are the colts that bear the Dawn.

Now let us come to Aeschylus and to Agamemnon's return home. Powerful and terrible indeed is the weight of the Aeschylean irony! More formidable to my mind is it than the neater, cleverer, more famous irony of Sophocles. But this huge, crushing, sardonic sublimity of Aeschylus moves and has its being in "worlds not realized." Among pillars and porches and altar-stones of an ideal Argos it gathers its "trailing clouds" of doom. A background of the symbolic traditions of a remote ritualistic art lies behind this Argos of fatal mysteries; whereas the "local habitation" of the house of Odysseus is as real and actual to us as are the colts of the Dawn, Lampus and Phaethon, whom the goddess holds back until that olive-tree bedstead has satisfied the longing that has been frustrated for twenty years.

But at this other home-coming let us hear the words of Clytaemnestra:

"And now, I pray thee, dear my lord, dismount from this thy car, but set not on common earth this foot of thine, my liege, that hath trampled upon Ilium. . . . Quick! With purple let his path be strewn, that justice may usher him to a home he ne'er hoped to see. . . ."

I am using the excellent prose translation of Dr. Herbert Weir Smyth in the Loeb Classics, with the original on the opposite page, and I cannot help wondering how many other unscholarly students will find it hard, after the large-rolling hexameters of Homer, to make the more jerky iambic metre fall as musically as doubtless it *should* fall, even upon our untrained ear.

Let me make an attempt to reproduce the difference between these two historic metres while the unlucky king is being persuaded to use these ill-omened carpets. He begins by uttering the following words, which in the original would sound something like this:

Ledas genethlon domatōn emōn phulax.

Dr. Weir Smyth translates this in his straight-forward prose: "Offspring of Leda, guardian of my house."

But had the original been an Homeric hexameter in place of what it is, we might have Englished it thus, in the Longfellow manner: "Lady, the daughter of Leda, who hast guarded my house in my absence."

While, as it is, we should be driven to content ourselves with this sort of spasmodic-sounding parallel: "Of Leda offspring, guarded hast thou well my house."

But the doomed monarch goes on:

"Pamper me not after woman's wise, nor, like some barbarian, grovel to me with wide-mouthed acclaim; and draw not down envy on my path by strewing it with tapestries. . . . I bid thee revere me not as a god, but as a man. Fame needs no carpetings and broideries to make her loud acclaim—"

But the murderess persuades him at last, though he insists on having his sandals removed: "Since I have been overborne to hearken to thee in this, I will tread upon a purple pathway as I pass to my palace halls."

I cannot feel that either Sophocles or Euripides had the grandeur of imagination that was needed to conjure up with such overpowering and primeval simplicity the scene that follows. The porch of that megalithic palace in Argos begins to tower before our imagination like some pre-historic "Caer"; and when the king has vanished—and it is the last we see of him—it is Cassandra of Troy, his royal captive, cursed by her lover Apollo with the prophetic gift that none will credit, who now becomes the protagonist of the play.

Darkly does the chorus of old men hint at the brooding horror that hovers over those unseen chambers with their bath of blood; but the wild-eyed captive girl, unwillingly persuaded by Clytaemnestra to leave the chariot where she has been crouching, screams aloud, desperate and reckless, her wild "Hell is murky!"

> CLYTAEMNESTRA: Nay, mad she is, and hearkens to her wild mood. . . . No, I will waste no more words upon her to be insulted thus.

And with that the murderess enters the palace; and Cassandra is left alone with the terrified old men.

Then the situation grows momently more tense. The young exile's horrible clairvoyance rises in gasping, choking screams, and the genius of the first and grandest of the Greek dramatists rises with it. It was a subject after his own heart. In his *Prometheus Bound* he went as far as his austere conscience allowed in his sympathy with the Titan's revolt; but he was caught—caught as fast as was his godlike hero in the iron rivets of his crucifixion on the Caucasus—by his sublime and terrible faith in the irremediable cosmic law!

There is indeed a grand and awful sense in Aeschylus of the utter hopelessness of meddling with the categorical imperative of the universe. It is more than puritanism this feeling in him. In some strange way it gives you the impression that he had a prophetic inkling of a moral power behind the world that is less amenable to supplication or propitiation than even *la somma Sapienza* of Dante or the "Almighty Father" of Milton!

In reading the *Prometheus Bound* of Aeschylus we experience something of that indignation with Zeus that we experience in our own life when the "President of the Immortals" behaves in an unpardonable manner; but it is clear that to the rugged and imperious soul of this Greek prophet a great deal of ordinary human sentiment and tender natural sympathy has to be sacrificed *and ought to be sacrified* if we are to make our will one with the implacable will of the universe.

And although, in the end of this terrific trilogy, the justice of heaven, by the intervention of its own glaucous-eyed daughter, consents to incarnate its verdict in that extremely human consistory known to us as the Court of the Hill of Mars, the feeling we are left with, when these three closely-linked plays, the *Agamemnon*, the *Choephoroi*, and the *Eumenides*, are brought to a close, is a fathomless sense of the horrible and devastating power of the human conscience. Yes, in the plays of Aeschylus the earthquake-and-glacier compulsion of the law of retribution cracks and crashes its way through the tragic heart of man; whereas in the drama of Job where the injustice of life is chanted on a far wider scale than the justice of the Areopagus, it is from deep calling unto deep beyond the reach of any moral order that the Lord answers his critics out of the whirlwind.

But on the other hand Aeschylus has a genius for a certain piled-up, richly-charged, purple-stained *sumptuousness of horror* which strikes us with a more sinister shock than anything in the drama of Job.

There is a touch, too, of something like Cyclopean humour at the end of the Watchman's speech and in the ominous part played by those ghastly carpets and the praise of their purple dye by the blood-brooding queen; but to my mind by far the most powerful portion of the whole trilogy is the dialogue between Cassandra and the chorus. The horror of this really becomes almost intolerable, and the whole Aeschylean conception of the figure of this daughter of Priam is charged with a significance that descends to the very roots of life.

Rejecting Apollo's love after beguiling him of the gift of prophecy the god cursed her by the fatal addition to his gift that her predictions should never be believed. Young and beautiful, and by the crowd held insane, she was the one of all the fair women of Troy that the leader of the Greeks chose for his prize, and the fact that Clytaemnestra took for granted that she was his paramour as well as his captive was enough to involve her in his doom.

One cannot help being struck all through these Greek dramas by the startling variations of quality in the choregic chants. And since so much depends upon the chorus, I would be tempted to hazard the view that though a stronger chorus saves a weaker situation a stronger situation does *not* save a weaker chorus.

In his grandest vein the choruses of Aeschylus compared with those of Sophocles resemble Pheidian sculpture compared with Praxitelean; while as compared with those of Euripides they resemble any sculptured figures *in the round* compared with the stirring flow of a rich, romantic, processional *relief*.

The Argive Elders in the *Agamemnon* make their appearance upon the stage with a prelude worthy of some vast heathen *Good Friday Mass*. "*Ailinon! Ailinon!* But may the good prevail! Zeus whoso'er he be—if by this name it pleaseth him to be invoked, by this name I call to him—"

It is interesting to note how closely in all these plays Zeus has come to represent what we moderns mean when we speak of God. This is a great revolution; for in Homer, though he *is* Sky-God and therefore the powerful All-Father of Gods and Men, Zeus remains a very clear-cut anthropomorphic figure, more so even than Milton's Jehovah, and he is not only invoked along with Apollo and

Athene but is very frequently roundly cursed and called
Sketlié—"Obstinate devil!"—by the angry heroes.

From a purely poetical and mythological point of view
there is something a little sad about this sanctimonious and
mystical change. It is true that in Homer he is not only the
great Sky-God, more powerful—as he himself explains in
extremely realistic fashion—than all the rest put together:
he is also the God of Suppliants, Strangers, Beggars, and
Tramps. Nevertheless in this simple stage of his development he left the profounder problems of good and evil to
the less human and more mysterious workings of Fate.

But how fascinating it is—whether one likes this change
from the poetical to the spiritual or not—to note the deep
intellectual disturbance that is going on in all three of these
great dramatists under the stress—Nietzsche would call it
the morbid and vicious stress—of this modernizing and
mysticizing of Olympus or, more strictly speaking, of this
desertion of Olympus for Eleusis! For in truth they all
reveal this trouble of mind; though it is the usual custom
among scholars to confine such agitation to the one of the
three who, as we gather from the foolery of Aristophanes,
was hand-and-glove with Socrates.

But in most of these plays—putting aside *Prometheus
Bound*, which has a freer, more elemental, more Homeric
atmosphere—it is *the mysteries*, these black-magical celebra-
tions and erotic-mystical initiations that give, at least to a
lover of the *Iliad* and the *Odyssey*, a certain blood-charged,
sex-charged, and—how shall I say it?—dimly-barbaric
shiver to these goat-chants of Dionysus.

One begins to remember, as one gets more deeply involved in these tragedies, that Dionysus was worshipped in
some of his favourite regions as the Devourer of Raw Flesh;
and if we take, as Keats did, and as Walter Pater and
Nietzsche did, all this significant mythology seriously, it is
impossible not to feel a certain satisfaction in recalling that

this blood-drinking vindictive effeminate divinity is only known to us in the epic poems as a terrified fugitive among the Nereids of the sea!

It is no petulant obliquity, however, for a devotee of the older poetry to stress the morbid and lurid element in Greek drama, for we may be sure that whither the horror-compass of modern psychology points, *there* incest, infanticide, and all the "*ailinon! ailinon!*" of the homicidal nerves of our race will be found and heard.

The choruses, in this great Aeschylean trilogy, differ from one another a good deal in the quality of their poetry; and the Furies are more passionate and moving than the Argive Elders or the Argive Slave-women.

One wonders a little, thinking of Keats' *Hyperion*, at the extremely calm way in which these pious citizens dispose of the great cosmic powers, Uranus and Cronos, who ruled the world before their spiritualized Zeus came into his own.

"He who aforetime was mighty, swelling with insolence for every fray, he shall not even be named as having ever been; and he who arose thereafter, he hath met his overthrower and is past and gone. But whosoe'er, heartily taking thought beforehand, giveth title of victory in triumphant shout to Zeus, he shall gain wisdom altogether—Zeus who leadeth mortals the way of understanding, Zeus who hath established as a fixed ordinance that wisdom cometh by suffering."

The chorus of Furies in the *Eumenides* takes, as indeed is proper with such old, dark, chthonian divinities, a very different view; calling upon primeval Night, its mother, in angry protest against the arrogant claims of these younger gods.

But the luckless Cassandra—to my mind, apart from Prometheus, the most moving of the Aeschylean characters —finds in these Zeus-loving Argive Elders a veritable crowd of well-meaning Poloniuses; and as, with her nostrils full of the smell of blood, and the cry, "Faugh! Faugh!" upon her lips, she parries with her sublime despair their conventional platitudes, all they do is to enquire grossly, putting their questions into one terrible Greek word, "Why—do—you—*faugh*—like—that?"

And what a deep-biting woman's wit lies in the retort which I will now set down, and set it down phonetically, so as to emphasize once more the metre of these plays:

Oudeis akouei tauta tōn endaimonōn!
"None who is happy is commended thus."

But I will quote the context:

CASSANDRA: The day is come. Flight would profit me but little.

CHORUS: Well, be assured, thou art patient and of a courageous spirit.

CASSANDRA: None who is happy is commended thus!

No, there is nothing in the *Libation Bearers* or even in the *Eumenides* equal to the moment when Cassandra, recalling the unspeakable Thyestean banquet and the sacrificing of Iphigeneia and predicting the death of her murderess, passes through the gate into that house of atrocity.

But the opening passages of the last of the three plays are as terrifying as anything in the whole literature of horror. What a scene the Aeschylean imagination conjures up as taking place in that mystic temple at Delphi!

The Erinyes, the Furies (for they are not as yet the Eumenides) are themselves made the chorus here, which was in itself as bold a stroke as any in Greek drama.

Lying huddled about the shrine to which Orestes is clinging, these loathly beings keep muttering an inarticulate gabble in their sleep, while the ghost of Clytaemnestra stirs them up to make sure that her son, already half-mad from their long pursuit, shall not escape.

"*Mugmos! Oogmos!*" gibber these chthonian abortions in their gradual awakening; and the grisly syllables are like the moan of lemurs round the morgue of a madhouse.

Nor has there been any relaxing of the pursuit of their victim by these Erinyes when they overtake him at Athens clinging to Athene's shrine.

> CHORUS: Here he is again! In shelter, with arms twined round the image of the immortal goddess. . . . Nay thou art bound in requital to suffer that I suck the red blood from thy living limbs. May I feed myself on thee—a gruesome draught!
>
> I'll waste thy strength; I'll hale thee living to the world below, that thou mayest pay recompense for thy murdered mother! . . . For great is Hades who holds mortals to account beneath the earth; and he surveyeth all things with his recording mind. . . . Nay, be sure not Apollo nor Athene's might can save thee from perishing . . . knowing not where in thy soul is joy, a bloodless victim of the powers below, a shadow of thyself!
>
> What! Dost thou not even answer, but scornest my words, thou victim fatted and consecrate to me? At no altar shalt thou be slain, but living shalt be my feast; and thou shalt now hearken to our song to bind thee with its spell!

Then follows the tremendous chant of the remorse-demons; and as they sing they clasp another's hands and dance; while among them clinging to the altar cowers Orestes.

> CHORUS: Come now, let us link the dance! O mother Night, mother who didst bear me to be a retribution unto the dead and the living, hearken unto me! . . . O'er our victim consecrate, this is our song, fraught with madness, fraught with frenzy, crazing the brain, the Furies' hymn—*hymnos ex Erinyon*—withering the life of mortals!

As the song of the Furies mounts up in intensity so do their leapings grow wilder; until so deeply does this whole

conception of the remorse-dance of the torturing conscience obsess the imagination of Aeschylus that he is inspired at last to communicate to the syllables they chant
something of the actual beat of their feet in "downfall
unendurable," as they proclaim themselves "separated
from the gods by a light not of the sun!"

Sophocles is undoubtedly, to an average unscholarly
mind, the most difficult to do justice to of these three great
poets. Lacking the huge cosmic sweep of Aeschylus, lacking
the obstinate questionings and voluptuous subtleties of
Euripides, he was in his own long prosperous life, and has
been ever since, what might be called the ideal Greek
artist.

Aeschylus, like the author of *Don Quixote*, was a veteran
soldier "in a war to save" Western civilization. He fought
at Marathon, and a decade later at Salamis; and though
he is rumoured to have been in philosophy a Pythagorean,
it is in the imaginative grasp of great momentous crises of
battle, murder, tyranny, revolt, both among mortals and
immortals, that the huge dim-smouldering imperious grandeur of his inspiration found its natural expression. Chosen,
on the contrary, for his unequalled beauty and his born
sense of rhythm, to lead as a boy the musical paean round
the trophy for the victory over the East, a friend of Pericles
and the favoured darling of the vast, wayward, critical
audience at the open-air theatre, Sophocles was in every
sense of the word a prize-winner in the lottery of life.

And it has been the same ever since! Lucky with his contemporaries, lucky with posterity, it is he our greatest critic
selects in that sonnet we are weary of hearing quoted, as
the one spirit of all time,

> *Business could not make dull, nor passion wild,*
> *Who saw life steadily and saw it whole.*

Does it not seem a little strange that this perfectly balanced dramatic artist, the flawless idol of Aristophanes, Aristotle, Virgil, Racine, Lessing, and all our university scholars, should have dominated the classic stage for so long, not, as in the case of the *Prometheus* of Aeschylus, with a figure who deliberately defied God, or, as in the case of the *Medea* of Euripides with a figure who deliberately defied man, but with this pious, well-meaning, human-too-human *Oedipus*, who, by pure chance, and in complete ignorance of what he was doing, murdered his father and married his mother?

I suspect myself that those who have a predilection for the epical will always prefer Aeschylus, and that those who have a predilection for the romantic, the analytical, the magical, will always prefer Euripides, but that it is the adepts and virtuosos of the pure art of the theatre who hold—just as the great Dionysian audiences did—that Sophocles is the master. What we call *Sophoclean irony* is not in reality an intellectual thing, like the irony of Anatole France, or an emotional thing, like the irony of Thomas Hardy—it is a *technical* thing, the creation of a particular dramatic tension by the use of a particular theatric device.

And indeed for the flawless handling of this device, and for the breathless suspense while this device is gathering momentum, *Oedipus Rex* stands out as the most *perfect tragedy* of the Greek stage.

The manner in which the audience watches him—knowing perfectly well whither it is all drifting—while he takes in his eager haste measure after measure to hasten the fore-ordained conclusion, reaches, I suppose, the superb limit of polished craftsmanship. One can see why Sophocles was the idol of Racine; and one can see also, I suspect, why it is that geniuses like Milton and Goethe—whose imaginative reach transcended and often outraged the laws of beauty—turned rather to Aeschylus and Euripides.

Dark hints of an alluringly equivocal character have been thrown out that the whole story of "Swell-foot the Tyrant," as Shelley in his literalness calls him, is a pregnant psychological symbol, indicating that to answer the riddle of the cosmic Sphinx it is necessary to have plunged into depths below our traditional conceptions of good and evil; but one thing may be said with certainty; that such was *never*, for one flickering second, the view taken by Sophocles. Sophocles has been praised—is *still* praised, and by others than Matthew Arnold—for his well-balanced religiosity and lovable piety, but it seems to me that such flawless craftsmanship and polished technique must in themselves, in the very nature of the case, tone down and smooth away those *desperate extremes* of deadly clairvoyance, that alone have enough "sacred madness," as Plato teaches, to reach the heart of things!

Sophocles was certainly of that balanced temper that sees life "steadily": but when I recall the Aeschylean *Prometheus* and the Aeschylean Hymn of the Fates I cannot agree with Matthew Arnold that he sees it "whole." In fact, one thinks of the fate of the mother of Dionysus who "saw it whole" for one blinding second and then became ashes, and of the experience of Faust who cried to the Life-Spirit he had himself raised: *"I endure not thee!"*

The truth is that Sophocles was so absorbed in his political business and his perfect art that he was spared the frightfulness of "seeing life whole"; an experience, as both Aeschylus and Euripides knew, not "intended" for mortal man.

The stylistic perfection of this great artist, combined with the difficulty of translating this perfection into English, is what has enabled, I suspect, a certain scholarly tradition about him to become a little supercilious; but if the test of the greatness of a writer be neither his popularity with professional critics, nor the balanced charm of his personal life, but the troubling, disquieting, inspiring effect he has upon the men of genius of the remote future, I am tempted to feel—in spite of Racine and Sir Richard Jebb—that the author of *Prometheus Bound* was a greater genius than the author of *Oedipus at Colonus*.

But putting aside the technical perfection of the machinery of the play and the polished balance of its style, let us proceed to quote from *Oedipus the King* at the supreme crisis, and see how the Sophoclean sense of horror compares with the Aeschylean.

It is the Second Messenger speaking:

> *"Laius," she cried, and called her husband dead*
> *Long, long ago; her thought was of that child*
> *By him begot, the son by whom the sire*
> *Was murdered, and the mother left to breed*
> *With her own seed, a monstrous progeny.*
>
> .   .   .   .   .
>
> *—With a shriek*
> *Burst on us Oedipus; all eyes were fixed*
> *On Oedipus, as up and down he strode.*
>
> .   .   .   .   .
>
> *"A sword!" he cried,*
> *"Where is the wife, no wife, the teeming womb*
> *That bore a double harvest, me and mine?"*
>
> *Then we beheld the woman hanging there*
> *A running noose entwined about her neck.*
> *But when he saw her, with a maddened roar*
> *He loosed the cord; and when her wretched corpse*
> *Lay stretched on earth, what followed—O 'twas dread!*
> *He tore the golden brooches that upheld*
> *Her queenly robes, upraised them high and smote*
> *Full on his eye-balls. . . .*

It is, however, in *Oedipus at Colonus* where he can describe his own birthplace and increase the glory of that very sanctuary to which the Furies of Aeschylus had been led that Sophocles is at his greatest.

We speak of it as a tragedy; but it is in reality like those final plays of Shakespeare, like *The Tempest*, for example, that you cannot attribute to any category. It lacks the dramatic poignancy of the passionate and heroic *Antigone*—that play which so specially enthralled the huge Athenian audience—for Oedipus' brave daughter and her less heroic sister Ismene play a passive rôle here; but the vanishing of the blinded king in this sacred spot, apparently under the forgiveness of the gods and the protection of the now thoroughly propitiated Eumenides, has a wonderfully solemn and tender power.

It has, in fact, the same effect as have certain Catholic Masses for the dead when the first despair is over. But if it is the nearest approach in Greek tragedy to that feeling of a "redemption of all sorrows" that comes to most of us now and again in life, it is a somewhat remote approach. In truth, when those two luckless daughters and sisters leave the place of his passing one hears still the echo of those Hardy-like words:

> *Not to be born at all*
> *Is best, far best that can befall.*

It is, I am afraid, almost impossible unless one is at least as good a scholar as Shelley to savour the peculiar quality of the famous Sophocles chorus in praise of his native village, which to our Dorsetshire ears is as if the folk of Stinsford and Bockhampton were to chant on Midsummer Eve a musically laconic and completely untranslatable lyric of Thomas Hardy's.

Not Shelley himself, or any other poet, can turn a Sophoclean chorus into real English poetry. No, our only hope, if we are not scholars, is a literal, word-by-word translation, a translation into the baldest prose, leaving the polished perfection to the muse of the imagination. We can get a certain satisfaction, and perhaps a little more than that, from noting such familiar flowers' names as *crocus* and *narcissus* and how the great playwright loves to linger over them, even as any of us, recalling the home of our childhood, might linger over cowslips and cuckoo-flowers; but the sad thing is that the more exquisite the Sophoclean perfection grows the harder it is to capture its special fragrance in the poetry of the Gothic North!

But now to turn to the one of the three about whose peculiar genius from the very start there has been anger and bitterness and controversy and dissension. Accused of championing women to a point of voluptuous nympholepsy, accused of hating women to a point of misogynistic mania, accused of an impious *apologia* for man against God, accused of a recantation of this impiety so reckless and shameless as to make one think of a villain in Dostoievsky, Euripides certainly lends himself to the feelings of us moderns as does no other genius of the ancient world. And he has paid the penalty for his modernity by being most freely and eloquently Englished in verse.

But eloquent as these poetic renderings of Euripides are, I cannot but feel that they alter the very spirit of this great genius. The truth is that they soften, loosen, weaken his savage and subtle intensity. For one thing, they change the characteristic short, violent lines of the choruses into long, flowing, rippling lines.

I must not dwell upon this, but let me in passing make the most vigorous protest against the Englishing of the fixed epithet of Dionysus, *Bromius*, into the sentimental adjective "Clamour-King." This is indeed a perfect example of the sort of thing that our eloquent versifiers of Euripides tend to do, and it is as bad on the side of his modern lovers as

Aristophanes' mockery of him was unfair on the side of his ancient enemies.

The thing to do is to get hold of a volume of the old Bohn Library, and then in your own imagination turn this literal prose into poetry resembling that of *Samson Agonistes*, poetry which certainly cannot be accused of melodious fluidity!

And the *Bacchanals* is the play to read if you want to capture the spirit of Euripides in its strangest, subtlest, and, if I may say so, most Russian vein. A recantation, is it, of his daring championship of humanity against the Gods? A recantation, is it, of his Strindberg-like sex-morbidity?

I am by no means so sure! It certainly could lend itself, without much special pleading, to precisely the opposite interpretation. The unhappy Pentheus who rules in place of the aged Cadmus is certainly no pleasing figure; but the way he is mesmerized by the god of frenzied women and the way he is transported to the wilds of Cithaeron to be torn in pieces by his own mother stirs up in us feelings of anything but a pious nature.

In her Maenad-madness the wretched woman takes his head for the head of a lion, till old Cadmus disabuses her, and lo! what she is carrying in her blood-stained arms has the features of the child of her womb!

The whole drama evokes such quivering pulses of pity for the house of Cadmus and such spasms of disgust at the vindictiveness of Dionysus that it is just as much propaganda for sober atheism as for the illumination of inspired belief.

The truth is that *both extremes*—a thaumaturgic ecstatic faith *and* a scepticism that corrodes the very navel of all religion—are instinctive with Euripides. A man of enormous nervous vitality, he was, if I may say so, like the fusion into one soul of the opposite souls of Nietzsche and Dostoievsky.

I confess it gives me a curious satisfaction to note how Euripides remains to-day the same stumbling-block to the conservative satirist, the same stumbling-block to the well-ordered scholarly mind, as he was in his own time.

But the great amateurs of scholarship, those who hold, as Milton and Goethe did, that inspiration is more important than either art or science, will always revert to Euripides.

Indeed, to my mind Euripides held a view of life similar to that of his friend Socrates, namely, that in all mythologies and religions there is some truth and in none all the truth. Certainly our modern fiction has been making of late a bold and sometimes an almost successful attempt to revive this great aesthetic *genre*, and doing it, too, rather on Euripidean than on Sophoclean lines; and yet I am not ashamed to confess that I would like to see some formidable modern writer make a Nietzschean attack on the whole tradition of Greek tragedy and thus prepare the way for a renaissance of the Homeric spirit. But this must be left to our descendants.

Meanwhile what could be more modern in its delicate cerebral sadism than the way the atheist is handled in the *Bacchanals*? The dressing up of old Cadmus and Teiresias in that equivocal womanish garb has in it surely a vein of the subtlest "miching malicho"; but when it comes to what I am now going to quote, how can it be that our scholars have not cried aloud with one voice: "*This* is no *apologia* for religion: this is the subtlest attack on the religious spirit that has ever been written!"

One is tempted, as one watches those noble and famous old heroes, the Homeric Teiresias, prophet for ever among the dead, and Cadmus, founder of the great city, leaving the stage in their skipping senility and pantaloon-piety, to quote those words of Oscar Wilde:

And the damned Grotesques made arabesques,
Like the wind upon the sand!

But the hypnotizing of Pentheus goes further still. It is as if Euripides had said to himself, "They have accused me of misogyny; they have accused me of atheism. Now I will show them what the hysteria of women and the cruelty of religion can do between them."

And the extraordinary thing is that the wild choruses in the *Bacchanals* are as lovely as any in Greek tragedy. But they are Bacchanals *from Asia,* and what Homer would have felt—not the false Homer of the *Hymns,* but the real Homer of the *Odyssey*—about such insidious delirium, is a question worth asking.

The thing Euripides was really doing was pressing the issue to the limit; and this was easy to him because temperamentally he was one who veered between reaction and revolution. But certainly in the process of releasing both these great suppressions of his soul very queer cerebral perversities come to light.

DIONYSUS: All Asians through these mystic dances tread.
PENTHEUS: Ay, far less wise be they than Hellene men.
DIONYSUS: Herein far wiser. Diverse wont is theirs.
PENTHEUS: By night or day dost thou perform the rites?
DIONYSUS: Chiefly by night; gloom lends solemnity.

Having completely mesmerized the unhappy man, Dionysus dresses him in women's clothes before leading him to his death; and at this point with a magical power over the dark phenomena of the underworld of mythology our poet makes Pentheus dimly aware that *the horns of the bull,* the god's *alter ego* in the orgies, have sprouted from the forehead of this sinister seducer.

PENTHEUS: Whose semblance bear I? Have I not the mien
Of Ino or my mother?
DIONYSUS: Their very selves I seem to see in thee.
Yet what? This tress hath from his place escaped,
Not as I braided it beneath the coif.
PENTHEUS: Tossing it forth and back within, in whirls
Of Bacchic frenzy, I disordered it.

DIONYSUS: Nay I, who have taken thy tire-maiden's part
Will rearrange it. Come, hold up thine head.
PENTHEUS: Lo there—thou lay it smooth: I am in thy hands.
DIONYSUS: Now is thy girdle loose; thy garments' folds
Droop not below thine ankles evenly.

And then when the Maenads have done their work and
the mother of Pentheus has learnt from Cadmus that the
bleeding head she carries is her son's, this strange play—
with a long passage completely lost to us, destroyed perhaps, who can tell? by some pious scholiast who caught
too well its blasphemous drift—reaches its conclusion in a
hint as to the fate of Cadmus.

Perhaps after the *Bacchanals*, the *Medea* is the most characteristic play of Euripides; and if he let his dithyrambic
psychology go to such lengths in celebrating the vengeance
of the women's god, he lets it go just as far in celebrating
the vengeance of a woman.

Not for nothing does he make his heroine the grand-
daughter of the Sun and the niece of Circe; she who alone—
when the voyage of Jason in the Argo would else have
failed—wins for him the Golden Fleece!

But in this play we find Jason on the point of taking a
new bride; and it is of the murderous fury of the woman,
of her slaying her rival, of her killing her own children, of
her robbing him even of the comfort of burying his dead,
that the story tells.

One cannot help remembering, as one reads Medea's
powerful defence, how Aeschylus in the *Eumenides* makes
Apollo bring forward in his plea for Orestes the supremely
masculine argument that it is the man who is the real parent
of a child, while all the woman does is to be the bearer and
the nurse of the man's seed.

Let us therefore hear how the misogynistic Euripides
presents the woman's point of view.

MEDEA: Surely, of creatures that have life and wit,
We women are of all unhappiest,
Who, first, must buy, as buys the highest bidder,
A husband—nay, we do but win for our lives
A master! Deeper depth of wrong is this.
Here too is dire risk—will the lord we gain
Be evil or good? Divorce?—'Tis infamy
To us: we may not even reject a suitor!

. . . . .

For the man, when the home-yoke galls his neck
Goes forth, to ease a weary sickened heart
By turning to some friend, some kindred soul;
We to one heart alone can look for comfort.
But we, say they, live an unperilled life
At home, while they do battle with the spear—
Unreasoning fools! Thrice would I under shield
Stand, rather than bear childbirth-peril once.

Thus does Greek tragedy, in these three great hands, pass from the drama of *Crime and Punishment* with a cosmic background to the drama of heart-rending human situations with the gods as accomplices, and from this move forward once again to the drama of lyrical psychology with the gods under critical indictment!

As we began our sketch with the Aeschylean hymn to the triumph of Zeus over Cronos, "who is past and gone," and over Uranus, "who shall not even be named as having ever been," it seems fair to close with another great puritan's hymn to the triumph of a yet younger Rebel.

The Oracles are dumb,
No voice or hideous hum
Runs thro' the arched roof in words deceiving.
Apollo from his shrine
Can no more divine
With hollow shriek the steep of Delphos leaving
No nightly trance or breathed spell
Inspires the pale-eyed Priest from the prophetic cell.

Dante

WHAT A HUGE and bleeding gap—like the extraction of an eye-tooth from the figure of Time—would be left by the removal of Dante from the literature of the world!

Speaking in Spenglerian terms, though not to Spenglerian effect, if Goethe is the supreme poet of the epoch that is now passing away, and Homer of the spring-time of all that we call classical, Dante is the perfect culmination of the Middle Ages.

It would be of curious interest if it were possible to apply a psychological *questionnaire* to the more intelligent among our Western youth of both sexes as to the precise and exact reaction of which they are individually aware, to these various world-geniuses.

One singular thing would, I believe, emerge; namely, that neither Rabelais nor Shakespeare seems as profoundly "dated" as these others.

And the way we use the adjective "Quixotic" would suggest that the same power of seeing life *sub specie aeternitatis*, that is to say, beyond all boundaries of any historic "culture," belongs to Cervantes too.

But Milton with his Protestantism and Dante with his mediaevalism *are* "dated"; though the miraculous vitality of the Catholic Church and her genius for adapting the old to the new, not to speak of her subtler metaphysic, gives the latter a tremendous advantage over the former.

Passionate moralists like Carlyle, as well as most typical academic students, love to assure us that Dante's spiritual attitude to our human situation, his tragic recognition of the difference between good and evil and of the infinite results of this difference, are things totally unaffected by the passing of time, totally unaffected by scholastic philosophy, and as essentially true to-day as they ever were; but I believe myself that this, like so many resounding moral and academic generalizations, is a treacherous fallacy, *in fact a lie*.

Catholics at any rate can hardly put their seal to this separation of Dante the moralist from Dante the believer, holding as they are bound to hold that his views of the nature of good and evil are inextricably bound up with his whole system of thought, a system which, with a few scientific and historic modifications, or, let us say, a few *changes of emphasis*, remains the Catholic faith of to-day.

What does remain unaffected by his mediaeval philosophy and his Catholic faith is his imaginative genius, his original and special way of reacting to sense-impressions, to the drama of history, to the phenomena of nature, to the mortal psychology of love and hate, and to that dangerous sex-nerve in human beings that is excited by cruelty. What would, in fact, remain the same had he been a free-thinker like Lucretius, with a philosophy completely hostile to all religion, is his unique personality, with all its peculiar attributes of deadly insight, exquisite tenderness, ferocious realism, savage disdain, imaginative intensity, sadistic cruelty, and, above all, an ecstatic power of ideal love. In other words, you cannot become a disciple of Dante in the metaphysical sense without becoming a Catholic; but you *can* become a disciple of Dante as a poet and lover and as the representative of a particular kind of imaginative response to life.

For though both the metaphysical and the ethical elements in *The Divine Comedy* are in their profound philosophical implications much more complicated and elaborate than the simple mingling of Platonism with Puritanism that inspired Milton; and though they revert, through the subtle medium of the great scholastic thinkers, to Plato's antithesis, Aristotle, who was to Dante as much "the master of those who know"—*il maestro di color che sanno*—as he has been from Chaucer down to quite recent times, to the scholars of Oxford, few of us laymen can use them for our cruder and more casual culture.

Except for men who have been trained for the priesthood in Catholic institutions, ordinary book-lovers are neither learned enough, nor unaffected enough by Goethe and Dostoievsky and Nietzsche to draw the inspiration of their secret life from St. Thomas Aquinas and Aristotle.

To speak personally, I confess to being much more influenced by the impassioned psychology of St. Paul than by any *"maestro di color che sanno"* in either classical or modern times.

But putting aside not only what Dante himself derived, through the mediaeval schools from Aristotle, but all that may have come our way in more recent revivals of such subtle methods of thinking, it still would seem that for non-Catholic readers—and indeed for both Catholic and Protestant readers who have not had a metaphysical training—the best approach to Dante is to concentrate on those original characteristics of his vision from which we can gather plenty of weapons for an attack upon life and a resistance to life, such as would serve our turn if we were a Turk, an infidel, or a heretic. Try the experiment then, reader—for you can easily slip back into your orthodoxy—of regarding Dante's religious convictions, together with his whole elaborate cosmology, as a fascinating, if painful and shocking *mythology*.

Regard the victims of the "*vendetta di Dio*" as if they were merely the victims—as the classical Capaneus, who so infuriated Virgil by his blasphemous defiance, actually supposed he was—of the thunderbolts of a ferocious Zeus.

Homer and Virgil have, both of them, given us descriptions of Hades, descriptions of which Dante is quick to take advantage whenever he gets the chance; so that it is only a fair return, since he Christianizes our mythology, that we should *mythologize* his Christianity!

The truth is there is a grievous inadequacy about what might be called "the psycho-poetical" appreciation of Dante, by which I mean the analysis of his genius in connexion with his psychological temperament.

Digging down into the elements of his unequalled style— this "*bello stilo*" which in a fit of passionate humility he swears, quite erroneously (for it is entirely his own), he learnt from Virgil—it becomes possible to be so deeply influenced by his peculiar life-illusion that we can actually appropriate it to ourselves and indeed make it our own to such a tune that the humblest of bookworms may acquire the right to utter the passionate words: "May the long zeal avail me, and the great love, that made me search thy volume!"

But this "secret" of Dante as applied to our ordinary and secular handling of life is the thing that has been most of all neglected. To concentrate upon it and to absorb it, we have to clear our minds of a deplorable burden of ambiguous moralizing by the Dante commentators, in fact—one might say—of pernicious moralizing.

And of the worst and most dangerous form that this sort of thing has assumed, it is not so much Dante's fellow-Catholics who have been guilty, as our own well-meaning Puritans.

John Bunyan believed in a material hell, and no doubt the unhappy Cowper did, quite as definitely, if not *more* definitely, than Dante, and believed in it too without the enormous mitigation of purgatory.

Indeed one cannot help thinking that it is because of purgatory, combined with a medicinal and casuistical metaphysic, that one seems more often to hear of Protestants than of Catholics going raving mad from fear of hell.

Our mid-Victorian exponents of Dante, led by Carlyle, fell into the unfortunate habit of referring to him in a solemn tone of sanctimonious awe, to clear the air from which it is certainly most salutary to turn to Voltaire, Goethe, Nietzsche, and, above all, Rabelais. To every "well-created spirit"—it is Dante's own expression—there is more magnanimous, humane, and in the deepest sense *evangelical* charity in any of the graver utterances of Gargantua or Pantagruel than in the whole *Divine Comedy*.

But on the other hand, how poor a wisdom to refuse to saturate oneself in Dante's "*bello stilo*" with its purged, clarified, and trenchant beauty, because this astounding poet's response to the most exquisite refinements is balanced by such a diabolical mixture of pride and cruelty!

In one aspect of this poetic vision, and in a certain sense it is the most important of all, he remains the supreme poet of the human race. Homer, Shakespeare, Milton are all inferior to him when it comes to this: to the condensation, namely, in a single line, of a huge volume of pity, of loveliness, of grandeur, of dramatic poignance.

Shakespeare *has* his magical, his tragical effects in this kind; but they come most often in gasping, desperate, broken half-lines. Milton requires a whole paragraph of eaglelike hoverings before he can reach his periodic, culminating flight, that goes soaring away over the coasts of time and the margins of space till it is lost in the infinite.

It is Shakespeare's own genius for giving imaginative and palpable form to the most complicated feelings that tosses him sometimes into such a conflicting sea of images that the sharp directness of the thought is almost lost in the waves of overlapping metaphors. Think of that famous soliloquy of Hamlet, for instance, about suicide, which closes with the words:

> *Thus conscience doth make cowards of us all,*
> *And thus the native hue of resolution*
> *Is sicklied oe'r with the pale cast of thought,*
> *And enterprises of great pith and moment*
> *With this regard their currents turn awry*
> *And lose the name of action.*

Or think of Macbeth's torrential speech at a crisis even more pregnant:

> *And pity, like a naked new-born babe*
> *Striding the blast, or heaven's cherubin, hors'd*
> *Upon the sightless couriers of the air,*
> *Shall blow the horrid deed in every eye,*
> *That tears shall drown the wind. I have no spur*
> *To prick the sides of my intent, but only*
> *Vaulting ambition, which oe'r leaps itself—*

And then consider the horrible clarity and appalling brevity of Dante's two verses describing the destiny, after their decease, of the easy-going harmless individuals that in England we call "gentlemen of private means" and in America "stuffed shirts":

These have no hope of death and their blind life is so base that they envy every other lot. Report of them the world permits not to exist; Mercy and Justice disdains them; let us not speak of them; but look and pass.

> *Questi non hanno speranza di morte,*
> *E la lor cieca vita è tanto bassa,*
> *Che invidiosi son d'ogni alta sorte,*
> *Fama di loro il mondo esser non lassa,*

Misericordia e giustizia gli sdegna:
Non ragioniam di lor, ma guarda e passa.

Compared with the feverish, tumultuous, and fanciful embellishment of human feeling that we get in Shakespeare and get too, as we have just seen, even at a dramatic crisis, how terrible, how startling is this simple directness!

And what a perfect example of the Dantesque spirit here at the very entrance to his infernal journey, are these beautiful and abominable lines denouncing all cautions and retiring adherents of the *via media*!

With this wholesale condemnation not only would Montaigne and Shakespeare and Charles Lamb and Emerson and Walter Pater have been damned, but the innumerable anonymous multitude of easy-going, helpless, indolent, drifting, harmless, human nondescripts, such as Gogol loved to depict and for whom Chekhov had such tenderness, would certainly at this moment be lifting up their voices in:

> Strange tongues, horrible outcries, words of pain, tones of anger, voices deep and harsh, and tumult of hands amongst them.

> *Diverse lingue, orribili favelle,*
> *Parole di dolore, accenti d'ira,*
> *Voci alte e fioche, e suon di man con elle.*

But with what a terrible and wonderful beauty—a beauty of pride, a beauty of contemptuous rejection, a beauty of sublime anger, a beauty of pity and terror, a beauty of the finality of brevity—is this wicked judgment uttered!

All that we have learnt from St. Paul as to the spiritual secret of the universe, whereby the weak and the foolish and the unresisting, yea! the things *that are not*, are dearest to the heart of great Tao is contradicted and gainsaid here from beginning to end.

Indeed, the largest element of the lofty spirit of the whole *Divine Comedy* lies in its Nietzschean loathing of the commonplace. His favourite word among all words is the word *disdain*. Disdain is clearly, to Dante's mind, the most marked characteristic of the Emperor of the Universe as it is of his angels.

It is also the most marked characteristic of the noblest of his damned. And this emphasis upon the terrible beauty of pride and disdain is *not* balanced—as Carlyle craftily suggested on behalf of his kindred spirit—by any *real* correspondent humility. He is humble before Virgil; he is humble before Beatrice; and he allows *some* purgatorial penance for the monstrously proud; but there his humility ends, and it is difficult not to link this complete absence from his deepest spiritual culture of the least trace of what Dostoievsky accepts as the essential Christian secret with the absence from *The Divine Comedy* of that quiver of personal emotion in the presence of the figure of Christ that many great writers display. He introduces Christ, of course; but where he does so his piety is conventional and theological rather than personal.

We are indeed forcibly reminded of the warlike Messiah in *Paradise Lost* when Virgil alludes in passing to the "harrowing" of hell by the Virgin's Son:

"I was new in this condition when I saw a Powerful One coming, crowned with the sign of victory."

> *Rispose:* "*Io era nuovo in questo stato,*
> *Quando ci vidi venire un possente*
> *Con segno di vittoria coronato.*"

But when once we have made the single necessary mental gesture without which the horrors of the "Inferno" are insufferable, I mean the gesture of detaching all this cruelty from the will of any deity but a mythological one, whose vengeance need trouble us no more than that of Zeus upon Tantalus or Sisyphus, the scoriated and savage sublimity of these tremendous inventions, the stripped intensity of these fuliginous vignettes, which follow one another as if upon a Tartarean film-screen, attain in their cumulative effect such a pitch of appalling beauty that we feel the like will never appear again.

The "Inferno" is an abominable vision, it is a shocking vision, it is a wicked vision, but it is a vision of overpowering beauty; and may it not be that all such extreme beauty in this chaotic world can only be attained by a measurable sacrifice both of the Good and of the True? May it not be that the greatest lie ever uttered was uttered by the most perfect of poets when he wrote:

> *Beauty is Truth, Truth Beauty; that is all*
> *We know on earth, and all we need to know?*

Incredibly arresting is the picture Dante gives us of the great spirits of antiquity moving sedately across their meadow of fresh verdure:

> On it were people with eyes slow and grave, of great authority in their appearance; they spoke seldom, with mild voices.

> *Genti v'eran con occhi tardi e gravi,*
> *Di grande autorità ne' lor sembianti;*
> *Parlavan rado, con voci soavi.*

It is indeed all in keeping with his huge disdain for the commonplace and for those "who have lost the good of the intellect"—*ch'hanno perduto il ben del intelletto*—that he communicates to us the glorious awe he felt in this exalted company who made him one of themselves.

And what a grand touch it is, that line which alludes to the proud adversary of the Crusaders! "And by himself, apart, alone, I saw the Saladin"—*E solo in parte vidi il Saladino.*

But not Shakespeare himself, no! nor Sappho *herself,* could write of the shivering symptoms of love as this poet of God's vengeance.

Having summoned the wind-tossed souls of Francesca and her lover to his side and having listened to the girl's words, Dante bows his head and holds it so low that his guide asks him what he's thinking.

> When I answered, I began: "Ah me! what sweet thoughts, what longing led them to the woeful pass!"

> *Quando risposi, cominciai: "O lasso,*
> *Quanti dolci pensier, quanto disio*
> *Menò costoro al doloroso passo!"*

And then, in response to a human sympathy such as she would never meet again throughout eternity, the girl utters the words that tell for all time the ever-recurring tale:

> "One day, for pastime, we read of Lancelot, how love constrained him; we were alone and without all suspicion. Several times that reading urged our eyes to meet, and changed the colour of our faces; but one moment alone it was that overcame us."

> *"Noi leggevamo un giorno per diletto*
> *Di Lancelotto, come amor lo strinse;*
> *Soli eravamo e senza alcun sospetto.*
> *"Per più fiate gli occhi ci sospinse*
> *Quella lettura, e scolorocci il viso;*
> *Ma solo un punto fu quel che ci vinse."*

> "When we read how the fond smile was kissed by such a lover, he, who shall never be divided from me, kissed my mouth all trembling: the book, and he who wrote it, was a Galeotto; that day we read in it no further."

"Quando leggemmo il disiato riso
  Esser baciato da cotanto amante
  Questi, che mai da me non fia diviso,
"La bocca mi baciò tutto tremante:
  Galeotto fu il libro, e chi lo scrisse;
  Quel giorno più non vi leggemmo avante."

Whilst the one spirit thus spake, the other wept so, that I fainted with pity, as if I had been dying; and fell, as a dead body falls.

Mentre che l'uno spirto questo disse,
  L'altro piangeva sì, che di pietade
  Io venni men cose com'io morisse;
E caddi, come corpo morto cade.

When we revert after this to any of the other great love-passages in literature we're conscious of the loss of a certain mystery of romantic feeling, wherein the metal of love has been passed through a crucible of such burning intensity that it has grown, in its white heat, into an element that not only no waters can drown or flame devour, but no Emperor of the Universe can cut in two. The nearest approach to this passage that I am able to bring to mind is that awe-inspiring sentence of Cathie's in *Wuthering Heights* where she confesses that though she "loves" her charming betrothed, *she is* the desperado Heathcliff.

The whole passage does indeed show what Christianity has done, in its mad life-and-death wrestle with sex, in the way of purging, refining, winnowing, but at the same time infusing with a tenfold charge of deadly magnetism, the sweet enemy with whose burning limbs it is entwined.

Not the most lavish celebration of Eros in classical poetry moves us like this, for the simple reason that between them and Dante lie the Middle Ages, where the phenomenon of the love of women, both in its idealization and in its renunciation, has become the chief miracle of life.

Everything is in the human mind—that is what is borne in upon us more strongly than anything else in reading Dante. The cruel First Cause, the everlasting torments, the quivering mountain of purgation, the rapturous orbits of the God-intoxicated saints, together with this two-natured human love-lute twisting and twitching in the wind as if strung with Eve's hair before Cain was born, all, *all* are to be found within the narrow bounds—and yet it is wider than the whole astronomical world!—of a man's or a woman's skull.

And when you come to think of it, how touching is the moral instinct in humanity which insists that all the motives, causes, urges, and impulses that lie behind every part of a great genius's work must be *good*!

Very often, on the contrary, they are extremely evil. A curious example of this is the eager haste we are in to assure ourselves that Filippo Argenti "of the old Adimari family" is for his snobbish insolence to be well soused in the infernal bog. It was humanity's universal love of punishing and revenging that created this same livid marsh, beyond the confines of whose reedy expanse glimmer the crimson pinnacles of the City of Dis.

Yes, humanity's are Dante's aggravated and twitching nerves; humanity's his righteous indignation yielding to this sadistic quiver. And it is because of this more poignant human psychology running all the way through it that the "Inferno" is so much greater a poem than the "Purgatorio" or the "Paradiso." It is more human; and *therefore* it contains more delight in cruelty, more malice, more revenge, more relish for excitement, for drama, for horror!

A supreme imagination, an incomparable style, if these are to be used to the best effect in the evocation of what we call beauty, must deal, it seems, with something in the world that is a little different from goodness, and not altogether the same as what we usually mean by "truth."

Any attempt to get all we can for our personal life from *The Divine Comedy* forces us indeed to come to terms with Goethe's great saying: "Live in the Whole, in the Good and in the Beautiful." And in fact it was with deep significance that Goethe used the word "the Whole" in place of "the True," and by thus balancing all three things side by side indicated clearly enough that in his view *they were by no means the same.*

Dante's terrific aesthetic vision when directed by the urge of savage anger is a very different thing from the "lacerated heart," the mad loathing of the disgusting and the base, which characterized the tortured soul of Swift.

What we can learn from Dante is the profound spiritual device of sublimating our natural human savagery till it becomes a medium for beautiful aesthetic vision.

But we must not deceive ourselves by any treacherous Carlylean moralizing into taking the position that because there is a terrible beauty in all these Dantesque horrors they are therefore propaganda for good against evil. They are the reverse of that! Their beauty is an *evil beauty*; and Dante, who is the most tremendous realist in all literature, uses the diabolic beauty of his realism to brand the Emperor of the Universe with the savage cruelty that was one of his own chief characteristics.

Listen to the details of the Filippo Argenti episode:

> Whilst we were running through the dead channel, there rose before me one full of mud, and said: "Who art thou, that comest before thy time?"

> *Mentre noi corravam la morta gora,*
> *Dinanzi mi si fece un pien di fango,*
> *E disse: "Chi se' tu, che vieni anzi ora?"*

And I to him: "If I come, I remain not; but thou, who art thou, who hast become so foul?" He answered: "Thou seest that I am one who weeps."

> *Ed io a lui: "S'io vegno, non rimango:*
> *Ma tu chi se', che sei sì fatto brutto?"*
> *Rispose: "Vedi che son un che piango."*

Pondering upon this passage it is impossible to miss the sublime beauty of these last words; and to the spirit of Carlyle, protesting that I am underrating the enormity of the sin that brought this wretch to this pass, I can only reply that for a sin committed in time a punishment throughout eternity, however it may lend itself to the beauty of poetic horror, is a contemplation for devils rather than for men.

But there is worse to follow; for the wretch who is now paying for the crime of what Shakespeare calls "the proud man's contumely" clings desperately to the side of their boat.

> And he put his arms round my neck, kissed my face, and said: "Indignant soul! blessed be she that bore thee."

> *Lo collo poi con le braccia mi cinse*
> *Baciommi il volto, e disse: "Alma sdegnosa,*
> *Benedetta colei che in te s'incinse.*

And the response to this horrible fawning, which must have been wickedly sweet to the poet's excited nerves, is not long in coming:

> And I: "Master, I should be glad to see him dipped in this swill, ere we quit the lake."

> *Ed io: "Maestro, molto sarei vago*
> *Di vederlo attuffare in questa broda,*
> *Prima che noi uscissimo del lago."*

Fortunately for us, by some sublime law of compensation in this beauty of frightfulness, Dante is compelled to transfer some of his *disdegno* and *dispitto* to the victims themselves; and what a relief it is to our profaner mind when the great Farinata, the Ghibelline, lifts his torso out of his burning sarcophagus and gives us an example of the power of the mind not only over the sufferings of the body, but even over the sufferings of what our Theosophists would call the "etheric" body.

> Already I had fixed my look on his; and he rose upright with breast and countenance; as if he entertained great scorn of Hell.

> *I' avea già il mio viso nel suo fitto;*
> *Ed ei s'ergea col petto e colla fronte,*
> *Come avesse lo inferno in gran dispitto.*

While we are comforting ourselves with this contrary side of Dante's mania for the emotion of *dispitto*, we find in the person of Capaneus, one of the victims of a former Emperor of the Universe, a splendid justification for our mythological attitude to *divine comedy*.

> "Who is that great spirit, who seems to care not for the fire, and lies disdainful and contorted, so that the rain seems not to ripen him?"

> *"Chi è quel grande che non par che curi*
> *L'incendio, e giace dispettoso e torto*
> *Sì che la pioggia non par che il maturi?"*

Could it be possible to find a better example of Dante's sadistic manner of gloating over these punishments than the monstrous humour of the phrase about the rain—*di foco dilatate falde*, "of dilated flakes of fire"—not "ripening" him? But after all we mustn't forget—and it is something to be the supreme realist of all literature, so that Petronius and De Maupassant are rude schoolboys compared with him—that it is Dante's own genius that evokes the pity and indignation we feel. We are, I suppose—at least I fancy myself to be so—like simple rustics at the play who take what they see as if it were *really* happening.

I know that for my own part, such is this man's appalling genius, I have continually to say to myself, "It is all mythological fancy!" lest my blasphemous fury against the First Cause should out-rail even Dante's damned.

And again we rustics at this terrifying play must remember that it is Dante himself who invents the retorts of these tremendous rebels whom Eternity's cat-o'-nine-tails *cannot* "ripen" though it fall never so lively.

> Ever restless was the dance of miserable hands, now here, now there, shaking off the fresh burning.

> *Senza riposo mai era la tresca*
> *Delle misere mani, or quindi or quinci*
> *Iscotendo da sè l'arsura fresca.*

But not a motion of any kind could this divine lashing draw from the incorrigible Capaneus. He had defied the heavenly tyrant of Olympus and he was prepared to defy this new master of thunderbolts.

"What I was living," he declares, in the very tone of Milton's Lucifer, "*that* I am dead!"—"*Qual io fui vivo, tal son morto!*"

The two poets' descent into the ultimate pit, the terrible Malebolge, on the back of the monster Geryon is most convincingly told, and after they have once landed and are slowly encircling the rocky ledges that surround the hollow cone of the torment of Judas—*tutto di pietra e di color ferrigno*, "all of stone and of an iron colour"—they make the acquaintance of far more unpleasant devils than those classical Furies of Dis who needed an angel absolutely composed of pride to quell them. Both Milton and Dante are proud men and they both enjoy describing pride; but it must be noted that it is Milton's *fallen* angels who show this peculiarity at its best, while with Dante it is the *unfallen*. Dante's devils are indeed the reverse of proud. They are as completely devoid of all dignity as they are of all decency; and they scrabble together and play scurvy tricks upon each other just like those "cart-loads of horned devils," the thought of which, in Rabelais, so obsessed the mind of the naughty yet extremely orthodox Panurge.

Like a horde of hideous gargoyles, leaping into monstrous life out of the indecent fancies of the ribald decorators of our cathedrals, are these Malacodas and Scarmigliones and Graffiacanes and Rubicantes; and it is a relief to think that is only when Dante and Virgil have left the chasm of the great sorcerers and have arrived at that of the official swindlers and grafters that this hellish gang appears.

Over the fate of these sorcerers—one of whom is Teiresias himself, who for Homer retains his full power and authority even among the dead, and another our old childhood friend, the Wizard of Scott's *Lay*—Dante cannot restrain his tears. What especially troubles him, and it is a touch of sublime anatomical horror worthy of an insane sculptor, is that these images of God are so contorted that *their* tears are compelled to roll down their "hinder parts at their division."

> Certainly I wept, leaning on one of the rocks of the hard cliff, so that my Escort said to me: "Art thou, too, like the other fools? Here pity lives when it is altogether dead. Who more impious than he who sorrows at God's judgment?"

For devoted bookworms whose conscience may refuse to allow them to dwell on the sort of spectacle that Dante loves to invent it is a comfort to remember what splendid confusion reigns among our greatest literary guides, nature pouring forth her multiple inspiration through so many masks that no man can say, "Lo! this is the Only Way!" Think what salutary and refreshing differences of view we encounter in this high sphere! The supremest of sages according to Homer is doomed by Dante to move and to weep with his face towards his rump.

Brutus, Caesar's virtuous assassin, is made a hero by Shakespeare; while his place in the "Inferno" is along with Judas in the very jaws of Satan!

And contrasted with Dante's proud contempt for the inglorious anonymity of the world's easy-going "honest cods," think of how Rabelais in his magnanimous and evangelical humour "puts down the mighty" in *his* next world!

"Their estate and condition of living," said Epistemon, "is but only changed after a very strange manner: for I saw Alexander the Great patching on clowts upon our breeches and stockins whereby he got but a very poor living.

"Aeneas was a miller.

"Trajan was a fisher of frogs.

"Hector a snap-sauce scullion.

"Julius Caesar and Pompey were boat-wrights and tighters of ships.

"Pope Julius was a Crier of puddings, but he left off wearing there his great buggarly beard.

"Lucretia was an ale-house keeper.

"Semiramis the beggar's lice-killer.

"After this manner they that had been great Lords and Ladies here got but a poor scurvie wretched living there below. And on the contrary, the Philosophers and others, who in this world had been altogether wanting, were great lords there in their turne. I saw Epictetus there, most gallantly apparelled after the French fashion, sitting under a pleasant Arbour with a store of handsome Gentlewomen, frolicking, drinking, dancing, and making good cheere—"

It was in the eighth circle of hell and in the seventh chasm of the Malebolge that the poets, in their gradual descent, encountered the sacrilegious thief, Vanni Fucci of Pistoia.

> Power of God! O how severe, that showers such blows in vengeance!

> *O potenzia di Dio, quant' è severa,*
> *Che cotai colpi per vendetta croscia!*

This poor wretch is punished by devilish serpents to such a tune that—as my English commentator observes—"he rises into a boundless pale rage, such as is hardly known in Northern countries."

For myself, however, for all my northern blood, I must confess to sharing something of this Pistoian's pale rage with the President of the Immortals.

> At the conclusion of his words, the thief raised up his hands with both the figs—*con ambedue le fiche*—shouting: "Take them, God, for at thee I aim them!"—"*Togli, Iddio, chè a te le squadro!*"

With a marvellous beauty however, before which all animadversion sinks abashed, does our poet, a little further on, bring it about that Ulysses, who is damned among the evil counsellors, should relate the manner of his death.

What a thing to note, the way this ideal adventurer has reincarnated himself! From Homer to Shakespeare, from Shakespeare to Cowper, from Cowper to Tennyson, from Tennyson to Lawrence of Arabia and James Joyce, he has mesmerized every type of human mind. We deal here with his mediaeval avatar in the "Inferno" of Dante; and Dante certainly rises magnificently and triumphantly to the occasion.

Like Shakespeare, whose Welsh friends claimed to be descended from the Trojans, Dante as an Italian is much more friendly to the Trojans than to the Greeks; but unlike Shakespeare he does heroic justice to those who "made the door," *ond' usci de Romani il gentil seme*—"by which the noble seed of the Romans came forth."

Ulysses and Diomed are entirely concealed in a pillar of moving fire; but addressing this rushing double-pointed flame in hurried fear lest it might dislike Dante's modern tongue, Virgil makes a courteous prayer to it to pause.

> The greater horn of the ancient flame began to shake itself, murmuring, just like a flame that struggles with the wind.

> *Lo maggior corno della fiamma antica*
> *Cominciò a crollarsi mormorando,*
> *Pur come quella cui vento affatica.*

How one realized at this point Dante's peculiar genius for condensing great events, great feelings, great dramatic issues, in a few bare, stripped, heel-upon-rock phrases, phrases that suggest hammer and chisel rather than the pages of a dictionary! Or, to change the metaphor, what could be harder than to convey in a dozen three-lined verses, each of them rolling forward on the swell and fall of recurrent waves of triple rhymes, as if on a tide that neither tires nor turns, the living spirit of the hero of the *Odyssey?*

Yet this is what he does; and indeed we are compelled to admit that in spite of the huge differences between Homer, Rabelais, Shakespeare, and Dante—differences so great that it seems sometimes as if they were writing for different planets—there are certain things in common between them.

Take the speech to his companions in his final adventure that Dante puts into Ulysses' mouth. Would not this— with some faint hint thrown in as to the amount of fair-girdled women and wide-browed oxen and beautifully worked vessels of gold and silver that the gods might incidentally add—fall aptly from the mouth of the Much-enduring?

"Consider your origin: ye were not formed to live like brutes, but to follow virtue and knowledge."

"Considerate la vostra semenza:
Fatti non foste a viver come bruti,
Ma per seguir virtute e conoscenza."

And here, not to speak of Shakespeare who uses almost identical words, or of Goethe, who calls upon us by our earnestness to "make life eternity," we find even Rabelais devoting page after page on these exact lines to the education of his great little giants.

Some of us however—and I am not referring to the wilful sad ones whose voices gurgle to eternity in bubbles out of the mud—will turn to Walt Whitman to escape this strenuous life, and Walt Whitman, countering both the classical and the mediaeval dogma, will tell us to imitate these same *bruti* in their undisturbed nonchalance, and to loaf and take our ease, "observing a spear of summer grass," or a strip of sea-sand, and giving both culture and ambition to the devil!

There comes a point now, however, as the two poets reach the tenth chasm of the eighth circle, when a very interesting episode occurs, nothing less than an indignant rebuke administered to Dante by Virgil for his too lively interest in the grosser aspects of human nature.

This occurs in connexion with the ferocious "back-chat" between Master Adam of Brescia, who was burnt alive in 1281 for counterfeiting the precious golden florins of Florence, and Sinon the Greek, who according to Virgil gave the Trojans, as a prisoner of war, counterfeit advice in the matter of the wooden horse.

Under Virgil's disgust at seeing him lap up with such eagerness every word of this repulsive broil Dante becomes

so speechless with shame and blushes so scarlet that he has
to be forgiven. But his friend tells him he must always in
future *count him by his side* when he's tempted to listen to
such filthy abuse—"for the wish to hear it is a vulgar wish":
Chè voler ciò udire è bassa voglia.

One does indeed, I think, detect a deep psychological,
if not a deep aesthetic difference, between gloating over a
base quarrel and gloating over scenes of torture, but
whether the former peculiarity is as likely to increase the
pain and evil in the world as the latter is a very different
question. Virgil praised Dante warmly for the pleasure he
took in seeing Filippo Argenti "well soused"; and it must
be remarked that on this occasion he doesn't blame him
for gloating over the ingenuity of *God's vendetta*; but only
for listening to the gross quarrel between its victims which
must at least have distracted their wretched minds for a
space.

The conclusion that a puzzled hyperborean is compelled
to reach therefore, as he ponders on this significant blush
between these two "Great Latins," is that cruelty can be
embraced with joy by the aesthetic sense while vulgarity
must not be touched; and this will be a conclusion which,
remembering all the "country matters" in Shakespeare
and all the tavern brawls in Dickens, he will have some
difficulty in accepting.

But our poets have now searched the terrible ninth and
last circle, and the absorbed reader who feels as if, like a
phantom third, he has been following them all the way
down, becomes aware of the frozen foundations of this
mythological universe. Certainly for a mathematical and
realistic materialization of the next world there is nothing
in literature like *The Divine Comedy*. Using all the science,
all the scholarship, all the faith, all the philosophy of his
time, using all the history of humanity *up* to his time,
selecting from among the dialects of his Italy the particular

one out of which he could best create the Italian language, Dante has branded upon the perilous stuff of the world's consciousness I will not say an everlasting vision of truth, but an unsurpassable picture of the last *complete unification* of the fathomless mysteries that will probably be attempted!

What a thrill of weird exultation quivers through us when we hear the horn of Nimrod, in this abyss! It makes us think of those terrific lines in the *Odyssey* about the great hunter, Orion. "Enormous," *pelorion*, is the Homeric epithet for him who has given his name to our grandest constellation; and with the weight of those huge syllables to help us we must struggle to imagine the vast primeval shape and the cosmogonic inarticulateness of this Hebraic titan.

Like a veritable howl from all the aboriginal creatures who have been engineered away and pioneered away and improved away and vivisected away comes Nimrod's cry: "*Rafel mai amech Zabi almi!*" And for myself I find great relief in repeating this defiant gibberish when in the presence of certain animal trainers.

But Virgil now makes of himself and Dante "one bundle," *un fascio er' egli ed io*, and lifted up by the giant Antaeus the two poets are set down in Cocytus, the ice-bottom of the world.

To describe this ultimate *fondo* of the universe is certainly not, as the poet well says, an enterprise for being taken up in sport, nor for a tongue that cries "Ma and Pop," *che chiami mamma e babbo;* but it is characteristic of Dante that it is for the reception of *traitors*, traitors to their kin, their country, their friends, their lords, and above all to their God, that this frozen pit has been reserved for eternity.

Oh, how characteristic it is of the fanaticism of human nature, and how completely in harmony with the savage hypocrisy of Carlyle's praise of a religion he didn't believe

DANTE ALIGHIERI

(From the fresco by Giotto in the Bargello, Florence)

for the sake of the violence he loved, that it should be for the heretics called "traitors," the predestined gaol-birds and hell-birds of all arbitrary régimes, that this frozen torture-chamber should have been designed! How characteristic of humanity that Dante should place in the lowest depths of all a person like Brutus whose character is the subject of *political* rather than moral controversy!

But the poet's own savagery in this icy Cocytus passes all bounds. He seizes one of the inmates by the scalp to satisfy his curiosity as to his name:

> I had already had his hair coiled on my hand and had plucked off more than one tuft of it, he barking and keeping down his eyes—*latrando lui con gli occhi in giù raccolti.*

Another implores the visitor to remove the icicles into which his tears have hardened, so that he "may vent the grief which stuffs his heart"; and Dante swears by the fate of his own soul that he *will* do this for him if only he admits his identity. But no sooner has the wretch given him the required knowledge and demanded the performance of this vow—"but reach hither thy hand: open my eyes"— than Dante, all his nerves twitching with the ardour of his pious cruelty, breaks his oath:

> And I opened them not for him; and to be rude to him was courtesy.

> *—Ed io non gliele apersi,*
> *E cortesia fu in lui esser villano.*

What a quaint example it is of that *sancta simplicitas* that so struck John Huss when he was being burnt that all our English deans and prelates and all our refined sensitive gentlewomen should have followed Carlyle in their praise of Dante as a *great moral force for good*! Oscar Wilde, however, took the right view when *he* praised this horrible scene for its beauty. That's what it is. It is at once abominable and beautiful!

And is it not a sad and a startling mystery that a thing as monstrous as this *should* be beautiful? I suppose it is beautiful—though the beauty of the appalling is a great mystery—because it lays clear and bare the tragic clash between the extremes of a merciless ideal and natural human pity.

But doesn't it show how right Goethe was in telling us to resolve to live in "the Good" and in "the Whole," *as well as* in this treacherous and beyond-good-and-evil "beauty"?

> . . . Livid, up to where the hue of shame appears, the doleful shades were in the ice sounding with their teeth like storks.

> *Livide, insin là dove appar vergogna,*
> *Eran l'ombre dolenti nella ghiaccia,*
> *Mettendo i denti in nota di cicogna.*

Half of the beauty of this is in its peculiar expression, so compressed and yet so imaginative, but the other half lies in the very monstrosity of the scene called up, the uncracked ice, in the tenebrous glimmering light, sown thick with livid gibbering human faces like the windrow of the sand with shells, or, as Dante himself says, like a village pond when the frogs hold their muzzles out of the water.

It is in fact the beauty of a stripped, superintense style, a style that throws into imaginative relief all that is conveyed by the most piercing, excavating, scooping, harrowing, disinterring *eye* that has ever been turned upon physical atrocity.

Oh, how often, when we hear in this our own day, of crimes resembling what we learn in this frozen pit to have been committed against Ugolino and his children, are we tempted to wish that Dante *was* in the right of it about the vengeance of God!

But these wishes are evil wishes and when a person has watched how "the world wags," as King Lear says, for a score or two of years, he will have found that evil for evil is only a vicious circle.

The moralists may tell us that "wherewithal a man sinneth by the same shall be punished," but something inexplicable in us, deeper than any judgment or justice, goes on muttering in its throat: "*Rafel mai amech Zabi almi!*"

It is indeed strange enough, and sad enough too, that unless we are passionate students of theological symbolism it is hard to retain our concentration of vision as fixedly on the "Purgatorio" and "Paradiso" as upon the "Inferno."

And I fancy it is not only the simplicity of our novitiate in metaphysics and ethics and the limits of our initiation into Catholic mysteries that produce this result. I think it is the old fate of average human intelligence, for which nature herself is responsible, that the tragic, the pitiful, the terrible aspect of beauty arrests us more, and holds us more, than her peaceful, her ideal, her happy expression. But let us steady and purify our disturbed nerves for a space anyway in the "Purgatorio." Full of a delicate symbolism that leaves a reader with the sense of having moved among the figures of some enchanted tapestry in an air scented with lilies—*Manibus o date lilia plenis*—or among the colours in some Fra Angelico fresco, where the gold and the green and the blue of the flowers in the grass are touched by the garments of lovely creatures who themselves have the faces of flowers, the Earthly Paradise at the top of this Sacred Mount seems to transfigure the burden of existence into all the day-dreams of all the young girls in the world!

This particular kind of intense ideal romance, like the lattice-casement thoughts on a May morning, of a maid who has read *Morte d'Arthur* before she slept and has left a jasmin spray between the pages at the place where Lancelot first meets the queen, is the most opposite human mood that could be imagined to the sadistic ferocity and deadly disdain of the "Inferno." But who among men knows not how true to the most secret and most hidden psychology of our nature these opposites are! Everything to do with the woman he loves in this tremendous amorist's mind, every detail of what she wears, of how she smiles—and no one but Leonardo has made so much of a woman's smile—every nuance in the way she lifts her hand or lowers her head, every flicker of the proud or shy or tender mood she is in, is registered as if in an illuminated Breviary.

We certainly realize as we read the "Purgatorio" all that women owe to the Middle Ages in intensifying the idealism, the subtlety, and the romance of love. It is conceivable, however, that we have among us to-day many damsels who would prefer the perilous life of the laughing white-armed classic maidens who attended Penelope and slept with her suitors rather than fulfil the high rôle that Dante demands!

But to sound the depths of this poet's own nature, it is essential that we should put the moment in the "Purgatorio" when he recognizes "the tokens of the ancient flame"—*i segni dell' antica fiamma*, and beholds his lady, "olive-crowned over a white veil, clad, under a green mantle, with hue of living flame," side by side with that other moment where he tugs at the scalp-hairs of Bocca degli Abati in the frozen Cocytus till he makes him bark like a dog.

Is it because of this very contrast that our delicately nurtured great-grandmothers would copy whole pages of this poet in their albums? Has the possibility of ferocity in a great man as much attraction for the feminine imagination as the possibility of reckless infidelity?

Certainly, in reading the "Purgatorio" and the "Paradiso," an ordinary book-lover, who has not been trained in philosophy, must feel, especially if he has a learned commentator to help him, astounded at the mental grasp not only of the poet who used them, but of the great Schoolmen he used. Any intelligent layman confronted by the metaphysical and moral subtleties of these mediaeval thinkers must be *awed* by the genius they possessed—must wish indeed that our modern philosophers, with a hundred times more help from the exact sciences, had a tithe of this sheer intellectual power!

Any shallow modern person who takes upon himself to cast aspersions upon the Middle Ages, using the very epithet "mediaeval" as a term of reproach, betrays a level of culture, and indeed a level of mentality, not a bit higher than that of the sly Pardoner laughed at by Chaucer.

At the same time, I'm not ashamed of confessing that in the midst of the ecstatic raptures of the divine pageant at the end of the "Purgatorio," I find myself wondering, when Dante turns for help, as was ever his custom, to his heathen guide—turns to him even from Beatrice herself—and realizes with tears that he has gone back to his place among those "who live in desire without hope," how exactly that *anima cortese Mantovana* made his return journey, and what mental consolation he derived from hearing again that welcoming cry:

"Honour to the supreme poet! His shade, which has left us, returns again!"

"Onerate l'altissimo poeta;
L'ombra sua torna, ch'era dipartita!"

And I find myself wondering, too, even at the very close of the "Paradiso," even while our author dissolves in adoration before those threefold circles of light that seemed to him "to be painted with our effigy"—*mi parve pinta della nostra effige*—how, after all, that "Love that moves the sun and the other stars" is to be reconciled with that other "*primo Amore*" whose decree carved the "*eternal I endure*" over the gate of hell.

Reconciled? "Squared," as they say, by the squaring of *such* a circle? Better a thousand times "return Him the ticket" with Ivan Karamazov!

And what, following the pragmatic method we have tried to sustain throughout these studies, is the value of Dante's appeal in the pressure of a modern person's life? What, apart from the Catholic faith, would a disciple of Dante's tend to aim at in moulding his mental culture?

I think he would in the first place destroy from his life-illusion that particular kind of vague pompous idealism, which is so easily shattered by any shock to one's moral and physical dignity! From this proud-humble egoist of realism he would learn to accept, and even exult in, as an essential part of the game, those bitter rebuffs to personal vanity that come to us all and make us wince and blush, even in the very thought of them! He would, I think, learn to accept without any of that morbid weakness, for which our catchword to-day is "the inferiority complex," every characteristic limitation, even the most grotesque, of his power, his courage, his appearance, his intelligence, nor allow these failings, however ridiculous, to abate one jot of his dramatic exultation at the contact of his poor battered, blundering, unlucky envelope of a living soul with the majestic panorama of the cosmos! How greatly most of us need some grain of that hard indissoluble Dantesque core kept intact under our fluctuations!

And a reader of Dante would also, I fancy, acquire a certain mental trick of linking up his consciousness of the unfathomable Macrocosm with every smallest episode and incident of his mortal days; and this would apply not only to his fortunate moments, but to those moments when he is completely routed and put to shame, and reduced purely and simply to the condition of "one who weeps."

And what about that inert misery, that disintegrating sense of fretful futility, which is the special curse of the Hamlets of our age, and which takes the heart out of tragedy, the spirit out of comedy, and by undramatizing the whole drama kills our basic response to life?

A reader of Dante—even if only by being roused to indignant rejection—would, one fancies, be "finely touched" to *some* sort of noble issue! And certainly a person who is prepared to go down those terrible circles again and again, will be a person who is unlikely to throw up his hands over his own minor miseries.

But—and this is a very important point—I do not believe we can get one-twentieth part of the secret *virtù* emanating from Dante's style without at least having the original Italian *before our eyes*.

For my own part, I find *all* poetical versions of *The Divine Comedy* intolerable; and I would strongly advise any one who, like myself, is no scholar to get hold of Dent's Temple Classics edition, which is a series of three small compact volumes with the Italian on one side of the page and a first-rate prose translation on the other.

Fortified with *something*—I am not prepared to define exactly what—that emanates from Dante's style, like the steam from the boiling blood where divine justice "to eternity milks tears"—*ed eterno munge le lagrime*—any human being, struggling through the pain and pleasure and indifference of one single ordinary day will find the central core of his soul more solitary and more independent. He will also, I think, acquire a peculiar anti-narcissistic awareness of his own particular skeleton, such as a tramp or a pilgrim might have, as he moves about his business, with only a thin time-screen between himself and eternity!

And this awareness of our skeleton, as the soul propels its body about its ordinary affairs, generally hides below the surface, if we have caught the real Dantesque secret, some ideal love or some secret cult of which we alone, in our unguessed-at pride, are the passionate repository.

And this hidden Ideal brings us in secret—always in secret!—an exultant sense of mystical romance, totally independent of the commonplace conditions of our life, totally independent of the shame and humiliations to which we are subjected. Yes, there is no doubt that any sensitive reader who acquires a mania for Dante's formidable destiny-charged style gathers a power to retain the sort of inviolable inner life that results from making a secret ideal or a secret romance, *or even a secret revelation*, something round which, unknown to the world, his whole existence centres. He acquires the power to hold this secret in the face of abominations that make him faint and sick with indignation, to hold it in the face of all God's ways to men and in the face of all men's ways to one another!

I am, as the reader has already perceived, struggling with an intimation that is very hard to express; but there is no doubt that a great many men and women in middle life, *nel mezzo del cammin di nostra vita* as Dante himself was when, supposedly in the year 1300, he visited hell, find the romance of their youth gone, the companions of their youth gone, the hopes of their youth gone, the strength and beauty of their youth gone. And then comes the moment for reading the "Inferno"!

And is it not strange? What remains in our mind as the final summary of it all is neither the cruelty of God nor the crimes of men. It is the staggering, awe-inspiring *endurance* of any ordinary human soul, whether such a soul be good or evil, whether it be in heaven or hell! Yes, whatever Dante's *doctrines* may say, the far subtler, the far truer emanation that proceeds from his *style* indicates endurance as the supreme human virtue.

> Therefore let fortune turn her wheel as she likes and the labourer his mattock.

> *Però giri fortuna la sua rota,*
> *Come le piace, e il villan la sua marra.*

For terrible and beautiful invention, for intensity of passion, for pure intellect and power, no poet who has lived can surpass Dante; but to praise him as a moral guide for those who are outside the Church is the most treacherous betrayal of the human spirit into which the academic mind has ever led us. Had the "Purgatorio" and the "Paradiso" been ten times more lovely, the mere fact that he could write as he has written in the "Inferno" would prove him to have condoned cruelty, justified cruelty, exulted in cruelty, gloated over cruelty, under the excuse that it was the will of Omnipotence.

All the horrible pain he describes as triumphantly inflicted by God upon His enemies *does* happen in this world, though not for ever; and the reading of the "Inferno" has at least this, that it makes us ashamed of our petulant pusillanimity, when other human beings, equally sensitive with ourselves, have endured and are still enduring what while it lasts partakes of the nature of eternity.

If therefore you say to me, "Why read the 'Inferno'?" I answer, "I read it because I get power from its power. I read it because the image of what pain *can be at the worst* is the best method of enduring it when it is far short of the worst. In other words, I read it so that I can compel the cruel spirit of its poet to do for me what Virgil before he went back to hell, did for him:

> Wherefore I do crown and mitre thee over thyself!

> *Per ch' io te sopra te corono e mitrio.*

Rabelais

To my way of thinking and feeling Rabelais is one of
the few supreme writers this planet has produced. I put
him higher than Plato or Cervantes or Montaigne. I put
him along with Homer and Shakespeare. And as with all
the greatest men of genius, you feel, every time you read
him, that no one has really properly interpreted him and
that, long ago as he lived, we are only beginning to understand him.

With a good deal of strain, and with a torrent of self-
conscious virility, Walt Whitman, on his own American
lines, has revived something of his cosmic optimism, just as
Balzac, with Gallic and phallic bravado, has echoed his
Cyclopean drollery.

But no one comes near him! The humour of Dickens is a
unique inspiration, human in the richest sense, racy, idio-
matic, irresistible; but its scope, though imaginative and
deep, lacks the huge tellurian swing of the Rabelaisian
orbit. The quaintness of character upon which it depends is
localized and particularized; nor, save for its impassioned
benevolence, has it got much mystical or spiritual background.

To drag forward the poetic satire of Aristophanes or the
misanthropic fury of Swift in relation to Rabelais is as absurd as to link him with the age-old tradition of literary
eroticism which moralists disparage under the abusive word

pornography. His attitude to the excremental is as different from Swift's as it is from that of the modern author of *Ulysses*; and only a mind with a most exceptional prep-boy obsession could derive aphrodisiac excitement from his colossal bawdiness.

Like all the true revelations of life the substance of Rabelais' book is at once very simple and infinitely deep. To maintain that he used his extravagant humour as a mere mask to placate authority and "get," as the saying is, "his message over," is to misunderstand the nature of his genius. His humour is *in itself* a complete philosophy. It is the essence of his doctrine diffused through his style, not a disguise to hide his thought. And it is humour of a very special and peculiar kind. It is not a mere playing with the comic or the ludicrous. It is more than merry fooling. Its scale is too stupendous. The laughter in it sinks down too deep. It is mystic humour, thaumaturgic humour, revolutionary humour. It is erotic and excremental; but with something over and above. It is evangelical, superhuman, cosmogonic; but its orgiastic revelry in the atrocious whimsies of life is not soured because of the enormous reformations it suggests, nor debased into mere satire because of the monstrous rascalities it exposes.

The genius of Rabelais is more critical, more militant, more, if I may say so, *evolutionary*, than the genius of Walt Whitman; because, for all the colossal gusto and relish with which it "accepts" life, it never seeks to force itself to "accept" the evil in life.

Rabelais could never have said, "Evil propels me and the reform of evil propels me. I stand indifferent. I moisten the roots of all that has grown."

What kind of a man was this *curé* of Meudon in ordinary life? No stickler for formalities of approach, at any rate, no rapper-out of carefully prepared aphorisms, or of pompous witticisms with a sting in their tails. You feel he would have talked easily, naturally, freely, to any one who came along, affecting no Socratic irony, no devastating Voltairian sarcasm, no gnomic oracles. A "penchant" for men of learning he must certainly have had, and an unwearied fondness for old wives' tales. But the chances are—as human character goes—that even in his cups this greatest of all humourists was of a shy, evasive, retiring disposition. Not perhaps looking on the ground as if to find a hare, as Chaucer says of himself, but prone to long brooding fits of amiable detachment from which his visitors had to rouse him.

What did he think and feel as he said his holy masses? Did he give more than evangelical comfort to the sick and dying? One is led on to dally with many curious speculations. What were the objects, for instance, that would arrest us in his house and kitchen? Did he plant shoots from his native vineyard in his vicarage garden? Did he, like Don Quixote, have a not too clever niece to make his bed? And during those final years of his life did he play the physician as well as the priest to his friends and neighbours?

Of one thing we may be certain; like all great men of genius he must have gathered from the most unlikely quarters grist for his mill.

His revolutionary correspondence with the more daring men of learning of his day is an established fact and the unfathomable impulse upon his mind of contact with the newly unearthed Greek classics.

In this matter of Rabelais' scholarship it is hard not to be struck by the crushing difference between his type of brain and that of so many later men of genius. Shakespeare's classical knowledge, comprehensive as it is, strikes nobody, except a few unimaginative pedants, as something out of reach of a lively, self-taught, alert intelligence. And how little of the true bookworm, how little of the impassioned scholar, there is in Dickens, in Balzac, in Tolstoy! Nietzsche, it is true, was a formidable philologist; but to-day, among our writers of startling originality, I can only think of James Joyce as coming anywhere near the colossal bookishness of Rabelais.

But this insatiable and extravagant scholarship of his—every ancient classic he got hold of being like a magician's wand to roll back the walls of the cosmos—can obviously have been only one of the stimulating treasure-houses his imagination exploited.

Another must have been to him an even richer quarry of magic lore, to be heightened and transfigured. I refer to his contact with quacks, empirics, alchemists, pedlars of freakish talismans, hawkers of fake elixirs, vendors of hedge-mascots, wandering astrologers, aphrodisiac-mongers, herb-sellers, and fortune-tellers.

But beyond both professional and unprofessional abstractors of the quintessence, he must have fed his terraqueous fancy and nourished his planetary humour from the random discourses, overheard in tavern and kitchen, of thousands of country wiseacres and village oracles.

To this singular ex-monk, to this pious-impious priest-doctor of humanity, must have come the most motley pilgrims; all of them bringing or seeking some kind of medical or botanical knowledge, some kind of philological or mythological enlightenment, and all of them anxious to discuss pro and con every new philosophical theory, every fresh antiquarian discovery, and every imaginable reform in morals, religion, education, statecraft and medicine.

Great combustible heretics must have come by night to that curious parsonage—worldly prince-cardinals with an itch for the classics, sly atheist-humanists masquerading under every sort of shaven poll.

Matthew Arnold said that Catholics had the secret of Jesus and Protestants his method; but this colossal worshipper of the "Great Pan"—"for He is our All"—this disconcerting accomplice of that "Circle, whose centre is everywhere and its circumference nowhere," seems to restore the "secret" of a lost Saturnian golden age and the "method" of a far-off Thelemic millennium.

There is undoubtedly a superevangelical, superindividualistic tone in Rabelais, a vein of huge, unctuous, homely piety, that has something of the best of Protestantism in it. But on the other hand what can the Puritan make of him?

We immoral bookworms know only too well how this "Book of Books," as his friend the Cardinal called it, is driven forth from our libraries to rest with queer companions in second-hand bookshops.

It is certain that Rabelais would have been on the side of Ivan Karamazov's Christ as against his Grand Inquisitor; but how he must have been against that vein of sublime spiritual asceticism in the New Testament which culminates in St. Paul's perverse and frantic wish that all sex-pleasure —even that of the marriage-bed itself—might be abolished from the world!

It is just here—in this primordial matter of sex-delight— that Rabelais, for all his tender respect for the tragic "Sansculotte" of Galilee, ranges himself quite definitely against the fundamental doctrine of Christian chastity.

And yet it would be a shallow judgment to class him in this respect with Voltaire or even with Anatole France. In fact, it is impossible to class him, in regard to this basic matter of his attitude to Christianity, with any other writer. His whole genius is dominated by his nature-inspired revolt against ascetic monasticism, but there is a thaumaturgical "lovingness"—it is hard to use any other word, except perhaps the Homeric *aganophrosunē:* for it has a touch of agapé in it, but an agapé thickened out by something gayer and grosser—diffused throughout his work, a sort of mystical apocalyptic *camaraderie* that has borrowed a great deal from the freemasonry of the "Communion of Saints."

I am thinking of some of the most characteristic elements in the tone of his cosmogonic life-worship when I say that it is this Christian tincture in his Titanic humour which separates it so completely from the thinner, more sapless, less magical well-being of the purely pagan hedonists.

To cut out from Rabelais his evangelical "love of God" and his equally evangelical *camaraderie* is to draw off, as it were, the very oil and unction of his spacious doctrine. The truth is, he has managed to retain the mystical quintessence of medieval piety, while making intransigent sport of its obvious abuses; nor does the colossal obscenity of his erotic jesting swamp or submerge the magnanimity of his sexuality, of the royal reciprocity—I had almost said the royal equality—of the relation he advocates between the sexes.

I am not ashamed to confess that I am not quite "hard-boiled" enough, or, if you must have it so, virile enough, to swallow with equanimity all those practical jokes of our friend Panurge. His street-gamin practices upon the lady of Paris, and the clodhopper way he scores off the rustic Ding-Dong, do not endear this honeysuckle rogue to my graver taste.

"We are not amused," as Queen Victoria would say, by these saucy games. But the less slapstick and clownish Panurge, the Panurge of the debate with Thaumast, the Panurge of the pros and cons of marriage, the Panurge of the apology for debtors, and, above all, the blubbering Panurge of the later books in his wit-combats with Friar John, jumps entirely with my notion of what is the true Rabelaisian touch.

As with all the deepest cosmic secrets revealed by genius, it is wise to take a circuitous flight round the tree of knowledge, hovering about the aromatic incense as it is diffused through the air and dwelling in the atmosphere of its revelation; whereas if you try to swallow every pip and stone of the celestial fruit you are likely to have to pay for your conscientiousness.

The more closely you read Rabelais the more intimately it sinks into your mind that there is diffused throughout these pages the very thing we are all craving for in this hard world; I mean some clue, however dim, to a way of enduring all the disgusting evils of life, to a way of distilling all the magical wonder out of life, as the chaotic mingling of these things in the great stream of existence hums by.

And to me it is as if this clue, this way, this secret, came welling up somehow from the inmost centre of each person's being.

But to get this life-spring into working order, to get this unconquerable flow of immortal ichor into play, a peculiar manner of thinking of it, or regarding it in the depths of oneself, seems to be essential.

And it is just here that the Rabelaisian piling up of excrement upon excrement, of sexuality upon sexuality, of wine and meat upon wine and meat, of book-learning upon book-learning, of magic upon magic, comes in to help us.

Everything is mental. Everything is personal. Everything depends on the mind. And this whole mystery of *the Rabelaisian way* depends on the mind's marriage with that irrational creative force we call the will. There is no word—modern psychology totally fails us where we need it most—for that godlike energy in the central core of the ego, that fighting-erotic energy, wherewith we wrestle with the cosmos when the mystic nuptials of mind and will take place.

We cannot at our simple pleasure call forth the exultant mood that in ordinary parlance we call ecstasy. But we *have* the power of summoning up in ourselves that fighting-

Brown Bros.

FRANÇOIS RABELAIS

erotic spirit which is, so to speak, the ethereal "laughing-gas" of ecstasy, even though it does not automatically culminate in ecstasy. In other words, there is such a thing as a constant, unintermittent *substitute* for these momentary ecstasies which are beyond the mind's power of creating for itself. But it would appear that for many sensitive and imaginative natures one of the grand obstacles to this gallant substitute for momentary ecstasy is the huge down-drag of the excremental processes and of the thick miasmic, grotesque weight of chemical matter in its foulest forms!

But if the fighting-erotic energy in one's inmost being can only manage to take this excremental accompaniment to life in a particular mood, a gigantic impediment in its path is at once removed.

Nor is the way of taking it into which Rabelais can guide a devoted reader a *realistic* or what we now call a "hard-boiled" way. Such a way would be totally beyond the power of a morbidly sensitive person—as most bookworms are! And it is of bookworms, that is to say of imaginative book-lovers, leading more or less sedentary lives, that I am especially thinking; for sturdy, active, healthy-minded temperaments take the excremental basis of life "in their stride," and to such persons this artificial and premeditated "substitute" for life's ecstatic moments is not required.

Their own well-constituted good spirits are enough. To natures of this kind Rabelais' monstrous humour presents itself as a fantastic exaggeration of a mere schoolboy's love of grossness and obscenity.

This is the whole point. Active, hard-boiled men of the world, devoid of bookish imagination, regard Rabelais as a somewhat tedious and scholarly edition of their own lively Pullman-car relater of indecent tales.

These are the persons who, in their sabbatical disguise as pillars of society, thrust forth this world-genius, as a mischievous scallawag, into the "forbidden" shelves of their public libraries!

I visualize the real Rabelais as the extreme opposite of this boisterous bawdy jester vociferously relating smutty stories to groups of uproarious nit-wits. I suspect him of having been an extremely shy and extremely sensitive scholar. The quintessential Rabelaisian humour is a very profound, a very subtle, and a very difficult way of taking those monstrous aspects of life that make it hard for sensitive people to re-create this chaotic world in terms of philosophical imagination.

Rabelais' book is a kind of apostolical epistle to the weaker brothers, the more timid and sensitive souls, among our Pantagruelian initiates, upon the subject of the soul's *evangelical ecstasy*, and how it can get the sexuality of the world, and the monstrous indecency of the world, and the bottomless disgustingness of the world, into harmony with the purer life of the spirit.

Like all great humour, the Rabelaisian way of taking the monstrous facetiousness of our fairylike cosmos is a way of philosophical and poetical exaggeration. And it is a humour saturated with the therapeutic oil of evangelical bawdiness, mixed freely and abundantly with the candle-ends of old wives' wisdom, but heightened throughout by an ethereal, translunar ichor, impossible to be defined, drawing its radiant and celestial quiddity from the very depths of the unconquerable spirit of man.

If it is optimistic, this Rabelaisian humour, like charity overcoming the world, 'tis an optimism that shrinks from no loathsomeness, no atrociousness, no horribleness that ordinary people encounter as they go through life; and it is profoundly and most richly the humour of a great scholar.

Passages recur again and again that bring this rich bookish joviality down to the earth. And at such times it is replaced—and one longs for more of these incomparable interludes—by a huge and friendly rusticity, a homely and yet royal humanity, the like of which is nowhere to be found outside this great book! Shakespeare and Cervantes, even Homer himself, show, as it were, *diminished* and in some indescribable way, *lessened,* both in bulk and weight when compared with the gigantic and simple homeliness of these godlike passages.

It is when we give ourselves up to the torrent of rich-echoing, symbolic, gnomic, oracular bookishness in Rabelais that we feel how slight a part the obscenity, the profanity, and all the monastic satire really play in this vast tide of tellurian humour.

If ever there was a great physician of the faltering human body and soul it is Rabelais. Mere contact with the unfathomable buoyancy of his spirit is a Pantagruelian medicine for the feeble heart. He himself hints as much in his comparatively serious dedicatory preface to the Fourth Book, where he refers, advancing into a mystery beyond even the wisdom of "our Father Hippocrates," to the occult effects of the mere presence of the physician, suggesting that actual telepathic sensations are "produced by a transfusion of the serene, or gloomy, aerial or terrestrial, joyful or melancholic Spirits of the Physician, into the person of the Patient, as is the opinion of Plato, Averroes and others."

It is characteristic of his unconquerable faith—a medical rather than a priestly faith but a no less *magical* one—in the efficacy of "the will to live" that Rabelais throws his Titanic weight, along with that of Pythagoras and Socrates and Goethe and Walt Whitman, on the side of those formidable and by no means cowardly masters throughout the ages, who, in confronting *le grand Peutêtre* at the bottom of our darkness, hold by *le bon espoir* of a joyful Resurrection from the Dead.

And, indeed, in reading Rabelais a curious feeling often comes over us, a feeling very hard to put into words, as if there really were some saving possibility some redeeming dimension of superplanetary force, not quite beyond human attainment, from which, if we could only tap its occult resources, a living assurance of immortality would flood our feeble and faltering lives.

But it must be noted that this underlying *bon espoir*, that runs like a deep fresh-water current below the overpowering salt waves, is a personal and mystical, not an orthodox or traditional faith. It springs from some secret reservoir in the depths of the individual soul and its *taste*, so to speak, is at once pagan and evangelical. And it is a significant and characteristic thing that this buoyant vein of mystical assurance adjusts itself so well to the huge, homely, monstrously gross humour, whereby he enlarges, heightens, and ennobles, with a sweet and godlike magic, the basic simplicities of earthly life.

Perhaps it is natural enough in the philosophy of a great physician that the ultimate essence of his attitude to the First Cause should be the joyousness of grateful well-being; of his attitude to morals the exuberance of abounding health; and of his attitude to immortality the intuition of an overbrimming vitality.

It is the affirmation of health against disease, of wisdom against ignorance, of magnanimity against meanness, of mercy against malice, of indulgence against resentment, of a free sex-happiness against depraved suppression, that culminates, in the dark deep question of the final alternative, in his preference for the Positive over the Negative, for the *open* over the *closed* door!

What Rabelais really does is to take our world, just as it is, with all its abuses, atrocities, injustices, stupidities, and monstrous ironies, and dig beneath it, until he can heave it up, roots, refuse, dung, offscouring, filthy rubble and all, and, lifted so, to let in upon it a luminous ether, a huge suffusion of celestial radiance, under which the whole chaotic spectacle falls into gigantic and friendly *homeliness*, no longer desolate and futile, but with all its piled-up abominations taking on a new significance. And as every human figure in his book grows more and more gnomic and mellow, he ends by convincing us with his Friar Johns and Carpalins and Epistemons and Trouillogons and Tribou-lets and Thaumasts and Gymnasts and Rondibilises, not to speak of Grangousier, Gargantua, and his great Pantagruel, that beneath all our viciousness and folly, it is of tough rind and sweet sap, of unconquerable humour and kindly resilience that our poor much-abused, much-enduring human nature is essentially composed!

Behind all human religions, behind the symbols of all creeds, behind the babble of all mystics, there does exist still, in spite of the negations of dogmatic science, an im-mortal spring of living water. This is the water that the Son of Man turns for ever into wine; and this is the wine, *tasting differently to all*, that this Arch-Thaumaturge and chief among heretics offers to us in his holy bottle! And how wholesome is the manner in which, like the old and great poet Raminagrobis, Rabelais would have us dismiss from the chambers of our spirit the pestilentious rakehells of all bigoted and cocksure orthodoxies, whether theological or scientific! *Keep all doors open*, of this mystery of life and death, is his free motto. And, like Raminagrobis, he would turn these bigots and dogmatists—of both sides—out of the fortress of his sweet thoughts and immortal contempla-tions! And to his bookish and book-loving readers his voice still comes, warning us against these same arrogant ortho-doxies—of both camps—with their waspish stingings. "Keep out of their courses, and eschew them, step forth of their ways and do not resemble them; and meanwhile let me be no more troubled by any of you, but leave me now in silence, I beseech you."

7

Montaigne

I⸰T⸰ IS of a peculiar interest to me as an elderly man to note exactly how I react to Montaigne now that, numbering the years of my life, I have managed to outlive the years of the great essayist.

I think he is, for all his gallant praise of youth as the heyday of our intellect, a writer peculiarly and especially adapted to old age. I had almost said to infirm old age; for though he fought stubbornly against it, and went on just the same, he suffered so abominably and for so many years from the anguish of the "stone," that we feel as we read him that his long contest with this wicked complaint must have played a considerable part in the conditions under which he expressed his maturest genius.

Certainly it seems to me that his work grows in interest the older *he* grows.

And how curious it is the way each great book of the world has its own special history with us, the successive stages of our own private life running parallel to our reactions to this particular mirror of the general life!

My own first acquaintance with Montaigne goes back to that profoundly subtle picture of the man and his ideas introduced by Walter Pater into the pages of *Gaston de Latour.*

But as I read him now, after this lapse of years, I feel as if I were encountering quite a different Montaigne from

146

that image of him which so kindled the imagination of young Gaston.

The Montaigne who arrests me now arrests me no more as a universal sceptic whose second thoughts, turning to the homely wisdom of the piety of the generations, subtly undermine his first, and by means of scepticism extract the sting of scepticism, and by doubting dull the edge of doubt.

He arrests me now as one whose chief wisdom has to do rather with the art of life and with the art of integrating one's essential personality than with any final conclusions of philosophic thought, whether sceptical or otherwise.

The secret I get from him now, as I brood over his words and seek to catch the dominant element in the floating solution of his drifting ruminations, is of far greater day-by-day value to me at my present age than the precise reasons why he could or could not accept the Athanasian Creed.

But let me refer at once to the element in Montaigne that I find myself instinctively dodging or hurrying past, so as to reach something more germane to the matter. He himself severely condemns all summarized, expurgated, condensed, abridged versions of great books.

Yet he confesses very frankly that in his own reading he skimmed and dallied with them, taking this, leaving that, and treating them all in an easy, capricious, lazy manner, digesting what suited his taste, what served his turn, and letting the rest go. He was indeed what Rabelais would call a great "abstractor of the quintessence," one who read for use rather than learning, and for life rather than knowledge; and this makes it legitimate to treat his own words in a similar way.

And for myself, though I have never seen such a volume and would only trust its compilation to a real lover of the *Essays* and one who had a temper of mind akin to their author's, I can well conceive that for the less dyed-in-the-wool devotees, not to speak of the entirely uninitiated, a version that deliberately eliminated the whole mass of historic anecdotes and classical quotations, and concentrated upon his personal habits, peculiarities, opinions, and above all upon his egoistic and philosophical whimsies, would make things much easier.

I suppose the idea that most English-speaking book-lovers have of Montaigne, unless they themselves possess an edition of Cotton's splendid translation, is that of the self-portrait of a magnanimous egoist, whose shrewd, kindly, earth-bound views upon our wrestling with the world are casually set down with an epicurean lavishness.

But if such a book-lover whom the accidents and chances of life have hitherto debarred from actually reading the essays in Cotton's translation *does* get hold of a copy, or even of an odd volume or two, and bringing it home with that peculiar thrill of pleasurable anticipation so beautifully described by Charles Lamb, *does* begin seriously to read it, I am prepared to wager he will suffer a grievous disappointment.

For in place of what he has been led to expect by such deep Montaigne-experts as Walter Pater, or my own brother Llewelyn, whose whole tone of writing, even to his use of that Montaignesque expression "the instinct of a well-descended spirit," is riddled with his influence, what our novice will stumble upon, unless he opens at the essay entitled "Of Presumption," or "Of Repentance," or "Of Vanity," or "Of Experience," will be page after page of historic anecdotes and of quotations from classical writers.

Of course the use of quotation *can* become a fantastical and artful adjunct to the living style of an author, as we note in *The Anatomy of Melancholy* and in the *Essays of Elia*, but Montaigne uses *his* quotations to quite other than stylistic effect. He uses them purely and simply for the curious and to his own mind fascinating nature of their contents.

Now to any intelligence resembling Montaigne's, with a passion for the classical authors, especially the Latin ones, and a mania for curious and monstrous human happenings wherever and whenever occurring, every page of the *Essays* must be full of salt and tang; but I profoundly suspect that Pascal and Walter Pater, both of whom saturated themselves in Montaigne's *philosophy*, were wont to skim over at great speed the bulk of these anecdotes!

Voltaire probably read every one of them with infinite relish; and so I dare say did Anatole France; but I have an inkling that William Hazlitt, our own egoistical essayist, was as wont to skip in following the great Gascon's circum-ambulatory strolls round his circular book-shelf as shame-lessly as I do myself.

However! Even if there does not yet exist a version of the *Essays* shorn of the anecdotes, and I suppose most Mon-taigne-lovers would scorn such a pimping concession, it is not, after all, so very difficult to turn over the pages till we come to some pungent opinion of his own that will pull us up short.

And as to the quarrel I have now with that incomparable summary of Montaigne's philosophy in *Gaston de Latour*, I only feel that it makes him a little too deliberate and pur-poseful in his particular kind of scepticism. Judging from the general drift of his work, and putting one inconsistency against another, it seems to me that there was much less of calculated metaphysic and much more of tempera-mental conservatism in those fluctuating *after-thoughts* of his, about which Walter Pater, assimilating, as we all will in such cases, Montaigne's attitude to his own, makes such an elaborate coil.

What a difference just a little shift of emphasis in these delicate psychological matters can make!

What Pater's young Gaston got from his host's epicurean discourse in that tower-library looking over the Perigord orchards was a system of thought far more deliberately rounded-off than what I at least am able to find.

And though I do dodge on my road, even as Bunyan's Christian might dodge a number of circus-caravans, all these classical fables and gossipping scandals, I cannot be persuaded that I lose the essence of his wisdom by this avoidance.

Pater's Montaigne with his notorious *que scais-je?* becomes indeed in ultimate matters as absolute a sceptic as Pascal was, apart from his desperate act of faith, and as Anatole France was, apart from nothing.

But on the basis, if basis it can be called, of this absolute scepticism Pater's Montaigne is prepared to accept as a conceivable "second thought" all the old traditions of the Catholic Church, finding support for this attitude in the wise obedience of simple people and in the unreliability of the Reformers with their "appeal to reason."

Certainly Pascal himself couldn't go further in his conviction of the weakness, helplessness, short-sightedness, and incompetence of human reason as a medium for truth, but on the other hand Montaigne declares over and over again that neither the fact that multitudes of people have believed a thing, or the fact that a thing has been believed for an enormous number of years, is able to make a thing true!

For all his passion for the classical Latin writers—and he is never weary of praising his father for having made Latin more natural to him than his mother tongue—I cannot find in the *Essays* the least sign that he wavered at any point in his simple, earthy, old-fashioned Catholic piety. He never, that I can find, speaks of God save with grave old-fashioned homely reverence, and his perpetually reiterated preference for old-established customs and old-established habits of thought suggests that his adherence to the Catholic Faith was much more a matter of an instinctive inborn conservatism than of any nice and subtle calculations as to the metaphysical wisdom of "second thoughts."

The idea that it was in some sort of Euripidean reaction to the religion of his fathers after a long excursion into absolute agnosticism that he made his wife send for the priest to celebrate Mass as he lay dying, has, as I read the *Essays*, no foundation at all. The old-fashioned piety of his death was, it seems to me, only the natural culmination of the old-fashioned piety of his life. He never erred, as he confesses his father did, in the direction of superstition, but his profoundest instincts—and he was one who always followed his instincts—were so massively and simply conservative that it does not seem as if in real philosophical scepticism he ever approached those depths of metaphysical doubt so familiar to Pascal.

Let the word be frankly spoken—Montaigne's wisdom is not a metaphysical wisdom or a wisdom concerned with what, in Nietzsche's phrase, we call "First and Last Things." It is a practical, moral wisdom, primarily concerned, as was that of Confucius, with the conduct of life rather than with its purpose or its remote cause.

The conduct of life and pre-eminently of his own personal life is the subject-matter of the *Essays*; and like Socrates whom he cannot praise too highly, and who, Greek though he was, was evidently dearer to him than any other classical thinker, his grand starting-point—and not only starting-point, for he is never weary of returning to it—is self-knowledge, the everlasting analysing of himself and his moods.

But even here we must advance cautiously and shrewdly in our estimate of Montaigne's everlasting preoccupation with himself. He takes advantage of the attitude of Socrates, both in regard to his oracle's "Know thyself," and in regard to his "I know nothing," but the longer you read the *Essays* the clearer it becomes that this ceaseless absorption in himself was a profound psychological, or if you are averse to such a tendency you can even use the word *pathological*, peculiarity of his whole nervous organization.

With what a gusto of life-deep relief, a relief that is spiritual, physical, and mental, does he speak of these felicitous escapes from his duties to others, from his duties to his country, from his duties to posterity, as he sinks back into himself!

It must be remembered he was a man of an extremely responsible conscience in all these things; but when he returns to himself in reaction from them it is as if he returned to the embraces of an adored lover.

Over and over again he celebrates these sinkings back into himself, making it clear from the variety of his descriptions of these self-orgies that they were an indulgence in a physical, mental, and spiritual narcissism so well constituted, so integral, so balanced, that, as a human phenomenon, it must be very rare.

For there wasn't a trace of vanity in the narcissism of Montaigne. He loved his old "grizzled face" not because it was handsome but simply because it was *his*. He emphasizes in his descriptions the purely physical enjoyment of himself, as when he broods lovingly over his bodily appearance, his physical peculiarities, his favourite processes of mastication, digestion, ablution, copulation; but he by no means rejects the pleasures of those "to whom to live is to think," *quibus vivere est cogitare*, in the intellectual "entertaining," as he calls it, of his wandering thoughts.

> Meditation is a powerful and full study to such as can effectually taste and employ themselves; I had rather fashion my soul than furnish it. . . . Nature has favoured it with this privilege, that there is nothing we can do so long nor any action to which we more frequently and with greater facility addict ourselves.

'Tis the business of the gods, says Aristotle, and from which both their beatitude and ours proceed.

In order to keep our strength, our energy, our real spiritual force for these heavenly moments when we make love to ourselves and fondle ourselves and chew the end of our contemplation of ourselves, it is best, he assures us, to be extremely lethargic and stupid, nay! even drowsy, in ordinary conversation, and above all avoid like the devil any attempts to show off, and lay down the law, or parade our pedantry or subtilty or cleverness.

I am afraid the impression he leaves is the un-Shakespearean one that the average persons we meet are not worth the effort of agitating ourselves!

'Tis in my opinion egregiously to play the fool to put on the grave airs of a man of lofty mind amongst those who are nothing of the sort; to speak by the book—*favellare in punta di forchetta*—"to talk with the point of a fork." You must let yourself down to those with whom you converse; and sometimes affect ignorance: lay aside power and subtlety in common conversation; to preserve decorum and order 'tis enough—nay crawl on the earth if they so desire it.

It is impossible to suppress a wanton curiosity as to what Mademoiselle Françoise de la Chassaigne whom he married when he was thirty-three, what their only surviving offspring, a girl called Eleonore, felt in their feminine hearts when Montaigne, in the year 1588, when he was fifty-five, entered into his close platonic relations with Mademoiselle Marie de Jars de Gournay, then in her twentieth year, who from that time forward became not only his literary editor but his adopted child.

Whatever it was they may have felt, this mother and this daughter, they seem to have kept it to themselves as far as we are concerned and very likely as far as the world was concerned; for, after his death in his sixtieth year, they forwarded from their château to this clever young lady in Paris all his final revisions for her special edition of his work.

Montaigne's attitude to women is entirely of a piece with the rest of his nature. It was a conservative masculine attitude. In the library we want wisdom, at the table wit, but in bed only beauty. He mentions as the best device to avoid the danger of being carried out of ourselves by a too violent infatuation for a lady the pleasant and simple trick of making love to another one.

And I dare say nothing would be easier or more agreeable than to follow this prudent method if a person were possessed of the cool heart, steady nerves, and lively senses of Montaigne. But for a different type of lover, of a more intense and passionate complexion, such a palliative would be of no more avail than striking a match upon a window through which we're staring at an eclipse of the sun.

But if Montaigne's attitude to women and to the love of women may not be altogether satisfactory to an intelligent lady of our epoch, there are passages in the *Essays* where he goes surprisingly far in the modern direction and deserts the gross masculine humour of those old days.

The essay in which we get both the two opposite tones in this matter is the one entitled "Upon some Verses of Virgil." Here, following with approval a recorded hint of Socrates he says bluntly: "Women are not to blame at all, when they refuse the rules of life that are introduced into the world, forasmuch as the men make them without their help. There is naturally contention and brawling betwixt them and us; and the strictest friendship we have with them is yet mixed with tumult and tempest."

Both these remarks fall congruously upon a modern ear, especially the suggestion that this "brawling" between the sexes is inherent in the "love-hate" of sex itself.

But how far Montaigne's feminine readers of to-day can approve of the length to which in his classical roguery he is prepared to go in offering judicial support to the famous decision of Teiresias in regard to the act of love is a lively and debatable question.

"My daughter," he remarks in this essay, "is now of an age that forward young women are allowed to be married at; she is of a slow, thin, and tender complexion, and has accordingly been brought up by her mother after a retired and particular manner—"

And he goes on to tell how he caught the girl's governess hurrying her with a too obvious anxiety and solicitude past a word they stumbled on in their book that had a double meaning. Commenting upon this, he declares it was his fortune once to overhear such talk between a party of young women as was too outrageous for him to repeat.

"By 'rlady," said I, "we had need go study the phrases of *Amadis* and the tales of Boccaccio and Aretin, to be able to discourse with them: we employ our time to much purpose indeed. There is neither word, example, nor step they are not more perfect in than our books: 'tis a discipline that springs with their blood: Venus herself made them what they are—*Et mentem ipsa Venus dedit.*"

But with all his broad talk about the relation between the sexes and for all his classical scholar's humour, Montaigne informs us that as a matter of fact he was more scrupulous under the covenant of marriage than he ever expected to be when he entered that condition.

Indeed, in the whole problem of morals, and the whole question as to what makes the difference between a good man and a bad man, there emanates from the *Essays*, for all their easy-going indulgence a very definite "stream of tendency" in the direction of honourable behaviour, kindly consideration, and solid probity.

And this vein of simple goodness in the man reaches us quite independently of his reliance on custom or his scepticism about custom. And it is independent, too, of his

Christian piety. Nor does it depend on outward opinion, as does the goodness described in those remarkable words of Penelope to her disguised husband in Homer:

Men are but short-lived. If one be himself hard, and have a hard heart, on him do all mortal men invoke woes for the time to come, while he still lives, and when he is dead all men mock at him. But if one be blameless, and have a blameless heart, his fame do strangers bear far and wide among men, and many call him a true man.

The grand passion of Montaigne's life was for his friend Etienne de la Boétie; but I cannot find the faintest trace of any homosexual feeling in his attitude to this grave and happily-married young man. It was a pure, unmitigated friendship between two original men—for they were no longer boys when they met—of kindred tastes, kindred opinions, kindred interests, kindred souls; and it certainly does seem as if the survivor were justified in his feeling that it was a unique and monumental bond, and worthy to take its place in the history of memorable human relations.

It was eminently characteristic of Montaigne's habit of putting friendship above love that he should have actually printed as a preface to *Plutarch's Consolation to His Wife*, which his friend had translated, a letter he himself wrote to Françoise to console her, or to remind her that Plutarch could console her, for the loss of a child of theirs who died in its second year.

One's inquisitive mind is tempted again to delve in imagination into the feelings of Françoise de Montaigne both when she first received this blunt but not unfeeling letter, and when she was called upon to produce it to serve as a preface to the learned tract of her husband's dead paragon.

To Mademoiselle de Montaigne:
My wife,—You understand well that it is not the part of a man of the world, according to the rules of this time, still

to court and caress you; for they say that a sensible man may
well take a wife, but that to espouse her is to act like a fool.
Let them talk; I adhere for my part to the custom of the
elder age; I also wear my hair in that fashion—

Nothing could be more characteristic than this whole
incident, showing the man's desire to link together the two
important emotions of his life by connecting Françoise with
his everlasting love for his lost friend, and incidentally pro-
claiming to the world his detestation of new-fangled ways,
both in matters of the heart and in matters of the toilet!

It is amazing how his refusal to sacrifice his independence
and integrity to either party in those murderous wars
between Catholics and Huguenots didn't lead to his ruin.
But there was evidently something so honest, so frank, so
downright and simple about the stand he took, keeping
open house to both sides, and even acting as a confidential
intermediary between the Duke of Guise and Henri of
Navarre, that disarmed the most frantic zealots of that
ferocious struggle. Twice, as he tells us in the *Essays*, he was
in imminent personal danger. On one of these occasions
his château was actually entered by a troop of armed men,
whose leader had planned his destruction. But, as he relates
with justifiable pride, his absolute unsuspiciousness and
easy friendliness of demeanour made these rascals thoroughly ashamed of themselves and speedily reduced them
to good behaviour.

It is indeed hard to overrate the moral and philosophical
importance of the particular kind of egoism advocated by
Montaigne.

It is *"the Ego and its Own"* of Max Stirner; only in Montaigne's case this superindividualism is mitigated by his
reverence for the laws of his country, by his love of the old
traditions, by his hatred of innovation, and by his profound distrust of the insane logic of that dangerous tyrant,
the human reason. His scepticism takes refuge from its

own corrosive undermining of all philosophical theories in a deep instinctive piety, according to the dictates of which he prefers to keep God and "His Holy Word" well out of reach of the wild antics of the human intellect.

As life renders itself by simplicity more pleasant, so, also, more innocent and better, as I was saying before. The simple and ignorant, says St. Paul, raise themselves up to heaven, and take possession of it; and we, with all our knowledge, plunge ourselves into the infernal abyss.

And again:

Whatever we undertake without His assistance, whatever we see without the lamp of His grace, is but vanity and folly; we corrupt and debase by our weakness the very essence of truth, which is uniform and constant, when fortune puts it into our possession.

And once more:

Now from the knowledge of this volubility of mine, I have accidentally begot in myself a certain constancy of opinion, . . . and since I am not capable of choosing, I take other men's choice, and keep myself in the state wherein God has placed me; I could not otherwise prevent myself from perpetually rolling. Thus have I, by the grace of God, preserved myself entire, without anxiety or trouble of conscience, in the ancient belief of our religion, amidst so many sects and divisions as our age has produced.

But, as I have hinted, though Montaigne's scepticism, by its undermining of the pride of reason, landed him on the bed-rock of old-fashioned faith, he apparently found nothing in this basic faith to conflict with his cult of self-realization. To shut himself up "like a tortoise in his shell" in the study of himself and in the enjoyment of himself was the supreme aim and purpose of his life.

His nature was so luckily constituted that no agitations of conscience, no qualms of superstitious fear, no spiritual wrestlings ever troubled his serene happiness, when once, retired within that shell of which his library-tower was the outward symbol, he caressed the most fleeting of his sensations and ideas as if they had been so many soft-furred pets.

He dared in fact, in the midst of that ferocious struggle between Catholics and Protestants, to give himself up to the sensuous deliciousness of a lifelong series of egocentric contemplations, stroking himself, tickling himself, stretching himself, making love to himself, while murder and fanaticism and treachery and massacre tore at his country's bowels.

It would be, however, to do Montaigne a grave injustice to accuse him of neglecting any of his public duties. It is true he registered a vow in his middle thirties, and went so far as to have it inscribed on his tower, that henceforth he would give himself up to study and the bettering of his mind; but this didn't prevent him in later life from becoming an indulgent, easy-going, but by no means incompetent mayor of Bordeaux; nor did it prevent him from playing a wise, honourable, and free-spoken part in the pacification of the kingdom.

But the *Essays* were the expression of his real life all the while, and not only the expression; for, as he says, this constant painting of his own portrait compelled him *to live up to* the lineaments he painted, while to the very last he was always adding some new and yet more revealing touch to the picture.

It would be possible, I suppose, to put forward a claim that Montaigne's constant expressions of faith in a God whose ways are not our ways and indeed are altogether beyond the soundings of our presumptuous, private judgment, was a crafty sop to Cerberus. But the longer I read the *Essays* the more strongly it comes over me that this faith in something "eternal in the Heavens," something unaffected by the tossings and "rollings" of human reason, was the thing that saved him from a sense of futility, and enabled him to present such a shrewd, earthy, solid front to this confused world.

It is not in regard to God but in regard to human custom that his feeling varies according to his mood; and in the endless examples he loves to give us of the grotesque and monstrous nature of custom he hesitates not to indicate his own corrective to that instinctive preference for old ways over new ways into which his ingrained conservatism led him.

In his opinion all the dictates of our conscience come from this too-human and often preposterous adherence to custom, and not at all from any categorical imperative in nature; but just at the point where we nihilistic moderns would for this very reason be tempted to relax our moral harness Montaigne invariably pulls himself up, and by some allusion to "God and His Holy Word" brings back his toppling and shaky conscience to its true foundation, a foundation entirely outside the shifty phenomena of time and space.

"This way of speaking in a Christian man," he remarks in his lengthy study of that discourse of Raimond de Sebonde on *Natural Religion* which he translated to please his father, "has ever seemed to me very indiscreet and ir-reverent: 'God cannot die: God cannot contradict himself: God cannot do this or that,' I do not like to have the divine power so limited by the laws of men's mouths; and the idea that presents itself to us in these propositions ought to be more religiously and reverently expressed."

Like Charles Lamb, and indeed like many another whimsical and antic confessor of his limitations, Montaigne loves to describe with a proud-humble relish and with that subtle self-justification which comes from being shamelessly frank, how helpless he is in most ordinary undertakings.

In music or singing for which I have a very unfit voice, or to play on any sort of instrument, they could never teach me anything. In dancing, tennis, or wrestling I could never arrive to more than an ordinary pitch; in swimming, fencing, vaulting, or leaping, to none at all. My hands are so clumsy that I cannot even write so as to read it myself. . . . I do not read much better than I write. . . .

I cannot decently fold up a letter, nor could I ever make a pen, nor carve at table worth a pin, nor saddle a horse, nor carry a hawk and fly her, nor hunt the dogs, nor lure a hawk, nor speak to a horse. . . . I am good for nothing: for I am of a humour that, life and health excepted, there is nothing for which I will bite my nails, and that I will purchase at the price of torment of mind and constraint. . . .

I have a soul free and entirely its own, and accustomed to guide itself after its own fashion.

There have been few famous writers, and still fewer men of the great world, who have had, and been at pains to express, such a loathing of cruelty. Montaigne seems to have felt as much repulsion at seeing animals suffer, even in the normal processes of what we call "sport," as any sympathetic person of our own day; and in the education of children he would have us cease once and for all our curst attempts to cudgel them into learning and virtue. He goes out of his way to reprobate the burnings and torturings of his time and no more vigorous protest has ever been raised by a great European writer against persecution for matters of opinion. Thorough Frenchman as he was and great devotee of Paris "the glory of France and one of the most noble ornaments of the world," Montaigne may be regarded as among the founders of a magnanimous internationalism.

Not because Socrates has said so, but because it is in truth my own humour, and peradventure not without some excess, I look upon all men as my compatriots and embrace a Polander as a Frenchman, preferring the universal and common tie to all national ties whatever. . . . Nature has placed us in the world free and unbound.

I have wondered, considering what a family of bookworms my own family is, which of all the great profane works of the world would lend itself best to be made into our secular family Bible; and I am tempted to think that Montaigne's *Essays* might be this book.

Certainly in following the subtle moods of my brother Theodore, as he wavers in his own peculiar way between piety and scepticism, I am often led to think of Montaigne; and I am continually being reminded, as I enjoy Cotton's robust turns of speech in this noble rendering, of my brother Llewelyn's deep-rooted hedge-parsley wayside chat.

In the essay called "Vanity," I light upon a passage where Montaigne plausibly defends—though for myself I am not converted—his inconsequential ramblings and everlasting anecdotes.

> I go out of my way; but 'tis rather by licence than oversight; my fancies follow one another but sometimes at a great distance, and look towards one another but 'tis with an oblique glance. . . . The titles of my chapters do not always comprehend the whole matter. . . . I love a poetic progress, by leaps and skips; 'tis an art, as Plato says, light, nimble, demoniac. . . . 'Tis the indiligent reader who loses the subject and not I; there will always be found some word or other in a corner that is to the purpose, though it lie very close. I ramble indiscreetly and tumultuously; my style and my wit wander at the same rate. . . . A thousand poets flag and languish after a prosaic manner; but the best old prose (and I strew it here up and down, indifferently for verse) shines throughout with the lustre, vigour, and boldness of poetry, and not without some air of its fury.

In what always seems to me to be his instinctive conservatism, though I can conceive of any reader—with an eye

upon our human love of torture as the best of all arguments
—regarding it as a perfectly legitimate and proper caution,
Montaigne defends the supreme miracles of our faith as
outside the realm of discussion; but when it comes to the
lesser miracles, miracles not mentioned in the Apostles'
Creed, he is the opposite of credulous. He is indeed heavily
and obstinately sluggish of belief: "To this very hour, all
these miracles and strange events have concealed themselves from me; I have never seen a greater monster or
miracle in the world than myself."

Well, upon this "miracle," Montaigne certainly fixed the
chief love, interest, delight, curiosity, and solicitude of his
well-spent days.

There are many kinds of narcissism in the world, and it
is possible to be an intense *self-lover* without being anything
of a self-admirer or having the least personal vanity.

Montaigne undoubtedly must have stared long and
tenderly at his "grizzled face" as he calls it, in the mirror,
but he felt towards every detail of his appearance as those
really devoted lovers do who derive a voluptuous joy from
the very defects of the loved object.

Indeed I regard it as one of his most endearing as well
as one of the wisest of his characteristics that his sturdy
egoism was not easily to be disturbed by a pretty face. If
he himself was no great beau, though his portraits *are*
better-looking than his idea of himself, it is hard to imagine
Mademoiselle Françoise as a very provocative belle; and I
have an inkling that the learned Etienne de la Boétie was
an excessively plain youth.

But plain or not, he was to his friend that sacred miracle,
a really kindred spirit, and as such Montaigne was ready
to risk cracking his "shell of a tortoise," risk being dragged
from his circular tower, risk forgetting his habits, customs,
ways, observances; in a word, risk losing himself.

And he was richly rewarded for this act of daring; for so completely was this cautious, solid, thoughtful, young student his *alter ego* that he became from loving him twice as much himself as he was before.

But it is clear that neither his wife Françoise nor his daughter Eleonore—and I doubt that it was really different with Mademoiselle de Jars de Gournay—had the power to make him "risk all for love," as he did in the case of his masculine friend.

"Wives, children, and goods," he says calmly in the essay "Of Solitude," "must be had, and especially health, by him that can get it; but we are not so to set our hearts upon them that our happiness must have its dependence upon them; we must reserve a back-shop, wholly our own and entirely free, wherein to settle our true liberty, our principal solitude and retreat. And in this we must for the most part entertain ourselves with ourselves, and so privately that no exotic knowledge or communication be admitted there; there to laugh and to talk as if without wife, children, goods, train, or attendance, to the end that when it shall fall out that we must leave any or all of these, it may be no new thing to be without them."

With our inquisitive modern presumption and our mania for facile pathological catchwords, the temptation, as I have hinted, to find a homosexual element in Montaigne's feeling for his friend, is hard to resist. Our tendency is to think that only an urge of that kind could explain this intensity of emotion in so balanced a gentleman.

But the long and minute account of La Boétie's death which the essayest writes to the elder Montaigne to my mind disposes of this completely. The relations between La Boétie and his wife—his pet name for her was "my Image" —were clearly much more intimate than those between our author and his Françoise; and indeed were of a kind to render the supposition to which I have referred wholly inconceivable.

And this letter to his father, whom, second to his dead friend, Montaigne loved best in the world, is of the most revealing interest in connexion with the high, grave, moral, classical key in which this famous friendship was pitched. It was a friendship of passionate intellectual reciprocity, a friendship that strikes us at its close, judging from the atmosphere of the final scene and La Boétie's constant use of Latin, as tuned to the dignity of a Roman death-bed.

The loss of La Boétie was the most disturbing event in the essayist's whole life; and the pathetic reality of the man's death, in these lines to his father, reach us still across the centuries with a vivid poignance.

A terrible sense of nothingness seems to have disturbed the grave young philosopher at the last.

> At this stage, he proceeded, among other things, to pray me again and again, in a most affectionate manner, to give him a place; so that I was apprehensive that his reason might be impaired . . . but he redoubled his outcry, saying, "My brother, my brother! don't thou then refuse to give me a place?" insomuch that he constrained me to demonstrate to him that, as he breathed and spoke, and had his physical being, therefore he had his place. "Yes, yes," he responded, "I have; but it is not that which I need; and besides, when all is said, I have no longer any existence." "God," I replied "will grant you a better one soon." "Would it were now, my brother," was his answer.

One thing is certainly clear about Montaigne's attitude to these *Essays* of his. It was—considering the extravagant extremes of feeling into which most writers fall about their work—incredibly cautious, guarded, and shrewd.

"Were these *essays* of mine," he writes in the one entitled "Vain Subtleties," "considerable enough to deserve a critical judgment, it might then, I think, fall out that they would not much take with common and vulgar capacities, nor be very acceptable to the singular and excellent sort of men; the first would not understand them enough, and the last too much; and so they may hover in the middle region."

After reading this it is pleasant to be in a position to remind ourselves that among the intellects in this "middle region" who exploited his wisdom to the limit, such names as Shakespeare and Voltaire are to be found. I believe, as I have hinted, that Montaigne's *Essays* are more adapted— by reason of the particular nature of their philosophy—to middle age than to youth. Certainly I am enjoying them now to an extent I have never done at any earlier period of my life; and yet, according to Montaigne's own estimate of these things, I am more than forty years declined from the zenith of my intelligence!

Most curious indeed is the great essayist's idea of when old age begins—he writes of himself at forty as if he were sixty, and at fifty as if he were eighty! And listen to this:

> For my part, I believe our souls are adult at twenty as much as they are ever like to be and as capable then as ever. A soul that has not by that time given evident earnest of its force and virtue will never after come to proof. The natural qualities and virtues produce what they have of vigorous and fine within that term or never.

Montaigne didn't live to read *Don Quixote*; but it does show, I think, a very serious lacuna in his imaginative power, if in nothing else, that he could dismiss Rabelais in so casual a manner.

"Among books," he says, "that are simply pleasant of the moderns, Boccaccio's *Decameron*, Rabelais, and the *Basia* of Johannes Secundus, if those may be ranged under the title, are worth reading for amusement."

Mr. W. C. Hazlitt, the editor of my brother's huge edition

of the Cotton translation, privately printed for the Navarre Society, remarks very pertinently upon this astonishing lapse:

> From the uncritical manner in which Montaigne has placed in juxtaposition three books so disproportionate and incongruous it is almost to be inferred that he had not attentively considered any of them, and that, as to Rabelais, he merely knew him from the common report, that he was a facetious and agreeable writer. His alleged occult moral would hardly have been revealed to Montaigne, and by his obscenity the latter would not have been gravely scandalised.

Putting aside his classical anecdotes which far outnumber the rest, what we cannot help noticing in the occurrences that strike him most shrewdly in his own day is their kinship to the kind of grotesque, exceptional, and gross playfulness of nature that would appeal to the interest of a not very squeamish rustic. They have, in fact, these objects of our sage's curiosity, I will not say the shockingness of the "freaks" at which we gape, in our bucolic wonder, among the booths of a country fair, but certainly a good deal of that physical repulsiveness from which Goethe, for example, or Emerson, or even Nietzsche, would avert their eyes, and, if they could, their mind and memory.

Close to the capacious breast of the daedal earth, undismayed by the spawning irrationality and monstrous shamelessness with which she pours forth her freaks and abortions from her multitudinous womb, Montaigne was certainly blest with nerves as tough and with curiosity as vivid as any notable jester who, as Rabelais would say, has ever drunk neat and eaten salt meat.

He whose piety consisted in keeping God "and His Holy Word" safe out of reach of our logical presumption had a stomach that was not easily turned by the obscene and pitiful curiosities that fall now and again from the hand of the Potter. He may have been no expert at hunting, but he certainly had, as Pater's young Gaston discovered, a most primitive and earth-bound affiliation with the habits and instincts of what we call "the lower animals," domestic or otherwise.

How feelingly he describes his games with his cat, who doubtless, as he says, fancied *she* was playing with him and not *he* with her, and whose conception of Providence would have taken, we may presume to add, a form still further removed than even his own from the proud features limned by human reason!

But it isn't his love of freaks, it isn't his sympathy with animals, it isn't even his loathing of the cruelties of fanatics, that has made the *Essays* such a creative force in the direction of the life of a humanity as yet unborn. It is his love of himself. When one turns the calm gaze of what might be called humanity's unsanctified *common sense* upon the world spread out before us to-day, with its bombings and shootings and murderous "ideologies" and its ferocious hatred of all unregimented, unhypnotized free souls, it begins to appear as if Montaigne's sensuous-psychic *love of himself* and obstinate concern with himself were quite possibly going to prove the chief oracular word for the next great psychological reaction.

Dante put this self-centred type of person in hell, along with a group of Montaignesque angels, who were neither "for God" nor "for the enemies of God" but *were for themselves*; and the great Erasmus would have suffered the same doom, and so most certainly would Walt Whitman, who refused to "take off his hat" to any spiritual authority or to find any sweeter flesh "than stuck to his own bones."

But the whole issue, raised thus boldly by Montaigne, goes deeper and further than almost any other human problem; and in estimating exactly to what this self-love, about which he makes such a clatter, really amounts, we must remember that egoism *à la* Montaigne is prepared to give to others all the privileges it claims for itself. His father brought him up to be able to rough it with working people and to rate all his advantages of wealth and birth as a mere accident of chance. He needed no one to teach him to be hostile to every sort of cruelty, hostile, above all, to the exercise of violence and torture where private opinions, whether religious or moral or political, were concerned.

That he was so opposed to innovation did not mean that he was blind to the unfairness of old customs; it only meant that he saw so many innovators become tyrants and so many innovations do more harm than good, that it seemed to him that the path of prudence, both in religion and politics, was "to let sleeping dogs lie."

Against this if you jerk the hands of time's clock forward a little and imagine Montaigne, with his shrewd merchant-squire sympathies, confronted by a starving people, a frivolous aristocracy, and so extremely different a king from Henri Quatre, is it not likely that even *his* rooted conservatism would have moved in its socket?

But the point for us now is not what he would have done in another age but what he did in his own; and *that* was to trim his sails to the wind, to cut his coat to his cloth, and though not exactly to run with the hare and hunt with the hounds, at least to keep his doors so wide open that if the hunt came in at the front the hare could slip out at the back. And all the while to "loafe and invite his soul," to stroke, pet, fondle, caress, and hug his identity, first for himself and then, in the *Essays*, for all of us who come after so that if we belong to that "middle region" not too stupid and not too subtle our laudable and righteous egoism can get the comfort and support it needs.

For myself, who had managed in my skimble-skamble way to hug and cherish myself even before I read Montaigne—for Nature hesitates not to give us all a push in this direction—I think this whole question of the individual against state, society, government, religion, is of the most sharp and stinging importance. My own private feeling, if under the aegis of a Mayor of Bordeaux I can gather up enough courage to express it, is that of all our political and economic theories the anarchist one is the one that eventually will prevail.

If our descendants have any libraries left, circular or otherwise, from which to collect anecdotes of our day and age, surely there will be, as they study the murderousness of our present national spirit, a reversion to Montaigne's self-centred cult.

Will not that remote and happy age feel that in the wise selfishness of the individual rather than in the ferocious and fanatical unselfishness of the public-spirited, the will of Heaven is revealed?

How curious it is that in our multiple form as nations, states, and governments, we are so much less scrupulous and so much more merciless than as individuals! Is this solely for want of a world-police? Or is it because *en masse* we are subject to the influence of the Devil, whereas as individuals we are subject to the influence of God?

But granting Montaigne's plea for this concentrated "living to oneself" as Hazlitt calls it, what tantalizes me as a travelling journeyman in this craft is the absence from the *Essays*—but I suppose I am demanding too much of that epoch—of the subtler undertones and overtones of our sensuous-psychic life. In his sturdy "skin for skin" encounters, in his unaffected humours, in his magnanimous indulgences, I confess I miss something very important, something that I might even contend is the most important of all! I speak of those obscure moods and intimations so feelingly described by Wordsworth, but not completely absent from earlier writers, where we come into contact with certain magical earth-memories such as I suspect are the experience of all men.

Now although Montaigne is always describing the *conditions* of his happy ecstasies of self-love, I cannot say I find him very illuminating as to their sensuous-mental *contents*.

And surely upon the quality of what they contain of magical and thrilling feelings half at least of their worth depends. I would find it, I confess, somewhat hard to defend this cult of the *moi* against all the thunders of religion and government if it couldn't "supply us," as Walt Whitman would put it, with spiritual, imaginative, and intellectual emotion equal to those bestowed on us by custom and by our service of State and Church.

I wonder if it can! In deep matters of this kind we have I think to consider the flickering across our mental landscape, like sea-gulls on the wing, of certain exceptional and unusual moods. After all, these *may* be more important than our ordinary ones.

For myself, for all my love of our secular family Bible, I note very clearly down at the bottom of my heart an irradicable tendency to admire Don Quixote, even though he never did any one any good, a good deal more than I admire Montaigne who has done us all so much good.

Now why is this? What we really need to help us clear up this nice point—perhaps the most delicate point in the whole of life's casuistry—is some tremendous modern Socrates, who would have the tolerance and the intelligence to analyse to the very bottom this inarticulate preference which we feel, at least which I feel, for the glow experienced when we read *Don Quixote* over the glow experienced when we fortify ourselves in our wise and humble egoism by reading the *Essays*!

But then Don Quixote is himself, as was Jesus Christ, the most reckless of anarchists. When he set the galley-slaves free he was certainly on the opposite side from all religions and all governments; and it is difficult to imagine how a community of tolerant Montaignes contemplating the world from their libraries could uphold the freedom of the soul without the help of a few desperate knights-errant. Or, alas! even *with* their help, unless some of them were shrewder in their valour than the Knight of the Rueful Countenance.

The truth is, this whole question of the amount of time, energy, and concentration we are justified in spending on "living to ourselves" is a very proper subject for one of those Platonic dialogues in which, question by question, Socrates leads us on, and in which the fluctuating *que scais-je?* of the Socratic "ignorance" guards us from any cock-sure conclusion.

After all, it was only because, thanks to his thrifty father and to *his* thrifty father, Montaigne was a well-to-do gentleman that he was able to live as he did; and it is life itself that with most of us sees to it that this cult of the self and its sensations and ideas takes a place of due proportion.

What we get from Montaigne is really a series of hints, and they are as shrewd as any to be found in the whole history of human culture, as to the way to use this precious margin of our existence wherein we live to ourselves and enjoy our classics and our classical histories, our philosophers and our philosophizing, so as to be fuller, happier, riper, wiser, and more tolerant human beings.

His grand "open secret"—and it is a secret revealed to most of us only after the most troublesome mental disturbances and miseries—is the importance of starting "from the ground up" and never losing touch with the ground. The spiritual trick of lying back upon our ignorance, of accepting our limitations, of taking mentally, as well as physically, "the lower seats in the synagogue," of ceasing to "lie awake in the night" repining about our sins, of creating a life-illusion of ourselves that shall follow the curves of all our weaknesses as the tide follows the hollows of its estuaries, is a trick not easily acquired.

MICHEL DE MONTAIGNE

Still harder is it to us to overcome that undue pressure of the race-conscience which makes us afraid of hugging ourselves to ourselves, in all our deformity, against the background of the cosmos, lest the jealousy of the gods smite us with a thunderbolt.

Every living creature has a divine right, as Goethe says, to those special and peculiar pleasures, uninjurious to its fellows, which its unique temperament *must* have, if it is to bear up under the common burden with any spontaneous resilience; and if for us the greatest of such pleasures is to make a cult of the half-mental, half-physical sensations that solitude invites, even as the windrow between sea and sand invites the gulls, the reading of Montaigne will certainly assist in keeping clear from conscientious invasion that narrow strip of spiritual independence which, just because it is free to all, can be made more entirely our own than anything else in the world.

8

Cervantes

AT THIS MOMENT of writing all the eyes of our Western world are directed, though by no means with the same emotion, towards Spain. In Cervantes' time Philip III was turning the Moors, where they had lived so long, out of the peninsula; but it was through the medium of an imaginary Moor, Cid Hamet, that the story of Don Quixote is told. The great original of the temper we call Quixotic, on which side of the present struggle would he range himself? Personally I like to think of him among the defenders of Madrid; but others, no doubt, just as we swing the figure of Christ first one way and then the other, would place him with the enemy.

But we have, anyway, as book-lovers, to face the fact that it is a Spaniard created by a Spaniard who is the most living, the most endearing, and the best-known character in all human literature!

How profound was the inspiration of the Italian philosopher, Croce, when he said that a great work of art is not *completed* until humanity itself for many generations has set its seal upon it!

Upon the figure of Don Quixote, of this ill-favoured, ill-starred, impoverished gentleman, who, as Tom o' Bedlam says, "knows more than Apollo," has been concentrated, beyond all parallel, this instinctive genius in our race which rounds off the invention of the individual.

Long ago—almost as soon as Cervantes invented him—
Don Quixote was snatched at by humanity and rendered
in a sense independent of his begetter. There are indeed
to-day three Don Quixotes—there is the author's, the
authentic original, from whose living reality the other two
draw their life-blood. There is the popular Don Quixote,
or, if you like, the mythological Don Quixote, who has
become a proverb, a legend, a universal symbol for all men.

And finally there is the Don Quixote of the *literary
disciples*, the Don Quixote who has been treated almost as
Jesus was treated, and has been turned into various mystical,
aesthetic, and moral Messiahs. Of all masks of this third
Don Quixote the most original as well as the most passionate
and fantastic is the one flung so desperately and defiantly
at the head of the rationalists by the late Unamuno.

The curious thing is that in both the popular proverbial
version and the literary-mystical version it is the *humour*
that chiefly suffers. The word "Quixotic" suggests, it seems
to me, something tragic, noble, and heroically foolish. Its
endearing comicality has been diluted to the vanishing
point. Yet it is surely this humorous endearingness of both
knight and squire that is the chief cause of our pleasure in
reading the book.

And the more we read it, the less, it seems to me, do we
feel that the chief element in it is the attack upon the
favourite books of the Knight of the Rueful Countenance.
It is the humorous contrast between Don Quixote's
essential nature and the essential nature of Sancho that
enchants us the most; and as the unequalled livingness of
these central figures grows on us we don't care an owl's
pellet how crazy the books were about knights-errant in
the world.

The humour of Cervantes reminds us sometimes of
Shakespeare and sometimes of Rabelais, and most of all,
especially in the details of its presentment, of the Russian

humour of Gogol; but the longer we share the experiences of Don Quixote the more definitely does the peculiar flavour of Cervantes' own turn of mind disentangle itself from these resemblances and leave upon our palates its own unique tang.

Up to a certain point what Goethe said of *The Vicar of Wakefield* applies to Cervantes. "That lofty and benevolent irony, that serene indulgence to all human faults and frailties, supplies us with the best way of taking life." But the humour of the Spaniard goes far beyond this. For one thing, it is much more than the humour of a scholar. It is the humour of an heroic and romantic soldier; and it is also the humour of a man well-stricken in years.

Before writing *Don Quixote* Cervantes had seen, as we say, history in the making. He had seen campaigns by land and sea, battles, imprisonments, treacheries, rescues, hairbreadth escapes, perils by land and water, desperate cruelties, life-and-death struggles, impoverishment, plottings, conspiracies, lawsuits, disparagements and running through it all the "insolence of office, and the spurns that patient merit from the unworthy takes." It is a book written not only by a poet, a gentleman and a wit, but by a battered soldier of fortune, a captive-slave of pirates, a "haggard and woe-begone" knight-at-arms; one of those "prisoners of the world" who like the faithful Kent in *King Lear* might say of what he wrote:

> *All my reports go with the modest truth,*
> *Nor more nor clipp'd, but so—*

But if the Don Quixote to the chiaroscuro of whose lean visage the infatuated disciples hold up their blazing torches be somewhat too nicely and narrowly conceived, somewhat too fantastically paragoned, what can we get from the stable-lanterns of the popular glimpse at him, that glimpse which has gone to the heart of the man in the street, such as may throw a broader light on those haggard lineaments?

A great genius often invents more than he wots of, and his creation, drawing new and unexpected life from the bowels of the human race, gets out of control, "gangs," as we say, "its ain gait," and leaving its author's original intention far behind, *becomes itself* a *creative power* and works strange wonders!

Now the most striking thing about this popular Don Quixote who has thus "run amok" by drawing on the heart's desire of humanity, is the somewhat startling fact, that, quite contrary to the author's avowed and reiterated intention of showing how fairy-tales could upset a good man's wits, *he is not a madman at all!*

It is true that he spears sheep, tilts at windmills, rescues galley-slaves, takes a barber's basin for a helmet and honest whores for princesses; but such has been the mysterious emotional accretion with which, as Croce so beautifully says, humanity rounds off and completes a work of art, that even these peculiarities do not turn him, no! not while his name endures, into a madman.

What, after all, *was* the "madness" which obsessed this great adventurer? We—author, disciples, and popular rumour—are agreed upon *that* point. Nothing less than the restoration of the lost golden age, that ideal age in the past—perhaps less imaginary than many think—when the *spirit* of knight-errantry, never mind about particular Amadises of Gaul or Palmerins of England, prevailed in the world.

"Why," argued Don Quixote, "if the world is out of joint, don't we try to save it by reviving this chivalrous, this heroic, this magnanimous ideal of individual behaviour?"

Whether it has come or not from reading this book at about the age when the author wrote it, but certainly under the spell of *Don Quixote*, it does not strike me as entirely impossible that some new spirit of knight-errantry, or the same spirit under another name, using airplanes if you like in place of horses and asses, might devote itself to the succouring of the oppressed and the overthrow of human giants and human enchanters.

The real defence of Don Quixote's wits is of course to be found in the text of the book itself; but that the common instinct of humanity holds the good gentleman to be of sound understanding though of eccentric behaviour is a convincing proof of Croce's theory about the multitude playing this decisive rôle in the creation of all supreme works of art.

The study of the text, however, at critical moments in the tale, is the best way of proving that a really mad Don Quixote is, if not a contradiction in terms, at least a blowing sky-high of the whole pith of the invention.

Take the scene of the penance in the mountain-glen after the thief has stolen Dapple. This is the scene in which the knight displays, according to the over-astute Coleridge, indications that his sanity has not disappeared so entirely but that there can still be found in him a sort of "twilight of the mind."

But an ordinary reader—and perhaps all the more shrewdly for being unburdened by psychological and metaphysical endowments—has only to read the conversation between the knight and the squire on the subject of Dulcinea to get the drift of the situation without resorting to any "twilights of the mind."

Here indeed it becomes apparent once and for all, that Don Quixote's so-called "madness" is nothing but his deliberate and perfectly conceivable, though somewhat unusual, passion, hobby, desire, or mania, for playing the part of a knight-errant, and indeed for restoring in our age of iron—for that age still continues—the nobler customs of the age of gold.

It is only when considered in this way that the whole trend of the author's method, his handling of each new situation as it follows the last, finds its deeper justification.

And, after all, why does this book have a more universal appeal than any other in the world? Surely because we all have a touch—though it is true that our successful men of action and powerful rulers tend to let that touch atrophy more quickly than others do—*of Don Quixote's own mania;* which is not merely, be it remarked, for helping the oppressed, but for helping them in a particular manner, that is to say by indulging our passion for whatever fantastical cult—in *his* case knight-errantry—satisfies our particular life-illusion.

It is a perfectly natural chance, when one considers the erratic motions of the best-balanced minds, and the secret fancies, weird imaginations, exquisite whimsies, surreptitious illusions, in which we indulge, that the most popular of all invented characters in the world's fiction should be this homespun gentleman of La Mancha. How deeply in harmony indeed with all nature's ways that this high destiny should have fallen to the lot of no great magnate, but of one "spare of flesh, dry of visage, a great early riser, and a lover of the chase," a third of whose substance was consumed in beef and salad, "a hotch-potch on Saturdays, lentils on Fridays, with the addition of a pigeon on Sundays," but whose mania for reading romances of chivalry was so great that he sold many acres of land to satisfy it, till at last "with little sleep and much study his brain dried up and he lost his wits."

Now it is, as I say, essential to the appreciation of Don Quixote's character and his relations with Sancho that we should take this "drying up" of the good knight's brain and this "loss of his wits" with what Sir Thomas Browne would call "a wide solution."

When the wind was not in the wrong quarter Don Quixote knew a hawk from a heron as well as another, and it is never *just* his illusion, but always his illusion *plus* the wind being north-north-west, that's the clue to the real quality of the situation! There is, in fact, so much method in his madness that it is constantly resolving itself into a quite conscious determination—like what children show when they are playing at being pirates to find matter for his crazy purpose from situations upon whose normal and and natural semblance he yet manages to keep at the back of his mind a shrewd weather-eye.

This is shown over and over again in his talks with Sancho, especially on the occasions when the latter's private mania about the governorship of the island is to the fore. Sancho's perpetual harping on this precious "island" becomes indeed a muted variation upon the main theme of the book, and it happens more than once that the knight shows himself the more realistic of the two. For example, on their second visit to the inn together, Don Quixote requires all his "dried-up wits" to make Sancho accept the crushing return to reality which occurs when the sprightly Dorothea sinks from the rôle of princess into that of a private and somewhat sportive lady.

Don Quixote achieves this in his usual crafty manner by a resort to enchanters, both friendly and hostile, and on this occasion the natural innocence of Sancho puts him into the curious position, as when he hunts about for the head of the giant after the pricking of the wineskin, of being madder than his master.

Upon this quaint reversal of the situation the author himself makes the appropriate comment; and he does it through the groans of their frantic host, to the effect that the squire's hunt for giants' heads in inn bedrooms is worse than the knight's dispatching of them in his sleep!

But the most delicate and subtle proof of my contention that Don Quixote's normal mentality—a mentality superior to that of everyone he meets—is never destroyed by his mania, lies in the way, after showing a little natural irritation at Sancho's obstinate literalness, he *is* prepared to accept the normal appearance of things—of the barber's basin, for instance, and even of the manners of Dulcinea— and confines himself with most profound sagacity to this felicitous theory of enchantment, whereby Sancho's "reality" remains true to ordinary vulgar eyes and yet does not interfere with that higher truth which is the truth for a knight-errant.

It is not in fact *only Sancho* who is hypnotized by the Don's powerful imagination; for, if I am not greatly mistaken, we all, as we read, begin to feel the solid ground of our normal apprehensions a little insecure. And indeed, the beauty of it is that by that splendid stroke when he makes the innkeeper and his whole family passionately and indignantly defend these debatable and dangerous books, Cervantes shows clearly how the popular mind itself, in its own simple mania for "better bread than is made from wheat," is always rushing to the defence of the knight's spiritual infatuation.

Though irritated and indeed "stung," as he himself confesses, by Sancho's teasing knowledge of Dulcinea in her homely reality, Don Quixote replies, in a vein of the profoundest philosophy, that the girl, *even as she is in Sancho's eyes*, serves well enough for the purpose to which it is essential she should be put!

How daintily too is it indicated by Cervantes that this worthy gentleman of fifty was *already*, before he decided to be a knight-errant, not a little in love with the original of Dulcinea! That the wench herself, so merry and tall, was ignorant of the "ingenious" Alonso's enamoured observation is natural enough.

We may be sure that the eccentric hidalgo was as tactful and discreet and courtly in his normal attraction as was the Knight of the Rueful Countenance in his abnormal infatuation.

The love of Sancho for Don Quixote was as deep as his admiration, and the homely display of this love, throughout all their escapes and imbroglios, is one of the most moving things in the book. If I may be allowed to say so, there is not a little in it of the peculiar bond that exists sometimes between a Negro servant and his master; and indeed we are struck throughout by the familiar intercourse between all classes in this Spanish book, compared with the separation between them which is so apparent in Shakespeare in spite of his rustic humours.

Spain was clearly in Cervantes' time exactly as it is now, not only a land of unconquerable individualism, but a land also of such courteous man-to-man familiarity that it submerged and overrode all the fantastic differences of rank set up by Church and State.

It is hard to imagine the emotional affection, the humorous understanding, the physical intimacy that bound Don Quixote and Sancho so closely to each other as existing between Englishmen of such different classes.

There ought to be some especial psychological and spiritual name for this breaking down of social barriers where social barriers of the extremest kind exist. But in truth it is much more than the breaking down of merely *social* barriers. It is the lifting up of all those dams and dikes of human *psychological reserve* that restrain us still in England.

In Gogol and in Dostoievsky this reserve breaks down, too; and we find something of the same kind in Rabelais, where it takes on an evangelical flavour, but for all our poet's love of simple folk it never really appears in the plays of Shakespeare. Prince Hal comes nearest to it, but that is simply a matter of condescending to the roguery of tavern and brothel.

What a mystery it is, this breaking down of psychological barriers between human beings! It resembles, only in a spiritual sense, that "uncovering of nakedness" spoken of in the Bible. In England it is made difficult because of the filtration of the dregs of class-consciousness into the very soul. In America it is made difficult because the soul itself is there so shy that it hides away even from its possessor's own consciousness.

It remains, anyway, that all through *Don Quixote*, just as all through Dostoievsky, there is a frank outflowing of the wildest and oddest peculiarities of the human soul, an outflowing that would have been impossible if its reception had not been guaranteed by some implicit feeling as to the underlying equality of all souls.

Sometimes it seems as if Sancho, in spite of his vigorous objection on one occasion to being compared to a woman, played in a real spiritual sense the feminine part between them.

On several occasions it is he, rather than the knight, who shows the more considerate, the more tactful, the more admirable, as well as the more sagacious instinct.

The truth is that almost all the familiar generalizations about this pair of friends, which we writers have so glibly repeated, would be crucially altered did we, as I am doing at this moment, read again, in middle age, or in old age, the work we rushed through when we were young!

One of these easy statements, which takes Cervantes' official words at the foot of the letter, is to the effect that the book was written to destroy the ill effects of the false, silly, futile, and sentimental books of chivalry.

Now one of the first things that surprises and startles a reader of *Don Quixote*, next to his discovery that the Don is not always a noble idealist any more than Sancho is always a gross realist, is the infinite trouble that Cervantes takes from beginning to end to distinguish and discriminate *between* these books of chivalry. Some he roundly condemns. Others he warmly and eloquently praises. But in either case, he makes it sufficiently plain that he is himself an imaginative, romantic, and passionate *reader* as well as an imaginative, romantic, and passionate writer.

As I have already pointed out, this unique book is the inspiration of long and harsh experiences. It is not only a work of maturity; it might even, considering how much earlier maturity came in those days be called a work of old age.

And yet it shows no trace of exhaustion. An unconquerable spirit emanates from every page. The reader seems, as he goes on from one part to another, from one chapter to another, to be tapping a fount of resistant endurance that sinks down beyond the bottom of life!

It is the book of an *old soldier*, literally and spiritually. "We enter war," said Voltaire, "when we enter the world—*On entre en guerre en entrant dans le monde*. And this battered, maimed, but undefeated warrior of old Spain communicates to the weakest among us a living drop of some celestial ichor that in place of making our gorge rise, like the knight's unlucky balsam, "works inward" through our most secret vitals, till it fortifies what one might call the very stomach of the soul.

And it does more than this; for the remarkable thing about the spiritual "aura" of Cervantes is that it makes us humbler and tenderer as well as of a stouter heart.

Nor does the magic stop there; for there still remains what we so lightly and hurriedly call *the humour of Cervantes*. Few literary undertakings are more enthralling, few more difficult, than a comparison between the nice and exquisite shades of difference that separate one great humourist from another.

Let us begin in this case by eliminating the particular kinds of so-called humour which are entirely absent from *Don Quixote*. Well! for one thing, in spite of a few fantastical parodies upon the rodomontade of the worst chivalric excesses, *Don Quixote* is free from satire. Adjectives like "satiric," "sarcastic," "sardonic," though so applicable to Swift and Voltaire and to James Joyce, are as out of place as applied to Cervantes as they are as applied to Shakespeare.

But come now to that peculiar form of humour that is called *cynicism*. Think of all the subtle philosophical connotations that lie hidden in this significant word!

Now the one thing most alien from the soul and style of Cervantes, as it was alien from the soul and style of Rabelais, is this same cynicism. Shakespeare, though he doesn't deal in satire, does I think, in *Measure for Measure*, *Timon of Athens*, *Troilus and Cressida*, and even here and there in *Hamlet*, approach cynicism.

But whatever Cervantes' humours may be, it is certainly not cynical. But what of the word "comic"? Would it be correct, above every other quality, to praise *Don Quixote* as the most comic of books?

Well, I suppose the oldest as well as the most popular form of comedy—only second perhaps to grotesque dancing—is pure knock-about farce; and of this there is so much in *Don Quixote* that a nervous bookworm like myself tends to squirm and fidget a little beneath this everlasting drubbing.

But in my childhood I was never tired of the bangings and pummellings in Punch and Judy; and no doubt there were plenty of grown-up people, a good deal more sophisticated than I, who to this day find no impediment to their enjoyment of the universal humour and tragic pathos in the inventions of Charlie Chaplin from the fact that they are so full of this oldest of all forms of comedy.

But the clue to the secret of Cervantes' real humour lies, I believe myself, in a certain universal *humility* which was intensified by his misfortunes.

It was in the year 1571 that he was so grievously wounded in the naval battle of Lepanto, where under Don John of Austria the high seas were made safe from the Turks. Since this maimed old soldier was nearly sixty when he published the first part of *Don Quixote* and nearly seventy when, ten years later, he published the second part, we are, as I keep repeating, confronted in this book, especially when we consider how much sooner people grew old in those days, with a work that, regarded relatively to our easier times, is the inspiration of an old man.

And not only of an old man. Of an old man who had known in his time most of the worst ills that flesh is heir to.

Now there is a certain endearing humility that is implicit in the character of a particular type of soldier, or sailor, and that a long life of hardship only intensifies. It is a quality exactly the opposite of that self-conscious mock-modesty, and pretence of despising glory, which we meet in a different type of heroic adventurer.

Like Don Quixote, one can very well imagine Cervantes talking proudly and eloquently in many an inn-parlour of the day he got his wounds under Don John. And why not? The unchristian, snobbish, and misanthropic conceit of being superior to tavern-boasting is the real sin, not this other.

And this instinctive humility which is perhaps the best gift Christianity gave us—for think what a different tone the boasting of Odysseus takes from that of Don Quixote!— is a thing that lends itself better than anything in the world to the deepest of all forms of humour. Satire, cynicism, sarcasm—nay! *irony itself*—are all signs of that innate sense of dignified superiority, of that refusal to recognize the equality of all souls, which is the last "infirmity" of noble minds.

It is a thing intimately connected with our *physical dignity* and our inability to allow this same physical dignity to be punched out of all recognition by slap-stick knock-about!

But that is precisely what has happened to the physical dignity of Don Quixote. What with sharing all the grosser details of life with Sancho—even to those which the latter so delicately calls "the lesser and the greater affair"—and what with being scratched and ducked and drenched and banged by every clown he meets, and what with being hung up even by little Maritornes, that no-better-than-she-should-be "slip-shoe Lovey," as Mr. Masters would say, there is no physical dignity, no artistic dignity, no intellectual dignity, no moral dignity, left in that rueful figure.

There is only left in it, what the world can neither give nor take away, the *dignity of the Holy Ghost*!

And it is—at least this is how this profoundest of literary problems presents itself to me—out of this lack of all dignity but the unconscious one of the equality with all souls that the real humour of *Don Quixote* springs.

Consider the causes, occasions, manifestations, and accompaniments of Don Quixote's outbursts of temper. In that Pharisaic superiority of self-control, which is often more malicious than a clap over the head, he is as lacking as he is in every other peculiarity of those of us who so gravely remember "what is owning to ourselves."

> "I am positive," said Sancho, "that this lady who calls herself Queen of the great kingdom of Micomicon, is no more so than my mother; for if she were what she says she would not go nuzzling at every turn of the head and every corner with somebody of the present company."
>
> Dorothea reddened . . . she was neither able nor willing to answer him a word. . . .

"I tell thee this, master," continued Sancho . . . "there is no need to hurry oneself saddling Rozinante or packing the ass or getting ready the palfrey, but we had better remain quiet, and let every trull to her wheel and us to dinner!"

Good Lord how mighty a rage was kindled in Don Quixote on hearing these unmannerly words of his squire! It was so great that with shaking voice and a stammering tongue, the live fire darting from his eyes he exclaimed:

"O villainous knave! uncircumspect, ill-mannered ignorant, blasphemous, foul-mouthed, audacious back-biter! . . . Out of my presence, monster of nature, magazine of lies, sink of rogueries! . . . Away with thee!"

Saying this, he arched his brows, blew out his cheeks, glared about him on every side, and gave with his right foot a great stamp on the ground.

But leaving the spiritual foundation of Cervantes' humour and coming to his lapses in the art of narrative, what a pity it is that after those ten years he forgot the upshot of one of his best scenes!

In the first part we are led to understand that though the real Dulcinea was ignorant of the impression she had made on Alonso the Good before he became Don Quixote, he *had* seen her, though only from a distance and with chaste admiration.

We are also told that Sancho knew her well. Nevertheless, on returning to his tale after this long interval, the author clearly states that neither the knight nor the squire had ever seen her and allows the former to be diverted by Sancho to the ill-favoured wench on the she-ass, outside the city of Toboso!

This reduction of the real Dulcinea to thin air, or at least to a person of hearsay, strikes us—at least it strikes me—with somewhat of a shock. And it does almost seem as if the author desired a complete change of atmosphere and tone at this point, for this lapse is followed by that portion of the

MIGUEL DE CERVANTES SAAVEDRA

work so frankly reprobated by Charles Lamb; the portion
that deals with the master and man's adventures at the
court of the unworthy duke and duchess. I say "adventures"; but as a matter of fact, what occurs is simply a
fantastically elaborate fooling of both Don Quixote and
Sancho by these aristocratic triflers.

Of course, it might be argued that the majority of the
people whom our wanderers encounter—including the
priest, the barber, and that malapert young popinjay,
Samson Carrasco—are perpetually playing on his mania,
and that what these idle magnates do is only what everybody else does. But when one bears in mind the extraordinary naturalness and inevitableness of Cervantes' highway inventions, and the convincing humour of Don Quixote's encounters with simpler people—with people like
the puppet-master and the showman with the lions—there
does slip into one's mind the feeling that our author has
begun to sail very near the wind when he throws the knight
and the squire on the mercy of these capricious and brutal
magnates.

Mr. H. E. Watts, whose admirable translation and ex-
haustive commentaries it would seem impossible to improve
upon, defends this long episode of the playful duke and
duchess on the ground that all possible highway adventures
had already been exploited and that we all needed a change.
For myself, I would simply say that it is hard to conceive
how even the inventive genius of Cervantes could get
Sancho his governorship without the aid of some such
objectionable and tricky potentate, and that for the sake
of seeing Sancho keep his integrity, *as he certainly does*,
even to the tune of turning the tables on his mockers, and for
the sake of the perfect passage at the end when he throws up
the job and goes off to put the saddle on Dapple again,
saying: "I am of the family of the Panzas, who are all
stubborn, and if once they cry odds, odds they shall be,

though they may be even, in spite of all the world," it *is* worth paying the price that Charles Lamb found too heavy.

Don Quixote is really a triumphant yet tragic apology for heroic illusion. Cervantes seems to hint that until some extreme pain makes us "lie howling" it is possible to bear up somehow under the whips and scorns of time as long as, in the teeth of every humiliation, we still can dance to the tune of our particular mania, Sancho to his, Don Quixote to his, and all to their own—"for let him twang who knows the strings and Saint Peter in Rome is well at home."

That nothing but the quality of our soul's inmost character, whereof our worst vices are but the lamentable defects, must be the secret of our universe, is proved by the art of Cervantes in this book to the most delicate point.

Has it been noticed how he anticipates all the cleverest, neatest, most convoluted conjurings with the mystery of *identity in change* in which our modern geniuses love to dabble?

The continuity of any living character and the necessity of its recreating the universe to fit its private illusion of life lie at the heart of Cervantes' daring scheme of introducing the *fictional* knight and squire to the notice of the *real* knight and squire, so that the projected image of themselves, as existing mentally in the minds of the readers of the *first part*, falls across their figures in the *second part* as if the shadows of Plato's cave by mingling with *that which throws them* had attained a double reality.

What, in other words, Cervantes has done in the actual process of the story is to anticipate what we ourselves are now doing in thickening out its extraordinary reality. He begins by thrusting Cid Hamet, his imaginary Moorish narrator, between his readers and himself, so that whenever he pleases he can introduce the phrase "the story tells"; but not content with this, he takes advantage of the ten years during which all Spain and indeed all Christendom had become acquainted with the knight and the squire to make them *see themselves* as the whole world had begun to see them.

Though the malignant and spurious version of the second part may have helped to keep him poor, it probably increased his public; and one even begins to get a curious feeling, when the knight is under the care of Don Antonio in Barcelona, that he has become so real to his begetter as to have almost reached the point of being too real to fool with, too real to be the subject of further fictional inventions! It is as if Don Quixote had come to life to such a point that his creator began to feel such a tender and scrupulous awe for him that he longed to take his hands off him altogether and leave him to his own devices!

That is really the impression you get that day in Barcelona, when the knight visits the printer's establishment. You feel that he has escaped, not only from the clutches of his friendly host, but from the presumptuous meddlings of the author himself!

And this triumph of characterization, which is likely to last as long as the world lasts, depends, it would seem, as much on the personal character as on the genius of Cervantes. How instinctively he took himself out of the way, and reduced his ideas, opinions, feelings, prejudices, fancies to the minimum in comparison with those of his creation!

And he didn't go to work according to any Flaubertian theory of objective art, but, if I may say so, according to his natural courtesy and instinctive disinterestedness; a disinterestedness which all the same it is hard not to regard as one of the subtlest of all imaginative weapons.

Shakespeare's disinterestedness went even further; went as we know to such complete self-effacement that, because of something queer about his signature and because he didn't go to Oxford or Cambridge, we are ready to give the credit of his work to almost any aristocratic incognito.

But this very quality in the book which is the secret of its author's greatness makes it hard for us earnest-minded Lollards of literature to disentangle in clear unequivocal terms the Spaniard's message to us all, and the moral interpretation of his living parable.

Great writers, like great moralists, are generally extremely willing to assist us in discovering their views upon God, immortality, free will, the nature of evil, and the origin, end, and purpose of the world. How easy it is for us to explain where the optimism of Meredith differs from the pessimism of Hardy or where the pluralism of Whitman differs from the Pantheism of Emerson! And though it is less easy to epitomize from the multitudinous secular stage of Shakespeare any definite prophetic gospel, there *is* a tone in the air, a many-voiced murmur on the wind, caught up from a thousand broken asides, that does protest, though without bitterness or laceration, against the cruel ironies of life and the unyielding mystery that surrounds them.

But the most patient and devoted Wilhelm Meister among us, unless endowed with "a heart of furious fancies" like the late Unamuno, will have difficulty in squeezing any very definite drops of metaphysical comfort from the brave humours and chivalrous inventions of this battered fellow-soldier of Don John.

Perhaps it is for this very reason that no nation has been more infatuated with *Don Quixote*, or has printed more volumes and brought out more editions of *Don Quixote*, than the British. From that first Elizabethan translation which may have supported the last years of Shakespeare, when "deeper than did ever plummet sound he drowned" *his* magic wand, to this gallant version by Mr. Watts which swings like a "good lantern" over the threshold of the present century, we have loved this work better than any.

Perhaps, as it says in the play, we're all so mad in these isles that we notice nothing unusual in this work. But at any rate, though we lack the French genius for criticism and the German genius for philosophy, we do seem able to steer our "dark steps a little further on" by the help of Rozinante and Dapple.

My only personal quarrel with the excellent commentaries of Mr. Watts is that he seems to me to permit himself a little too much stress upon the *irony* of Cervantes.

Now irony, as we all know, is a very ticklish thing, and a thing of a thousand shades and inflections. In its airier and more diffused forms it melts so delicately into a certain sturdy and amused acceptance of life's absurdities that its self-consciousness, as an animadversion on these absurdities, is lost in imaginative relish of their very monstrousness and grotesqueness.

Now to a realistic English intelligence, few things are more repellent than the grosser aspects of the popular faith in the efficacy of relics. Long before the Conqueror tricked Harold into perjuring himself upon such gloomy fragments of mortality, the Anglo-Saxon mind had felt for these things a certain distaste, a distaste that culminated in the movement called Lollardry.

And so, to my English commentator upon *Don Quixote*, the following argument as to the rival claims of sanctity and knight-errantry seems purely ironical.

"Which is the greater," said Sancho, "to raise a dead man or to kill a giant?"

"The answer is plain," replied Don Quixote; "it is a greater thing to raise a dead man."

"I have caught you now," said Sancho. "Then the fame of those who bring the dead to life, who give sight to the blind, straighten the crooked, and heal the sick, and before whose tombs there are lamps burning, and whose chapels are full of devout folk who kneel before their relics, is a better fame for this and the other life than such as all your heathen

Emperors and Knights Errants have left or will leave in the world."

"That also I confess to be true," answered Don Quixote.

"Then this fame," continued Sancho, "these favours, these privileges, or what you call them, the bodies and relics of the saints have who, with the approval and licence of our Holy Mother Church, have lamps, candles, winding-sheets, crutches, pictures, eyes, legs, periwigs, whereby they enlarge their Christian reputation."

. . . . .

"All this is so," Don Quixote made answer. "But we cannot all be friars, and many are the roads by which God carries His own to heaven. Chivalry is a religion. There are sainted Knights in glory."

"Yes," responded Sancho; "but I have heard tell there are more friars than Knights Errant in heaven."

"That is because the number of those of the religious profession is greater than of the knightly," said Don Quixote.

Now this is a very good example of what my admirable translator calls the "irony" of Cervantes; and he is hard put to it to account for the fact that Inquisition authorities, though more lenient in the days of Philip III than of Philip II, allowed this sort of thing to pass.

But, Heavens! think of the colossal sport made of monks and friars in Rabelais, compared with this harmless passage! Surely to get the clue to the exact tone upon religious matters taken in *Don Quixote* it were wiser, instead of using the ticklish term "irony" which makes one think of Voltaire and Anatole France, first to remember Shakespeare's tone in these things, a tone too profoundly agnostic ever to approach irony; and then to think of the attitude to religion in our own personal experience of the most long-enduring, long-suffering, humble-minded man of action we may happen to know. I suspect that such an one will probably be a patient humorist, one who has made up his mind once and for all and long ago as to the limitations of the human intellect and especially of the intellect of those we call powerful original thinkers.

There is such a thing as taking for granted both the superstitions of the vulgar *and* the errors of the judicious, while we retain a modest attitude to our own mental endowments.

A veteran observer of the mad panorama of the world may surely be one who could enjoy the fantastical spectacle of the clash of human character without bothering very greatly about the clash of human ideas. It may even be that the necessity of heresy, like the necessity of logic, is an attribute of a mind that cannot get on without an intellectual system, whereas a tougher intelligence, especially a humorous intelligence and one that has long suffered "the slings and arrows of outrageous fortune," may acquire a kind of unprincipled relish for the very chaos of human opinion.

As I have hinted, what we call irony is usually the sign of a deep sense of personal superiority to the ordinary run of people, and I confess it is hard for me, though I dare say like Don Quixote he fought his battles over again in many a village inn, to think of this ex-captive of the Moors assuming that supercilious sense of superiority to the superstitions of the vulgar that heightens the wit of Voltaire's *Candide* and rounds the periods of Anatole France's *Jérôme Coignard*.

Among the curious experiences of Don Quixote in Barcelona, as he nears the close of his adventures, is the one of the oracular head, an episode of no very pungent entertainment.

Now I fully and completely share my English translator's horror of the abominable crimes of the Spanish Inquisition; and I share his view that nothing can excuse such atrocities. I also share his feeling borne out by what I saw in Spain before the war, as to the harm done to the country by the church.

But it seems to me as improper for us sturdy islanders to make Cervantes a rationalist as it is improper for Unamuno to make him the blood-thirsty Christ of the mystical Spanish spirit.

> But it being spread about the city that Don Antonio kept a magic Head in his house which answered all questions, fearing lest it might reach the ears of those watchful sentinels of our faith, he gave an account of it to the Inquisitors, who ordered him to take it to pieces and use it no further, so that the ignorant vulgar might not be scandalised.

Now since it is the lawful and uncontrovertible right of commentators to come to blows over their author, our English commentator challenges the Spanish commentator at this point to explain how this allusion to "those watchful sentinels of our faith" could possibly be taken as other than ironical. Well, I cannot tell!

But I seem to visualize Cervantes as more like Shakespeare than like Voltaire; and I can easily imagine Shakespeare, just as I can imagine the late Thomas Hardy, casually referring to some magisterial bench as "those watchful sentinels of our morals," without any unctuous respect, but also without any particular ironic emphasis.

No, this whole business of analysing the ingredients of the humour of a great writer is a very ticklish one. The humour that is the deepest, the most mysterious, as well as the most difficult and the most imperishable is not satire or sarcasm or ludicrous farce or even intellectual irony; it is and was, and always will be, one thing only, the creation of humorous character.

Like Falstaff and Pecksniff and Panurge and Uncle Toby, only a hundred times more so, Don Quixote and Sancho justify the ways of man to God, if not of God to man, in the simplest of all possible modes, *by being themselves to the limit;* and what an inspiration it was that made the knight catch the habit of rattling off proverbs from the squire, and the squire catch the trick of poetical eulogy—as for instance the famous one upon sleep—from the knight!

What I feel when I close *Don Quixote* is that we are all the imaginary characters of some great Cervantes of the cosmos, and that nothing in the external world, whatever power of giving buffets it may have, is as real as the passion, or the mania, or the illusion, that we each of us carry in our own head!

As we read this unique book we certainly get the feeling that the dominant life-illusion in a person's head, whether we're mad or sane, is more real than the heat of fire, the cold of water, the damp of rain, the slipperiness of ice, the obstruction of marble, the beat of waves, the wash of air, or the boundless recession of the infinite sky!

Even under the pressure of his hungry governorship and of all his pinches, blanketings, drubbings, and lashings, Sancho will utter his incorrigible proverbs; and even under the spear of the malapert Samson Don Quixote will utter those words that Heine thought the most beautiful in all literature.

My English commentator quarrels with Heine because this latter says that Don Quixote was overthrown by Master Nicholas the barber instead of by Master Samson the bachelor. For myself I can see no more "buffoonery" in his being overthrown by a conceited young scallawag, with a smattering of learning from college, than by an honest barber, his old neighbour and familiar gossip.

But what matter such bagatelles? I owe far too much to Mr. Watts to take any real exception to his protest. That the knight was done for is the crying point. We know too well that both the barber *and* the bachelor survived him. Indeed, they survive him still.

The egregious Avellaneda, whose spurious "Second Part" has, I presume, never appeared in English, ended his version, Mr. Watts tells us, by confining Don Quixote in the Toledo Lunatic Asylum.

Reserved by his true creator for a kindlier fate, Don Quixote actually encounters towards the end a character taken bodily out of Avellaneda's pirated version. By playing these tricks with time and space and with what might be called the different dimensions of fictional reality, we are compelled to feel that Don Quixote and Sancho have an existence and a being not only independent of the injurious Avellaneda but independent of Cervantes himself. It is a master conjuring-trick; and though several clever moderns have tried their hands at a similar device, *their* homunculi remain as unreal in their new objective masks as they were in the laboratories of their makers.

But never was there a situation, before or since, like the one Cervantes now imagines; for this poor "revenant" from the lewd brain of Avellaneda, who must have felt like one of those dissolving *shells* of the dead, that theosophists speak of, who hover over cemeteries, is anxious, the moment he sets eyes on the real knight and squire, to suck fresh vitality from their imperishableness, and to affirm— poor ghost!—even before the mayor of the town, "that I have not seen what I have seen, nor has there happened to me what has happened."

But it is not only the knight and squire to whom Cervantes gives a triumph over the treachery of time, equal to, if not more perdurable than his own. Horse and ass, Rozinante and Dapple, share this deathless survival; for what animals, historic or otherwise, have got themselves lodged in the human brain as these two?

And when you come to examine the art by which this miracle has been achieved it is just as hard to arrest this sorcery, and to catch its magic between crucible and retort as it is to catch Providence itself in *its* workshop.

One thing, however, seems clear. It is partly done by emphasizing the *inconsistencies* of both men and beasts. Had the knight been always the unruffled but deluded hero, Sancho always the affectionate but greedy clown, they would never have been "clothed upon with immortality," and the same thing applies to their four-footed companions.

The essence of *Quixotism* is its war with what we call "the World," and Don Quixote himself, when he listened to Sancho's praise of the relics of the saints, spoke as if there were something corresponding to knight-errantry that already, apart from its failures in time and space, "had overcome the World."

But one of the most beautiful and subtle touches in the whole book is when Don Quixote feels that it is incumbent upon him *to pretend to be mad* for the love of Dulcinea. With this in view he is anxious to perform certain crazy pranks, the tale of which Sancho is to convey to the sprightly wench Aldonza.

"I trust to your worship," said Sancho . . . "for I intend to start at once without witnessing the mad pranks which your worship is going to play, for I will say I saw you perform so many that she will want no more."

"At least I should like thee, Sancho, and because it is essential . . . to see me stripped, and go through a dozen or two of mad things, which I will despatch in less than half an hour—"

"For the love of God, dear master, let us not see your worship naked, for it will raise in me so much pity, and I shall not be able to keep from crying; . . . but if it is your worship's pleasure that I should see some mad tricks, do them with your clothes on—short ones, and such as are of most account. . . . For how should it be suffered that a Knight Errant so famous as your worship should go mad without why or wherefore for a—let not my lady make me say the word, for by God I will out with it and scatter it by the dozen. . . ."

"In faith, Sancho," said Don Quixote, "it would seem that thou art no saner than I am."

"Not so mad, but more peppery," answered Sancho.

Whether Charles Lamb or whether my scholarly commentator is in the right of it over the elaborate fooling that our adventurers suffer at the hands of the frivolous duke and duchess, it certainly remains that both Don Quixote and Sancho come out of the ordeal with their integrity unabated and their dignity enhanced.

Not only does Sancho astonish these silly play-actors by his shrewdness and mother wit, but his master reduces them to silence by some of the noblest justifications of the profession of knight-errantry that appear in the whole book.

The part of the episode that I myself like least has to do with the author's deep-rooted prejudice against those unlucky elderly ladies, spinsters or widows, called *duennas*. Mr. Watts seems to hint that, as an impoverished soldier and a poor proud gentleman, Cervantes may easily have suffered in the houses of certain patrons of letters from the backbiting spitefulness of this duenna class.

It certainly shows the extraordinary livingness of the story that a detached bookworm like myself should suffer a positive pang of vexation when Don Quixote's gallant championship of this luckless duenna and her seduced daughter comes to nothing owing to the duke's capricious meanness, so that the girl, instead of being married to her enamoured lackey, is clapped into a convent; but, after all, these shocks to the less tough reader occur all the way through the tale, and it is hard to point to a single instance, right up to the very end where the knight's interference does any good. Possibly the release of the luckless chain-gang—but even there the ungrateful Gine rewards his rescuer by making off with Dapple.

Gentle and courteous as his hero was, with his mania or

without it, Cervantes himself can hardly be called a writer of squeamish sensibility.

The return home at the last is as curious as it is sad, and I confess it does appear here as if Mr. Watts had justification for his contention that the great writer had, as we say, his knife into the Inquisition. Certainly to dress up Dapple at that moment in the institution's famous flames and mitre does seem going a bit further than a thoughtless jest.

But if to see the ass in the terrible *sanbenito* is a pleasure to a humane conscience it is painful, at least to one reader, when Don Quixote gives back the hunted hare to her pursuers.

> "Your worship is a strange one," said Sancho; "let us suppose that this hare is Dulcinea del Toboso and these hounds are the vagabond enchanters. . . . She flies; I catch her and place her in your worship's power, who hold her in your arms and caress her—"
>
> . . . . . .
>
> Then the huntsmen came up, and asking for their hare Don Quixote gave her to them.

It is curious to notice how Cervantes resembles Rabelais in his miraculous memory for popular proverbs. Sancho is the grand adept in this kind, but though applied in a more judicious manner, as he himself hesitates not to point out, they are used by Don Quixote, too, and to fine effect.

But it is Theresa Panza who rounds off her argument with these rich oracles most neatly of all, using them more sparingly than her husband and less sententiously than his master.

> "I tell you, wife," said Sancho, "that if I did not think to become governor of an isle before very long I would drop dead upon the spot."
>
> "Not so, husband," cried Theresa. "Let the hen live though it be with the pip. Live you; and let the Devil take

all the governorships that are in the world; without a government you came from your mother's womb; without government you have lived till now, and without government you will go or be carried to the grave when it shall please God. How many in the world are there who live without a governorship, yet for all that do not give up living and being counted in the number of the people!"

Now if any one were to ask me, what in my opinion was the most humorous remark in all literature, I would be tempted to try and remember this speech, ending with, "for all that they do not give up living and being counted in the number of the people!" And yet the whole thing is only an extension of her own homely proverb: "Let the hen live, though she *has* the pip."—*Viva la gallina con su pepita!*

But doesn't it seem as if this inexhaustible memory for old wives' sayings which Cervantes shares with Rabelais is a shrewd indication as to the nature of their common inspiration, tapping, as they both do, the bottomless reservoir of folk-wisdom?

Here are a baker's dozen of these "unvalued gems," filched at random from this book, and the reader must not suppose they are all Sancho's.

> Whether the pitcher strikes on the stone or the stone on the pitcher, it is bad for the pitcher.
> It's no good to look for flitches where there aren't even hooks.
> The pure woman and the broken leg are best at home.
> The honey is not for the mouth of the ass.
> Another's ill hangs by a hair.
> Don't name rope in the house of the hanged.
> He is safe who sounds the bell.
> Behind the Cross stands the Devil.
> God grant it and Sin be deaf.
> To an ill wind goes *this* grain.

Not with whom thou art bred, but with whom thou art fed.

St. Peter is very well at Rome.

The dog saw himself in linen breeches and did not know his companions.

Let folks laugh, so I go warm.

When they offer thee a calf run with the rope.

How impossible it is not to wonder, when we read of Don Quixote's adventures in Barcelona, what the Knight of the Rueful Countenance would feel to-day about events in Spain! He was certainly glad enough to escape from his luxurious imprisonment with those idle patrons.

"Liberty, Sancho, is one of the most precious gifts which Heaven has bestowed upon man. With it no treasure can be compared which the earth contains or the sea conceals. For liberty, as for honour, one can and should adventure life. . . . In the midst of those high-seasoned banquets methought I was suffering the straits of hunger, for I enjoyed them not with the same freedom as if they had been mine own; for those obligations, which benefits and favours received impose, are bonds which will not let the mind range freely. Happy the man to whom Heaven has given a crust of bread, without the obligation of thanking any for it but Heaven itself!"

Tiresome and silly though the pranks were that those rich idlers played on our wanderers, we at least owe to them the piquant situation of the thousands of lashes which Sancho had to inflict on himself for the disenchanting of Dulcinea.

It is I think partly owing to what might be called the "skin-for-skin" intimacy between master and man—as when Sancho suddenly looks at Don Quixote and bluntly expresses his wonder that any wench could be excited to amorousness by such a figure, or, on the other hand, when with the utmost delicacy of consideration he gets him out his cage in order that he may do "what we can only do for ourselves"—that the livingness of the pair attained to such an *absolute of reality*.

It is in connexion with the putting off of this "disenchanting" process that Sancho bursts into his famous eulogy upon sleep.

> "O squire without pity! . . . Through me thou hast seen thyself a Governor and through me thou seest thyself in near expectation of being a Count . . . for *post tenebras spero lucem.*"
>
> "I know not what that is," replied Sancho. "I only know that while I sleep I have no fear, nor hope, nor trouble, nor glory; and good luck to him who invented sleep, a cloak which covers all a man's thoughts, the meat which takes away hunger, the water which quenches thirst, the fire which warms cold, the cold which tempers the heat; to end up, the general coin with which all things are bought, the balance and weight which levels the shepherd with the king, and the fool with the wise man."

Certainly if it were the sweet perilous drug of romance that sent Don Quixote crazy, Cervantes took a strange way of combating it. Why, he has set an eternal advertisement of it among the stars!

It is as if, when he took up that pen of which he speaks so touchingly, to attack this thing, the real Don Quixote, armed at all points, appeared at his elbow. Did he appear *in vain* at his elbow when it came to that final recantation?

Oh, how many simple readers there must be, who, like those the indignant innkeeper told his clever guests used to listen spell-bound, must have relucted from their deepest hearts at Don Quixote's death-bed "sanity"!

Well, it matters not. Alonso the Good may make his will as he pleases, and may thank God as he pleases that he dies in his right mind. *To us he is not the man.* From that unreal death-bed, from all the unreal death-beds of imperishable romance, comes the voice of the real Don

Quixote, still reversing all the values of this plausible world, still putting invisible things in the place of visible things, still declaring, in defiance of all the vivisecting science of all the schools: "Dulcinea del Toboso is the most beautiful woman in the world and I the most unfortunate Knight upon earth; and it is not well that my weakness should discredit this truth."

For my own part I cannot help thinking that however triumphant Sir Homo Sapiens, our constantly reborn "Bachelor from Salamanca," may prove to be, there will always be some pair of arms, some pair of legs, even if no braver than Sancho's, to follow that faint voice, though it *is* as feeble and weak "as if out of the tomb."

> *With a Knight of ghosts and shadows,*
> *I summoned am to Tourney:*
> *Ten leagues beyond*
> *The wide world's end;*
> *Methinks it is no journey.*

Shakespeare

THERE is surely something significant in the fact that the personalities of the most universally human of all poets—Homer and Shakespeare—should be so completely lost in their work.

In Homer's case the huge gulf of time must of course count for much and the fact that a poet, unlike an Egyptian king, has no power to build monuments in everlasting stone, and have them inscribed with his glories.

To Achilles, to Hector, to Odysseus, the poet himself— acting like a god—could give a life as lasting as the hardest granite; but his own personality—save in the tone and temper and scope of his art—*that* he could not save; *that* he had to leave to a few rumours of legendary ambiguity and a few tags of popular gossip!

But in Shakespeare's case there is no such gulf. In Shakespeare's case we are confronted by a phenomenal obscurity that presents itself as a psychological rather than a historic riddle.

Far earlier, far remoter writers are clear, definite, unmistakable personalities. Dante, Rabelais, Chaucer, we know well; and the identities of his own contemporaries, Spenser, Marlowe, Sidney, Ben Jonson, stand out in unquestionable outline.

Does it not seem likely that just as, with the aid of the "iniquity of oblivion" and the "scattering" of time's "poppies," the very genius of Homer aided the dissolution of his personality, so the very genius of Shakespeare has assisted in this blurring of his mortal lineaments?

Poets who are able, as Keats said of himself, and they are the greatest of all, so to lose their identity in the thing they are contemplating that they cease to possess the contours of personal character, do they not, for that very cause become the clearest-sounding reeds, the most transparent mediums, for our universal humanity?

In other words, is not the obscurity of Homer's and Shakespeare's personality the inevitable result of the quality of their particular greatness?

For what, when you consider it, is the nature of the emphatic personality which stands out so formidably in Dante and Milton? Precisely that towering and belligerent egoism whose urge in writing is what we now would call self-expression or even propaganda, whereas the words of Hamlet to the players, about holding the mirror up to nature and showing "virtue her own feature, scorn her own image, and the very age and body of the time his form and pressure," are a shrewd hint of a completely different urge, the urge, namely, I will not say to justify life, but to *present* life, and to present it rather as an aesthetic spectacle than as any sort of personal problem.

Both Homer and Shakespeare have suffered from a curious subterranean *jealousy* in intellectual critics which is the counterpart to the equally untrustworthy *idolatry* among the masses. For these extremes of opinion spring really from the same source, namely, humanity's inability to believe in the *natural power* of supreme genius; the critics attributing Homer's work to a crowd of anonymous minstrels and Shakespeare's to anybody rather than the unlearned actor-manager from Stratford, while the vulgar are tempted to turn them both into legendary figures of supernatural inspiration and fairy-story prowess.

Between the jealous critical view, getting its curious and morbid pleasure in devastating iconoclasm and the idolatrous popular view, piling up legend on legend, it seems that the latter is, on the face of it, likely to be nearer the truth.

The quarrel of so many intelligent people with the accepted Shakespearean legend has at the bottom of it the clever person's instinctive distrust of the miracle of genius.

How could the son of a small-town butcher even if he did pick up a smattering of law in a small-town law-office, who certainly never went to the university and who joined a play-acting troop when the social position of actors was anything but respectable, how could such a man acquire the knowledge of the world and the knowledge of the classics, and of court and camp and law-courts such as is revealed in the plays?

And then, once assuming that the player from Stratford *couldn't* have been the man, what is more adapted to the robust intelligence of truth-seeking critics than to hunt about for some one who *was* experienced in all these high matters, and to light first on my lord of Verulam, and then on the earl of this or the earl of that, who would be, or might be, or could conceivably be, just the person "if he had the mind" to throw off in his leisure moments such trifles as *King Lear*, *Hamlet*, *Othello*, *Julius Caesar*, *The Tempest*, and so forth?

Nothing is more beautifully illustrative of that mixture of jealous scepticism as to what genius can do and an infinite credulity as to what cryptograms and counterfeits and cozening conspiracies can do, than the history of what is called the Baconian theory. I love the mental image— who wouldn't?—of a mysterious bastard of Queen Elizabeth, whose power of dramatic creation was only equalled by his power of legal chicanery, and his scientific originality only surpassed by his passion for cryptograms; but to the humblest bookworm with any respect for the mystery of style, it is simply impossible, notwithstanding the evidence of mountains of cryptograms, that out of the same spiritual workshop, even if the playwright lifted whole passages from the latter, should have come the plays *and* the *Essays*.

The psychological truth is that when once you cut yourself adrift from the homely wonders of common tradition and let your astute rational logic go to the limit, you find yourself landed in far wilder possibilities than that a man could write *Hamlet* without going to Oxford or *The Merchant of Venice* without being lord chancellor.

Ben Jonson would have had to have been in the plot, and the whole elaborate conspiracy against posterity would have to be attributed to the snobbish desire of the great personage not to be known as anything so gross, so vulgar, so ungentlemanly as the supreme dramatist of his time.

The literary rival who in his own day derisively sneered at this "Shake-scene" must have been as much fooled as we are; and it is certain that John Milton—no mean judge of stylistic subtleties—when he wrote:

> *If Jonson's learned sock be on.*
> *Or sweetest Shakespeare, Fancy's child,*
> *Warble his native wood-notes wild,*

would have been astonished, if not extremely angry, to learn that his favourite poet was not an honest commoner from the Warwickshire woods at all, but a titled "Malignant" of a sycophantic court!

The enemies of our Stratford Shakespeare evidently differ from Milton as to wherein consists the essential quality of the poetry of the plays. Milton—and I cordially agree with him, though I boggle at the word "warble"— evidently thinks that the essence of Shakespeare's style lies in the way his images are drawn from the country side and the way his imagination is steeped in the sounds and sights of English earth and water; whereas it is clear that what these opponents hold to be the important element is the number of allusions it contains to the classics, to jurisprudence and geography, to international statecraft, and to the political history of the world.

The things, in fact, that our literary Sherlock Holmeses, in their exposure of this actor-poacher of the wild woods, who signed his name anyhow, care nothing for and understand nothing of are the mysteries of poetry.

That there should be words and even whole phrases in common between Shakespeare and Bacon is little to Milton or to Keats or to any other poet who knows the depth of the spiritual and literary gulf that divides the plays from the *Essays*.

The appeal in this matter is from the detective school of criticism to what might be called the school of poetic tradition; but the final issue as to whether the vagabond-actor from Warwickshire, with his "wood-notes wild," could write what we know as the "plays of Shakespeare" depends on one's faith in the sheer power of genius to override all handicaps.

There is one argument, however, on the Stratford actor's side that seems to me of no mean weight; and that is an argument concerning the technical structure of the plays.

Putting aside their rhetorical and poetical seductiveness, no one will be found to deny the unique effectiveness of this vast mass of plays as extraordinarily artful theatrework. This is proved by the successful experiments that have recently been made of playing them in modern dress, and it has been proved again and again during the last three hundred years by their professional popularity, not only with "stage-stars," but with the rank and file of the entertainers of the people. Nor can we discount in this connexion what might crudely be called their box-office success.

Now one is continually being reminded of the difficulties encountered by poets who try to write for the stage without a working knowledge of stage-craft; and it seems on the face of it more unlikely that some young Elizabethan noble-man, not to speak of a busy statesman-lawyer, could acquire this intimate stage-craft, and acquire it as none other has ever done, than that a country-born actor of unexampled genius could pick up from his aristocratic cronies and scholarly patrons enough classical and historical material to body forth his inspired imaginations.

Listen, reader, to our actor-poet's own words:

> *Alas! 'tis true I have gone here and there*
> *And made myself a motley to the view,*
> *Gor'd mine own thoughts, sold cheap what*
>   *is most dear,*
> *Made old offences of affections new;*
> *Most true it is that I have looked on truth*
> *Askance and strangely—*

Does not this sonnet most perfectly suggest the early years of one who before he put off his "motley" was des-tined to "look on truth" through the eyes of the greatest number of impassioned "masks" ever brought upon a human stage?

Surely it is the most natural of all things that the greatest of playwrights should have been an actor; and indeed all the most characteristic touches in the plays are not only an actor's touches but those of an actor who has come from the country.

We get the impression from the sonnets, and it is fully borne out in the plays, of a man swayed by every wind of erotic passion, a man tormented, ravaged, scoriated by love, and also of a man who inevitably uses country sights and sounds to express their feelings.

We are made aware of an ideal passion for some lovely youth of the poet's own sex, and of a far more dangerous and less exalted feeling for some very seductive, very witty, and very treacherous woman.

All this falls in naturally with the life of a daring adventurer from Warwickshire, *saturated*—as we cannot conceive a fashionable young nobleman or an ambitious law-student to have been—*with country things*. His favourite books, too, seem to have been just the ones that an adventurous young actor would naturally prefer. Plutarch's *Lives*, the works of Rabelais—for the reference to the "mouth of Gargantua" in *As You Like It* is far more suggestive of a real intimacy with this book of books than the rather contemptuous and stupid reference made to it by Montaigne—the *Essays* of Montaigne himself, and the works of his own contemporary, Christopher Marlowe.

It might have been better for him if he'd read Rabelais with even greater care; for he might in that way have gone deeper than he does in *Love's Labour's Lost* into the "bettering of the mind," and have come to recognize even more than he does, in Hamlet, the philosophical absurdity of national wars. He might also, incidentally, have come to see the intellectual superiority of the Greeks over the Romans!

Granting him then to be the actor-manager going up to town from Stratford and returning to Stratford to buy the New Place and to plant mulberry-trees and to sue "Old Double" for fourpence halfpenny, and to play backgammon in the tavern, and to pet his daughter, and to leave his lady the bed on which we may suppose, thinking of Venus and Adonis, she seduced him as a young lad, it is easy to see how his lack of Greek—and indeed I think some queer accidental prejudice that could only have grown up in a self-educated man was the result of this—limited his response to Homer to an idealization of that "sweet warman" Hector and a rooted, almost rustic hostility to Helen, whose "lips sucked forth the soul" from Marlowe's Faust.

And it is still easier to see how inevitably it happened that while his poetry is so often entangled in the elaborate flights of an overclever verbal wit, he should instinctively resort, when his feelings are most deeply stirred, to snatches from old country ballads, things that few great court-noblemen and few learned university wits would naturally pick up, a traditional vein that is different from the familiar Border-ballads, and seems to carry with it the rural atmosphere of the more purely English shires. The mellow humour of those Gloucestershire scenes, too, when Falstaff goes recruiting, and we are introduced to Justice Shallow and Master Silence, leave a taste in the mouth hard to regard as the evocation of any one not steeped in country ways; and the same applies to this:

ROCHESTER: An Inn Yard

Enter Carrier with a lantern in his hand.

FIRST CARRIER: Heigh-ho! An't be not four by the day I'll be hanged; Charles' Wain is over the new chimney, and yet our horse not packed. What, ostler!

OSTLER (*within*): Anon, anon.

FIRST CARRIER: I prithee, Tom, beat Cut's saddle, put a few flocks in the point: the poor jade is wrung in the withers out of all cess.

Enter another Carrier.

SECOND CARRIER: Peas and beans are as dank here as a dog, and that is the next way to give poor jades the bots: this house is turned upside down since Robin Ostler died.

FIRST CARRIER: Poor fellow! never joyed since the price of oats rose, it was the death of him.

But leaving this defence of Shakespeare as an actor-manager come up from the country, we now find ourselves confronted by one especially vague and unsatisfactory spot in all the huge mass, the ever-increasing mass, of Shakespearean interpretation.

It seems to me that every conceivable aspect of Shakespeare's art has been intimately discussed except what is surely the most important of all—I mean that mental and emotional reaction to human life, which in unsophisticated circles is called a writer's "message."

And that this essence of the whole matter has been so thinly and vaguely interpreted is not merely due to the fact that our impassioned reformers of society fail to find in him the sort of rounded-off system for improving our mortal lot that seems to them alone worthy of the name of "philosophy"; it is also due to the fact that, as with Homer, Shakespeare's philosophic "message" is so diffused throughout his poetic rhetoric and throughout the humours, dilemmas, fancies, and poignancies of his "wood-notes wild," that it requires a spellbound intimacy not only with the temper of his style and the accents of his voice but with the spiritual implications of his habitual stresses, silences, reserves, and avoidances, to catch the drift of the tide.

To my mind the most illuminating interpretations of Shakespeare's "philosophy" are to be found in certain careless and casual remarks scattered through the essays of Lamb and the letters of Keats; while among more pretentious works I confess to having found the audacious and lively study by Hamlet's fellow-national, Georg Brandes, the most rewarding.

The vast shelves of books upon Shakespeare in our own tongue are, as I have presumed to hint, at their weakest in this most important aspect of the subject. His characters have been discussed to a point of weariness, his allusions to every mortal subject have been catalogued, his sources collated, his dramatic art explained, and here and there—

though much more rarely—a poet like Coleridge, or a critic like Hazlitt, has thrown light upon the technical secrets of his actual poetry, but the mere fact that such a simple expression as "the philosophy of Shakespeare" is calculated to give a scholarly student no slight shock is a proof of what little headway has been made in the essence of the matter.

In the few cases where such an attempt has been undertaken one is conscious of a moral idealization that leaves, if I may coin such an expression, a hollow sweetness in the mouth, and not only this but an uncomfortable feeling that the man has been made so completely "everything," that like the Deity in a logical pantheistic system, he hovers on the brink of the antinomic "nothing."

What I would like to suggest in this place is that it is just as possible to be a disciple of the philosophy of Shakespeare as to be a disciple of the philosophy of St. Paul or Dante or Rabelais or Goethe; nor do I think that the fact of his being a playwright need throw any insurmountable difficulties in the way.

Surely a reader of the plays endowed with any degree of intelligence can catch through the seductive clamour of opposing voices a clear drift of the author's personal reaction to life, a drift revealed not only by the thousand floating straws and bubbles and foam-wisps and revolving eddies upon the surface of the tide, but by the unrevealing nature of the "murmurs and scents" of the unknown sea towards which it is moving.

And how would a person, who, in the company of Platonists and Epicureans and Stoics and Christians, declared himself to be of "the school of Shakespeare," define his emotional and intellectual attitude?

In the first place he would, I think, declare himself an individualist; one, that is to say, who finds in the character of the individual, rather than in any collective or standardized "ideology" as we call it now, the chief redeeming element in the world and the best hope for the well-being of humanity.

And when we inquired what particular aspects of personal character are to be regarded as fundamental, it seems to me that even the most modest of Shakespeare's disciples would be forced to reply, "courage, magnanimity, and an open mind." Carrying our presumptuous inquisition from the social into the metaphysical sphere and inquiring of our reserved Shakespearean disciple about the existence of God and of a life after death, we should merely be answered in a final and absolute, "Nobody knows!"

Nothing, in fact, emerges more unmistakably as the attitude of Shakespeare to these crucial questions—Has the Universe an underlying purpose? Does man's soul survive death? Is there an overruling conscious Intelligence?—than an undeviating agnosticism. And this agnosticism, as it gradually takes possession of us in reading the plays, turns out to be no more than a heightened poetic emphasis upon the average individual's normal instinct.

Talk to any ordinary person, lucky or unlucky, the first comfortable citizen you meet, or the first tramp you meet, and you will soon catch them referring to God in the precise Shakespearean tone—that is to say, in a tone that blends natural superstition, conventional reverence, egotistical emotion, with complete agnosticism.

Talk to them about the mystery of evil, and their tone will be the same, a combination of universal human superstition, traditional morality, individual passion, and a wistful incorrigible feeling that *nobody really knows*.

And then, finally, bring up the subject of death; and behold, with one universal sigh and shrug of the shoulders, from the Hebrides to Land's End you'll get the true Shakespearean answer: "He's out of his troubles," or, "She's safe from it all now"—and "the rest is silence."

But you will protest, at this point: "How can you call it philosophy when Shakespeare goes no further about God and immortality and good and evil than the average well-meaning citizen and the average much-enduring tramp?

"Isn't it precisely to enlighten this primitive ignorance, to purge these traditional superstitions, to make logical these irrational hopes, that the great thinkers have rounded off their vast systems, and that Plato and Aristotle and Kant and Hegel have received so much honour?"

Ah! but that is the whole point! The philosophy of Shakespeare is of such great value just because, with an originality that is the more startling the more you realize what it means, he *does* catch the common accent, the common tone, the universal mingling of superstition with agnosticism, which is the average man's instinctive response to the mystery of the universe.

Shakespeare, in fact, held in sober earnest what the Catholic church claims in dogmatic theory—*securus judicat orbis terrarum*—"the whole world's opinion is a safe guide." Did he hold this philosophical brief for the common man's philosophy, as some have claimed, in order with subtle equivocations to wheedle us back into the arms of Mother Church?

Was Shakespeare, in other words, the inspired inventor of the fascinating conjuring-trick of Mr. Chesterton? I cannot think so. Indeed, it seems to me that there is as much difference between using the average man's instincts as a jumping-off board for submission to the Church, and using them as an Aeternum Organum in themselves, as there is between the monastical piety of St. Thomas à Kempis and the evangelical piety of Rabelais.

It has been inevitable that having poetized with an unequalled glamour the philosophy of the man in the street, Shakespeare should receive some shrewd buffets

from the more daring among our modern "intelligentsia."
Tolstoy regarded him as an unholy supporter of a degenerate aristocracy and as a hot champion of the world, the
flesh, and the devil; and in our own day his individualistic,
one might almost say his anarchistic indifference both to
political reform and political standardization would clap
him into gaol in any other country but ours.

But luckily his philosophy is so widely shared in Great
Britain, and we have got so much of his distrust of "Great
Thinkers" and their rational conclusions, that this humorous agnostic attitude of his, combined with his reverence
for tradition, strikes us all as *so natural* that we tend to just
take it for granted, without bothering our heads about its
somewhat startling implications.

And startling indeed these implications are!

Here we have a mass of plays, comical, historical, his-
torical-tragical, greater in bulk, higher in quality, more
appealing in poignance, more seductive in style, than those
of any other dramatist; a mass of plays to find a counter-
poise for which from the classical world you would have
to add Sophocles to Euripides and both to Aristophanes,
and what is their subject-matter? From first to last the
palpable, visible, secular, human, too-human spectacle! No
wrestling with the cosmological problem, no reiterated and
obstinate delving into the problem of good and evil, no
desperate fathoming of the social problem, no introduction
of gods or devils or messiahs, or demigods or prophets or
saints; and finally, as Ruskin says, not one single hero
whose character is not weakened and thwarted by obvious
and most disastrous faults!

At the same time, and this is of the very essence of the
matter, none of our stout rationalists, positivists, material-
ists, determinists, atheists have ever thought of claiming
Shakespeare as a kindred spirit.

In some extraordinary way the man has become an

inspired medium, an undistorted, untwisted human reed, through whom the natural man—an entity rarely found, perhaps never found in actual life, but of whose nature we all have something—can express his spontaneous reverence, his recurrent scepticism, his undying hopes, his fluctuating despairs, his intermittent faith, his treacheries, and his loyalties.

One frequently hears a person say, "I couldn't stand it, if it weren't for my sense of humour."

Now I am tempted to think that what these people mean by their "sense of humour" is not exactly that they see themselves as ludicrous or comical in their predicament, still less that they see their persecutors or persecutions as something funny. What I think they mean is that they "couldn't stand it" if they hadn't by some lucky mental device the power of detaching themselves from the painful situation, and contemplating it as *drama*. It is indeed, I suspect, by our dramatic instinct, the mysterious comfort we get from seeing ourselves, and those who make us suffer, from the vantage-ground of a certain interior balcony-seat, that enables us to endure. In other words, as long as we don't know what is going to happen next, as long as the play of our life remains a play, we can stick it out.

It is when it ceases to present itself to us in the likeness of a play, with unknown "acts" and "scenes" before us, and we looking on, and watching ourselves behaving like ourselves and the others behaving like *themselves*, that we commit suicide.

It has ceased to be a play. We have lost "our sense of humour." It has become reality. And no man can face reality and live.

As Ibsen so beautifully hinted in *The Wild Duck*, we must hang on to our life-illusion by the hair of its head. We all must "save our face," to ourselves. And this "sense of humour," which is in reality a sense of drama, is one of the means by which we "save our face."

Falstaff "saved his face" by his life-illusion of being "not only witty but the cause why wit is in other men"; and it is a device that all shrewd people learn, to dodge the shame of their cowardice by what they would call "humorously" admitting it.

Now the whole mass of Shakespeare's plays is an impassioned chorus of eloquent life-illusions and humorous admissions. He is the supreme dramatist because he found in this clashing discord of multitudinous life-illusions a mystic harmony, a strange and abysmal beauty. His genius was of that particular nature which enables a person to *become* other people, and become several other people at the same time.

This power of becoming a medium, a reed, a wind-harp, an unblemished mirror, approaches the extremely ambiguous power of yielding ourselves up to obsession or possession, or, as the spiritualists say, to being "controlled."

And one feels this "control" of the poet by the anonymous generations of common men and women more than anything else in the plays. Shakespeare *becomes* all his hapless and desperate and eloquent characters. *They* possess him. Not *he* them. He becomes Lear. He becomes the Fool in Lear. He becomes Prospero. He also becomes Caliban. He becomes Hamlet. He also becomes Ophelia. He becomes Falstaff. He also becomes Henry V condemning Falstaff. He becomes Caesar. He also becomes Brutus killing Caesar. His genius is that it can be obsessed by the simple equally with the subtle, by the feelings of a woman equally with the feelings of a man.

And it seems as if this in itself throws more light than a thousand anecdotes could do on the personality of the man. He *couldn't* have had the preoccupations of a scientist or a statesman. He *couldn't* have had the dignity and egoism of a poet like Dante or Milton.

He may very well have been—in fact I suspect he certainly was—of a weaker, airier, more emotional, less compact, more flexible nature, than Montaigne or Cervantes.

It is Georg Brandes who shrewdly remarks that his genius itself gives one the impression of being composed of a stuff of *lighter weight* than that which composed the genius of Rabelais; and no one, I think, can read the sonnets without being aware of a nervous, high-strung, quicksilver temperament behind this impassioned sequence that is the reverse of everything strong, steady, well-poised and calm, the reverse in fact of all that Matthew Arnold calls him—"self-scanned, self-schooled, self-honoured, self-secure"!

But returning to what a person would aim at who decided to become a disciple of Shakespeare rather than of Dante, say, or of Milton, or of Goethe, or of Dostoievsky.

In the first place, such a one would be what you might call a fluid and malleable individualist; that is to say an individualist whose egoism is tempered by such simple virtues as generosity, mercy, loyalty, courage, and gentleness.

In the second place, such a one would retain an unwavering agnosticism towards all the great ultimate questions, such as whether there is a life after death, whether the universe has a purpose, whether such a purpose takes cognizance of man, whether evil is a positive or a negative power, whether matter is eternal, whether God is a person who thinks and loves or a blind creative force.

In the third place, such a one would hold the view that the usage and customs and traditions and conventions of ordinary humanity contain more wisdom than the most logical systems of the profoundest philosophers.

In the fourth place, such a one would avoid every kind of extravagant, violent, quixotic, fanatic virtue; remaining infinitely indulgent both to his own lapses, weaknesses, and indolences, and to the lapses, weaknesses, and indolences of others.

"Be not over-righteous, nor take upon thyself to be over-wise. Why shouldest thou destroy thyself?" is the Shake-spearean attitude; and like all other great mental attitudes, it can be deliberately and consciously cultivated; and the more a person cultivates it the more he will limit his faith, limit his trust, limit his confidence amid all the contradic-tions and paradoxes of life to the basic human qualities of courage, magnanimity, and an open mind.

It is impossible to saturate yourself with the plays of Shakespeare as a few great actors and a good many im-passioned bookworms have done without acquiring a sort of—what shall I call it?—a sort of interior *emotional bias* which beneath all personal cowardice, meanness, and bigotry points like a compass-needle to courage, magna-nimity, and an open mind!

And this generous "open mind," which is the dominant emotional result of reading these plays, takes to itself, the more a person's private experience thickens, some ex-tremely startling and revolutionary aspects.

It becomes, in fact, a mental method, beyond all logical definition, of dispensing with all philosophical systems, yes, by heaven! and I might almost say of *dispensing with philosophy itself*!

The secret we learn from Shakespeare is, in fact, the magical and wanton gift—like the note of a fairy-horn sounding in the brain of a witless younger son—of catching the spirit of life upon the wing, rather by means of a brave heart, a naughty fancy, and an irresponsible generosity than by studying Taoism or Buddhism or Catholicism, or by making a cult of hedonism. It is, of course, by means of a mixture of good health and a certain blessed stupidity that so many dare-devil rogues of both sexes scramble through life with a minimum of insanity.

Well! What the sophisticated and the sensitive among us can get from soaking themselves in these plays is the crafty and celestial trick of making a certain fanciful humour and a certain airy imagination, as these are born like wanton elves in the detached intelligence, serve just as well as the good digestion, the hard heart, and the thick-skinned callousness of these honeysuckle rakehells.

Now the substitution of poetic fancy and wanton humour *for philosophy* is the supreme gift of the mixed race inhabiting our British Isles; and what Shakespeare has really done, in thus substituting humour for philosophy, and the imagination for reason, as the ultimate weapons of the soul, is merely to make an unlimited human universal out of a limited insular particular.

He is only doing here in the moral sphere what he does in regard to nature in the material sphere; for although he rarely mentions a flower, a tree, a plant, and still more rarely a beast or a bird, that couldn't be found within a few miles of Stratford, this provinciality of flora and fauna, and of the changing expressions of earth and sky and land and sea, becomes so universal in his hands that it seems perfectly natural for Antony to pursue Cleopatra up the Nile like a "doting mallard" from Squire Lucy's great pond, or for Ophelia to sink to her muddy death at Elsinore with the "long purples" of Avon-bank loosestrife in her arms.

All through these plays the greatest philosophical dilemmas, the profoundest philosophical antinomies, are just fancifully *played with*; and almost always when matters get intolerably tragic it is with a word like the "ripeness is all" in *Lear*, or "the rest is silence" in *Hamlet*, or "this parting is well made" in *Julius Caesar*, or "rounded with a sleep" in *The Tempest*, or "then I defy you, stars!" in *Romeo and Juliet*, or "all our yesterdays have lighted fools" in *Macbeth*, that the open door and the magnanimity and the courage of his message are preserved.

What Shakespeare does in all his ultimate tragic moments is to indicate the whole burden of human life in a brief or a broken sentence, a sentence that is like a sigh or a cry or a start or a sob or a spasm or a groan; but is anything rather than the sort of philosophical summary of the situation we get with the Greeks or the sort of rounded ethical apologue we get with the French.

Tolstoy attacked Shakespeare on the ground that he was a propagandist for the aristocracy against the masses; and it is impossible to deny that over and over again he seems to do his utmost to make the crowd, the mob, the multitude, "hoi polloi" appear fickle, cruel, changeable, gross, and ridiculous.

We feel this about the mob in *Julius Caesar*, about the mob in *Coriolanus*, and, above all, about poor Jack Cade's motley followers in *Henry VI*.

But though we have just to accept this dislike of the mob, a dislike which almost appears, judging from the tone he habitually uses, to amount to a nervous mania, the fact remains that the moment he dramatizes any *individual* member of this same mob his genius for throwing himself into the heart and inwards of any living human creature, and of reacting to the whole gamut of life from that creature's mood, forces him to come to terms with what his personal mania heartily dislikes. Thus in spite of a fastidiousness that would strike Rabelais as shameful and totally unworthy of a noble intellect, the moment any of these gross-mouthed "honest cods" from the labouring classes come to life under his touch they become not only witty and entertaining, but most formidably humorous at the expense of his fine ladies and gentlemen!

This whole attitude of his is summed up in the contrast between Caliban and Prospero but it is diffused throughout a hundred scenes; and in the figure of the Homeric Thersites, through whose bitter tongue he delights to make these famous Greeks, of whom he was probably weary of hearing learned men talk, look like hulking bully-boys, he lets himself go in a vein of farcical rustic profanity.

The truth is that his reckless wit was continually, as Ben Jonson protested, bursting all bounds. He is the supreme example of genius with the bit in its teeth, with the bridle flung down on its neck, of genius knowing no law but its own humours; and when, as in all the supremely tragic moments, the whirlwind of passion begets its own "temperance and smoothness" one feels that this is not due to any consciously restraining art but to the inherent nature of passion itself, made simple and direct by its own intensity.

Nothing controlled his imagination but those technical necessities of the theatre itself in which he was both a practised master and a daring experimenter; and it is clear to-day from the way his plays are cut that no age but his own, and no audiences but the audiences he must have had, would have endured the licences he allowed himself. His imagination, his fancy, his flickering, serpentine, convoluted wit, his towering rhetoric, were ready to burst out at any moment and on all occasions; and over the tumultuous chaos of the hoarse, rasping, bewildering performance whereof Providence itself is the stage-manager he was for ever flinging, from an inexhaustible fount within himself, the seductive music of a unifying orchestration. How well one comes to know the peculiar Shakespearean literary devices, some absolute in their perfection, like his passion for broken tags from old songs, old saws, old proverbs, old Mother-Goose oracles and nursery-rhymes, introduced when the emotional tension is so extreme that only wild, mad, babbled nonsense could give it its true expression, but others most curiously confusing, like the extravagant fantasies and punning fribbles of his early comedies, and the tortuous intellectual convolutions of his later romantic melodramas.

These latter are indeed so packed with image upon image and thought upon thought that they make Henry James and Meredith seem simple and obvious in comparison. And as for the themes of his plays, he snatched at them from every direction; but he always gave them his own peculiar twist, his own tone and overtone.

Upon English and Roman history—known to him from our own chroniclers and from Plutarch—he played as if upon the virginals, stressing what notes he pleased and exaggerating all manner of original predilections.

What, for instance, put it into his head to make the abused Glendower into such a hero? What put it into his head to turn the heroic and learned Lollard, Sir John Oldcastle, into Sir John Falstaff?

One of his most interesting plays, from a psychological point of view, though in dramatic construction it is one of his worst, is that same farcical *Troilus and Cressida*. Here he gives vent not only to a violent reaction against his own attitude to women, but to a reaction against one of the chief poetic cults of his time. Surely this market-tavern treatment of the Homeric Greeks is a sufficient proof that he was anything but a learned and courtly aristocrat!

In an age when Chapman was translating Homer, what earthly excuse, save some savage Swiftlike laceration of his own feelings, and possibly a humorous desire to please his Welsh friends by praising their reputed ancestors, the Trojans, had he got for the wayward, mischievous, cynical, and ribald tone he took by this play?

But it is, for all that, one of the most fascinating of his works; and not only from the point of view of its personal revelation and its incorrigible pessimism. Just consider the reactionary and scandalous conservatism in that startling speech of Ulysses about class and place and degree, and observe how he carries it off!

And what man-satisfying cynicism in making Cressid

into a really flagrant whore! In no other play does he allow his curious passion for convolutions of verbal wit to carry him quite so far. He "lets himself go," as we say, with complete moral, emotional, and aesthetic irresponsibility; and few of his real lovers will begrudge him this one single sweet dark plunge into the less magnanimous, the less courageous, the less indulgent portion of his heart!

Troilus and Cressida represents, indeed, that "one touch of nature"—and we must remember that this famous line itself comes from this queer play—which "makes the whole world kin," by giving to the woman-hating, culture-hating element that exists in most men's natures, at any rate in most Englishmen's natures, a gross, cynical, stable-yard expression after its own heart!

As I have hinted, it hardly seems conceivable that it was only to please his Welsh friends—though he undoubtedly *does* hold a brief for both the Welsh and their Trojan ancestors—that he turns Achilles into a mean and spiteful ruffian, Patroclus into an effeminate minion, and Ajax into a clown.

Yes, it must have been that he had suddenly become irritated by some overweening group of young university aesthetes, with Homer for ever in their mouths; and that this singular production, championing the "sweet war-man" Hector, is his retort.

One thing is clear. We certainly shouldn't be shocked if any other dramatist had turned so savagely upon women in the portrait of Cressid; and this itself is significant.

Think of the number of women that play a dominant part in these plays; and save for Regan and Goneril, where are the wicked deceivers, the cruel intriguers, the shameless whores, the treacherous light-of-loves?

Outside a few termagants, and the desperate and heroic Lady Macbeth, and the Queen in *Cymbeline*, for one feels only sympathy for Gertrude of Denmark and poor Doll

Tearsheet, while Cleopatra is simply Cleopatra, the women in Shakespeare are undoubtedly the noblest, sweetest, wittiest, cleverest, loyalest, and most entirely lovable women in all literature.

And what does this mean? Why does he feel so tenderly for, and believe so whole-heartedly in, all the daughters of Eve?

Had he more of the woman in him than other writers? Is it a usual characteristic of a man who can idealize a youth of his own sex to the tune he does in the sonnets to feel for women like this? Is it not rather the very thing in him which I have attempted so fumblingly to hint at as the quintessence of his peculiar genius, his rooted distrust of logic and of all that is usually called philosophy?

Is it not, in fact, his "open mind" towards intimations, intuitions, and instincts, *as against reason*? In any case, his personal cult of magnanimity and courage must have enabled him to handle women rather in the spirit of Hardy than in the spirit of Strindberg. Nor was his humour of the kind—as was the humour of Rabelais and Cervantes and Sterne—that puts women at a disadvantage. His humour was composed, in almost equal parts, of poetry and wit. It was the kind of humour that lends itself to the presence of women and that goes well with women.

Doll upon Falstaff's knee feels an authentic pang of pure grief when the old reprobate has to go to the wars. Between Cordelia and the Fool there was a most tender and romantic link. His humour is indeed as closely linked with that quality in him that got him the appellation of the "gentle Shakespeare" as it is linked with the airy, wanton, village-fair tone in which he alludes to "country-matters."

And just because of this "gentleness" in its grossness, and this poetry in its realism, the Shakespearean humour lends itself, above all other kinds, to the presence of tragedy. This is not the case with Rabelais' humour. Think of the death of the noble Badebec, the mother of Pantagruel! Had Shakespeare had the handling of that great scene there would have been, I admit, less unequalled unction of homely gusto over the giant's lusty progeny, but there would have been something else—a touch of we all know what—in the good old drinker's eulogy on his lost lady!

But after all has been said of the nearness of this stirrup-cup humour to this mounting tragedy—which is only a return to the cosmic-comic goat-song at the beginning of the theatric art—it remains that what overwhelms all readers of Shakespeare, what drugs us into such beatitude, what magics us and medicines us into such oblivious felicity, what carries us away to such a tune that all criticism seems a pimping and paltry irrelevance, is his poetry itself—the cumulative music of the style in which he writes. The style of Shakespeare is indeed one of the three—or is it seven?—artistic wonders of the world.

And you can, with easy infallibility, discriminate it from the other Elizabethans. I don't say it is always better than these others. It is sometimes worse. But it's always different and recognizable. There's a certain rending, blood-stained, shivering cry in some of Marlowe's lines that he never reaches. There's a majestic and rolling reverberation, like the echoes of celestial thunderbolts on satanic shields, in some of Milton's lines that he never reaches. There's a melting absorption of syllabic sound into ecstasies of taste and touch and scent, into subtle intimacies of atmosphere, in some of the poems of Keats that he never reaches.

But for headlong plunges into the wild heart of things, for airy swallow-flights over the magical surface of things, for the fusing and the melting together of image with image, emotion with emotion, memory with memory, till the beat of life's wings, the pulse of reality's blood, the shock of all that our race's nerves have ever recorded, catches us up and whirls us away, there is nothing in literature like Shakespeare at his best!

And he can work his charm with the fewest of simple words:

> *In such a night*
> *Stood Dido with a willow in her hand,*
> *Upon the wild sea-banks, and waft her love*
> *To come again to Carthage:*

or with a veritable hurricane and tempest of piled-up words, words drowning and swallowing each other in the fury of their onset:

> *Wilt thou upon the high and giddy mast*
> *Seal up the ship-boy's eyes and rock his brains*
> *In cradle of the rude imperious surge*
> *And in the visitation of the winds*
> *Who take the ruffian billows by the top*
> *Curling their monstrous heads and hanging them*
> *With deafening clamours in the slippery clouds,*
> *That with the hurly death itself awakes?*

No poet can be simpler, or more direct; no poet can be more elaborate and more indirect. Simile follows simile like hand-clasped nymphs on the dancing-lawns of the dawn.

Metaphor follows metaphor like wind-spirits melting into fire-spirits on the sunken shore-reefs of the sunset. The scattered armouries tossed on the tidal-waves of his language, the towering avalanches of his vocalization of mortal feelings, impressions, thoughts, imaginations, are constantly being intermitted by brief, laconic, pregnant sentences that fall to the rainy earth like shot birds.

And the supreme use to which we can put this multitudinous, many-sounding ocean of feeling, this mounting, sinking, ebbing, flowing, racing, lingering river of human passion, is to have sailed on it, and swum in it, and drifted with it so long, that at every crisis in our life there shall reach our ears, with a living smack of that deep tide, a rich Shakespearean echo, consonant with, or at least contiguous to, the perilous stuff of our particular occasion.

And it is the rounded firmament of the ultimate doubt, it is the huge convexity of the overhanging "perhaps," that gives to the radiant-dark secularity of the Shakespearean stage its heart-strung poignance. Courage, magnanimity, and an open mind towards a dark sky—such is the burden of this mighty fog-horn from the coasts of Albion, while the hurricanes "drench the steeples," and "night's black agents to their preys do rouse."

Were some young person to ask you, reader, from which of all Shakespeare's plays can we get the rarest essence of his genius, which one would you name?

I suppose most people would at once say *Hamlet*, but for myself I should say *King Lear*.

Hamlet is a subjective tragedy, the whole poignance of which—with Ophelia as its victim—depends on the character of the protagonist. For this very reason it is the play towards which our disillusioned modern intellects instinctively turn, finding in it their anger, their bitterness, their sardonic humour, their cynical futility, their sophisticated pessimism, their bursts of "miching mallecho," their sick weariness of the whole game of living.

How natural, how inevitable, on such lips sound these wild and whistling words, these tags and snatches of tormented pride, these mocking bubbles of the heart's blood-stained foam!

HAMLET:
> *Why let the stricken deer go weep,*
> *The hart ungalled play;*
> *For some must watch, while some must sleep:*
> *So runs the world away.*

Would not this, sir, and a forest of feathers, if the rest of
my fortunes Turn Turk with me, with two Provincial roses
on my razed shoes, get me a fellowship in a cry of players,
sir?

HORATIO: Half a share.
HAMLET: A whole one, I.
    For thou dost know, O Damon dear
    This realm dismantled was
    Of Jove himself; and now reigns here
    A very, very—pajock.

But in *King Lear* we are swept away, out of our private,
self-lacerating, procrastinating, antisocial morbidities, into
the vast pity and terror of the whole world's grief, the whole
world's wrongs.

What a gloss upon the wily Ulysses' praise of "degree" in
this chance-ruled life are the bed-rock commentaries upon
the "pathos of difference" between man and man in *Lear*!

Ha! Here's three on's are sophisticated; thou art the thing
itself; unaccommodated man is no more but such a poor,
bare, forked animal as thou art. Off, off, you lendings!

I cannot feel that for the depths of tragic human emotion
anything in literature can touch certain passages in *Lear*,
except perhaps that unbearable scene in Dostoievsky's *Idiot*
when the two talk together over the body of Nastasia, or that
other occasion in his *Possessed* when Shatov is lured away to
be murdered just as his returned wife is in the pains of
childbirth.

CORDELIA: How does my royal lord? How fares your majesty?
LEAR: You do me wrong to take me out o' the grave;
Thou art a soul in bliss; but I am bound
Upon a wheel of fire, that mine own tears
Do scald like molten lead.

And even Homer, when Odysseus is known by his dog
and his nurse, and even Hardy, when Tess and Angel are
together at the last in that shuttered room, do not approach,
no! not by a fathom of salt tears, the scene where father and
daughter are led away to prison.

> CORDELIA: We are not the first
> Who, with best meaning, have incurred the worst.
>
> .   .   .   .   .
>
> Shall we not see these daughters and these sisters?
> LEAR: No, no, no, no! Come, let's away to prison;
> We two alone will sing like birds i' the cage:
> When thou dost ask me blessing I'll kneel down,
> And ask of thee forgiveness; so we'll live,
> And pray, and sing, and tell old tales, and laugh
> At gilded butterflies, and hear poor rogues
> Talk of court news; and we'll talk with them too,
> Who loses and who wins; who's in, who's out;
> And take upon's the mystery of things,
> As if we were God's spies, and we'll wear out,
> In a wall'd prison, packs and sets of great ones
> That ebb and flow by the moon.
> EDMOND: Take them away.
> LEAR: Upon such sacrifices, my Cordelia,
> The gods themselves throw incense.—Have I caught thee?
> He that parts us shall bring a brand from heaven,
> And fire us hence like foxes. Wipe thine eyes;
> The goujeres shall devour them, flesh and fell,
> Ere they shall make us weep; we'll see 'em starve first.
> Come.

No, there has never been, and it is hard to believe that
there ever will be, a mimic representation of human life
equal to the plays of Shakespeare. To get an effect similar to
the effect of reading this volume you would have, in some
impossible way, to roll together all the great novelists of the
world; and *then* you wouldn't get it, because over this tossing

sea of kings and clowns and warriors and honeysuckle rogues and Bedlam fools and lovely women the very firmament seems to melt in such a starry ether of magical poetry that all this pathos and passion, nay! all these conspiracies and crimes, seem played out to the music of the spheres for the delight of the "young-eyed cherubims."

And since courage and magnanimity, tossing on a "sea of troubles," touched by a poetry that "redeems all sorrows," and at the last "rounded by a sleep," is Shakespeare's reaction to our human predicament, it is natural enough that his genius should gather itself together in its most inspired force in the attempt to portray the opposite of courage, the opposite of magnanimity: and thus we get those two overpowering figures, Falstaff, the philosopher of irresistible and bewitching cowardice, and Iago, the incarnation of fathomless malignity.

It is curious to note, in spite of the sonnets, how deep what we now-a-days call sex-normality goes with Shakespeare. When you come to consider his whole conception of these opposites to courage and magnanimity you touch, not some morbid and perverted twist of the nerves as with so many writers, but a universal weakness, a universal wickedness.

To the former he is tender, with an infinity of humorous relish for an old sensualist's incorrigible wit; but as we remember that, "I know thee not, old man; fall to thy prayers!" he cannot exactly be accused of condoning such a temper.

And in Iago's case it is the same. That "motiveless malignity" in him, noted by Coleridge, is no abnormal neurosis. Is it not what, if we were honest—like "honest, honest Iago"! we would have to confess—we all, I say *all*— in some degree and measure, share?

I would go so far as to suggest that in a sublimated form it is what some of our most characteristic modern writers are tempted to betray.

"I will set down the pegs that make this music, as honest as I am." Does not a stir, a motion, a flicker, of this *revenge upon life* by undermining the sweet raptures of its happy innocents, give the devil's own tone now and again to the words of our mouths and the meditations of our hearts?

Yes, we all have "the Iago" in us, as when we say: "Drown thyself? Drown cats and blind puppies. Put money in thy purse"; just as we all have "the Hamlet" in us, when the whole visible world seems to us a "pestilent congregation of vapours."

But the best of all instances of what I might call Shakespeare's *abnormal normality*, the thing in him that made him such a perfect medium for "all weakness that impairs, all griefs that bow," is his treatment of lust.

He dealt with this aspect of universal human nature very early in his life. In *Venus and Adonis* we have a woman's lust; in *The Rape of Lucrece* a man's; while one of the most effective of his sonnets is entirely devoted to the thing's normal psycho-physiological accompaniments.

And how does he deal with it? Exactly as he does later with jealousy, with ambition, with revenge, with cowardice. He gives it its full reach of seductive, eloquent, irresistible *apologia*, and then, coming full circle with a "dying fall" of poetic realism, he indicates the character of the mortal "wisdom" that follows such mortal "excess."

It seems to me that without having recourse to anything outside the plays themselves we can form a pretty adequate idea of Shakespeare's personality. There are certain characters among the rest that seem to have the very trick and favour of their begetter about them, so exquisitely, so delicately, and with such a seductive and beguiling sympathy are they described.

The man must surely have had something in him of the melancholy Jacques, of the incorrigible Mercutio, of the desperate Timon, of the betrayed Troilus, of the "mad"

Hamlet, of the detached and remote Prospero. He must have been swayed by his passions, precisely as his "good Horatio" and his upright Brutus were *never* swayed; and he must have suffered from the "rack of this tough world" exactly as the weakest and most unphilosophic among us suffer.

Yes, among the great writers of the world, for all his love of kings and warriors and fair women, none but Gogol and Dickens give you such a sense of reverence for that "quintessence of dust," unaccommodated man, just as he is, with all his faults thick upon his head.

Dead or alive it is the same. "Beat not the bones of the buried; when he breathed he was a man."

Is there not a curious comfort after listening to the well-constituted preachers and the bragging optimists and the inviolable stoics to turn to so different a voice?

"With a heart of furious fancies" he had followed, if ever man had, those fatal enchantments of beauty and wit that are to be found, in this world, as Walter Pater says, "in small measure or not at all"; and it is because he is the voice of the reckless and the passionate rather than of the wise and the prudent, the poet of lovers rather than of philosophers, that he is nearer to the heart of humanity than any other.

"Think of living!" says the greatest of our modern sages; but when in less lucky quarters we catch the sigh, "I wish I were dead!" is there no significance in recognizing this as a *natural wish* of Shakespeare's?

> Tired with all these, for restful death I cry,
>   As to behold desert a beggar born,
> And needy nothing trimm'd in jollity,
> And purest faith unhappily forsworn.
> And gilded honour shamefully misplac'd,
> And maiden virtue rudely strumpated,
> And right perfection wrongfully disgraced,

WILLIAM SHAKESPEARE

(From the tomb bust, Stratford on Avon)

And strength by limping sway disabled,
And art made tongue-tied by authority,
And folly—doctor-like—controlling skill,
And simple truth miscalled simplicity,
And captive good attending captain ill;
   Tir'd with all these, from these would I be gone,
   Save that, to die, I leave my love alone.

Milton

ONE wonders how many people there are who have it in them to be more thrilled by the poetry of Milton than by any other poetry in our language, but who for one reason and another have never made any real effort to do him justice?

I fancy there are more sensitive and receptive persons in this condition—a condition of *accidental* ignorance—than any one would believe possible; and I fancy, too, that the chief cause why such people dodge, avoid, and instinctively sheer off any attempt to read for pure pleasure poems that I suppose most of them were forced into some acquaintance with at school, is an absurdly simple one, the fact that they link his genius with everything that has been most unpleasant to them in the Christian religion.

This feeling would not apply so much to Catholics; though I dare say *they* are tempted to regard the cruder elements of Milton's creed as a perfect example of the disastrous effect of heresy upon a noble mind.

Certainly it is astonishing what violent and scandalous lapses from any discreet tolerance of his orthodox opponents this great "combustible" heretic allows himself!

Not only Roman Catholics but every brand of traditionalist, ritualist, sacramentalist, prelatist, and sacerdotalist must feel in every line of Milton's work that they touch here their arch-enemy! And he *is* their arch-enemy. But on the other hand he is certainly no favourite of rationalists. His position would be indeed rather like that of Spinoza, save that an unfortunate vein of gross materialism betrayed him now and then into a grotesque anthropomorphism.

But I suppose there are few congenital haters of ritualism in religion who have not been entertained by the ferocious iconoclasm of Milton's limbo. It is not a retort in kind to Dante's treatment of heretics. It shows more easy-going contempt than inquisitorial mercilessness. But I will quote the passage, for it really is extraordinarily effective; and the desolate rondure and shivering convexity which he imagines to exist *at the back of the stellar world* is a wonderful "locale" for a limbo of this sort. In this and in all future quotations I will use the Oxford edition taken from the old texts so that the reader can get the poet's own particular spelling.

> *All th' unaccomplisht works of Natures hand,*
> *Abortive, monstrous, or unkindly mixt,*
> *Dissolv'd on earth, fleet hither, and in vain,*
> *Till final dissolution, wander here,*
>
> .   .   .   .   .
>
> *Embryos, and Idiots, Eremits and Friers*
> *White, Black and Grey, with all thir trumperie.*
> *Here Pilgrims roam, that stray'd so farr to seek*
> *In Golgotha him dead, who lives in Heav'n;*
> *And they who to be sure of Paradise*
> *Dying put on the weeds of Dominic,*
> *Or in Franciscan think to pass disguis'd;*
>
> .   .   .   .   .
>
> *And now Saint Peter at Heav'ns Wicket seems*
> *To wait them with his keys, and now at foot*
> *Of Heav'ns ascent they l'ft thir feet, when loe*
> *A violent cross wind from either Coast*
> *Blows them transverse ten thousand leagues awry*

Into the devious Air; then might ye see
Cowles, Hoods and Habits with their wearers tost
And fluttered into Raggs, then Reliques, Beads,
Indulgences, Dispenses, Pardons, Bulls,
The sport of Winds: all these upwhirld aloft
Fly o're the backside of the World——

But it is undoubtedly because the word "Milton" instead of reminding us, as perhaps it ought, of his lovely early poems, or even of his "Titan angels, Gabriel, Abdiel," calls up a harsh and unsympathetic theology which it is distressing to think our ancestors accepted, that so many of us sheer off. It is almost as if there were some sinister kind of bruise at the back of our inherited consciousness upon which the particular tone he adopts seems to press with painful severity.

All this may be, and I think in a large measure it is, unfair to him. The "sublime notion and high mystery" of the "sun-clad" Chastity he praises in *Comus* is much more a Platonic than a Puritan attribute, and the infant Christ-God of the "Nativity Hymn" is celebrated in a mythological rather than a scriptural manner. But the fact remains that what our humanity, our civilization, our life has suffered, both in Great Britain and in the United States, from puritanism has left such a deep hurt, that, as the paramount puritan poet, Milton pays the penalty.

Devoted readers of Milton, however, cannot, it is clear, dismiss the whole subject of his religion with the weary sigh with which we dismiss the cruder and more repulsive aspects of the creed of our Protestant ancestors. An intelligence as powerful, a genius as commanding as his, must, we feel, have had some inner light to live by, true enough, real enough, inspired enough to feed his deeper soul, and not as incommunicable to us, or as totally unacceptable by us, in our present perplexities, as are those grosser aspects of the puritan creed.

One thing stands out clearly enough. Both Milton's personal temperament—something proud, cold, and "translunar" in the noblest part of his nature—and his indignant vision of the evil in the world, militated against his stressing that tender love of the Father of which Jesus speaks. Nor did the orthodox doctrines of the Incarnation and Redemption mean very much to him. He was, to speak plainly, what Panurge would call "a resolute formal Heretic, a rooted and combustible Heretic."

But though his solitary pride and his ungullible recognition of the prosperity of evil rendered him cold to the doctrine of God's fatherly love, he did, one feels, from the very bottom of his soul *believe in God*. But the God he believed in—and held by heroically to the very last—was never the God of Jesus, nor of Paul, nor of John. He was the God of Milton; and in many respects resembles Allah rather than Jehovah. Where, however, he differs from both Allah and Jehovah is that while remaining a "God of Hosts," never quite forgetful of his lonely champions in a world given over to Baal and Dagon, he is also the great ultimate Spirit of Life, the *Creator Spiritus*, the nameless, mysterious eternal *Tao* behind the whole astronomical universe.

But as with many another solitary "God-fearing" sage, this high, cold, heroic, inhuman faith in the First Cause is not a faith calculated to be popular with normal men and women.

Another obstacle, if I am not mistaken, to the pure pleasure that *can* be derived from his poetry springs from its inherent nature, from the subtle and recondite character of the particular harmonies he creates. But what poetry can be called superior to Milton's at his best? Simply as a poetical artist, overcoming in a way that seems as miraculous as it is beyond all imitation, the obstinate resistance of words, his only rivals in our tongue are Keats and Shake-speare.

When it comes to descriptions of nature, to what Matthew Arnold so aptly calls *natural magic*, Keats is at the top of all. Even Shakespeare cannot equal him. There is a rich vegetative intricately flowing life-sap in the slow cadences of his music. The evening rains soften his rhymes and his words melt into the dew of the morning. They cease to be words. They become odours and touches and tastes. They become presences felt through the pores of the skin and upon the palate of the mouth. The flowing of his syllables conveys the very life of green-growing things, the hush, the in-held breath, the atmosphere around them, the ineffable bloom upon them, the long patience of their "cool-rooted" vigils.

The quivering expectancies of his forest trees, "branch-charmed by the earnest stars," the "embalméd darkness" of his "verdurous glooms" hold a magic that even Shake-speare cannot invoke.

Passages like the latter's

> *O Proserpina!*
> *For the flowers now that frighted thou let'st fall*
> *From Dis's wagon! daffodils*
> *That come before the swallow dares, and take*
> *The winds of March with beauty;—*

have a lighter, airier, freer, more dramatic, more balladlike freshness, but they are surpassed by the younger poet's power of communicating to us what the shy indwelling genius of each of these living things *actually feels itself* in its leafy seclusion as the wandering airs caress its sap-warmed growth. The great dramatist, in his reckless and arbitrary inspirations and his wanton Elizabethan fantasy, will fling off his classical allusions and snatch his easy human metaphors and then must needs on with the passions of his tale; and thus his

>—*violets dim*
>*But sweeter than the lids of Juno's eyes*
>*Or Cytherea's breath; pale primroses*
>*That die unmarried, ere they can behold*
>*Bright Phoebus in his strength, a malady*
>*Most incident to maids;*

do not measure up, lovely as they are, to the other's

>*Fast-fading violets, covered-up in leaves.*

For the particular feelings evoked in us by winter and spring Shakespeare I admit comes very near to him, but for the peculiar sensations of autumn, for that rich-swooning indescribable hush, for instance, when

>—*in a wailful choir the small gnats mourn*
>*Among the river sallows, borne aloft*
>*Or sinking as the light wind lives or dies.*

I think Keats leaves him some distance behind.

But this kind of earth-brooding realism, this rare sensitivity to "natural magic" is not the only form great poetry can take; and Milton in his own special sphere is as unsurpassed as Shakespeare and Keats in theirs.

And what is his special sphere? Alas! it is only in the first two books of *Paradise Lost* that we learn what it is; and here all poets except Homer take a second place. It is the invention of what you can only call *cosmic scenery*, and it is the peopling of these huge and monstrous regions with superhuman presences, awe-inspiring and terrific as their boundless background. Michelangelo had something of this power. It is a totally different thing from what Dante did. It requires a *larger* imagination than Dante's but a much less intellectual one, and apparently one with less power of being protracted and drawn out.

But over this latter point one hesitates! Dante certainly *seems* to have more unwearied creative intensity, as he certainly has more architectural realism; but, after all, Dante's invention lacks the enormous horizons of Milton's, and his more philosophical scholasticism saved him from the appalling handicap of Milton's anthropomorphic theology. On the other hand the *terza rima* of the Italian could never in its inherent nature carry its rider across the "wasteful deep" with those cumulative soarings and sinkings, those condor-winged hoverings and towerings of the Miltonic Pegasus.

Nor had Dante—though he had a good deal—as much power of conjuring up, by the thaumaturgic *names* of mythic-historic persons and places, such vistas of old romance as Milton possessed.

Let us cling to the wings of Lucifer in two of his flights—

> *—som times*
> *He scours the right hand coast, som times the left,*
> *Now shaves with level wing the Deep, then soares*
> *Up to the fiery concave touring high.*
> *As when farr off at Sea a Fleet descri'd*
> *Hangs in the Clouds, by Æquinoctial Winds*
> *Close sailing from Bengala, or the Iles*
> *Of Ternate and Tidore, whence Merchants bring*
> *This spicie drugs; they on the trading Flood*
> *Through the wide Ethiopian to the Cape*
> *Ply stemming nightly toward the Pole——* .
>
> .   .   .   .   .
>
> *—all unawares*
> *Fluttring his pennons vain plumb down he drops*
> *Ten thousand fadom deep, and to this hour*

Down had been falling, had not by ill chance
The strong rebuff of som tumultuous cloud
Instinct with Fire and Nitre hurried him
As many miles aloft; that furie stay'd
Quencht in a Boggie Syrtis, neither Sea,
Nor good dry Land; nigh foundered on he fares,
Treading the crude consistence, half on foot,
Half flying: behoves him now both Oare and Saile.

The truth is, Milton's technique is such that although there is never the least obscurity in what he writes or any doubt about his meaning, the secret of his style is so recondite, so remote, so unusual that it requires a different ear from that which most of us possess before its supreme quality can have justice done to it.

This supreme quality lies undoubtedly in a far-reaching complicated harmony, which displays itself to fullest advantage in long organ diapasons and vast aerial flights, but which *can* concentrate itself with surprising artfulness in short lines and short poems.

No poet who has ever lived, not Homer or Dante or any other, has such genius for suggesting unlimited horizons, horizons either in space or in time; and the curious thing is that he can create the *effect* of such unlimited horizons in what you might call the reverberating echoes of lines that in themselves are brief, concise, laconic. This is an inspired trick of his, and one that must always return upon the ear of a poetic connoisseur with a fresh and startling thrill. He changes his style consciously and deliberately as he grows older; and it is curious to note what elements of harmony are preserved from beginning to end and what are deliberately dropped.

Let me set down a specimen of his earliest religio-mythological poetry and of his latest.

From the "Nativity Hymn":

> *Such Musick (as 'tis said)*
> *Before was never made,*
> *   But when of old the sons of morning sung,*
> *While the Creator Great*
> *His constellations set*
> *   And the well-ballanc't world on hinges hung,*
> *And cast the dark foundations deep,*
> *And bid the weltring waves their oozy channel keep.*

From *Samson Agonistes:*

> *But he though blind of sight,*
> *Despis'd, and thought extinguish't quite,*
> *With inward eyes illuminated*
> *His fierie vertue rouz'd*
> *From under ashes into sudden flame*
> *And as an ev'ning Dragon came*
> *Assailant on the perched roosts,*
> *And nests in order rang'd*
> *Of tame villatic Fowl; but as an Eagle*
> *His cloudless thunder bolted on thir heads.*
> *So vertue giv'n for lost,*
> *Deprest, and overthrown, as seem'd*
> *Like that self-begott'n bird*
> *In the Arabian woods embost,*
> *That no second knows nor third,*
> *And lay e're while a Holocaust*
> *From out her ashie womb now teem'd*
> *Revives, reflourishes, then vigorous most*
> *   When most unactive deem'd,*
> *   And though her body die, her fame survives*
> *   A secular bird ages of lives.*

Since both these fragments contain rhyme and alliteration
and assonance, it is interesting to note how, with the years

of furious controversy intervening between them, the sound of their rhythm differs.

In both cases, and this alone suggests some special musical quality in them, you find your lips instinctively moving as you read; but this *silent reading aloud* is not the same. The first fragment has such an undulating, swinging, reef-bell rhythm that it calls for a monotonous chanting intonation, whereas the other lines are so full of artful turns and abrupt condensations of dramatic intensity, such as "cloudless thunder bolted on their heads," that it is hard not to imagine yourself some great Hebraic herald with the star of David upon your tabard as you declaim them.

But apart from the style of his poems there is something about Milton's dominant tone that is so lonely, so defiant, so contemptuous of common opinion, so self-absorbed and self-sufficing, that the reader has always to advance a considerable distance to meet him; whereas in the case of Shakespeare and Keats, *they*, so to speak, advance that same distance towards their reader.

Milton's ego is constantly narrowing, hardening, and intensifying itself *against* fate or chance or God or Satan or the crowd or against life or against death; while Keats and Shakespeare are constantly resolving themselves into all these things and many more, losing their identities in what they contemplate, becoming what they write of, merging themselves in the huge pluralism of the world.

Milton stands away from humanity like some great pharos-tower mocking the huge sea with its search-light, whereas Keats and Shakespeare seem to slip out of the circle of all personal consciousness and to enjoy—as many of us *can* at various moments—a large diffusion of their individual being in response to the common glamour, the common romance, the common tragedy of life.

Milton's poetry tends when it is most characteristic to monumentalize itself into certain great negative gestures;

the gestures for example of some planetary hero-god, devil, or poet—defying legions of stupid, contemptible, but implacable foes! Shakespeare's poetry on the contrary resembles the careless commentary of some vast impersonal being, brooding on the ways of a world too pitiful to be damned, and too mad and wicked to be saved.

And unless we can identify ourself with the negative heroism of the Miltonic superman it is natural that we should find the many-sounding blessings and cursings of Shakespeare's multitudinous chorus easier to appropriate and to absorb.

Milton's poetry divides itself, as his life did, into his thoughts, feelings, and ideals *before* Cromwell's death, and his thoughts, feelings, and ideals *after* Cromwell's death.

Before the Civil War he was a late Elizabethan, a Platonic reformer, a Spenserian puritan, full of lyrical hope for the world. After the Civil War he was the blind prophet of a lost cause, plunged in despair about the world, with nothing left but his proud individual conscience, his unconquerable faith in a God made after his own image, and his undefeated will.

The whole process was a process of tragic stiffening, of tragic hardening, of tragic narrowing-down. In his earlier poems his interest radiates outwards in a passionate student's response to the loveliness of nature, to the reformation of abuses, to pride in England as the protagonist of liberty, to the beauty of Diana-like girls and the culture of charming Rousseauish women.

During the Civil War and the Commonwealth he poured forth his savage hatred of secular and religious tyrants, his unbounded hopes for his country's greatness, his indignant revolt against legal customs that cripple the freedom of domestic happiness. His prose is more savage and chaotic than his poetry. He defends divorce. He defends freedom of thought and speech. He passionately defends the regicides.

But the Milton of the Restoration, when all he had struggled for was defeated, and when worldly and cynical wits were clipping the locks of his Samson-England and loosening the limbs of his heroic Muse, is the Milton we know best, the Milton whose solitary and austere grandeur repels as much as it attracts, the Milton towards whom it is *we* who have to advance like Adam to meet Raphael, if we are to enter the ensorcerized terrain of his "guarded mount."

Emotionally his life grew more and more tragic, though steadily calmer, steadily more stoical and resigned, as it advanced to its close.

And poetically it grew grander and sterner and always less compromising, until it culminated in the towering Phoenix-flight of the end of *Samson Agonistes*. It gives one a strange feeling to turn back to "L'Allegro" and "Il Penseroso" after following him to the end. These gay, "richly-dight," dainty fancies are like the flutings of some young Enceladus before the gods throw a mountain upon his head. "Doric delicacy," as the wise Provost of Eton said, could scarcely go further; but I feel confident that lovers of the rarer and scarcer elements in poetry will always prefer *Comus* and *Lycidas*. *Comus* is like an impassioned nocturne upon the two Eleusinian secrets that in his youth interested him most; the "high mystery" of chastity and the "high mystery" of music.

There are cadencies in this poem, sounds melting into translunar silence, and silence precipitating itself into quicksilver drops of sound, that might almost be said, if you allowed the wings of Psyche to embrace the wings of Eros, to reach the pure plenilune of the Platonic vision. Anticipations of Shelley blend here with echoes of Spenser; but the fingers on the lute-strings of this Olympian Israfel are firmer, stronger, more deft and definite in their touch, than either of those other Platonists.

> *At which I ceas't, and listened them a while,*
> *Till an unusuall stop of sudden silence*
> *Gave respit to the drowsie frighted steeds*
> *That draw the litter of close-curtained sleep.*
> *At last a soft and solemn breathing sound*
> *Rose like a steam of rich distill'd Perfumes*
> *And stole upon the Air, that even Silence*
> *Was took ere she was 'ware, and wist't she might*
> *Deny her nature, and be never more*
> *Still to be so displac't. I was all eare,*
> *And took in strains that might create a soul*
> *Under the ribs of Death—*

But if *Comus* reaches forward and backward in its bewitched vistas of moonlit Platonism to Shelley and Spenser there are fairylike touches that suggest Shakespeare's *Tempest* in lines like these

> *—els O Theevish Night*
> *Why shouldst thou, but for som fellonious end,*
> *In thy dark lantern thus close up the Stars,*
> *That nature hung in Heav'n, and filled their lamps*
> *With everlasting oil, to give due light*
> *To the misled and lonely traveller?*
>
> .   .   .   .   .
>
> *What might this be? A thousand fantasies*
> *Begin to throng into my memory*
> *Of calling shapes, and beckning shadows dire,*
> *And airy tongues that syllable mens names*
> *On Sands, and Shoars, and desert Wildernesses.*

Every great poet suffers from certain congenital defects, which if not the fatal and inevitable "defects of his quality" are deep parts of his inherent character.

The worst defect, to my mind, in Milton is a certain incurable *materialism*. I use this word deliberately rather than the word "realism"; because both Shakespeare and Keats are extremely "realistic" without ever being in the remotest degree "materialistic."

But Milton is just that; and not seldom! It is a certain *heaviness* in the wings of his imagination, that, while it serves him to good purpose in his huge planetary flights, tends sometimes to brush away some impalpable petal-dust from the "purfléd" parterres of his Muse's pleasance.

Indeed, so heavily do these great wings flap sometimes among the flower-beds of his Arcadia that the frail *genii loci* are "with sighing sent" to more secluded retreats. In the beautiful lines I have just quoted, for instance, there lurks, in spite of their Shakespearean audacity, a touch of this cruder handling. Let us put it plainly. It is, in fact, a tendency to fall plumb down into the grotesquely *prosaic*; and thus it is something totally different from those startlingly realistic words in Keats and Shakespeare which only enhance the poetical effect.

Consider the word "clammy," used by Keats in the "Ode to Autumn":

"For summer has o'er-brimmed their clammy calls." How perfectly in harmony with the spirit of the hot misty, wistfully languorous weather he is describing is that allusion to the wax of the honeycomb!

But though Milton's "dark-lantern" has a Shakespearean ring, I confess to relucting at the introduction of oil-lamps into the firmament. The word "everlasting" may have a certain biblical congruity with the word "oil," but surely the homely Shakespearean, "There's husbandry in Heaven: their candles are all out!" suggests those flickering points of stellar light more appropriately.

And I cannot resist the same sort of feeling about that expression "gay wardrobe" applied to the flowers in

"Lycidas"; and worse even than that—at least to my Celtic taste—is the passage describing the frugivorous feast offered by Eve to the angel in Eden, when the poet hastens to remind us that there was no danger of such a banquet growing "cold."

It is, I think, always in foreground descriptions that this curious element of prosaic materialism in Milton's fancy emerges. The moment his landscape broadens and expands, the wings of his imagination gather power. His spirit must have been for ever craving wider horizons than ordinary life gave him; and this very clumsiness may have sprung from this. Shakespeare's greater swiftness of imagery and bolder rush of metaphor carry off a good deal that wouldn't bear the captious scrutiny of lumbering and literal pedantry and it is true that Milton's incomparable music often serves him the same good turn; but even the music of such a line as "a thousand liveried angels lackey her," in the great passage in praise of chastity, only *just* saves us from this prosaic grotesqueness. The same quaint emphasis upon well-attired attendants—and even there I find it obnoxious —occurs in the "Nativity Hymn" in the passage about the bright-harnessed angels "in order serviceable."

Lovely as his praise of chastity in *Comus* is, it is, I think, not uncharacteristic of the heroic belligerency of his proud spirit that the *negative* side of the great duality should be emphasized, and that it should be rather the defeat of evil than the triumph of good that rings out in grandest blast.

> *But evil on itself shall back recoil*
> *And mix no more with goodness, when at last*
> *Gather'd like scum, and settled to itself*
> *It shall be in eternal restless change*
> *Self-fed and self-consum'd, if this fail*
> *The pillar'd firmament is rottenness*
> *And earths base built on stubble——*

JOHN MILTON

But it is in "Lycidas" where Milton is at his very best; and I shall have many sympathizers when I call this poem the loveliest in our language. Nor is its perfection—unequalled by any single ode of Keats or by any single passage in Shakespeare—made less by the formidable outburst of wrath against the unworthy shepherds of the people.

And how curious to note that the finest rendering of one of the most characteristic marvels of our rocky coasts—the whirling revolutions of sea-gull flights round the precipitate cliffs, should appear in this most *unnaturalistic* of scholars, whom even the city-bred lexicographer scolds for his lack of observation. I refer to the lines;

> *And questioned every gust of rugged wings*
> *That blows from off each beaked promontory——*

for this is surely as good—and in *their* special province, too—as any "realism" of Keats or Shakespeare. "Lycidas" is so drenched in the magic of the ancient poets that for those among us who are ignorant of Greek and Latin it comes miraculously near to being an *adequate substitute* for the classics, seducing us with the very accents of those siren tongues!

For inspired skill in conveying the evasive nuances of the fond, wistful, and yet even faintly playful "second thoughts" with which we soothe our sorrow after a death that touches us but doesn't touch too nearly, this poem is perfect. It conveys every lightest sigh and every long, long thought, and every shift of mood and every wayward fancy, under such a loss.

And it does this in so dulcet-delicate a way that the orchestral flow of the rhythm, as if "the wizard stream" herself were carrying the bard's voice, goes on unbroken to the end.

Where were ye Nymphs when the remorseless deep
Clos'd o're the head of your lov'd Lycidas?
For neither were ye playing on the steep,
Where your old Bards, the famous Druids ly,
Nor on the shaggy top of Mona high,
Nor yet where Deva spreads her wisard stream:
Ay me, I fondly dream!
Had ye bin there—for what could that have don?
What could the Muse her self that Orpheus bore,
The Muse her self for her inchanting son
Whom Universal nature did lament,
When by the rout that made the hideous roar,
His goary visage down the stream was sent,
Down the swift Hebrus to the Lesbian shore.

Am I not justified in finding in this passage the very genius of a master grammarian; the poet's use in fact—as a painter might use perspective and anatomy—of the most exquisite technical niceties, so that every vibration of his turns of thought should be revealed?

One can see here too how down to the very depths of his being Milton's nature, his whole habit of thought, was subjective, egoistic, fastidiously antisocial!

This image of Orpheus being hounded by blustering bacchanalians is one that occurs more than once; and what a depth of dislike for his fellow creatures in their riotous moods does it display! For all his adamantine armour one detects "the lady of Christ's" in this nervous shrinking.

The truth is Milton's life was a classical tragedy, and a tragedy attuned to Apollonian music in the true Nietzschean sense. Vain is it—vain as the waftures in his own limbo—to wonder what poetry he would have written had he not been driven by fate to fight for liberty, religious, political, and personal. I doubt if it was only the war that kept him from his first projected theme, the epic upon King Arthur. War and love and the enchantments of Merlin would never altogether have satisfied him. He was a born rebel, a born reformer, an uncompromising individualist. No ideal-minded Spanish anarchist of the present hour believes more passionately than he in personal liberty, in the inevitable wickedness of kings and priests and governments.

I have confessed to my reaction against that peculiar vein in him which I have called "prosaic grotesqueness," but I am tempted to wonder whether the extraordinary effect—unlike anything else in literature—produced by the sardonic humour, ferocious wit, and colloquial inspiration of his controversial sonnets, may not be due to a hammer-blow materialism not unconnected with this offending element. And after all, there must be savage and malignant moods unsuitable to a great poem which can be used to excellent effect in the heat of controversy; moods, too, that beautifully lend themselves to what you might call the brutalities of scholarship.

The more curious of us will not have forgotten how in that fluent Latin of his which he must have written as easily as Conrad wrote English or Oscar Wilde wrote French, he twits his Continental opponent in the most bawdy and brutal vein for a harmless sexual lapse, the sort of lapse of which it would be a singular comfort to the impartial historian to be in a position to accuse *him*! And though this personal hitting below the belt is anything but civilized, it is possible that the shameless downrightness of this defect is what gives something of their engaging quality to these colloquial sonnets. But it is more than that! Milton shows in these sonnets an ear for such original musical effects, reached through such crashing discords and sledge-hammer harshnesses, that the like of it will never be heard again. Poets have with more or less success imitated the style of Shakespeare's sonnets; but to imitate Milton's is much harder; and to imitate the ones in this sardonic-belligerent vein totally impossible. They are indeed a poetic "genre" quite by themselves, and a "genre" of extraordinary potency.

The mingling of ribald abuse with Satanic pride and both these things, with a liberal Englishman's passion for self-restrained individualistic freedom, make an amalgam that leaves a unique taste in the mouth.

> *I did but prompt the age to quit their cloggs*
> *By the known rules of antient libertie,*
> *When strait a barbarous noise environs me*
> *Of owles and Cuckoes, Asses, Apes and Doggs.*
> *As when those Hinds that were transformed to Froggs*
> *Raild at Latona's twin-born progenie*
> *Which after held the Sun and Moon in fee.*
> *But this is got by casting Pearl to Hoggs;*
> *That bawle for freedom in their senceless mood,*
> *And still revolt when truth would set them free.*
> *Licence they mean when they cry libertie;*
> *For who loves that, must first be wise and good;*
> *But from that mark how far they roave we see*
> *For all this wast of wealth, and loss of blood.*

What a mystery *style* is! To *that* we are driven back again and again in reading Milton. You feel as though the very physical constitution of the man and all his little mortal habits embody themselves in the way he picks and chooses his words and balances his syllabic pauses and regressions! You feel that his custom of fencing so furiously for exercise, you feel that his tight, compact, slender, nimble, hard-fleshed figure, you feel that his delicately tended locks, his brilliant early-doomed eyes, his inability to compose at his best save in the autumnal equinox, his mania for long lonely hours of organ-playing, you feel that his very custom of smoking a pipe of tobacco to make him sleep when his passion for old books killed by his blindness no longer could out-watch Hesperus and greet great Lucifer, are all, every one of them, part of the miracle of his style!

How many tags and shreds and echoes from these sonnets keep returning upon us!

. . . . . .

Till the sad breaking of that Parlament
Broke him, as that dishonest victory
At Chœronéa, fatal to liberty
Kil'd with report that Old man eloquent. . . .

. . . . . .

The great Emathian conqueror bid spare
The house of Pindarus, when Temple and Towre
Went to the ground: And the repeated air
Of sad Electra's Poet had the power
To save th' Athenian walls from ruine bare.

. . . . . .

Men whose Life, Learning, Faith and pure intent
Would have been held in high esteem with Paul
Must now be nam'd and printed Hereticks
By shallow Edwards and Scotch what d'ye call. . . .

. . . . . .

Threat'ning to bind our soules with secular chaines:
Helpe us to save free Conscience from the paw
Of hireling wolves whose Gospell is their maw.

. . . . . .

Nor to their idle orbs doth sight appear
Of Sun or Moon or Starre throughout the year,
Or man or woman. Yet I argue not
Against heavn's hand or will, nor bate a jot

Of heart or hope; but still bear up and steer
Right onward. . . .

.   .   .   .   .

. . . Why is it harder Sirs than Gordon,
Colkitto, or Macdonnel, or Galasp?
Those rugged names to our like mouths grow sleek
That would have made Quintilian stare and gasp.
Thy age, like ours, O Soul of Sir John Cheek,
Hated not Learning wors than Toad or Asp;
When thou taught'st Cambridge, and King Edward Greek.

.   .   .   .   .

But to come to *Paradise Lost* : how many plays of Shakespeare would we give in exchange for Milton's masterpiece? How many plays to make *Paradise Lost* kick the beam?

For myself I would pile *Othello* on *Macbeth*, and *Julius Caesar* on *Othello*, and *A Winter's Tale, Cymbeline, Coriolanus, Measure for Measure, Richard II, King John, Antony and Cleopatra*, on *Julius Caesar*, and add some half a dozen more on the top of those, before the vibrating Parnassian scales would hang level!

And yet the faults, "faults," do I say? the monstrous woolsacks of error, the gigantic ash-heaps of mountainous perversions to be discovered in this heroic work, are more dumbfounding than those in any other poem of equal magnitude.

But think of the hugeness of excellence that is here to outweigh these equally huge blemishes! I would certainly say that the first Two Books, including the address to Light in the first page of the Third Book, contain what—even if you took it as a disconnected fragment—is a mass of poetry superior to anything *of the same unbroken continuity of length* in Shakespeare, or Dante, or Virgil, or Aeschylus, or in all the poetry in the world except Homer.

But with the close of the Prelude to the Third Book, with the close of the lines

> *—all mist from thence*
> *Purge and disperse, that I may see and tell*
> *Of things invisible to mortal sight——*

This unequalled continuity of supremely great poetry suffers a collapse into something so inferior that the change can be hardly endured.

From the words I have just quoted down to the words "nor from thy Father's praise disjoine," it is no longer a great poet speaking, though it is the voice of a formidable enough man.

But beginning with his sardonic description of limbo Milton recovers his mastery again and all through the Third, Fourth, Fifth, and Sixth Books remains worthy of himself, though not I think, nearly equal to what he was in those first two Books. In fact, do what we can to pretend otherwise—and many of us long to do it as ardently as we long to uphold the character of our own parents—the remaining bulk of the poem is *not* on the same level as the incomparable opening; and though the battle in heaven and the temptation and fall of Adam and Eve, and Raphael's story of the creation are characteristically Miltonic, and contain passages of intermittent splendour, the unique sublimity of those earlier pages has created a taste in us that remains unsatisfied to the end.

When Matthew Arnold declares that from start to finish in *Paradise Lost* Milton never sinks from the "grand style"—whereas Shakespeare frequently—sinks from this proud level, he must be referring to the technical flawlessness of his long-flowing rhythms. But no flawlessness in rhythm, no unflagging mastery of syllabic and paragraphic sound, can lift and sustain a subject-matter that contains in its very essence something as unreal, as unnatural, and as unlovely as the dogmatic theology he was exploiting. It was indeed this miserable misfortune of having a theological in place of a *mythological* foundation to his scheme that lowered the key upon which he pitched those first two books. Nothing that even *his* genius could do—and what he did with such material is a wonder—could conjure the living and magical sap of poignant reality into the heavy and monstrous creed beneath whose weight, like Atlas holding the globe, his genius staggered.

And the unfortunate thing was that his worst weakness as a poet—that tendency towards a grotesquely prosaic materialism—was precisely the one of all others that would best lend itself to the theology that limed his wings and hampered his flight.

Take, for instance, this description of the Son of God leaving the bosom of his Father to wage war upon Lucifer. The Son himself is now speaking:

> *"But whom thou hat'st, I hate, and can put on*
> *Thy terrors, as I put thy mildness on,*
> *Image of thee in all things; and shall soon,*
> *Arm'd with thy might, rid heav'n of these rebell'd,*
> *To thir prepar'd ill Mansion driven down*
> *To chains of Darkness and th' undying Worm."*
>
> .   .   .   .   .
>
> *So said, he o're his Sceptre bowing, rose*
> *From the right hand of Glorie where he sate.*

It is curious that so stout a Republican as Milton should make so much of God's regality as an Oriental potentate. Even in his touching sonnet upon his blindness we get the same thing: "His state is Kingly; thousands at His bidding—" And yet all the while one feels that what he really worshipped in his heart was not this "kingly" tyrant, but the great spirit "that from the first wast present . . . brooding on the vast abyss."

The truth is we need no reminder by William Blake that Milton—without knowing it—was on the side of Satan. The issue goes deeper than that; touches indeed the tragic heart of the old immemorial difference between the poetry of conquest and the poetry of the unconquerable endurance of defeat. Milton was on the side of good, which in the only world we know is ever being defeated by evil. But the theology he used implied the defeat of evil by good: and his incorrigible materialism drove him to give this defeat a palpable semblance. Thus the uttermost law of poetry and of life, namely that to nobly endure defeat is more dignified, more beautiful, than to conquer with power and acclaim, rises up in the secret heart of every reader to thwart, distort, disparage, and even render a little ridiculous, this materialistic triumph of the Son of God over the despairing heroism of his antagonist.

Milton was not so much blindly fighting for Satan against God as he was deliberately and wilfully struggling against the profoundest law in the nature of poetic beauty, namely that the heroic endurance of defeat is more moving than the most resounding victory. Compare, for instance, our poet's description of the two hosts, the host of the victorious angels and the host of the lost angels.

Of the former we read,

> *Messiah his triumphal Chariot turn'd:*
> *To meet him all his Saints, who silent stood*
> *Eye witnesses of his Almightie Acts,*
> *With Jubilie advanc'd; and as they went,*
> *Shaded with branching Palme, each order bright,*
> *Sung Triumph, and him sung Victorious King,*
> *Son, Heire, and Lord, to him Dominion giv'n,*
> *Worthiest to Reign: he celebrated rode*
> *Triumphant through mid Heav'n, into the Courts*
> *And Temple of his mightie Father Thron'd*

On high; who into Glorie him receav'd,
Where now he sits at the right hand of bliss.

But of the damned, of the devils, of the eternally defeated, of those who "cannot win," listen to the infinite wistfulness and grandeur of what he says:

Others more milde,
Retreated in a silent valley, sing
With notes Angelical to many a Harp
Thir own Heroic deeds and hapless fall
By doom of Battel; and complain that Fate
Free Vertue should enthrall to Force or Chance.
This song was partial, but the harmony
(What could it less when Spirits immortal sing?)
Suspended Hell, and took with ravishment
The thronging audience. In discourse more sweet
(For Eloquence the Soul, Song charms the Sense,)
Others apart sat on a Hill retir'd,
In thoughts more elevate, and reason'd high
Of Providence, Foreknowledge, Will, and Fate,
Fixt Fate, free will, foreknowledge absolute,
And found no end, in wandring mazes lost.

. . . . . .

And while hell becomes in this manner a much more civilized and sympathetic place than heaven, others among these devils explore the infernal scenery, and far away through that deep Cimmerian twilight we catch the long roll of the familiar Homeric waves:

—along the Banks
Of four infernal Rivers that disgorge
Into the burning Lake thir baleful streams;
Abhorred Styx the flood of deadly hate,
Sad Acheron of Sorrow, black and deep;
Cocytus, nam'd of lamentation loud

Heard on the ruful stream; fierce Phlegeton
Whose waves of torrent fire inflame with rage.
Farr off from these a slow and silent stream,
Lethe the River of Oblivion roules
Her watrie Labyrinth, whereof who drinks
Forthwith his former state and being forgets,
Forgets both joy and grief, pleasure and pain.

I think you have to be a man who like one of D. H.
Lawrence's erotic desperadoes can be idolatrously enamoured of his feminine companion and yet proudly and
austerely independent of her, to do justice to the Miltonic
Adam and Eve.

Everything in our particular generation—our undomesti-
cated sophistication, our undersexed fastidiousness, our
attraction to all the impotent and perverse sexual cults, our
fanatical feminism alternating with our sadistic misogamy—
unfits us from appreciating the simple and natural humanity of Milton's description of our first parents.

But as I read again of their dalliance, their pathetic
arguments, their quarrels, their reconciliations, I confess I
feel as much admiration and surprised wonder at the poet's
insight as I feel inability to share his moral-amorous glory-
ing in their portentous nakedness. Into his description of
the verdant background to this ill-starred pair he throws
all his rich, fanciful, sumptuous, but it must be confessed
not very magical descriptive power. Tennyson declares
that these "brooks of Eden mazily-murmuring" are his
favourite portion of the poem and though most of us will
have been too "spoilt" by the more atmospheric, the more
intimate, the more interpretative imagination of Keats and
Shakespeare to share this opinion, we must admit that the
poet's voluptuous picture of the Garden, with its rich
Poussin-like formality and its roses "without thorns," is
more poetical than anything he puts into his Archangel's

mouth about the creation of the world. We have, I feel, a real grievance against him that he did not invoke more of his grandest inspiration in regard to these creation passages. Personally, I would have relucted most of all at the use of the *Golden Compasses* he speaks of, regarding them as a grotesque, hand-to-mouth excuse to escape the effort of spreading his eagle-wings and plunging again, as he did for Satan's sake, into

> *—the vast immeasurable Abyss*
> *Outrageous as a Sea, dark, wasteful, wilde,*
> *Up from the bottom turn'd by furious windes*
> *And surging waves, as Mountains to assault*
> *Heav'ns highth, and with the Center mix the Pole,*

did there not come into my mind that terrific drawing of Blake's of the cosmic architect using just such instruments!

But it was the necessity that bound him, or that he re-solved *should* bind him, of following, planetary day by planetary day, the precise words of the Bible that gave a predetermined *schedule* to his vision such as would have totally ruined the inspiration of any one else.

Most curious and profound has been the impression of the Miltonic Adam and Eve upon the imagination of the English race. A queer atmosphere, made up in part of childish desire, in part of Puritan suppression, in part of the vulgarest aspect of Anglo-Saxon humour, hangs about these fair and tragic figures.

There surged up indeed in Milton's own nature a strange blending of emotions, feelings, prejudices, when he came after an impassioned description of the beauty of their bower to describe their first nuptial embrace. He fully realized the dramatic and historic momentousness of this event, the first consummation of mortal love between man and woman on our tragic globe; and his first instinct as an

insatiable lover of the old mythology is to tell us that
Eve is—

> *More lovely than Pandora, whom the Gods*
> *Endowd with all thir gifts, and O too like*
> *In sad event——*

But, as with all human beings, and poets most of all, he
cannot approach this inflammable and touchy matter of
sex-love without releasing from the recesses of his being a
torrent of violent prejudice. Covering his Puritan nicety
with the unlovely word "connubial," he launches into a
defence of our Anglo-Saxon ideal of the married state, at
once against "free love," mediaeval courtly romance, and
monastic ascetism.

There is much to be said for the position he takes; but
something—how shall I put it?—something of the perilous
stuff out of which ballad poetry is made, something of the
tragic desperation in the essence of poetry itself, rises
up in revolt.

And it is surely significant of the presence of some element
in Milton that was being suppressed just then that he seems
unable to write of this married love, this—

> *Perpetual Fountain of Domestic sweets*
> *Whose bed is undefil'd and chast pronounc't*

in the way in which Homer writes of the reunion of
Odysseus and Penelope, after the hero's adventures with
Circe and Calypso.

And yet there is something honest and simple and
Arcadian, such as would please Rousseau, about his
attack on

> *—Court Amours,*
> *Mixt Dance, or wanton Mask, or Midnight Bal,*
> *Or Serenate, which the starv'd Lover sings*
> *To his proud fair, best quitted with disdain.*

Unlike many Puritans he certainly doesn't gloss over the sensual delights of the "domestic sweets" thus pronounced "chaste"; but one is permitted to suspect that many modern women overburdened by the fruit of such lawful sensuality would prefer the less Biblical attitude of mediaeval chivalry, and even, in spite of the risk of being sold for so many head of cattle, the greater scope offered them in Homer. The handling of the personality of Eve, for in depicting Adam all he had to do was to look into his own mirror and into his own heart, was indeed, since Homer described Helen of Troy, the most difficult task any poet had attempted.

But in one important respect Milton was curiously fitted for it. The Fall took place, we are led to understand, before any child was begotten or conceived; so that although this young mother of us all had already known the pleasure of love—"nor Adam from his fair spouse turned, I ween," she was completely untaught in the pains or pleasures of maternity.

Now Milton, lover, as we can see from *Comus*, of the Artemis type of virgin, had no poetic response to make, no response of any kind to make, to the beauty and mystery of motherhood.

And thus, though not to be fascinated by the miracle of maternity when you are writing of the mother of all men might seem odd, it left him free to treat Eve as if she had been the Flower-Bride of Celtic romance. He was probably like the tempter in *Comus*; extremely conscious of the attraction of maidenhood; so conscious that we can allow ourselves to play with the speculation that he made a deliberate moral effort to paint his Eve as *matronly* as he could, so that as with Giorgione in his *Fête-Champêtre* the main purpose of his work should not be side-tracked by other emotions.

But he was such a shameless egoist that he must have

used without any scruple all his own experiences of women; and I believe a modern reader returning to *Paradise Lost* after a lapse of years, or even entering that happy Garden for the first time, will be startled by the dramatic naturalness and genuine poignancy of both the man's and the woman's words at their supreme and fatal moment.

"Heav'n is high," the hapless girl says to herself when the deed has been done; and it is not hard to catch a multiple echo of that pitiful whisper!

> *—Heav'n is high*
> *High and remote to see from thence distinct*
> *Each thing on earth; and other care perhaps*
> *May have diverted from continual watch*
> *Our great Forbidder, safe with all his spies*
> *About him. But to Adam in what sort*
> *Shall I appear?*

And then having dismissed the temptation of increasing her charms by "the odds of Knowledge,"

> *—the more to draw his Love*
> *And render me more equal, and perhaps,*
> *A thing not undesirable, sometime*
> *Superior: for inferior who is free?*
> *This may be well: but what if God have seen*
> *And Death ensue: Then I shall be no more,*
> *And Adam wedded to another Eve,*
> *Shall live with her enjoying, I extinct;*
> *A death to think—*

she decides to tell him the whole story and give him a chance to share her fate.

A quaint touch follows, curiously characteristic of that vein of courtly *politesse* in Milton that may have been one of the reasons why among his rude Cambridge companions he received the nickname of "the lady"; for just as he makes

Adam, for all his primeval nakedness, receive "the affable archangel" with a decorous bow, and just as he makes the only begotten Son bow "over his sceptre" to his Begetter, so now he even goes so far as to make his heroine, for all her nakedness, drop what I suppose was a seventeenth-century curtsy to the terrible Tree,

> —as to the power
> That dwelt within, whose presence had infus'd
> Into the plant sciential sap, deriv'd
> From Nectar, drink of gods.

Meanwhile Adam, in a most charming and loverlike way, "waiting desirous her return" had busied himself in weaving a garland "to adorn her tresses . . . as Reapers oft are wont thir Harvest Queen," and it was across the scattered roses of this garland which soon fell, in his blank horror, to the ground that the unhappy man uttered his gallant and reckless resolve.

> How can I live without thee, how forgoe
> Thy sweet Converse and Love so dearly joyn'd:
> To live again in these wilde Woods forlorn?
> Should God create another Eve and I
> Another Rib afford, yet loss of thee
> Would never from my heart; no, no, I feel
> The Link of Nature draw me: Flesh of Flesh,
> Bone of my Bone thou art, and from thy State
> Mine never shall be parted, bliss or woe.

Having finally "justified" after his own fashion, a fashion more Biblical than orthodox, "the ways of God to men," Milton ends his terrific task in the same grand, calm, restrained manner in which he began it.

> They looking back, all the Eastern side beheld
> Of Paradise, so late thir happie seat,
> Wav'd over by that flaming brand, the Gate

With dreadful Faces throng'd and fierie Armes:
Some natural tears they drop'd, but wip'd them soon;
The World was all before them, where to choose
Their place of rest, and Providence thir guide:
They hand in hand with wandring steps and slow,
Through Eden took their solitarie way."

In *Paradise Regained* the cosmic issue is at once deepened and narrowed. It is deepened by the fact that the whole drama becomes a psychological and spiritual one. It is narrowed by the fact that the huge duality of good and evil which in the longer poem was diffused and scattered through infinite space is here concentrated in a universal-particular struggle between a superhuman personal Protagonist and a superhuman personal Antagonist.

Though it might be argued that because of its narrower scope there is less here of the abysmal injustice and un-fathomable arbitrariness of real life, there is certainly more of that ideal verisimilitude which we have come to feel is all the greater "art" because, in place of trying to reproduce the inchoate pressure, the amorphous incon-gruity, the blind waywardness of our experience, it gathers up our intimations of some ultimate explanation and rounds them off into an intelligible symbol.

The spiritual grandeur of *Paradise Regained* lies in the fact that it would not be difficult to take the "Christ" and the "Satan" of this world-deep dialogue, and turn them into the two opposing personalities of which we are all aware at the bottom of our individual hearts.

The "Temptation" of Christ by Satan is thus abstracted from its place in definite circumstantial history, and pro-jected into the timeless, the universal, the eternal. I find no single place, when the "President of the Immortals" has finished his tedious prelude, where the high tension of the interest flags, as it does over and over again in the theological and scientific talks between Adam and Raphael; and though none of the sublimest inspirations of Milton enter this poem, we never find ourselves, when once the too-familiar voice of Jehovah ceases, shocked by that material grotesqueness into which he falls so often in *Paradise Lost*.

It is the same with *Samson Agonistes*. Indeed, the Milton of these two last poems rises up out of the pages, grand and stoical and defiant, undefeated by treachery within or foes without, a living monument, not of Christian sympathy, but of towering heathen patience and abysmal resignation. *Paradise Regained* is intrinsically a moral-philosophical poem, with a mythical background; and though he uses the Biblical story he uses it in an original manner and to his own purpose.

Like Goethe's *Faust* and Nietzsche's *Zarathustra* and Dostoievsky's *Idiot*, it is an attempt to propound, with a superman as its hero, the writer's conception of the war of the spirit, his revaluation of the values of earthly life. To get this great poem into true proportion and perspective what we have to do is to tear away the whole theological scaffolding, and recognize the contrasted Christ and Satan as the two ultimate personalities in the bosoms of us all.

In place of the scriptural duality of which one pole is the Son of God and one His grand Antagonist, we may think of these opposed forces as the two basic emanations from the actual system-of-things to which all human experience points.

Not a living soul among us but has the Christ and the Satan in him, and the contest between them is lifted to the true height of tragedy because in the real cosmos each is necessary to the other and the only life we know feeds upon the flame of their struggle. The interest of this cosmic debate lies in the fact that as it advances the issue between the two grows deeper and deeper.

Quickly enough are the lower antinomies of sense and

spirit transcended. The crude advice of Belial, "Set women in his eye and in his walk," is speedily exposed by the master of more spiritual evil. The subtlety of the real tragic clash only begins when the will-to-power and the will-to-knowledge are confronted by that Inner Light not of this world wherein the spirit of man, without calling philosophers or priests or armies or science to its aid, can sink back upon *what is kindred to it in the Power behind the universe* and in the quietness of that contact can rest in peace.

We need not be misled as to the ultimate issue between these voices from the deep because one of them, as Matthew Arnold would say, "Hebraizes" and the other "Hellenizes." *That* particular clash of opposed cultures is a small difference compared with the real gulf between them, the gulf between those who follow "the traditions of men" and those who follow the nameless "spirit-like" power behind the universe.

> *Think not but that I know these things, or think*
> *I know them not; not therefore am I short*
> *Of knowing what I aught: he who receives*
> *Light from above, from the fountain of light,*
> *No other doctrine needs——*

Who but Milton, however, can read the heart of the will-to-power and the will-to-knowledge when that heart, rejecting the light within, devours itself in its huge Luciferian pride?

> *I would be at the worst; worst is my Port,*
> *My harbour and my ultimate repose:*
>
> .   .   .   .   .
>
> *If I then to the worst that can be haste*
> *Why move thy feet so slow to what is best?*

It must be the Protestant-Puritan in our blood—so difficult to eradicate—that prevents our doing justice to *Para-*

dise Regained. If we could only treat the whole story of the vindictive Jehovah and his humane and sympathetic Son and his conquered but unconquerable Rebel exactly as we treat Greek mythology, we could enjoy this incomparable style, these rolling lists of magical names, this yawning gulf between proud philosophy based on the egocentric core of "I am I," and the lovely quietism of losing of ourselves in the Power behind the cosmos; just as we can enjoy the beauty, the moral values, the problem of good and evil, in the *Odyssey,* without taking too seriously the fairy-story fury of Poseidon at the slaughtering of his sacred steers or the fairy-story interferences of Pallas Athene.

Milton himself in his own life is much more like a mythological Titan than he is like a Hebrew prophet. He is like the sort of tragic demigod, Theseus, Orion, Heracles, Odysseus, who has to bear blow after blow from chance and destiny and fate without wincing or yielding. Step by step, ledge by ledge, he was driven backward by the murderous irony of life. One by one he lost in the struggle all the mental and emotional and physical possessions he valued most. He lost his women, his friends, his sight, his cause. All the way through *Paradise Regained* and even in certain places in *Paradise Lost* the grand emphasis is laid upon patience, upon resignation, endurance, *quietism,* upon a Quakerlike submission to the invisible spirit who prefers "before all temples" the conscience of the good and just man.

In place of any Buddhist indifference to both pleasure and pain, in place of any stoical lying back upon "nature," Milton's faith in the nameless non-human spirit behind the cosmos gives him the strength to "steer right onwards" even though like Samson he is blind among enemies, even though he has given up all hope, even though he has come to the conclusion that except in the far-off miraculous future evil must of necessity be stronger than good.

I seem to divine—judging purely from his own poems—
that he was most delicately sensitive to feminine charm,
but, like Strindberg and unlike Blake, completely devoid of
that restraint, that indulgence, that massive ironic tact,
which it is unsafe even for a Caesar or a Napoleon to be
without and fatal for a man of Milton's ferocious imagination.

In these subtle psychological reactions, the law of opposites plays, I suspect, a much greater part than is usually
divined. Many people think of Milton as a person infatuated with the idea of *fatherhood*; his own benevolent and
stern father, his own thwarted desire to be the father of a
son endowing the mere idea of the *heavenly* Father with an
appeal that swallowed up all other human relationships.

Now there is, only too obviously, much to be said for
this view: but may it not be that the passionate zest with
which he describes Satan, who throws, it must be confessed, all other attempts to depict creation's grand Adversary into the background, betrays the fact that the whole
business of the "father-cult" in these poems was one of
those curious cases worthy of the analysis of Dostoievsky
where you revenge yourself upon what you suffer from by
piling up—Pelion upon Ossa and both upon Olympus—the
particular qualities in the object of your reaction that make
you suffer the most?

Is it not possible that the real clue to the odiousness of
the Miltonic Heavenly Father lies, not as Mr. Tillyard
quoting from M. Saurat suggests—namely, that Milton
believed in a First Cause *who was both bad and good* and who
consequently allowed a portion of his Absolute Being to go
its way to everlasting damnation—but in a certain feminine
sensitivity in the poet's own nature, the quality that got
him the nickname of "the lady," which urged him on in a
sort of morbid obsequiousness, that was not free from something hysterical, to utter, along with the angelic hosts his
hollow hallelujahs.

It is a puzzling question, but one full of a curious interest, and we are confronted by a not very dissimilar difficulty to-day; only with us the question of future damnation doesn't enter; and the difficulty is to reconcile a merciful, unrevengeful Deity with the horrors of the actual world round us. To accept Blake's idea that *without knowing it* Milton was on the side of Satan would almost imply a half-deliberate malignity in the way he exaggerates the servility of the seraphic court; but the fact that the wearisome adulation of these sycophantic harpings destroys all poetry would rather suggest, considering to what lengths the piety of quite sincere women will go, that it was the numbing and stupefying effect of sanctified masochism rather than unconscious hostility.

But, as I keep repeating, the surest ground we can go upon is to regard Milton's inmost feelings—that inspiration that made him able to "steer right onwards" in his darkness and defeat—as an authentic spiritual power, supporting his lonely conscience, and reaching him from outside the whole created world. If not unconsciously malignant, his paeans of praise to Jehovah are completely unpoetical, and *that alone* is a proof that they do not spring from the depths of his being; whereas his sublime invocation of the eternal spirit that "sat'st brooding on the vast abyss and mad'st it pregnant" and his grand appeal to the Inner Light and to Urania, the Muse beyond the Muses, carry with them the whole passion of his soul. No, it was not that he was on the side of Satan against the Father, but rather that, in his greatest moments, he *transcended both*, transcended all the traditions, all the authority, all the creeds of men, and sank down and back and away, into the nameless, formless, timeless spirit behind it all, and in the power of that Spirit obtained the strength to "only stand and wait."

There is nothing forced, nothing obsequious, nothing unworthy in *Samson Agonistes*. The hero's angry rejection of

Delilah is a rejection of the weakness in himself that made him yield to Delilah. It is a return to the things "that no gross ear can hear." The dominant note in *Samson Agonistes* is not contempt for Delilah but contempt for himself; and if his patience "at the mill with slaves" is rewarded beyond all hope at the last by so great a triumph, the implication is that with or without that triumph he would have perished in the faith that in the final issue "the Eternal not ourselves that makes for righteousness" would overcome Dagon.

I cannot but feel that in the closing passages of this unique poem, a tragedy in the true Promethean sense, we get his final word upon the confused treacheries of earth-life.

One thing remains, not a Protestant faith, not a Catholic faith, not a Hellenic or Hebraic faith; but the faith of a man confronting a world given over to Dagon, in the strength of the eternal Spirit behind all worlds.

> *Nothing is here for tears, nothing to wail*
> *Or knock the breast, no weakness, no contempt,*
> *Dispraise, or blame, nothing but well and fair.*
> *And what may quiet us in a death so noble.*

Goethe

IT WAS at Cambridge that I was first brought under the influence of Goethe; and though still ignorant of the German tongue, so that I cannot enjoy in connexion with him, as I can with Homer and Dante, those intimations of new worlds of feeling that we get from a foreign language, I certainly can say that no writer, no thinker, no teacher, has influenced me more all my life long.

I do not at all agree, though no one could be less of a linguist, with Emerson's theory that you can get the essence of any foreign genius through a translation. Translations of poetry are, to my mind, usually worse than useless; for not only do you get no adequate idea of the poet in that way, you often get a *wrong* idea, which may cling to you all your life.

In prose it is quite different. Few of us can do more than glance cursorily at the French of Rabelais, but I have a shrewd inkling that Sir Thomas Urquhart's translation runs it close; and I cannot believe that our Authorized Version of the Old Testament falls far short of the original Hebrew.

If, however, there *is* an exception to the rule that poetry is untranslatable I would say such an exception exists in the case of Goethe's *Faust*. Both the First and the Second Parts of this great drama are crowded with ideas that belong to the whole human race; and in addition to this the sex-interest in the Gretchen tale is of peculiarly universal character. Then there is the world-embracing folk-lore, deeper than any merely local legends, out of which Goethe builds up his symbolism.

And may it not be, too, that Goethe's thought does not wed itself so intricately and absolutely to the syllabic sounds he is using *as to be undetachable from them*, or, when detached from them, to be unrecognizable?

I am not one of those who in praising the First Part of *Faust* disparage the Second Part. Except for Proust's masterpiece, and by reason of his dying so young *his* "Second Part" was necessarily a little hurried, it is hard to think of another literary work—I mean a work that is more than mere "essays" or "confessions," a work that forms an imaginative projected whole—into which a crowded personal life of thoughts and feelings, experiences, disasters, redemptions, has been caught up.

The Divine Comedy itself might be called a *static vision* as far as Dante's own spiritual and intellectual development is concerned, and even the history of humanity implicit in it is visioned as subject to an inflexible *schedule*, a schedule, it is true, with a complicated metaphysical framework, but a schedule that allows but little for the dim, obscure, living mystery of organic growth.

Although *The Divine Comedy* visions the invisible world as threefold, its Purgatory is only a temporary preparation for its Paradise, and between its Hell and its Paradise there is no interchange of experiment, experience, or condition.

All is over, all is done for and finished at the fatal moment when the soul leaves the body. "The rest is silence"; but it is the silence of a Purgatorial ascent to Paradise, or of an irremediable perdition.

But the essence of Goethe's *Faust* is that it is a living growth, a progressive development, full of something vast and blurred and dim and dark and mysterious, something completely *beyond any schedule*, something where good is mingled with evil and evil is mingled with good and where both of them are surrounded by huge natural and supernatural mysteries, at present unsolved and perhaps insoluble.

Goethe began *Faust* when he was twenty and finished it when he was eighty-three; and every time he came back to it after a lapse of years he threw into it some new experience, some new intellectual or aesthetic discovery, some new hint of intercourse between Heaven and Hell, some new vibration of the mountain of Purgatory, unforeseen by the angels at either its summit or its base!

What makes *Faust* so great a work, taking its place along with *Lear* and *Hamlet*, along with *Paradise Lost* and *The Divine Comedy*, among the universal poems of the world, is its constant preoccupation with "first and last things," and its treatment of these things with the highest imagination and the deepest realism.

In solid philosophical weight it has the advantage of Shakespeare's tragedies, because it offers a more definite intellectual system. Shakespeare's art, though closer to common human experience, is like a many-sounding ocean of mortal outcries, lashed and tossed into foam by the crisscross winds of "crass casualty."

And Goethe is a greater help to us in our modern life than Milton or Dante because the burden of orthodox religion is loosened, lifted, broken up, diffused, dispersed, lightened of its dogmatic necessity.

Shakespeare's attitude, when you come to examine it, implies no more than a poetical acceptance of religious tradition as an undertone in life, with its inevitable reaction upon moral issues and dramatic emotions. What absorbs him is the visible spectacle of the secular world, its exultations, its humours, its despairs, its struggles, all of them "rounded" by the silence of death and riddled with insoluble mystery.

When you come honestly to think of it, how hard it is to draw from any of these other famous works, from *Paradise Lost* with its Protestant theology, from *The Divine Comedy* with its scholastic metaphysic, from *Hamlet* and *Lear* with their pessimistic reserve, any real help in our secret inner wrestlings with life!

A word of sad resignation here and there:

> *Man must abide*
> *His going hence, even as his coming hither:*
> *Ripeness in all.*

or of patient fatalism:

> *There's a divinity that shapes our ends,*
> *Rough-hew them how we will.*

or of a desperate hope-against-hope in the far-off Heavenly Father:

> *All is best, though we oft doubt*
> *What th' unsearchable dispose*
> *Oh highest wisdom brings about,*
> *And ever best found in the close;*

or of unquestioning obedience to Holy Church:

> *Avete il vecchio e il nuovo Testamento,*
> *E il pastor della Chiesa che vi guida;*
> *Questo vi basti a vostro salvamento.*

> Ye have the Old and the New Testament and the Shepherd of the Church to guide ye; let this suffice ye unto your salvation—

such is, as honest John Ruskin long ago complained, about the best we can get, in our complicated mental and emotional difficulties, from these great poets.

And many hold that it is absurd of us to crave for more. Over the turbulent arena of our earth-life, rounded by unbroken silence, Shakespeare scatters the ineffable balm of an imagination that gives to the worst—or to *almost* the worst—a magical "Fata-Morgana" beauty.

In a world dominated by Moloch and Baal and Dagon, Milton stands and waits in blind trust that the "Eternal not ourselves who makes for Righteousness" will one day bring down their circus-roof upon the heads of the ungodly. While to satisfy his insatiable lust for a divine malediction upon human malefactors Dante sees the atrocity-workers of the earth condemned to a despair worse than any they have inflicted.

> *Bestemmiavano Iddio e lor parenti*
> *L'umana specie, il luogo, il tempo et il seme*
> *Di lor semenza e di lor nascimenti.*

They blasphemed God and their parents, the human race, the place, the time and the seed of their engendering and of their birth.

But, as the indignant Ruskin says, it *is* hard, when we ask the greatest geniuses of our race for bread, that they should give us these stones, give us in fact the same wistful resignation, the same blind trust, the same implacable resentment, that we know only too well in the weakness of our own hearts!

But in *Faust* Goethe does, I think, come a little nearer than Dante or Shakespeare or Milton to offering us some more solid assistance in our mental and emotional quandaries.

It is, of course, a well-known trick of the cynical conservative mind, aimed against youth's impatient wrestlings with life's riddle, to praise with an air of fatuous maturity the philosophical reserves of Shakespeare and his careless acceptance of life's tragedy at its face value. As a matter of fact, one could easily gather evidence from his plays to prove Shakespeare a pessimist of a brand so extreme that the people who praise his well-balanced normality would be aghast at the morbid desperations of his spirit.

But the fact remains that Shakespeare's genius does lie rather in throwing a magical glamour over the figures of our life and its appalling predicaments, than in trying to get behind the drama to any secrets of the Management.

Perhaps it is impossible to get behind the drama, but the door is not shut yet; and from the first to the last line of *Faust*, into which, as he told Eckermann, Goethe "put his whole life," we get a deliberate and concentrated attempt to throw into symbolic form all that he—our wisest sage since Rabelais—thought and felt of the general human situation.

The four-square *satisfactoriness* of *Faust*, its suggestiveness for any sceptical and yet religious mind lies in the depth of its mysticism, in the vitality of its symbolism, in the huge reservoirs of religious mythology it conjures up, and finally in its magical closeness to nature.

The religious problem is at the bottom of it all; and in his occult wisdom Goethe has frankly followed the natural instincts of his soul even where they break down in their overbrimming vitality the brittle ramparts of logical reason.

And it is here, above all, that he is so significant for us to-day. Not to feel a certain unfulfilled craving for religious satisfaction in the face of all our specialized science is to confess yourself a thin, atrophied, desiccated, abortive nature, a nature only half-developed, a nature blighted and withered in its flowering.

There is hardly any natural religious impulse whether pantheistic, pluralistic, monotheistic, pagan, or Christian, that does not find its appropriate symbol in *Faust*. The "Chorus Mysticus" at the close, which sounds like the voice of the Nameless itself, heard faintly from beneath the waves of the tossing ocean of being, declares that the whole stream of life is but a symbol of what lies beyond.

And this idea, that all our religious instincts, infinitely various as they are and mutually conflicting, are representative, each in their own way, of the Indescribable, is exactly what we most need just now, to put both theological and scientific dogmatism in their place. A gentle mind turns in weary distaste from the arbitrary jealousies of the cruel Father of men as Milton's obsequious hallelujahs belaud him. It turns with an even deeper reaction from the "*somma Sapienza e il primo Amore,*" of Dante's ferocious "Emperor of the Universe."

But the tyranny of science, with its withering of individuality, its contempt for the difference between right and wrong, its vivisectors and gas-poisoners, is worse than the tyranny of Jehovah, save that its regime is ended by death.

And Goethe treats science with the same freedom as he does religion. *Faust* is the most agnostic poem in the world, and yet it is the most religious! Its whole tone and temper does exactly what at this day and hour we most need should be done. It *dedogmatizes* Christianity, turning its nobler elements into the beautiful mythology they are; not treating them for that reason as untrue, but as humanity's culminating symbol in a world where *everything* is a symbol!

In these days when the traditional churches and their worship are becoming a no man's land of conflict between reactionaries and revolutionaries, it is most salutary to return to the atmosphere of *Faust*, wherein if all "houses made with hands" for the cult of the Invisible were destroyed, the religious impulse would still remain, and the cosmos would be as full of magic and mystery as it ever was.

The essence of religion—that is to say the feeling of wonder and awe in the presence of life and of the unknown powers behind life—is, according to *Faust*, the supreme and highest virtue of man. This is what Goethe was never, never weary of repeating. The more reverence the more culture: the less reverence the less culture! And thus, in an age when a smattering of extremely questionable scientific "truth" is assumed to justify a human soul—a soul that has entered into its inheritance of the inspirations of the noblest minds of ten thousand years—in taking up a negative attitude to everything beyond the scope of the senses, there is every reason why we should return to Goethe.

A mind inspired by *Faust* would not be overwhelmed with dismay even if revolutionaries did destroy every religious edifice in the world. Such a person would neither fight to defend churches nor to destroy churches; for he would know that *all* churches in the world, together with all the gods and all the demons invoked or exorcised therein, are to be found in *the mind of man* out of which they arose, and in which, though all their priests and black-and-white magicians were slain, they would still survive and beget innumerable progeny.

Any modern intelligent person if he never entered a church, and confined his reading to Homer and Rabelais, would find plenty of scope wherein to cultivate that religious awe which is the highest attribute of man.

And the devotees of the inexhaustible gold-mine of human wisdom to be found in Goethe will, of all things, most avoid the negative attitude in religious controversy. Life is *more* religious, not *less* religious, than the orthodox hold it to be. It is the vicious, malignant, negative aspect of God that Goethe rejects; but even *that* he doesn't so much fight against as subsume, sublimate, and hypostatize in the figure of Mephistopheles, the enemy of creation and life, but in spite of himself the minister of creation and life.

In one's reaction from the too-human behaviour of

Jehovah one tends, especially after reading Milton, to feel that it is a mark of intellectual superiority to worship God as a Great Spirit rather than as a Person who loves and hates. But one sometimes grows aware of certain serious doubts about this intellectual superiority of believers in "spirit" over believers in "personality." "Spirit," after all, is only a metaphor drawn from the wind; and one feels sometimes a little doubtful whether as a worshipper of the Ultimate in the form of wind one is superior to those who worship it in the only form of which we have any experience *from inside*, the form of personal consciousness.

But the satisfactoriness of the Goethean attitude to religion, as we allow it to sink into us in *Faust*, is that it finds room for everything. Goethe himself declared that he had it in him to be a pantheist when need were, a polytheist when need were, and if his nature at any time required a personal god, "there was room for *that* also."

No remark could be more infuriating to dogmatic believers than that! To come to the feet of the Living God as lightly and casually as this, is, they feel, a greater insult than to deny His existence. But, after all, it is only because Goethe was so absolutely certain in his own mind that the Ultimate Power of the universe was not on the look-out for petty insults, nor had any resemblance to a touchy parent, that he wrote of it as he did, and felt towards it as he did.

What Goethe felt was that though it transcended human personality by as large a gulf as eternity transcends time, there was no reason why it should be something *less*. There were, however, a great many reasons against accepting the orthodox view of the three Persons of the Trinity; and in this sense Goethe remains a heathen.

There seems to be some law of life by which it is impossible for a great work of art to come into being by the arbitrary "fiat" of a single brain, working independently of any deep human tradition. Shakespeare, indeed, broke this law and achieved this impossibility, for though both *Hamlet* and *Lear* were drawn from old chronicles, their stories were just insignificant folk-lore episodes, without any mass of popular legends behind them.

But *Faust*, like the *Odyssey* and *Paradise Lost*, had behind it a huge agglomeration of mythological tradition and medieval legend, each of them of the sort that are of all most appealing to the superstitious instincts and rooted sex-manias of average humanity.

Save for our own Marlowe, however, no great genius had made use of this rich mine of popular appeal; and even in his hands the legend still kept its grosser, cruder, more sensational aspects. But Goethe changed the whole thing. He purged it of all its meaningless sensationalism and where he retained its grosser and more grotesque elements he forced them into subjection to the main stream of his symbolic thought.

The Gretchen episode was a pure inspiration of his own, and in all the Gretchen scenes he surpassed himself and attained a dramatic poignancy that Shakespeare himself has never excelled; but, for the rest, all the way through this huge creation he gathers his materials from the deep mass of our demonology and mythology.

But into the heart of all this, giving it a vivid modern interest, he flings, in the figure of Faust, all his own erotic intensity, all his own titanic supermoral struggle after the secret of life.

The whole work—the two parts taken together—forms a vast mythological cathedral; for in spite of the Greek folk-lore and the Helen episode of the Second Part his mystic-realistic treatment of these classical legends, with its incurable bias to the grotesque, is in reality profoundly *Gothic*, and for all his yearning after classical balance and proportion is much more Düreresque than Raphaelesque.

The First Part of *Faust* with the piteous tale of Gretchen's earthly fate—for the undying spirit of one girl plays its part in the final redemption—is like a sort of Lady-chapel to this great Gothic pantheon; and its heavier, darker, more mediaeval vaulting accords most suitably with the romantic magician's cell in which Faust is first discovered.

The device of bringing the Lord and the Devil together in a confederate colloquy is, though borrowed from Job, profoundly significant of Goethe's intimation that good and evil are both necessary in the evolution of life; and while the Daedalian chantings of the archangels, suggestive of the music of the spheres, gives the drama its planetary background, it is the Lord himself who in philosophical detachment strikes the non-moral key-note to the whole symphony. In the sentence "While man strives he is bound to stray," we receive the first hint of Goethe's meaning. It is made still clearer when this is added: "In his own dim impulse a good man has an instinct of the true way"; and it receives its final emphasis when this extremely unbiblical pilot of the system-of-things indicates his ambiguous method of keeping up what you might call the tone of evolution by temporary "liaisons" between Heaven and Hell.

> *Man's efforts lightly flag, and seek too low a level;*
> *Soon doth he pine for all-untrammelled sloth.*
> *Therefore a mate I give him, nothing loth,*
> *Who spurs and shapes, and* must *create, though Devil!*

How portentously upon the ears of every lover of the world's great plays fall the famous opening words of *Faust*, as they indicate in unmistakable terms the sort of intellectual mystic yearning to drink deep at the breasts of life which in his own experience had led Goethe such a dance!

Philosophy and Medicine have I studied
And Jurisprudence and Theology . . .

.   .   .   .   .   .

And I have found that all we know is nothing!
Therefore to magic will I turn my mind.

.   .   .   .   .

The youthful Goethe himself "turned his mind to magic" at one epoch of his life, and all the way through both parts of *Faust* there runs an umbilical cord, linking this huge work with his own personal adventures and his own cultural development. It was no doubt from his own remorse concerning more than one "Gretchen" that he drew the *emotions*, though not the facts, of this particular girl's fate. It was himself who turned, just as Faust did, from an impassioned study of books to a more vital but not less mystical contact with nature. And again it was himself, who, like the early scholars of the Renaissance but still more like the yet earlier medieval magicians, forced his way into the undying underworld of classic symbols and ravished with his volcanic-Gothic passion the calm loveliness of the Hellenic ideal.

The thrilling power exerted upon us by Faust's invocations as he bends over his magic book is due to the fact that we all conceal within us, inherited from an immemorial past, a secret yearning to enjoy by some magical short-cut the hidden potencies of nature. A responsive pulse begins to beat irrepressibly within us when Faust makes the sign of the Macrocosm; for there is not one among us for whom the idea of forbidden sensual joys and an unnatural power over the forces of nature has not got a seductive appeal.

It is in fact just in that very quality in *Faust* which has troubled certain rare and pure minds that we must look for its real greatness; for Goethe brings to the whole problem of good and evil a planetary detachment that is not a little disturbing. It is true he never, as Walt Whitman claims to do, "moistens the roots of all that has grown" in the sense of celebrating the evil *equally* with the good; but he rejects the evil in so cold-blooded a way and acknowledges the Lord's use of the evil, to bring forth more good, in so shameless and unshrinking a manner, that though no doubt both St. Paul and Dostoievsky would have understood him, Nietzsche seems to have been deceived by his demonic detachment into taking for granted that he was a good deal more "beyond good and evil" than in reality he was.

But if *Faust* is not altogether pleasant reading to the simpler kind of moralist, it cannot be much more pleasant for the rationalistic type of scientific thinker. The calm planetary eye he turns upon Nature, that *physiognomic eye* of which Spengler speaks so eloquently, is a very different approach—at once more mystical and more realistic—from that of average mathematical or chemical science.

Faust remains an imperishable refutation of our modern preference for a mathematical universe over a magical one. I am not referring merely to all the thaumaturgic paraphernalia which of course was implicit in the Faustian legend, but to what might be called the living magical element in the mysterious processes of nature herself.

When Faust falls back in weakness and terror from the apparition of the earth-spirit, at whose occult breast his book-magic had been suckling for so long, we touch what was one of Goethe's most subtle intimations, namely that nature, in a manner totally beyond our comprehension, possesses a consciousness of her own, a consciousness not less but *more* than human, which she expresses all the while through the multiform tongues of all her children, but in a language that not one of these children understands.

Like many another despairing human intellect wrestling with the insoluble riddle, the Goethe-Faust of this moonlit

Gothic cell feels a sudden inspiration that it is death rather than life which holds the ultimate clue; and few situations in the roll of the world's great plays are more dramatic than where the Easter bells recall him to life, and with the stars of the morning announcing the tidings of Christ's birth he dashes the death-cup from his lips.

Not a little suggestive of these temporary "marriages of heaven and hell" by which according to Goethe the tricky First Cause works his evolutionary scheme is the fact that our commentators leave it, as Mr. Latham says, "to the reader" to decide whether the spirits who cry out, "Thou has shattered it all, the beautiful world! Build it again fairer than before!" are good or evil spirits.

Faust now walks abroad with his "famulus" Wagner among the springtime crowds pondering upon the strange nature of his own soul—the soul of Goethe—which, unlike his worthy companion's, is torn by two insatiable contradictory passions, one for the visible world of the senses, and one for the invisible world beyond the senses; and it is at this crucial moment, as he realizes the full implication of this duality within him, that Mephistopheles appears.

"*Dost see yon black dog?*" But the good Wagner—for the abysmal spirit of futility is unknown to the average man—sees nothing more than an ordinary dog, a teachable dog, a patient obedient dog, a well-behaved dog, just suited to be a scholar's pet.

Nor is it insignificant that as soon as Faust is back again alone in his cell with this docile pet, his total disillusionment with everything else in life drives him, as a last resort, to the Gospel of St. John.

Helped in his interpretation of the most crucial metaphysical passage in the world, "In the beginning was"—by more than one spiritual power, for his black pet is now becoming extremely lively, he rejects the "Word" and the

"Thought" and the "Might" for the heretical but perhaps more modern version: "In the beginning was *the Act.*"

So many commentators have had their fling at interpreting *Faust* that the book has become, like the philosopher's stone, a Mecca of mystery for all occult pilgrims.

Certainly as we come back to this tremendous work, to its ironies within ironies, its secrets within secrets, its revelations within revelations, we are left staggered at Goethe's weight of genius.

It is the only play—Shakespeare's *Hamlet* is a hurried sketch beside it and the *Prometheus* of Aeschylus a broken torso—that rivals the Book of Job as a philosophical commentary upon the ways of the First Cause; and for myself, as the latest "famulus" to *Faust*, I find its contents far more useful as a guide to the cosmos than Job's *Apologia pro Deo.*

Of one very interesting aspect of man's life, not referred to at all amid the terrific imagery of the Book of Job, Goethe makes a great deal. I refer to the magic power over both the spirit of evil and the spirit of despair exercised by what one might almost regard as an erotic passion for the elements. One feels sometimes, especially in the first scene of Part Two, as if one were on the tantalizing edge of an actual formula for the seduction of the powers behind the forces of nature, for these Sylphs and Ariels and Undines and Salamanders, whose non-human embraces can erase the troubles of the mind.

There is something in Faust as there was something in Goethe, that remains strange and weird and inexplicable; but his mysticism differs from other mysticism by being rooted in a curious realism, by being a matter of personal experience rather than of theory. It is this emphasis upon real experience that gives such integrity to his irrational instincts, even to that most irrational one of all, his obstinate belief in personal immortality.

The precise terms of the bond that is finally arranged

between Faust and Mephistopheles are of Faust's own making. The magician, not the Devil, suggests them, and their nature reveals the whole Goethean super-moral, or, if you like, sub-moral attitude to life. They follow the line suggested in the Prologue by the Lord himself, namely that the essence of good is *to strive* and never be content, while the essence of evil is to give up striving and to rest in the enjoyment of the moment.

As soon as Faust can be persuaded to call upon the moment, as it flits past him, to stay and immortalize itself, then the Devil is to have him. "Let Pain and Pleasure come and go as they will," Goethe declares, "it is only by eternal striving that man fulfils life's law."

Here we get a definition of the difference between good and evil which may well indeed set us thinking! I cannot tell what other disciples of Goethe may feel about it, but for myself I can state my attitude with extreme clarity. Theoretically I entirely disagree with Goethe. Theoretically I find the essence of good in harmless happiness, in the harmless happiness of rapt contemplation, while I find the essence of evil in frivolous curiosity, in malice, and in cruelty.

I must confess, however, that in practical experience I have found it very difficult to call upon the moment to stay. Devilish thoughts, devilish fears, a deep devilish restlessness, have urged me on, have urged me to let the moment go; and, do what I can, this same troublesome servant of the Lord goads me still into this same action and striving.

Cleverer "Wagners" than I will have to reconcile as time goes on Goethe's words in *Wilhelm Meister*, "To act is easy, to think is hard," with all this praise of action; but it may be the "thinking" he had in his mind was very different from the psycho-sensual quiescence that Faust rejects as he plunges into the ocean of experience to test and taste all;

and it may also be that the opposite of this sacred striving is not calm contemplation but vicious negation, and what might be called *malicious inertness*.

As I have already hinted not only is *Faust* uncomfortable reading for theologians and puritans; it is also extremely disturbing reading for average scientists. Goethe is the grand enemy of the mechanical-logical-mathematical school of scientific thought.

While Faust is getting ready to set out to see the world, Mephistopheles, disguised in his doctor's gown, interviews an eager student and mockingly bids him study logic, but closes his mockery with true Goethean seriousness and hatred of soulless dissection.

> *He who some living thing would study*
> *Drives first the spirit out of the body,*
> *And then the parts he holds in his hand*
> *And there fails him but the spiritual band,*
> *ENCHEIRESIS NATURA!——*

Never failing to keep a close contact with the historic symbols of humanity, Goethe liberates from each one of these as he touches it that living essence whose reality lies in the actual experience of the individual. Just as the cry, "Christ is risen!" at which the death-cup falls from the lips of Faust celebrates the birth of life out of death which is within the consciousness of all the children of men, so the drunken revel in Auerbach's cellar, with its notorious flea-ditty, stirs up that sediment in the breasts of us all which is the water-become-wine of the Rabelaisian holy bottle.

But further down still, among the unsanctified dregs of creation, must this Goethe-Faust soul be conducted by his graceless guide, before he is in the right mood to enter Gretchen's chamber. "Fie upon such fantasies!" cried Charles Lamb, when he was made acquainted with the "he-ape" and "she-ape" of the Witch's Kitchen; but as with all the other grotesque details of this gargoylish Gothic pandemonium there is natural truth enough in the devil's having to "aphrodize" his adventurer's book-benumbed senses with the prophetic crystal and philtre before the casual sight of a simple girl upon the pavement can create in such a master of magic the imperishable Illusion.

When once, however, with the Devil's help and that of the lively Martha, the lust-drugged wanderer has destroyed Gretchen's peace of mind, who but Goethe can describe to a nicety the miraculous change from lust to love, and the seducer's romantic-ideal attempts to leave the girl before he ruins her?

Deep indeed is his reading of his own heart and through his own of the universal masculine heart, as in that scene entitled "Woodland and Cave," which follows the girl's cry, "I know not what he can find in me!" he struggles with his infernal comrade and recalls his discomfiture before the earth-spirit's apparition, and "sees, not feels" the pure beauty of nature.

But we are soon given proof, as the Lord hinted in the Prologue:

> *That a good man, by his dim instinct driven*
> *Of the right way hath ever consciousness;*

for it is after he has gone back—in spite of his ideal resolutions—to complete her seduction, that we find him pouring into her startled ear what is no less than Goethe's ultimate religious faith.

Hitherto I have been using Albert Latham's translation in the Everyman edition; but I now quote from Bayard Taylor's version:

> *"Who shall dare, 'I believe in God' to say?*
> *Ask Priest or Sage the answer to declare,*

And it shall seem a mocking play,
A sarcasm on the asker.''

"Then believest thou not?"

.   .   .   .   .

"The All-upholder, the All-enfolder,
Folds and upholds he not, thee, me, himself?
Arches not there the sky above us?
Lies not beneath us firm the earth?
And rise not on us, shining,
Friendly, the everlasting stars?
Look not eye to eye on thee, and feel'st not
Throbbing through head and heart the force,
Still weaving its eternal secret
Visible, invisible about thy life?
Vast as it is, fill with that force thy heart,
And when thou in the feeling wholly blessed art,
Call it then what thou wilt—Call it Love, God, Life!
I have no name to give it—Feeling is all in all—
The name is sound and smoke,
Obscuring heaven's clear glow."

The story of Gretchen's seduction seems to call forth every sympathy, every idealized memory, every imaginative instinct that Goethe possessed; and so natural and convincing is the figure of the unhappy girl that even the most cynical reader must feel a shock of moral—or immoral—reaction, from the deep-rooted social conventions that bring about, even without the help of the Devil, these world-old sex-tragedies!

Nowhere is a writer's most secret nature revealed more searchingly than in his handling of this ancient and pitiful theme. The helpless docility of Ophelia in regard to her father and her lover evokes what is perhaps a more *individualized* though not less poignant figure, and every touch, in every successive scene, that *her* poet adds to her picture intensifies this brooding passivity till it finally emerges as something definitely recognizable in the lineaments of a particular maid.

And not only does Ophelia become, just because of this touching dependence, a clearly defined personality, but her madness and half-accidental death take on a certain poetic inevitability. Her very pliableness in the hands of each one of the people of her life prevents the wavering, hesitant, inner romance of her nature from betraying itself, until, as Goethe himself has hinted, it is pitifully released by the unsettling of her brain.

But her personality from the beginning is so particularized in its shrinking receptivity that it is impossible to think of any future for her when her world trembles under the shocks of mischance; whereas, if things had gone otherwise, it is easy to imagine a most natural future for Goethe's Gretchen. Touch by delicate touch Ophelia's poet evokes her fragile lineaments, till they limn themselves as clearly in our mind's eye as the reflections of the "pendent weeds" in the water where she sank.

But what Goethe does with *his* young heroine is very different. With hardly less inspired art, but to a quite other purpose, he concentrates in her figure all the most characteristic qualities of her sex, adding stroke after stroke to make her as much of a universal symbol of susceptible and innocent girlhood as a young German woman—and no women lend themselves better to this—could possibly be made.

It is the fleeting charm of youthful femininity *in general* that he struggles to capture rather than the individual characteristics of a *particular* young girl; and he achieves this with such success that for stage purposes Gretchen must always be the easier of the two to play.

In a sense *all* young girls are Gretchens; at least they all have something of Gretchen in them, whereas Ophelia is a rare, baffling enigmatic entity, a unique human soul, such as it may, or may not, be our luck to encounter in real life.

But how cunningly Goethe goes to work in his task of creating a living symbol of tender, trusting, unsuspicious girlhood! Not a word she speaks, not a song she sings, not a prayer she utters, but enhances with a new magic this universal embodiment.

To every crisis in the Gretchen tragedy—and how easily one false note, too much sensuality here, too much sentimentality there, would have spoilt it all!—Goethe rises with easy, inspired mastery. Faust's emotions in her chamber when with Mephistopheles he is secreting the tempting casket and they catch the sound of her step below, his outburst of remorseful shame, "Away! Away! I never will return!" the girl's entrance:

> *"How sultry 'tis!*
> *. . . I know not what comes over me . . . what*
> *a silly, timorous girl I am!*
> *'There was a king in Thule*
> *Was faithful to the grave*
> *Him she that loved him truly*
> *A gold cup dying gave—' "*

and the scene a little later where she plucks off the daisy's petals . . . "loves me . . . loves me not . . . *he loves me!*" and all this followed so quickly by the heart-sick love-plaint at her spinning-wheel and then, when a maid no more, by that cruelly natural dialogue with her companion at the well where they chatter, just as Hardy would have made them do, about another girl who "has got herself into trouble," all these things as they mount up, adding here a little and there a little to this world-old pitiful tale, certainly leave us with the feeling that never again will the classic theme, "the woman pays," be treated according to its demands.

No one can accuse Goethe of dragging in unessentials where Gretchen's fate is concerned. Scene by scene—from her desperate prayer to the Virgin's picture on the Town Wall to her brother's denunciation of her as a whore, and from her despair in the Cathedral when the organ plays the *Dies irae, dies illa*, to the final moment in her prison— this supreme outrage upon great creative nature, wrought by society and religion, and by women themselves in their selfish trades' unionism, is exposed and immortalized.

And this is done by the one of all others best fitted to do it, both from his own relations with women and from his superhuman understanding of that mysterious creativeness in the heart of nature which he himself calls *the Mothers*.

But everything else apart, what an inspiration it was to introduce the witches' orgy in the Harz Mountains between Gretchen's despair in the church and the last scene in her prison!

Here again Goethe defeats all rivals in yet another terrific piece of symbolic universalism; but it is by the black-magic cult of obscenity this time—of obscenity in relation to the essence of life and of its *necessity* in regard to the highest purposes of life—that he shows the connexion between monstrous grossness and the most quivering tendrils of spiritual clairvoyance. The vision of Lilith, and that other vision whom his guide names as Medusa but who reminds the distracted Faust of Gretchen *paying the price of infanticide*, are so weird and terrible in their appeal that it seems strange that he could have brought along with them such a puerile topical jest as Herr "Proktophantasmist," the local bookseller, exorcising his demons by putting leeches to his rump!

But after all there are occasions when our own imaginative writers sail as near the wind as that, and there are certainly moments in the lives of us all when we would be willing to recognize this or that familiar face on the top of the Brocken!

As for that absurd "Intermezzo" or what he calls "Walpurgis-Night's Dream," it is incredible that he should have inserted these preposterous jibes, these frivolous and vulgar broad-sheet skits, between pages of sublime inspiration that he must have known would be read for a thousand years! If he wanted a greater weight of contrast with what was to follow why couldn't he have carried further his Witches' Sabbath?

More Saturnalian obscenity would have been perfectly in order; more about the "apple-tree" and the "cloven-tree." He might even have brought his he-ape and she-ape on the scene again. But these foolish "Zenia" epigrams—what strange element of solemn clownishness was it that allowed him to drag them in?

In one sense it is an illuminating phenomenon that he did so, for it proves that in a man of supreme creative genius the critical faculty *can* sink into complete abeyance!

The truth is that with all his perpetual preoccupation with "art" there has seldom been a genius with a less sure artistic instinct. He says himself that no laborious effort can produce the best, but that our inspired thoughts must come like happy children, and cry, "Here we are!" And certainly few great men have been more dependent upon nature, and chance and the urge of the immediate occasion than Goethe was.

Successful artists are as a rule far more remarkable in their art than in themselves. Goethe was the reverse of this. Like Leonardo da Vinci, he was far greater in himself than in anything he achieved. One wishes there had been a score of devoted Eckermanns to record his most casual sayings, for no human being has uttered so many profound oracles. And there was always something so indifferent to our ordinary human ideas of success of life and success in art about Goethe's methods, that you feel sometimes as if he were a changeling from another planet. He cared nothing what the mass of people thought; and when you consider the shock he deliberately gave the ceremonious Weimar court by his proletarian marriage, you can see that his interest in high society that caused such pain to Beethoven was only part of what nowadays we would call a polite Proustian curiosity!

It was the same in everything. Not one single moral passion of the crowd, not one single electric mass-prejudice but he deliberately flouted it. Patriotism meant very little to him. "How can I hate the French," he said, when they were actually occupying his province, "while I owe so much of my intellectual culture to Voltaire?" He classed the symbol of the Crucifixion with tobacco and bugs as his three greatest aversions; and his attitude to the science of his day was as detached and critical as his attitude to its morality and religion. He passed through human life as if it were all of equal interest; of an interest that was on a level with the engaging peculiarities of nature, but not of *more* interest than that.

But if he was free from the normal prejudices of humanity he was also free from its abnormal obsessions. Think of the part played—since those names were coined and probably before—by what we now call sadism and masochism in the history of human genius!

Goethe is absolutely free from the faintest trace of either of these perversions. One sees this clearly enough in comparing the way in which Victor Hugo, Balzac, Thomas Hardy, and so many others delight in *hunting down their feminine victims* with Goethe's treatment not only of Gretchen in *Faust* but of Mignon in *Wilhelm Meister*.

Scientific psychologists will smile at such a remark but it seems to me as if the inmost organism of woman's being was expressed in some of Gretchen's most simple outbursts, while it is society, not any sadism in the author, that drives her into madness.

The closing scene of the First Part of *Faust* seems to me as fine as anything in Shakespeare; and not only so but it rivals Shakespeare upon his own peculiar ground; I mean in being permeated by the *ballad element*.

No quoted fragment could do justice to it: the reader must turn to the book; but might we not be allowed to suggest that it was just because of that Saturnian detachment from ordinary human passions, making him both so startlingly unselfish and so startlingly selfish, that he was enabled to keep this flawless scene—perhaps the most moving scene in all human drama—free from any lapse into either sentiment or cruelty? And here, at his best, how little of the classical there is! How little of the influence of Voltaire, or of Sophocles either! The end of the First Part of *Faust* is pure romantic hyperborean ballad tragedy, and could have been written nowhere else but in the Gothick North.

The Second Part of *Faust* begins with an Interlude in which, throwing his soul into those vast cosmic reservoirs which are beyond both good and evil, Faust bathes his despair and remorse in the elemental sea of dawn, where the spirits of air and fire and dew are giving new life to the earth. The voices from his victim's death-cell, "She is condemned!" "She is redeemed!" together with that terrible commentary of Mephistopheles, "*She is not the first*" are absorbed and sublimated now, not in any human pardon but in the vast primordial forces that urge life on, be it the life of the good or the life of the evil, into eternal mystery and eternal change.

In their new rôle as court magician and court fool to the Holy Roman Emperor it soon becomes necessary—their poet flinging into their quest his own life-nostalgia for what

JOHANN WOLFGANG VON GOETHE

the Gothick North could *not* give—to call up from the
classic past the Homeric Helen herself, the embodiment of
what life appears, when it is seen as neither moral nor
immoral, neither good nor evil, neither vicious nor spiritual, but simply and solely as an "aesthetic spectacle."

And to bring back this shameless, mysterious, terrible
loveliness to the divine-Satanic Nordic world Faust's
companion explains to him that he must descend to
the *Mothers*.

Here we touch one of Goethe's tremendous inspirations,
an inspiration of which, when Eckermann pressed him, he
had no rational explanation to offer.

Interesting indeed would it be—for do we not touch just
here one of the profoundest mysteries of imaginative creation?—to follow the precise emotional process that made him
feel such reluctance to confess to his faithful "famulus"
anything more about the Mothers save that he found a passing reference in Plutarch to their worship in the town of
Engyon in Sicily. In his notes to the Everyman translation
Mr. Latham connects these Powers of the abyss with Plato's
archetypal Ideas in the *Timaeus*; but for myself I prefer to
think of them as belonging to that remote human tradition,
of which we find traces in Crete, and even—according to
Sir John Rhys—in certain queer survivals in the Welsh
language, concerning some prehistoric cult of the Feminine
Principle, regarded as the origin of all things.

If this is so it would connect the Mothers with that gnomic
word with which the "Chorus Mysticus" rounds off the
whole thing; and we would be justified in regarding that
oracular expression, "the woman-soul leads us upward and
on," which follows the words, for I desert my fellow countryman's version at this point for the American poet's,
"the Indescribable, here it is done," not as commending
any definite attribute of mortal women for our human
example, but as suggesting that above and beneath all the

vast evolutionary cycles of being, where all is transitory and symbolic, the feminine principle dominates the cosmos.

Faust's guide to the "Classical Walpurgis Night"—which is as much a prelude to his encounter with Helen, as the "Nordic Witch's Kitchen" was a prelude to his encounter with Gretchen—is not Mephistopheles nor the Mothers, it is *Homunculus*, the little artificial being created by the patient toil of the pedantic Wagner.

Thus when it comes to the actual reviving of classical antiquity Goethe is too true a Teuton to refuse the most important rôle to the hard-working, one-track-minded scholar; nor is there wanting a real touch of pathos when the little newly-formed being, unable to leave his crystal container without perishing, compels this gleaming receptacle to carry him through space and time like a flying electric globe and ungratefully forsakes his humble creator.

For my own part I find this Pharsalian field of mythic shapes—as if Lemprière's Classical Dictionary had been struck with a magic wand!—more pleasing, though less awe-inspiring, than the Brocken revel; nor do I feel that Goethe's passion for the particular part played by water in place of earthquakes in our planet's geography detracts in the least from the magical feeling one gets of being present at some universal Daedalian dance of the evolutionary forces of the world. Homunculus' suicide—if such it be, rather than a fusion with some imperishable life-force—by breaking his glass globe against Galatea's beautiful shell evokes once more that curious excited uneasy feeling that Goethe's conceptions so often produce—as if we were contemplating the secrets of earthly life through the eyes of some superhuman or, if you like, some subhuman creature, who is not afflicted with the same afflictions or stirred by the same sentiments as we are ourselves.

Just as the soul of this Goethe-Faust, journeying through the cosmos after leaving Gretchen's call, purges its remorse by bathing in the dew of the morning, so Mephistopheles puts off the Gothic terror from his Satanic soul and by sharing her body with the third Phorkyad assumes that more disgusting and realistic hideousness which is the price we have to pay for accepting life simply as an aesthetic spectacle.

And so we come to what has been to some minds a great stumbling-block in this portion of the poem, the introduction of the *Kabiri*.

For my part I accept whole-heartedly Küntzel's interpretation of these symbolic totems and entirely refuse to regard them as a mere satire upon a fantastic controversy. The historic Kabiri seem to have been mysterious divinities of Samothrace, probably of a chthonian character; but Goethe—always pursuing his evolutionary idea of making everything come from the sea—uses these occult *Fetishes*, who, although only idols of clay,

> *To the Inexplicable*
> *Forward still are yearning,*
> *Hunger-bitten, ever-burning,*
> *For the Unattainable,*

as symbols; for according to his magic-illusionist feeling about life, the whole stream of things is only a series of symbols of the divine reality.

And the mysterious Kabiri, each one a stage in the evolution of religion, rise like all other living things out of the sea, out of the shell-cradle of the mother of Eros, and as symbols of all the mystical creeds of the world, the last of which, though it hasn't yet incarnated itself in any material form, is the religion to which the whole world is groping, are found here in characteristic Goethean significance, in the hands of Nereids and Tritons!

This is no satire. This is the truth; and to any one who has come under the secret spell of Goethe's occult yet realistic method of handling nature there is a profound satisfaction in seeing these great, proud, troublesome, historic world-religions presented to us as the fetishes and totems and transitory playthings of the universal unknown Divinity, whose garments—although as Goethe calmly remarks, "if you require personality *there is room for that also*"—are the water and the air and the earth and the fire!

Goethe lived—like Spinoza who so deeply influenced him—in a sphere of thought and feeling as much above that of ordinary scientific men as of ordinary religious men. And so although in both science and religion he was a master adept, his methods in them both appear to the average scientist and the average pietist as grotesque and fantastic. He hated mathematics. He despised all the lower levels of logical and rational understanding. Not through dissection or vivisection, or metaphysical abstraction, or any other narrow specialization, was Nature's secret revealed. Nature was magical not logical in her ways; and she refuses to betray her secrets to those who fail to recognize her divine spirit.

In 1829 he spoke as follows to Eckermann; and his words might have been chanted by those very Nereids and Tritons who bear the Kabiri to Homunculus.

> Without my attempts in natural science I should never have learned to know mankind as it is. In nothing can we so closely approach pure contemplation and thought, so closely observe the errors of the senses and the understanding, the weak and strong points of character. All is more or less pliant . . . but nature understands no jesting; she is always true, always serious, always severe; she is always right, and the errors and faults are always those of man. Him who is incapable of appreciating her she despises and only to the apt, the pure, and the true does she resign herself and reveal her secrets. The understanding will not reach her; man must be capable of elevating himself to the highest Reason, to come into contact with the Divinity, which manifests itself in the

primitive phenomena (*Urphänomenon*), which dwells behind them and from which they proceed. The divinity works in the living not in the dead; in the becoming and changing, not in the become and the fixed. Therefore reason, with its tendency towards the divine has only to do with the becoming, the living; but understanding with the become, the already fixed, that it may make use of it.

The third act of the Second Part, describing the union of Faust and Helen has a more purely *poetic* beauty than any other portion of the whole drama. This act offers us more of the peculiar tone, temper, atmosphere, more of the curious fatalistic resignation, of the old Greek stage than you'd suppose could possibly be reproduced in a modern tongue, still less in one modern tongue translated into another.

What deathless vitality these old Greek gestures and attitudes and turns of feeling must have, to be capable of such diffusions and dilutions and yet remain so dynamic! Those old poets must have carved their rendering of human passions upon an uncrumbling granite monolith of aesthetic response that has the power, like some immortal stone quarried from a nobler planet than ours, of yielding an echo that resounds through eternity.

The fourth act of the Second Part is, on the contrary, unendurably tedious. Nothing but the pedantic architectural necessity of accounting for Faust's favoured position under the Emperor, as a reclaimer of fertile land from the salt-marshes, seems to justify its existence and its stiff and wooden and unrewarding expanse, like pasteboard upon which some solemn child is arranging his tin soldiers, has as its only interest the psychological problem as to *what it was* in Goethe that lent itself to such tedium. But this is not the only occasion when he works like a man made of sapless wood. The close of *Wilhelm Meister* has the same lack of inspiration. One can only suppose it came from some

weight of cosmogonic rubble in this colossus that a little
Celtic quicksilver or a grain of Gallic roguery would soon
have transmuted!

But the moment we come to the fifth and last act of the
whole play we find him gathering himself together in the
strength of all his most disturbing wisdom. In his extreme
old age we discover the world-weary Faust rejoicing in the
material benefits to posterity of his marsh-reclaiming ex-
ploits. It would have seemed natural for Goethe to have
let him die just so, acclaiming in a final *nunc dimittis* the
satisfying perfection of the passing moment; while by the
nature of this perfection he slips out of his hell-fire pact.

But Goethe's everlasting refusal to forsake the shocking
mixture of good and evil in life forbade so easy a close, and
by the aid of his black magic Faust proceeds to evict the
amiable old couple whose defiant homestead, like Naboth's
vineyard, has long been taunting his satisfied mind. In this
eviction both the old people perish; and once more it becomes his destiny to endure the misery of remorse; remorse
not quite as extreme as he had felt over Gretchen, but
enough to surround him with spectres of horror.

In his dialogue, however, with one of these ghastly
visitors, who to keep all distraction away now adds blindness
to these devastating thoughts, he has an opportunity to
indicate what Goethe's own methods were when fear and
horror and loathing attacked his mind.

Most sensitive natures, at one time or another, have to
pass through a period when the three kinds of fear, physical
fear, mental fear, and what in homely fashion we can only
describe as "the horrors," come gibbering at their threshold
and plague them with mystic panic and physical loathing.
With a natural psychology wiser than most of our risky
modern conjuring-tricks, Faust defies these spectres of remorse and terror by a yet more savage plunge into work,
into yet heavier work, into desperate Lethe-bringing
struggles with the resistance of matter.

And in these final struggles, which are simple and practical enough, and indeed are no less than what all pioneers
have to do in unreclaimed wildernesses, the old eroticist
and illusionist finds he can forget his guilty conscience.

For he alone deserves liberty, as he alone deserves
life, who every day conquers it afresh.

It is with a very Gothic ecstasy that Faust winds up his
contract with the Devil, and in so doing makes a fool once
more of that queer son of negation, who "*willing the evil* is
for ever furthering the good."

What "the Lord" said in the Prologue turns out now to
be literally true:

A good man, by his dim impulse driven
of the right way hath ever consciousness;

and Mephistopheles is cheated of his rational and logical
victory.

Faust has brought about the ruin of Gretchen and her
people and the wretched deaths of Baucis and Philemon,
and yet when he contemplates his final practical achievement he bids the "fair moment stay," and falls triumphant
into the grave dug by the Lemures. It thus becomes significant that while Shakespeare, the pessimist, makes his
powers of evil conquer Macbeth by a superficial equivoca-
tion, Goethe has his evil one defeated by a more spiritual
quibble. But this extraordinary poem—which is nothing less
than the greatest autobiography ever written—doesn't end
with Faust's death.

While the soul is not yet free Mephistopheles utters his
word of everlasting futility which, for it springs from the
same abyss as the word of life, cannot in the nature of
things find any logical refutation. Here is Mr. Latham's
admirable rendering of this Satanic self-justification.

CHORUS: *'Tis past and over.*
MEPHISTOPHELES: *Past! a stupid word.*
Why past and over?

Past and pure Nothingness! The same and wholly one!
What boots us then Creation's endless travail?
Created but to nothing to unravel!
'Tis past! From that what meaning can be twisted?
It is as good as had it ne'er existed
And yet in cycle moves as if it were.
Eternal Emptiness would I prefer.

Thus does Goethe drop his plummet into the void, into the *other side* of the mind of *the Mothers*, into the inert malice of the Absolute; and in comparison with this indrawn breath of Brahma, in comparison with this abysmal sigh of "the Thing in Itself," how frivolous does most human pessimism appear!

In fact, Mephistopheles, though defeated by Faust's irresistible share in the creative energy that evolves the world, is never *in his own nature* put to silence. He remains to the end the eternal protest of *not-being*, which, as Hegel says, is the necessary compliment to *being*.

And how characteristic of that non-moral element in Goethe's own nature that has always been such a stumbling-block to certain minds, and that made even his admirer Carlyle more than once throw down *Wilhelm Meister* in despair as he struggled with it, is the way the pretty boy-girl angels steal off with Faust's soul while their Adversary is absorbed in his satyrish lust for their lovely limbs!

The poem ends as it began in superterrestrial regions; and among the ecstatic worshippers of the celestial Life-Force—represented, be it noticed, by *the Mother*, not the Son, of God—we are permitted a vision of the redeemed Gretchen.

The Indescribable,
Here it is done:
The Eternal Feminine
Leads us Upwards and on!

12

Wordsworth

MORE critical energy has been lavished on Wordsworth than upon any other modern poet. And yet how clear it is that nothing approaching the final word about him has yet been said!

No one is to blame for this but himself. His work is like the multifarious impressions, the sluggish half-physical thoughts, the monotonous unappealing objects, together with the transporting thoughts and the divinely magical objects, of which any of us might grow aware, during a long tiring walking-tour through town and country.

There is something hard and tough, cold and self-centred, at the core of the man's nature, something isolated, selfish, and stiff, the sort of thing we are accustomed to call "unsympathetic," something that would make a neighbour say to himself as he heard that cottage door close, or that drive gate click, "There goes Mr. Wordsworth, off for one of his walks. I don't think I'll bother him to-day."

Stirred to the depths by the French Revolution, a natural emotion that was, as we now grow weary of being reminded, intensified by a still more natural emotion, his passion for a French girl, it is plain enough that at bottom Wordsworth was a born and instinctive conservative.

Browning's well-known arraignment of him is patently unfair—there are plenty of "handfuls of silver" to be got in the opposite camp, and "ribands to stick in our coats," too! There is indeed abroad at the present hour a curious conscientious fear of not being on the side of progress and of being caught with old-fashioned moral prejudices, that makes many a timid, well-meaning soul hide his natural God-fearing simplicity as uneasily as if it were an anarchist's bomb.

And if to our radical nerves there is something infuriating about what we feel to be his stupid piety, tedious morality, irrational optimism, to our equally tense medieval-reaction nerves his idealism seems easy, obvious, vague, windy, lacking aesthetic subtlety, lacking that desperate "I believe because it *is* impossible," which has so strong an appeal to our recondite perversities.

Ah! Browning, Browning, if your psychological insight had been a little deeper you would have had the wit to see that thanking God for Legacies and Controllorships and Poet Laureateships is not the only hypocrisy in the world, any more than the composing of Ecclesiastical Sonnets and Sonnets advocating Capital Punishment is the only literary crime.

The way to get at the earth-rooted rock-bottom of Wordsworth's best poetry is to analyse the nature of his particular kind of simplicity.

We have our "simple" poets on both sides of the Atlantic, such as A. E. Housman and Robert Frost, but how sophisticated, how premeditated, these poets' artlessness is compared with Wordsworth's when he was really driven to let himself go! It was in him to be spontaneously grandiose and diffuse and rhetorical, just as it was in him to elaborate the most complicated and metaphysical reasons for being puerile and dull; but when the breath of the spirit touched him, and that emotion "remembered in tranquillity" was stirred within him, his simplicity is like the water of life flowing from the eternal hills! It is not only "simple"; it is

majestic, inevitable, unalterable. It has the magical directness of the gods of the early world, talking to another from
mountain to mountain, in the silence before the dawn.

To reach the essence of a great poet's work it is necessary
to consider his physical nature, his normal character, his
average being, independently of his peculiar type of
intellect and imagination.

Wordsworth had a solid weight of healthy physical being.
He had, too, a solid weight of stubborn, obstinate, massive
character, that, like the cloud to which he compares his
reserved old leech-gatherer, "moveth altogether if it
moves at all."

The neurotic, the quick-witted, the morbidly sensitized
temperament with which we are only too familiar to-day, as
the dominant stuff out of which genius is made, how is it
possible for such electric waywardness to do justice to the
massive single-hearted impulses of a poet as normal, as
tough, as unconciliatory in his conservatism, as Wordsworth?

But just as the great winds of night and day can make a
more majestic music when they bend the branches of a
rock-rooted Scotch fir than when they rustle the foliage of
poplars or willows, so, when the spirit does take hold of this
man and his sluggish nature vibrates under its touch we
get an inspiration beyond all beauty of artifice or even of
art; and the winds and the waves and the water-brooks
respond to what is akin to them in ourselves.

It goes deeply against the grain with me to listen to glib
aspersions upon what is called the "optimism" of Wordsworth. However much you may sympathize with attacks
upon his tedious old-fashioned piety, it would seem that a
man who regarded suffering as a deeper and more perdurable thing than pleasure is a somewhat grim and
austere optimist. You might as well call Dante an optimist!
I do not know any writer except Hardy who indicates more
tenaciously and with a sterner hand what you might call

the "bend sinister" of the boughs of the tree of life, and the contortion of rigid endurance that binds animate and inanimate together, in the long travail of the world.

For good or evil Wordsworth regarded the business of being a poet as something very different from the composition of "pretty pieces of paganism." He set out to convey in poetry a philosophy of human happiness that was of necessity a philosophy of human endurance; and he deliberately based it upon the senses. From the senses came all those overtones and undertones that transported him so constantly to that region, to that dimension rather, where we feel the presence of the Something else, the "Something far more deeply interfused" that lies "too deep for tears," too deep for words, too deep for reason.

It was Shelley, I believe, who said that in Wordsworth *the senses think*. And this is true; but they not only think. They become ministers of grace in the sternest endurances of the spirit. This is where Wordsworth is indeed unique among poets.

In Keats the magical and immortal loveliness of nature where "youth grows pale and spectre-thin and dies, where but to think is to be full of sorrow and leaden-eyed despairs," is *contrasted* with the tragedy of human life; whereas in Wordsworth there are always the simpler, austerer, lonelier presences of nature, which like a shadow on a way-side stone, or a raven crossing a mountain chasm, or the cuckoo's cry "breaking the silence of the seas," or a twisted thorn on a desolate moor, or a tuft of feathered grass stirred by the wind upon a ruined wall, blend themselves with the refusal of the stoical heart to abate one jot of "resolution and independence" under the shocks of untoward fortune.

It is not necessary to journey to the Lake Country, where he was born and lived, to catch the essence of his revelation.

Many of his most characteristic poems were written elsewhere. Wherever a wave breaks or a wind blows, wherever
the sun rises or sets, wherever a highway crosses an upland
unto the wide unknown, wherever the moonlight falls on
the works of men's hands, wherever a roadside ditch reveals
a flowering weed, or the smoke mounts from a human
hearth, or a girl sings at her work, or a child "leaps up on
his mother's arm," or "a single field, of many, one" arrests
us with its mysterious shock of obscure memory, the spirit
of Wordsworth's poetry abides.

What he communicates is deeper than the potency of the
picturesque, or even, in the ordinary sense, of the beautiful.
It is of those mysterious feelings that come to us all now and
then, and lift us out of ourselves and out of our sorrows,
with vague intimations of something in the mere experience
of life, beyond luck, beyond ill-luck, that his poetry keeps
hinting; and it is for this reason that he is at his best in
writing of the very old and the very young. What he is
for ever fumbling and groping towards is nothing less than
what, in another medium, is the main preoccupation of
Proust's convoluted prose, the secret of existence caught, so
to speak, on the wing among the most casual, accidental,
and fleeting of our sense-impressions. The fever of the
world, rather than any suffering or loss, is what dulls our
inner sense to these rare feelings; and though to make much
of them no leisured detachment from the burden and the
heat of the day is required, they do seem to arrive most
naturally to the especial sensibility of feminine youth and
masculine old age.

Certainly with Wordsworth—and this is deeply involved
with his peculiar temperament—it is from the brooding
receptivity of girlhood and from the outward-gazing contemplation of aged men, that the most powerful elements
in his inspiration are drawn.

On the other hand no poet has written as poignantly as

he has done of the tragic intensity of the maternal passion. "Women labouring of child" and women with infants at the breast play a part in his poems second only to that of young girls and old men; and the noticeable thing is that in all these cases it is upon what one might call *the passive state of being* rather than upon any state of action that the emphasis is of necessity laid.

Clever analytical natures, as well as those in whose existence the aesthetic element dominates, will never be naturally attracted to Wordsworth; for the whole drift of his poetry concerns those simple but fleeting and mysterious sensations that are beyond analysis and have to do with the normal continuity of ordinary life.

One might indeed say that the abiding subject of Wordsworth's poetry is the most difficult of all subjects, as well as the most important; for it is nothing less than an attempt to put into words those obscure feelings of half-physical, half-mystic happiness, that come to all of us in ordinary life, and come from quite casual impressions, and yet when they come sweep us away into strange vistas of unearthly exultation.

And the miracle is that whenever he does succeed in catching these vague, subtle, fleeting feelings, his language takes on a magical directness, an unaccommodating austerity, a simplicity like that of polished pebbles under moonlit water. What we must remember is that the same honesty, the same grave realism, the same absence of the affected or the artificial, that accounts for his grandest poetical effects, also accounts for those things in his work that strike the un-Wordsworthian mind as dull, puerile, ridiculous, grotesque, and idiotic. What really confronts us in Wordsworth is a strong, hard, self-centred, unsociable temperament that has the power of responding to the inanimate and the elemental as if it were itself tough as a gnarled tree, hard as a weather-beaten stone, majestic in its inhuman aloofness as the motions of dawn and noon and night.

The way to get at his real value, his abiding quality, is not to draw back from the mass of moralistic tedium and ponderous sermonizing, but to wander over the surface of all this with a sensitized divining-rod; for through all of it runs, like an underground river, that startling intimacy with the voices and the silences of the inanimate that brings us close to the cosmic secret.

We need no unusual cleverness, no particular gift of taste, no especial luck in our chance-given abode, no favour from the gods in our fate-chosen companions, no exceptional power of mind or spirit, to saturate ourselves in Wordsworth's way of life. Surrounded by dulness we can touch the eternal. Surrounded by the commonplace we can feel the infinite. All that we need is a certain stoical self-centredness, a certain aloofness from the world, a certain sacred stupidity, a certain consecrated and crafty detachment from the lively interests of the hour, and a tendency, I might almost say, to share the subhumanity of rocks and stones and trees, to watch the grass growing till we grow with it, the way-side stones waiting till we wait with them, to walk with the morning as with a companion, with the night as with a friend, to catch the pathos of the human generations from the rain on the roof, and the burden of the mystery that rounds it all from the wind that voyages past the threshold.

Yes, the thing to do with Wordsworth is simply to disregard his conventional virtue, his conventional piety, his ponderous moralizings, and to treat all these as a wholesome and reassuring proof that his inspiration, when it does arrive, is unique in its integrity; for with him it is not the premeditated originality of a poet trying hard to say something that has been never said before, but the voice—

against the grain of his own conventionality—"of what was and is and is to come."

Every great genius makes use, either positively or negatively, of what might be called the defects of his character. It is for this reason, that the faults of a man of genius are of the utmost interest and worthy of the closest scrutiny. Now Wordsworth's most obvious fault is a certain hard, stupid, wooden imperviousness implying a lack of porous human sympathy. But when one comes to analyse this limitation down to the depths one finds that it is this very hardness, as though some nervous fibre in him had turned into stone, that helps him to give a clear pure echo to the overtones and undertones of the sense-feelings of the generations.

It is difficult enough for the individual to put aside the distractions of action so as to yield himself to the purer sensuous impressions of diurnal existence; but it is more difficult still to put aside, along with the distractions of action, those personal, emotional, subjective reactions which prevent us from being a perfectly detached medium for the primal feelings of life, as such feelings have been repeated for countless centuries.

Now it is the very hardness and imperviousness in this great poet's character that saved him from all those nervous susceptibilities, both physical and metaphysical, such as proved so deadly to his friend Coleridge. But it did more than that. It made it easy for him to echo back—as if from the surface of a hard mountain rock—all those primeval murmurs of our normal responses to life, overtones of the universal senses of man, which the distractions of more sensitized individual nerves, as well as the obvious distractions of action, prevent our hearing. To isolate, in other words, "the still small voice" of the universal sense-feelings of the generations amid the uproar of the world it is necessary to be as tough as wood or as hard as stone.

WILLIAM WORDSWORTH

But there is often brought against Wordsworth, by people whose "sense of humour" is no more than a cheap awareness of the ludicrous, the charge of being outrageously ridiculous. This, among the critical wags of his own day, must have been the prevalent "clever" reaction to such curious poems as "Peter Ball," "The Idiot Boy," "Goody Blake and Harry Gill," and even to "The Last of the Flock" and "The Thorn"; all of which are poems wherein a certain tragic intensity is combined with a grotesque childishness.

Now, any one who has known country life in England until it has grown into his bones knows that there is a grim bed-rock humour there, such as might be called "the humour of the human skeleton," something which lurks in the very ground-element of rural intercourse, something which must inevitably strike a jocular outsider as grotesquely childish and a sensitive outsider as crazily repulsive.

The element I am thinking of is indeed the aesthetic inverse of that stark realism of the country which undoubtedly does have an aspect that is hard and pitiless, if not actually brutal and terrible.

As I have hinted above, the groundwork of Wordsworth's own psychology was the extreme opposite of the sentimental or the "artistic." It was essentially tough, austere, stoical; possessing the terrible patience, under one's own *and others'* suffering, of old trees, old animals, old men, and old women.

And what in these grotesque lyrical vignettes of tragic endurance attains its grandest utterance in poems like "Michael" and "Ruth" and "The Affliction of Margaret" and in the noble verses about the aged leech-gatherer, whose "head and feet," so bent he was, were "coming together in life's pilgrimage," finds a diffused and long-winded expression in those lengthy productions that only the real initiate in the Wordsworthian secret is able to get through. I refer to *The Prelude* and *The Excursion*, where the poet's own lumbering and egoistic evolution is revealed— not without a North Countryman's crafty reserve—in all its instinctive earth-bound sagacity, its integral debouchings, its tough and hard-sinewed piety.

Most poetry-lovers are content to enjoy Wordsworth's poetry, when from a purely *poetic* point of view it is at its best, as in "Intimations" and "Tintern Abbey," and in so many of the sonnets, and in such magical outbursts as "The Highland Reaper"; but my own feeling is that quite apart from these grander heights, apart even from his cosmic intuitions with regard to the "Something far more deeply interfused," there can be discovered, scattered amid the incredible tedium, banality, and sheer silliness of so much of his work, hints and suggestions towards a way of taking life which can prove of unspeakable value even to minds that are forced to reject with indignant aversion the tra-ditional foundation of his old-fashioned piety.

To have made our senses not only *think* for us, but supply us with vistas of strange feeling, down which, like gossamer galleons charged with the afterthoughts of a thousand generations, the long broodings of our race can drift, was no negligible achievement. It was to open the door, it was to lift the sluice, it was to roll back the horizon a little further, for every child of man; so that without idealism or romanticism or any of the affections or novelties of art, a simple unintellectual man or woman, however closely bound to the wheel of matter and the iron of circumstance, may catch sometimes from the least promising aspects of our earth-life and the least engaging aspects of the inani-mate around us, a breath of what, if it is neither ecstasy nor hope, is at least a reciprocity of endurance. A plain man or woman, bearing up under a monotonous and weary exist-ence, can get small comfort from being told "to live in the

Beautiful, the Good, and the True," but concealed beneath
the weight of Wordsworth's too frequent tediousness lies
a secret that can bring to such burdened spirits a startling
and masterful release, a trick of tapping, in the response of
our senses to life on its barest level, a well-spring of inscrutable strength, in the power of which—just as if, only a
little way below our barest sense of being alive, there
flowed, along its own mysterious channel-bed, an unfathomable stream of formidable life-force—our soul can
dispense with what love and art and cleverness add to life,
and can touch in its stripped and lonely integrity what
might be called "the Thing in Itself," that primal energy
of creation, of which the common inanimate and the common elements are the simplest embodiment, and in contact
with which we grow aware of something in ourselves whose
power of endurance is at once subhuman and superhuman.

The essence of Wordsworth's inmost teaching is totally
apart from his traditional piety. It is a stoicism that draws
its strength from forces outside humanity. It is a stoicism
that endures as rocks and trees and plants and animals
endure; but inasmuch as it is an inhuman stoicism, it
endures as in the presence of something beyond the cate-
gories of human thought. It endures, like the sleepless eye
of the whole astronomical world, in a cosmic expectation
as undisturbed by hope as it is untroubled by despair.

Casually turning the pages of any complete edition of
Wordsworth's poems the heart of even the most devoted
adherent must often sink in weariness, if not in actual
indignation. Never was there so much dulness, so much
convention and tedium, so much sluggishness, so much
uninspired wordiness.

Expurgated indeed he must be, unless you are a reader for
whom it is enough if words rhyme; enough if some kind of
a metre reminding us of poetry is kept going.

And, heaven help us! it is an expurgation from the dull,

not the indecent, that is required! "He who uttered nothing base," wrote the good Tennyson of him in fatuous praise. As if the most blasphemous scurrility would not be a relief after such heavy purity.

And yet for a reader who has once got on the track of the Wordsworthian secret no selection is really quite satisfying. In some queer way it seems a sort of homely reassurance against the kind of artistic premeditation and forced originality one has come so deeply to distrust that the man should remain so sublimely, so obstinately, so stupidly *natural*! The best way is to regard all this mass of pontifical meandering as the only soil, thick enough, heavy enough, weedy enough, clayey enough, *unconscious enough*, to produce the particular kind of enchanted root, which the immortal gods called *Moly*, and which the Messenger gave to the much-enduring Odysseus, so that he might enjoy unbetrayed the perilous embraces of the daughter of the Sun, and learn from her how to hear without losing heart "the still sad music" of the unnumbered nations of the dead, who shall see that Sun no more.

13

Dickens

IF SOME Saturnian Micromegas were to visit our earth to make a study of the various types of human genius represented by our different nations and races and languages, what would he set down in his planetary note-book as the supreme contribution of the English? Surely he would only hesitate between two grand qualities that throw all others into the shade: *magical poetry* and *idiosyncratic humour*.

By "magical poetry" Micromegas would have to explain, when he returned to his Saturnian Academy, that he meant poetry *in its purest quintessence*, whether in ballads and songs, or in particular passages from longer poems.

And by "idiosyncratic humour" he would have to explain to his learned colleagues that he meant humour that was neither wit, nor satire, nor comedy, nor sarcasm, nor irony, nor farce, but a humour entirely and absolutely *dependent upon character*, that is to say upon the whimsical effect produced by every mortal thought, gesture, word, and *even silence*, of a person of either sex who could be described as a character.

"But for Heaven's sake inform us," the Saturnian Academy would enquire of their ambassador, "what you mean by a 'character'? Are we 'characters'? Could this high quality of the planetary tribe to which you allude be said to emanate from *us*?"

But at that point, like other intellectual explorers returning home, our traveller would be forced to change the subject; for the probability is that in that august assembly there would be more Wilhelm Meisters than Dick Swivellers and more Jean Christophes than Falstaffs.

But Micromegas to make a diversion would proceed to illustrate what he meant by this *humour of character* by passages from the English geniuses who possessed it, brief passages from Scott and Jane Austen, and much longer ones from Shakespeare and Sterne. He would even read a few excerpts from Charles Lamb, to show how this "humour of character" could be diffused through the most random sallies of discursive fancy, and remain unspoilt by the most bookish wit.

And then to illustrate the nature of "magical poetry" as distinct from other sorts he would quote from Shakespeare and Keats and Coleridge and Matthew Arnold and from the old ballads.

"But I beg you to note," he would say, "that while the special English humour to which I refer appears at its best in Shakespeare and Sterne and Dickens, it does not appear in complete isolation. In Shakespeare it is mixed with tragedy, in Sterne with sentiment, and in Dickens with melodrama; but since there is a larger and a more exuberant mass of it in Dickens than in these two others, I must announce to you," Micromegas would conclude, "that as Keats represents one of the two supreme gifts of this tribe, the most irrational and unphilosophical tribe to be found on this mad globe, from whose Bedlam—and not without relief—I returned yesterday, Dickens represents the other."

Passing from the analysis of Micromegas to our own attempt to get into focus something of what this name "Charles Dickens" represents, it seems as though to do the man full justice we have to consider the extraordinary handicaps under which he laboured.

In the first place, unlike Shakespeare, he had no "uni-

versity extension" culture to fall back upon, no Mermaid
Tavern frequented by learned wits, no encounters with
rich young bloods fresh from a Renaissance court or from
"swimming in gondolas."

In the second place it was London, and not the country,
upon which his imagination had to feed. Think of the implications of this! The whole trend of British literature from
Shakespeare to Hardy has been countryward rather than
cityward. Practically all the great novels before Dickens
have either country towns or country villages as their background. This is partly, of course, because cities as we know
them now, and even as Dickens knew them, are things of
recent growth, creations of the Industrial Revolution; but
London was there, London with her streets, her river, her
docks, her bridges, her squares, her markets, her churches,
her shops, her offices, her slums; but how seldom—and then
only incidentally—did our earlier novelists make any real
imaginative use of her!

No one has caught the spirit of London like Dickens;
of foreign writers, describing great foreign cities, none can
touch him except Dostoievsky. Balzac himself is not *quite*
at his best when dealing with Paris. In his Paris scenes,
through all the smouldering and dusky magnificence,
through all the intricate contrasts of the sumptuous and the
sordid, through all the passion-drugged procession of sweet
innocents and fuliginous devils we seem to miss, at least so
it appears to me, something of that unequalled street magic,
so rich, so thick, so convincing, that we get from his provincial towns. The smoky trail of his Arabian-Nights' demons,
the super-gangster *Treize*, is enough in itself to blight with
its fabulous brimstone the homely truth of the *Cousin Pons*
and *Cousin Bette* element; while round the thunder-scarred
brows of the tremendous Vautrin hover mephitic flames
sufficient to reduce to a neutral pallor the shrinking tapers
of reality.

No, in the whole of human fiction there are, from my point of view, only two novelists who give us the real ineffable magic of a vast metropolitan city. Zola deliberately sought to do it, but he lacked the imagination; and if, as I have hinted, Balzac was always being side-tracked by his passion for superhuman rascals, Victor Hugo was too deafened by his own grandiose virtue to catch those whimsical oracles that like elfin half-wits drift with the dust about the doors. Dostoievsky and Dickens alone, to my thinking, hold the clue to the mystery of a great city, of *any* great city; and they achieved this by the possession of a certain imaginative power that suggests, as only the most magical poetry can do, the real relation of the animate to the inanimate.

Neither of these writers troubles greatly about style, neither of them bothers much about "documented" realism, neither of them is afraid of the wildest melodrama. It is true that on one occasion Dickens goes out of his way to prove the literal truth, from historic evidence, of the phenomenon known as "spontaneous combustion"; but as the higher truth of the imagination absolutely demanded this unusual event, such an excursion was quite superogatory. What Dostoievsky and Dickens have in common is a quality singularly difficult to define, as are all great imaginative essences, but it is a quality at all events that has to do with the porousness of human souls to inanimate objects, and it is as richly charged with the magic of streets and houses as is the poetry of Keats and Shakespeare with that of land and sea.

It is I think no far-fetched fancy to note yet another resemblance between these two—the fact that they are so ensorcerized by the sayings of Jesus. Here they differ from both Shakespeare and Hardy; and is it fantastic, considering the derivation of the word "pagan," to look upon this as the natural result of the kind of "sorrow" that is "barricaded evermore," as Wordsworth says, "within the walls of cities"?

It is ever in the country that the old gods linger, ever through the crowded towns that the new religions—Communism among them—carry their spiritual flames; and there is little enough of the heathen worship of the earth in either Dostoievsky or Dickens. Over the Nevski Prospect of the one, over the Whitechapel of the other, hover the outraged lineaments of "le Bon Sansculotte" and whether it is done with Russian mysticism or with English radicalism every aspect of religion except the desperate paradoxes of Jesus is torn to shreds with the sound of the tearing of many parchments.

The more you read Dickens—skipping, as a grown-up person, *some* of the tenth-rate sentiment—the more his resemblance to Dostoievsky expands and deepens. And his amazing genius is shown in the mere fact that this is the case *while he dodges every problem of sex*. To create a world of supertruth, whose roots are plunged in nature while it goes beyond nature in carrying out her most erratic ventures, and yet to dodge the quicksands of sex, is indeed an achievement.

But putting sex aside—and one feels that this ban was largely due to the umbilical cord of personal sympathy that bound him in such a glow of reciprocity to his huge audience—Dickens resembles Dostoievsky in his complete disregard of almost all the labours by which humanity lives! Office-work and needlework are the only forms of human activity at which we are permitted to be present. Here we contemplate at their job, no carpenters, no plumbers, no weavers, no dairymen, no miners, no ploughmen, not even any fishermen, except the Peggotty family; and the plots turn, just as Dostoievsky's do, upon the arbitrary benevolence, or the arbitrary miserliness of people who in some unexplained manner have large sums of money in the bank. The activities of lawyers and of lawyers' clerks play a tremendous part, and the offices of old merchant houses; but of the actual processes of business or of finance, such as Balzac and in our own day Dreiser find such joy in describing, we hear little or nothing. We are led to assume that many specious rascals are occupied in many sinister enterprises, but the nature of these enterprises, except in the case of money-lenders and rent-collectors, are left obscure.

Dickens does indeed play two most rewarding cards, if I may put it so, neglected by the great Russian. I refer to his descriptions of various little shops, full of various fantastic objects, and to his absorbing passion for itinerant showmen. It is "bread and the circus" indeed—the poor man's intermittent paradise. And this mania for showmen, which extends to every type of theatric entertainer, has no rival in his love except endless potations from the flowing bowl and feverish consumption of buttered toast. Certainly when you think of Dostoievsky's murderous vodka-orgies and deadly samovar-metaphysics there is a Gargantuan reassurance about these harmless circus-people and their innocent collations.

But though in place of these Russian philosophers wrestling with God and the Devil over their stoves and their vodka we have the prodigals and the misers and the half-wits of London frying their bacon and buttering their toast, there is in both these writers the same dark, brooding, atmospheric tension, full of the creakings and shufflings of the padded feet of fate.

Take the chapter in *Bleak House* which introduces us to Mr. Tulkinghorn and at the same time gathers up the whole "milieu" of the law-courts and their victims into a revolving cloud of smoke and dust and powdery papers out of the heart of which the old lawyer's ruby glass of solitary port gleams like a ubiquitous eye, and note how the transfusing imagination that gives these scenes their organic unity answers to the watchful atmosphere that hangs about the Karamazov home, where the doomed old man is waiting, always waiting, for Grushenka to come to him!

When one considers how much easier it is—for an English novelist, anyway—to blend the majestic processes of nature with his narrative than to give to the inanimate objects in a dust-begrimed city their apocalyptic significance, it indeed makes one feel that a master thaumaturge is at work, to enter any of these Dickens habitations. In every pause of the action, in every lull of the talk, you are aware of the crowd of inanimate witnesses that surround these bizarre people, surround them with mockings and beckonings, with leerings and oglings, as though from a world of presences living a subhuman life parallel with ours.

Where he is far below Dostoievsky as a novelist, and even below Scott or Balzac, is in his unfortunate sentimentality. His is a sentimentality worse even than Sterne's, though it is more sincere; for Sterne's sentiment, as in the case of Maria and her goat, and the caged bird, and the ass with the macaroon, is a deliberate aesthetic cult, whereas with Dickens it is simply the popular warmth of an unsophisticated heart. It is, in fact, unmitigated bad taste—parallel with the lapses of the popular cinema; and at its worst it assumes a sanctimonious religious form, as when Agnes at the death of Dora raises a saintly finger and points upwards at the ceiling.

The truth is that in reading Dickens an ordinary intelligent person has to do what he does when reading Wordsworth—unless he has a malicious relish for the lapses of genius—discreetly hurry on. For in Dickens we are faced—and there is I think no parallel example among great novelists—with two collaborating authors, one of whom is, after Rabelais, the supreme humorous genius of the human race, and the other a tenth-rate, I might say a twentieth-rate composer of newspaper serials for young ladies.

Of course there has always been a mysterious psychological link between humour and sentimentality. We find it in Hans Andersen; we find it in Heine; we find plenty of it in such an admirable modern author as Neil Lyons. And above all we find it in Charlie Chaplin. But this is an utterly different thing from the Sunday-school claptrap in Dickens. Dickens *can* be touchingly poignant with the old immortal catch in the throat of the undying clown, and here he is often at his very best, as when Dick Swiveller plays cards *à deux*.

"Tell upon you!" said Dick. "Do you mean to say you were looking through the keyhole for company?"

"Yes, upon my word I was," replied the small servant.

"How long have you been cooling your eye there?" said Dick.

"Oh, ever since you first began to play them cards, and long before."

Vague recollections of several fantastic exercises with which he had refreshed himself after the fatigues of business, and to all of which, no doubt, the small servant was a party, rather disconcerted Mr. Swiveller; but he was not very sensitive on such points. . . .

. . . . . .

"Now," said Mr. Swiveller, putting two sixpences into a saucer, and trimming the wretched candle when the cards had been cut and dealt, "those are the stakes. If you win, you get 'em all. If I win I get 'em. To make it seem more real and pleasant, I shall call you the Marchioness, do you hear?"

The small servant nodded.

"Then, Marchioness," said Mr. Swiveller, "fire away!"

The Marchioness, holding her cards very tight in both hands, considered which to play; and Mr. Swiveller, assuming the gay and fashionable air which such society required, took another pull at the tankard, and waited for her lead.

Passages of this kind—and there are a great many of them—are on a par with the famous "So am not I" of Sterne's dropsical scullion, and they form a sort of link between Shakespeare and Charlie Chaplin.

But there are utterances of Dickens' humorous characters all the way through his works that are beyond all dialogues in fiction; that are superior, because more spontaneous and less witty, to most of the humorous utterances in Shakespeare. And when these beyond-all-art sentences occur, what you might call a perfect smoke-ring of supertruth mounts up; and as far as humour is concerned the absolute is reached, as it is reached nowhere else save in Rabelais.

We students of human history—and especially we students of literature—are so conventional in the motions of our mind that because neither Dickens nor Rabelais has composed thoughtful treatises on sociology we fancy that they have contributed little or nothing to the serious progress of the human race. On the contrary, they have contributed everything. They have contributed between them *the one single panacea* that goes to the root of our trouble; and not only so, but together they have indicated the one and only path by which humanity can become more and more itself—that is to say more and more *humane*. The whole of Rabelais and the whole of Dickens is one vast *skit* upon the folly of our clever rulers, our clever bureaucrats, our clever lawyers, our clever generals, our clever scientists, our clever politicians, and our clever patriots. And it is a skit upon these as against the *men of good will*. It is a skit that contains the startling suggestion that only when the "men of good will," that is to say men who refuse to do evil that good may come, *are in possession of the power*, will humanity be set upon its true path—the path not of science *or* religion, for both have failed us, but of *humanity*!

But not even yet have I arrived at what to most of his

readers is the culmination of Dickens' genius: the livingness
of his characters. Many of us feel, and not without reason,
that the invention of living characters, of symbolic characters, of characters that gather into themselves whole avatars
of eternal recurrence, is the proudest, if not the most godlike
achievement of the human mind.

I have myself a malicious prejudice against the glib use
of the word "creative" as applied to the lesser arts. I do
not presume to be offended when a milliner uses it for a
lady's dress, but it does annoy me when it is applied to
pieces of dainty bric-a-brac. This is probably a rustic
prejudice; for in nature there are many tiny sea-shells as
lovely if not as dramatic as the grandest cataract; but it is
a prejudice that has a considerable human tradition behind
it and I have a suspicion that to the end of time, in our
race's estimate of works of imagination, size, length, magnitude, quantity, as well as the weight of human significance
will continue to overawe the mind. Thus we surely must
consider the invention of Don Quixote or Panurge or Falstaff or Hamlet or Uncle Toby or the Idiot as of greater
importance than to compose even such a perfect sonnet as
"Since there's no help, come let us kiss and part," and
equally we must regard the invention of this host of characters as a greater achievement than a perfectly written book
like *Henry Esmond* or *Madame Bovary*.

But let me hint at a certain doubt I feel just here. I
would like to appeal to every reader of *The Enjoyment of
Literature*, when they reach this point, as to whether, deep in
their hearts, they wouldn't sooner have invented Don
Quixote than all the characters in Dickens put together?
This categorical question is not however really a fair one;
for there is no other human "creation"—and here indeed
we have a right to use this godlike word—in the least
comparable to Don Quixote. To keep *him* the human race
might well offer up Falstaff and Panurge and Hamlet and

Uncle Toby as well as all our Dickens puppets. Indeed, to
find a counterweight for Don Quixote you would have to
leave the inventions of individual men altogether and pass
into mythological regions where the anonymous genius of
humanity itself has been at work.

Dickens is undoubtedly, for all his ban on sex, what
Nietzsche would call a "Dionysian." Here he resembles
Rabelais; and it is for this reason that one still encounters
nervous and fastidious persons, devotees of Walter Pater or
of Henry James, who "can't read Dickens." In Rabelais
you have to put up with the mountains of excrement, with
the colossal slaughterings, with the cosmic bawdiness, while
in Dickens you have to endure, what is even harder to
many, a great deal of boisterous bad taste and an exuberance that in avoiding indecency plunges into vulgarity.

And you have to endure so much unmitigated *ugliness*.
If Doré's illustrations of Rabelais are sufficient to frighten
away many timid spirits, what must be said of the veritable
revel in human distortions that we encounter in the original
illustrations of Dickens?

Gazing at these goblins—and I protest that sometimes
they dehumanize our wretched mortality to a point of
terrified disgust—we have the sensation of being present at
a "Walpurgis night" of domesticated Lemurs, whose
swarming masks are far more shocking than any of the he-
apes or she-apes of Goethe's fancy. Those burning eyes of
Dickens missed nothing of the pantomime distortions of our
mortal bodies, nothing of the devil-dance masks of our
pitiful "mugs," but the illustrators of Dickens set out to
imitate humanity still more abominably; caricaturing cari-
catures, till these wretched images of God become like
those revolting "valentines" which superseded the tender
missives of an earlier age.

There must be a vein of enjoyment of the monstrously
vulgar in our national psychology, else how did those hor-

rible "valentines"—worse than anything that even Swift's race-loathing could conjure up—ever come into being? But one approaches the same thing, or used to when I was young, in some of the "comics" that children love. And perhaps there, and there alone, lies the explanation! Children are not as sensitive to the hideously grotesque as some older people, especially those among us who purged our taste—or depraved it if you will—with the sinful line of beauty in Beardsley's delicate erotica! There certainly existed in Dickens a great deal of that strange immunity to the horror of ugliness that seems to be a characteristic of children; and is it possible that his suppression of sex, which his loving reciprocity with his Victorian public encouraged, helped to develop this childish immunity to disgust-phobia?

But against all this, have we not reason to be proud that the most English of all our men of letters surpasses all the writers of the world in his genius for describing children themselves? It is indeed impossible to exaggerate the child element in Dickens' imagination. If it is this curious chastity in the driving-force of his demonic urge that accounts for his freedom from the *disgust-phobia*, it is surely this same quality that endows all his inanimates with such abounding life.

And I think, too, that all this must have a definite connexion with the absence from Dickens' personal culture of any influence from the classical world. The smallest smattering of such an influence encourages in us a diffused erotic fastidiousness with regard to the human body. But Dickens' characters seem, if I may say so—and the deliberate grotesqueness of the old illustrations intensify this effect—*to have been born in their costumes.*

It is a shocking thought, an indecent thought, to imagine any of these vivacious, hilarious, fiendish, angelic, gesticulating puppets *without their clothes.* Nor is this merely that

Brown Bros.

CHARLES DICKENS

so many of them are elderly. The poor lean mortal frame
of Don Quixote, do we not know it, in its crazy nakedness,
as well as Sancho did, and reverence it more, just as we
reverence a naked medieval saint? Scott's Baron Bradwar-
dine could strip himself to the skin and none would wink an
eyelid; so could Meg Merrilies, the old gipsy, or Flora
Mac-Ivor, the Highland beauty; but it is as inconceivable
to think of a naked Agnes or Dora as it is revolting to think
of a naked Micawber or Pecksniff or Quilp!

Every great original genius is a rock of offence, an in-
cendiary's torch, a sword for the dividing of souls, and I
know well that my particular reaction to Dickens must
inevitably excite contempt as well as sympathy.

I am aware myself of the same antipodal emotions
towards the instinctive reactions of others to him! How it
used to outrage my feelings at school when certain literary
masters amused themselves by composing examination
questions upon *Pickwick*! How it annoys me still to hear a
certain type of unctuous and jocular, and to my mind
totally undiscriminating reader, put this same *Pickwick* on
a par with Rabelais! To confess my own secret thought, I
believe that all this fuss over *Pickwick* has done real harm
to the appreciation of the far subtler and quite as characteristic excellences of Dickens' later books.

Oh, we have to go much deeper than this merry-andrew
vein which for all its racy inventions offers us little beyond
inspired farce, before we reach the Aladdin's cave of his
extraordinary imagination!

For myself I find him at his best, not in *David Copperfield*,
and certainly not in *Martin Chuzzlewit*, but in *Bleak House*,
Little Dorrit, and *Our Mutual Friend*. It is in these books, to
my notion, that we get a certain atmospheric feeling that
has no parallel in literature.

If this impression is connected with the emotions of childhood it is no more connected with any *particular* children

than it is in his other books. In all his books there are children, and they serve him, as Puck and Ariel served Shakespeare, as mediums for this atmospheric secret. And it is curious that it should be in Dickens, where reign ugly and grotesque powers rather than beautiful ones, that children play such a dominant rôle; while with Shakespeare and the Greeks—where the ruling spirit is the spirit of beauty—they hardly appear at all!

There are singularly few children in Balzac, or in Scott either, and one feels that here again Dickens and Dostoievsky are together, and together as the only great novelists who in the profoundest sense of all have caught the secret of the spirit of Jesus. Yes, the grandeur of both Dickens and Dostoievsky is that they dare to make a frontal attack on exactly the same worldly and false "reality" that Jesus attacked. The tragic psychology of the one and the infinite humour of the other were both directed against, not the flesh or the devil, but *the world*, the world of logical cause-and-effect, the world of "efficient" work, the world whose hard self-made gods are the gods of knowledge and power! Among Dostoievsky's drunkards, whores, degenerates, and madmen move his disturbing saints, such as the Idiot and Alyosha. Among Dickens' performers, entertainers, showmen, clowns, devils, and misers, move his wistful all-enduring children. Over and over again in both their works there are gathered together queer groups of human oddities; with the all-levelling metaphysical samovar in the one case, and the all-levelling unmetaphysical punchbowl in the other, unloosening hearts and tongues. And in both cases the reader grows aware of "something else"; of "somebody else" present among these queer ones, creating a glow, a warmth, a melting together of the knotty husks of obstinate human selfishness! Again and again in both of them the reader has the sensation that a power beyond humanity is melting the isolation, the pride, the self-complacency, the proud efficiency of the righteous in the presence of some little accidental human gesture, some chance-blown natural light falling upon some negligible inanimate object. And then, and then, with a tragic burst of tears, *à la russe*, and a wild and whirling jest, *à la Londres*, lo! the impossible happens, the fairy-story comes true, two and two make five, and the Kingdom of Heaven is among us!

No great pagan novelist brooding bitterly upon life's futility, or clinging passionately to the sweet anodynes of beauty and sex, can shake the walls of our solemn cause-and-effect Consistory, as Dostoievsky does when Rogozin flings a million roubles into the stove, or Captain Cuttle conjures up the lost Wal'r—"he's drownded, ain't he?"—into little Florence's arms. Something breaks in *from outside* in the work of both these prophets of the millennium, disturbing our modern star, the star Wormwood, in its rational courses and interrupting the orderly sequence of the tragedy "Man." These two great masks, in these "lonesome latter years," put the match to the gunpowder under our "brass-tacks" reality, till the "world as it wags" which Lear told Gloucester you could see with the "case of eyes" begins to heave and crack.

There is round the work of all great geniuses a certain aura or emanation, made up of the winnowed essence of the writer's most characteristic vision; and I always feel this when I look at any volume of Dickens; and I remember feeling it at school in spite of that dubious fuss over *Pickwick*.

From the covers of any of Dickens' books emerges a cloud, like the cloud from the unsealed bottle where the genie was imprisoned; and to me this magic cloud has always represented a thick smoky mass of tall dark houses, narrow streets, dim alleys, winding stairways, dingy courts, under a forest of chimneys, alongside of a moaning, desolate, slippery river-wharf. And this smoky mass of lurid habitation always seems to me to be able to thicken itself, and deepen itself, within itself, so that there is no end to its occult and enchanted recesses. By its long contact with humanity the actual masonry and woodwork of this mystic mass has taken on an indescribable livingness of its own, so that as it is perfectly congruous for any member of its goblinish inmates to perish of spontaneous combustion, so it seems natural for any portion of its own fabric to fall into instantaneous dust; for between the inanimate body of this creaking and whispering masonry and the human elves and the human fiends and the more than human children that inhabit it there is an organic affiliation.

This particular vision of a Dickens' book as a dusky fragment of a labyrinthine world of stone and slate and brick, that recedes into a fairylike infinitude, is what makes me so particularly attached to *Little Dorrit*. I always think of the weird house where Mrs. Clennam eats out her heart in self-torture while her soul like a lapping cat licks its saucer of remorse, and where Mr. Flintwinch runs his Affery by the scruff of her neck up and down the creaky stairs, the house that finally falls into powder, as a perfect symbol of that almost physical porousness of human mortality to the bricks and mortar about it which is like a recurrent strain in his vision of life.

But first and last it is in *imagination*, that highest of all human gifts, that he surpasses all competitors. It is real imagination, not just the play of fancy or invention, whereby he created, out of the casual hints and random strokes of chance-encounters, this magic-lantern metropolis. And returning to his pages from the novels of our own age, how lacking we seem in this magician's gift! Philosophy, psychology, sociology—our great writers abound in all of these, but where are the "dramatis personae," where are the *characters*?

In Joyce's great *Ulysses*, Daedalus and Bloom and Bloom's wife are all symbolic focuses of whirlpools within whirlpools of inspired psychic discoveries; but their very weight of mythological and cosmic suggestiveness detracts in some way from the clear-cut outlines of their personalities. There are so many irrepressible, questing, vulgar, lecherous, kindly Blooms, there are so many earthy, shameless, fecund, unfastidious, maternal Mrs. Blooms, that these particular specimens of these planetary types merge the lineaments of their single never-to-be-reproduced identity in the recurrent truth they represent. The universal, in other words, swallows up the particular!

And the same is true of D. H. Lawrence. The grotesque and pathetic and never-to-appear-again outlines of a unique human creature, how completely swamped and absorbed and lost they are in these representative and symbolic sex-reactions! The new psychological science has done precisely what the old physical science is always doing. It has levelled out and drained away the mysterious uniqueness of all separate living persons.

If one of our chief "pleasures" in reading fiction—and it is a legitimate and very ancient one—consists in adding to our list of real acquaintances a vast array of *imagined* acquaintances, what a meagre satisfaction we get—putting the unequalled Proust aside—in present-day literature! They don't *stand out*, these dissected perambulatory pathoids. They puke and pine, they mime and mow at one another, they reveal to a wonder their "streams of consciousness"; but their loves and hates are like the loves and hates in fish-ponds and aquariums. The psychology of sex has dehumanized them. We do indeed feel ourselves into every amorous motion of these fishy universals, but when we've closed the book, we've forgotten their very names. They are ourselves, or rather they are that portion of ourselves which we share so widely—for we are all sadists and masochists and complex-bitten madmen—that the heart of the matter, every man in his unique humour, and every man expressing that unique humour in every unique gesture he makes, has melted away.

Were Dickens to come back from the dead and write to-day, think what he would gain from our greater freedom of speech in sexual and religious matters. But he would use that freedom to outline, to clarify, to emphasize, even further than he did, the abysmal gulf that divides personality from personality, the gulf that is the only true cause of the only true humour—the humour of differentiated character.

The social cruelties that this great Radical attacked have changed their form. The Bounderbys and Gradgrinds of our generation use new moral shibboleths to take the whims and the fancies, the vagaries and the wantonness, in a word *the heart*, out of the lives of men and women. But the solemn sanctimoniousness is the same. The unrelenting self-righteousness is the same, the cock-sure dogmatism is the same; and there is present in all these new "ideologies" the hard eye of Mr. Murdstone, whipping us into line.

It is the old puritan blasphemy, against which, and it is the one single place where he speaks sharply in person, Shakespeare himself protested; the blasphemy of sacrificing the sublime irresponsible mystery of being alive at all, to some damned ulterior purpose, a purpose which in its essential definition can never be more than a means to an end.

The one human spirit that in its divine "escapism" will always baffle these moral slave-drivers of the world is the spirit of humour. It is because the English beyond all others possess this gift—a gift which springs up spontaneously from the depths of their souls—that they "never, never will be slaves"! Slave-drivers can dragoon artists, make prophets recant, make philosophers prevaricate, make scientists serve them with blameless devotion. The one type of free soul that will baffle them and defy them to—well! as

Rabelais would say—"to the fire exclusively," is the soul
of the humorist.

All this goes far and deep. It is a spiritual secret, shared
with that mysterious "love" and that equally mysterious
"equality of all souls" taught by Jesus. Nor can I feel as if
it is mere "miching mallecho" in me when I contend that
after the Fifth Gospel of Dostoievsky our only real Evangelists have been Charles Dickens and Charlie Chaplin. And
both of these great geniuses excel in the little side-scenes
and side-shows where the misfits and the derelicts and the
dotty, all of them candidates for scientific liquidation, utter
their inopportune sentiments.

These side-issue scenes, which have—as far as Dickens is
concerned—very slight connexion with the "classic unities,"
are often passages of the purest inspiration. After reading
them a person feels an impulse to "shake his superflux,"
as Lear says, and "show the Heavens more just." Little
Dorrit is relating a fairy-story to her friend:

> "Hospitals," interposed Maggy, still nursing her knees.
> "Let him have hospitals, because they're so comfortable.
> Hospitals with lots of chicking."
> "Yes, he had plenty of them and he had plenty of
> everything."
> "Plenty of baked potatoes, for instance?" said Maggy.
> "Plenty of everything."
> "Lor!" chuckled Maggy, giving her knees a hug. "Wasn't
> it prime!"

Where Dickens like Charlie Chaplin is in an absolute
sense the spokesman of the People against the Privileged
is in the relish he expresses for the three grand "desiderata"
of a destitute life—food and drink, warmth, and some rare
and startling occurrence.

> Supper was not yet over, when there arrived at the Jolly
> Sandboys two more travellers. . . . One of these was the

proprietor of a giant, and a little lady without legs or arms . . . the other, a silent gentleman who earned his living by showing tricks upon the cards and who had rather deranged the natural expression of his countenance by putting small leaden lozenges into his eyes and bringing them out at his mouth. . . . The name of the first of these newcomers was Vuffin; the other, probably as a pleasant satire upon his ugliness, was called Sweet William.

"How's the Giant?" said Short when they all sat smoking round the fire.

"Rather weak upon his legs," returned Mr. Vuffin. "I begin to be afraid he is going at the knees."

"That's a bad lookout," said Short.

"Ay! Bad indeed," replied Mr. Vuffin, contemplating the fire with a sigh. . . .

"What becomes of the old giants?" said Short turning to him again after a little reflection.

"They're usually kept in caravans to wait upon the dwarfs," said Mr. Vuffin.

"The maintaining of 'em must come expensive when they can't be shown, eh?" remarked Short, eyeing him doubtfully.

"It's better *that* than letting 'em go upon the parish or about the streets," said Mr. Vuffin. "Once make a giant common, and giants will never draw again. Look at wooden legs. If there was only one man with a wooden leg what a property *he'd* be!"

"So he would!" observed the landlord and Short together. "That's very true."

"Instead of which," pursued Mr. Vuffin, "if you was to advertise Shakespeare played entirely by wooden legs, it's my belief you wouldn't draw a sixpence."

"I don't suppose you would," said Short. And the landlord said so too.

It is impossible to overestimate the part played in Dickens' work by his mania for the *theatre*. Like Dostoievsky, what delights him is to gather the most opposite types of character together, each with all his characteristic gestures and familiar tags of speech well-established, and then make them "act" in concerted contrast; but whereas in Dostoievsky this clash quickly becomes a spiritual and symbolic one, with Dickens it either tightens into extravagant melodrama, or dissolves into a delirious glow of pentecostal love.

But whether the tension is tightened into lurid drama, or relaxed into a melting love-feast, one is always aware of the huge personal relish with which the stage management is being conducted; and this leads me to the gulf there is between writers whose "art" is always being *felt* and writers whose creative energy is always carrying them away. For the catholic-minded there is a special pleasure in both; but I think the latter kind has this advantage, that you feel that the personality behind the work is larger and greater than any particular thing he does. The "artists" at this job seem indeed to have a clear motive behind their work. And they do what they want to do and have their reward. But Dickens was the opposite of an artist. His theatricality, his sentimentality, his reckless humour, were all used shamelessly and carelessly for propaganda purposes, propaganda on behalf of the irresponsible against the responsible, of the irrational against the rational, of the helpless against the competent, of the foolish against the wise. "A miracle! A miracle," we may cry, with Homenas, of this man; for if like Don Quixote he could turn windmills into giants, by God! he could turn water into wine.

Whitman

THE most striking characteristic of Walt Whitman's poetry is surely its astounding optimism.

And the curious thing is that it is an entirely heathen and profane optimism. Now we all know that pagan poets have very frequently either from stoicism or from cynicism been what you might call *cheerful*; but one would hardly call any of them exuberantly optimistic.

In England, William Blake, I suppose, though he included Jesus in his mythological pantheon, is our nearest approach to a triumphantly optimistic pagan poet. And it must be remarked that both Whitman and Blake are extravagant mystics. In fact, one wonders sometimes if it is possible for any pagan poet to be rapturously happy in this world who is *not* a violent mystic.

Browning, of course, was optimistic enough; but Browning's optimism was based on his individual interpretation of orthodox Christianity, and though extremely personal it certainly cannot in any sense be styled pagan.

But Whitman's optimism is pagan through and through. No poet since the Christian era has been less influenced by Christianity. The anti-Christian quality in his work goes down to its deepest roots. This can be seen in its undeviating pluralism and polytheism. Where Christian poets rejoice in the spirit of God, or, if they have a pantheistic bias, in the inspiration of some great Over-Soul or *Anima Mundi*,

342

Whitman rejoices in the individual souls of the multifarious populations—human, subhuman, and superhuman—that crowd with their diverse identities the whole fathomless ocean of life and being.

Instead of calling on us to worship God, or to imitate Christ, he calls on us to "follow the Great Companions"; an allusion, I take it, simply to the souls of all the dead, who are all exempt, as Pantagruel says, from the scissors of Atropos, but have by no means all been famous heroes! Where his originality shows itself as most staggering to the rational mind is in the vast scope of this mystical pluralism.

The implication is that the secret of the system-of-things is to be found altogether in the *Many* rather than the *One*. It is a sovietization of the Absolute. His universe, is, in fact, not a universe at all, but a *multiverse*; the sort of world for which William James had so decided a predilection. A "multiverse," if one can speak in such terms, lends itself much better to the magical and the miraculous, and to all the vagaries of chance and accident and free-will than a world made "of one piece" or a "block-universe," as William James rather disparagingly called our ordinary scientific cosmos.

It is of course this world "of one piece" that lends itself so smoothly and satisfactorily to the rational determinations of both orthodox science and orthodox religion.

Walt Whitman's world, in fact, for all its gigantic realism and cosmogonic proportions, is like a fairy place in comparison with the world of logical physics and metaphysics. Another striking thing about it is its triumphant response to the natural heart's desire of the ordinary man.

One of the reasons why the idea of death is so unpleasant to most of us is that we are faced with a choice between the complete extinction of our personality according to scientific law, and a moralistic Judgment Day according to religious law, both of which alternatives are extremely disconcerting to the human ego.

We have no wish to lose our personality, and we have still less wish to pay a heavy price for our dalliance with the world, the flesh, and the Devil.

But Walt Whitman's mystical fairy-world gives us all exactly what we want. It encourages us to assert our natural egoism while we live, and it assures us that no amount of "mortal sin" will debar us from continuing to assert our natural egoism after we are dead. In a word, Walt Whitman's poetry is an exultant and prophetic affirmation of all that the normal heart of man would like to believe *if it dared*.

And it is not only we mortal men who are to have the immortal satisfaction of our profligate hearts. Like St. Paul, Walt Whitman never allows himself to forget the "whole creation groaning and travailing in pain together"; and without having recourse to any religious or any moral redemption that would confine its benefactions to the chosen few this unexampled Heracles of Felicity opens the gates of what might be called a fourth-dimensional paradise to every living creature in the teeming cosmos. Would it be a malicious question to ask how far this surprising soothsayer honestly and confidently felt in his secretest heart that the system-of-things really *was*, as he declared, prepared to satisfy to the full the egoistic yearning of all the children of life?

It is a fascinating psychological problem, anyway—whether malicious or not—to ponder on the relation between an optimistic poet's heroical utterances and those lapses into ordinary human doubt and despondency which must often have put down the "pegs" that made such tremendous music. Only once or twice in *Leaves of Grass* does our author confess to such despondent moods.

But I fancy, when they *did* come, the collapse of these

Gargantuan certainties must have been a lamentable land-slide. And indeed when he does confess his doubts he certainly does so without beating about the bush. "Bloody flukes" are what rise to the surface then, as if from the spoutings of some cosmic "Moby Dick," whose writhings, as the harpoon gores its side, "the multitudinous seas incarnadine, making the green one red." In its terraqueous vastness and huge *camaraderie*, in all its grossness and piled-up compost, in all its measureless and mountainous rubble and slag, Whitman's world resembles the world of Rabelais.

But while Rabelais drew the rich unction of his life-acceptance from a large, lazy, easy belief in an indulgent and bountiful God, who is "in all and through all and behind all," Whitman celebrates the innumerable host of "all souls," human, subhuman, superhuman, who, like the *ideas* of Plato, fill the multitudinous reservoirs of imperishable being.

It seems to me then that Walt Whitman's optimism is the life-blood of his poetry, and that the boldest and most heart-satisfying mysticism ever projected by a poet's "will to believe" is the life-blood of his optimism.

But Walt Whitman's optimism has a physical as well as a mystical basis, and it is curious to notice how his bodily self-consciousness causes a particular kind of nervous irritation in certain types of people, an irritation that must be extremely comprehensive, for such persons feel disgusted with him when he talks of the smell of his arm-pits, and equally disgusted with him when, with a carefully washed shirt open at his tanned neck, and his loose, free, easy, athletic limbs clothed in spotless workman's trousers, he appears before us with an almost sailorlike nonchalance, but obviously with an intense narcissistic enjoyment of his healthy body in its clean linen.

But this is all part of his deepest life-illusion; and whether he annoys us by his dandified elementalism or shocks us by talking of the hairs on his chest I cannot see how we can avoid the recognition that he is one of the greatest poets in our language. Like Homer, like Dante, like Keats, like Wordsworth, he has a "secret" to communicate which is as much more than a "message" as the blood in a man's veins is more than a mole on his cheek.

And as in the case of Rabelais this "secret" is diffused through every word and every cadence of his style, so that even if he had never actually stated it we should know perfectly well what it was.

And what is it? What is the grand secret of Walt Whitman? I think it is to be found in the emotional extension of our personal ego till it enters the inner identity—all those other personal egos—of each object that surrounds it. And what separates him in this respect from all other poets is that these external objects, through whose inner identity his ravishing spirit flows, are just simply all the objects, accidentally selected and without any aesthetic discrimination, that happen to be around him when the spirit takes him by the beard and says,"Prophesy unto us, Walt Whitman."

Thus the beauty and magic of this secret is that we learn by degrees from it how to enjoy a most secure and impregnable happiness that is independent of our human affections: the only happiness which neither the jade Fortune, nor any other Queen Whims or Fata Morgana can take away or destroy.

It is a happiness of a peculiar kind, a kind which all men know at moments, but few cultivate, and wherein our prosperity depends in almost equal measure upon a certain premeditated sensitiveness and a certain premeditated insensitiveness.

To take the latter point first, there is required in this business a particular toughening and hardening of certain nerves, so that the endless occasions for sick disgust and

weary distaste that we encounter can be warded off by our
natural animal resilience. And then with regard to the sort
of sensitiveness needed, what we have to do, if we are to
catch the secret of this "mystic trumpeter," is to cultivate
a response to things that are not in the ordinary sense either
beautiful or even particularly appealing.

Every great poet reveals some aspect of the inanimate
world which save for his insight we might have missed, or
caught only in unconscious snatches. And the aspect of the
inanimate revealed to us by Walt Whitman is of all others
the least attractive to senses that only respond to the sunny,
the cheerful, the ingratiating. It is, in fact, an aspect of
things that strikes many of us as we go through the world as
bleak, and forlorn, devoid of bloom and fragrance, all, in
fact, that is left over, when what most beguiles, endears, and
seduces has been washed away, as if by a salt tide.

It is the litter and the debris omitted by Homer. It is the
slag and the offscouring, the rubbish and the desolations,
that Wordsworth put aside to enjoy the clear-cut shadow
of a flower upon a stone, or the reflection of a naked moon
in a mountain tarn. It resembles the sort of thing that
would be found in the path of one of Dostoievsky's lacerated
spirits, as on the outskirts of a town he leaves his mud
planks for a muddier tow-path.

But the lover of Walt Whitman sees these things with an
exultant eye, and with a heart that responds to this ooze
and mud and murk, as if there were an immortal soul in
such desolations.

And we learn from him how to let our human ego flow
forth like a disembodied vapour through the heaps of grey
stones and the dusty weeds, through the disordered scatter-
ings of wayside rubble, through the rain-soaked palings and
the broken shards, through the tidal drift and the flotsam; in
fact, through all those backwaters of matter that he loves to
call the "measureless float." He can isolate when he wants

to—who better?—the lilac in the door-yard, the lonely
bird in the sea-swamp, the solitary star above the horizon;
but what he prefers to concentrate upon are the things
neglected by other poets, the things that have hitherto
seemed in their essential nature to be the extreme *opposite*
of the poetic. And he loves to see these casuals and castaways and transients of the workshop of life thrown accidentally together in large, loose, vague heaps and neutral
accumulations; for not a bank of them, not a murky pool of
them, but sinks down and away, into other dimensions of
mystic being.

> *Melange, my own, the seen and the unseen,*
> *Mysterious ocean, where the streams empty!*

He doesn't botanize or geologize; he doesn't paint delicate
symbols in artful gradation, or etch vignettes and silhouettes
against appropriate backgrounds.

Over the "growth by the margins of pond-waters," in
all their chance-flung anonymity, he lets his spirit hover.
Over the brown manure-heaps of ramshackle farmyards he
lets it loaf. Over the windrow of sea-debris between shore
and ocean, that trail of "little corpses," that no man's land
of broken shells and sea-gluten and driftwood he sends his
soul, till the miracle of his own identity, "floating the
measureless float" sinks into the mystery of the sea-scum and
the sea-wrack, the submergings and the dissolvings, the
derelicts and the tangle, all with something immortal in
them ready to debouch into another dimension.

And as he lets his soul brood over the melancholy salt
ooze and bitter salt mud, as he lets it embrace the trailing
smoke from the factory chimneys and the mounds of ghastly
slag and the broken and blackened sheds, and the interminable monotonies of begrimed shanties and the iron
spikes of the factory palisades, and the spoutings of the
blast-furnaces, and the filthy pools and the fire-bitten

WALT WHITMAN

cinder-paths to the pit-heads, he hears the "ho-honk" of the wild geese of eternity.

And all this comes to us as we read these tumultuous pages not merely in oracles and soothsayings, though there are plenty of such, but in the strange originality of the words he uses, often of the words he coins, and always of the rising and falling of the musical lilt that carries them.

When his inspiration is full upon him no poet surpasses him in the staggering appropriateness, the intimate, fluid, miraculously identifying appropriateness, of the words that come into his head.

Wordsworth selects noble and simple words that isolate the elements he writes of with heroic austerity, and make his clouds and waters and suns and moons and all the motions and aspects of his dawns and twilights take on an inevitable and awe-inspiring grandeur; but Whitman, with a reckless American audacity and shameless realism, is not content with this. He seizes upon these dignified simple traditional words and melts them into flowing vapour and splashing spray; he pounds them into scoriac dust; he freezes them into arctic ice, he gouges them into burning craters; he makes them sob and surge and gibber and groan and whistle and whimper. His pluralistic mysticism, with its vistas and avenues of progression, its rebirths and transfers and promotions, gives a soul to every living identity; a soul to abortions, a soul to raving maniacs, a soul to embryos, a soul to all the quintillions of vanished corpses since the world began.

Everything that hath breath, everything that hath being, purging the unspeakable "compost"—it is his own word—of the cast-off scurf of mortality, he sees it rushing forward, along with hosts upon hosts of indestructible spirits, into an exultant redemption.

And the peculiar and unique words he uses, while they convey the tang and taste and smell and heave and sob of the thing's bodily reality, are melting words, decomposing words, dissolving and metamorphosing words, undulating and fluctuating words, such as suggest in their very tone and cadence the birth-pangs of corruption putting on incorruption, of mortality putting on immortality.

Absolutely pagan as he is in his exultant and shameless acceptance of the lusts of the flesh, absolutely anarchistic, as he is in his attitude to the authority of the state or the dignity of omnipotence, no one has ever worshipped more passionately what Emily Brontë so boldly describes as the god within our own breast. This is where his mysticism has both its triumphant root and its beatific consummation; and it is on the strength of this that he makes his indiscriminate bow to all the gods and saviours of the world, not forgetting, as in that queer poem "The Square Deific," to celebrate the Holy Ghost in Taoistic fashion as "Santa Spirita," and Satan, in the style of William Blake, as the heroic, cosmic Prometheus.

And it is in the strength of this god within his own breast that his defiant and heathen Quakerism mounts up by degrees to that sublime mood—let the frivolous blaspheme as they please!—wherein he becomes more than the bearded darling of Manhattan, more than the elemental child of fish-shaped Paumanok, more than the representative of America and the Average Man; in which, in fact, he becomes—and only a great spirit would *have the gall* to assume such a rôle—something uncommonly like a mythological being himself!

And why not? He has already announced to each of us, even though we are the viciousest and miserablest wretches on earth, that there is no position, not even the position of being a god, that is closed to our transmigratory progress!

The tone he adopts in these proclamations is a superhuman one. It sounds as if— But having thus "sovietized" the Absolute, and substituted the Many for the One as the ultimate reality, why shouldn't he in his role of Atlantean medicine-man to the wide West, *feel himself into* this super-human mask of planetary guru?

There are two kinds of "symbolic figures," as we say, among human writers. The inferior kind are "symbolic" in a gaudy, spectacular, worldly sense, like Beckford or Byron or Oscar Wilde, while the superior kind, like Blake and Nietzsche and Whitman himself, have the power of actually feeling themselves to be great occult influences in the history of our race.

And perhaps they are what they claim! Walt Whitman goes beyond even Nietzsche in the extravagance of his self-assertion; but since he remains a good anarchist and claims almost as much for everybody alive, it is impossible to take it as mere megalomaniacal boasting.

> *This the meal equally set, this the meat for natural hunger,*
> *It is for the wicked just the same as the righteous, I make appointment with all. . . .*
>
> . . . . .
>
> *I am he that walks with the tender and growing night,*
> *I call to the earth and sea half-held by the night.*
>
> . . . . .
>
> *Smile, O voluptuous cool-breath'd earth!*
> *Earth of the slumbering and liquid trees!*
> *Earth of departed sunset, earth of the mountains misty-topt!*
> *Earth of the vitreous pour of the full moon just tinged with blue!*
>
> . . . . .
>
> *Far-sweeping elbow'd earth, rich apple-blossom'd earth!*
> *Smile, for your lover comes—*
>
> . . . . .
>
> *You sea! I resign myself to you also—*
>
> . . . . .

> Sea of stretch'd ground-swells,
> Sea breathing broad and convulsive breaths,
> Sea of the brine of life and of unshovell'd yet always-ready
>   graves,
> Howler and scooper of storms, capricious and dainty sea,
> I am integral with you, I too am of one phase and of all phases.

·   ·   ·   ·   ·

> Unscrew the locks from the doors!
> Unscrew the doors themselves from their jambs!
> Whoever degrades another degrades me
> And whatever is done or said returns at last to me.
> Through me the afflatus surging and surging, through me the current
>   and index.
> I speak the pass-word primeval, I give the sign of democracy,
>   By God! I will accept nothing which all cannot have their counter-
>   part of on the same terms.
> Through me many long dumb voices,
> Voices of the interminable generations of prisoners and slaves.

·   ·   ·   ·   ·

> Of the deformed, trivial, flat, foolish,
> Fog in the air, beetles rolling balls of dung.
> Through me forbidden voices,
> Voices of sexes and lusts, voices veiled and I remove the veil,
> Voices indecent by me clarified and transfigured.

·   ·   ·   ·   ·

> And as to you Life, I reckon you are the leavings of many deaths,
> (No doubt I have died myself ten thousand times before)
> I hear you whispering there O stars of heaven
> O suns—O grass of graves—O perpetual transfers and pro-
>   motions,
> If you do not say anything how can I say anything?
> Of the turbid pool that lies in the autumn forest
> Of the moon that descends the steeps of the soughing twilight,

*Toss, sparkles of day and dusk—on the black stems that decay in
 the muck,*
Toss to the moaning gibberish of the dry limbs.

. . . . .

The last scud of day holds back for me,
It flings my likeness after the rest and true as any on shadowed wilds,
It coaxes me to the vapor and the dusk.
I depart as air, I shake my white locks at the runaway sun,
I effuse my flesh in eddies, and drift it in lacy jags.

It is curious that there should be anything in common
between two such very different contemporaries as Matthew
Arnold and Walt Whitman; but I cannot help feeling that
both these great poets are philosophers in the *ancient* Greek
sense, in the sense in which Empedocles or Heraclitus were
philosophers rather than Plato or Aristotle.

And it is interesting to note, too—for all their extreme
differences—that Matthew Arnold, like Walt Whitman,
can convey a magical impression of reality by the use of a
certain easy, careless, unmelodious juxtaposition of prosaic
details. A casual aside like this, for instance, reminds one of
certain digressions in *The Scholar Gipsy*.

*Now by the post-and-rail fences, where the old stones thrown
 there, pick'd up from the fields, have accumulated,*
*Wild-flowers and vines and weeds come up through the stones
 and partly cover them.*

But it should be noted, too, that Walt Whitman's oracular
proclamations of hope for every possible identity, his proud
anarchistic attitude to all authority, his feeling of himself
as a triumphant medium for the unseen forces through
which all the broken, baffled, frustrated abortive souls in
the world pass on to higher dimensions, are intimately
linked with what might be called his supersexual amorousness. Shrewdly reticent as he always was as to his *particular*

love-affairs, whether of a normal or abnormal character, he lets himself go to the limit in the expression of a free and flowing sexuality *in general*, a sexuality both passionately physical and spiritually vulnerable, and which is confined to neither man nor woman, though its poignancy culminates perhaps in regard to his male companions.

The curious thing is that though he always celebrates his sexual excitements *in the abstract*, and, as one might say, *anonymously*, he uses the most physiological, and from the view-point of even our modern censors of such things, the most shamelessly realistic imagery. No poet has ever been at once so reserved and so portentously unabashed in these erotic ejaculations.

What elements of ordinary romance appear are certainly of a homosexual character, but with a shrewd prophetic instinct he has made it impossible to particularize even this; and his magical way of gathering together in one wild sobbing refrain all the tragic-exultant passion, all the desperate, surging, pent-up longing that the whole planetary ocean of sex, as it heaves and pulses and churns and foams and breaks, lets loose in its ecstasy, sweeps all the traditional psychological differences between normal and abnormal into a cosmic level where they seem negligible, unimportant, transfigured.

And after love, after this supersexual ecstasy, in which the surge and the sob and the world-obliterating embrace open, shall we say, the final seventy-seventh heaven to the lowest of the low and the weakest of the weak, it is death that stirs him the most.

No one has felt for death what Walt Whitman felt. The power to feel so must have come to him because of all the deaths he had watched and soothed when he was in those field hospitals in the war. Death has upon him an effect that resembles the effect of love. It seems the fulfiller of all

that is unfulfilled in love, it seems the answer to all that is
dumb in love, it seems the grand *dénouement* of love and the
rounding-off of love's broken circle.

And now we can see why, if we are to do justice to Walt
Whitman, it is necessary to shake off the sterile mystery-
drained doctrine that our telescopic, microscopic, astro-
nomic universe is all there is. And with this limited conception of the cosmos, Whitman's "serenely arriving" death
sloughs off from us the fret and gnaw of the world and the
contemptible ambitions of the world. This divine life-
enfolder, this transforming and transfiguring mother of
life, is the very touch of the dimension we see not, the very
embrace of the secret we cry for. The world hates death.
But love does not hate death. Love has something of death
in it. Love and death together are stronger than all the
meanness and silliness of the world. The world can vulgarize
life and is always doing so, but death and love when they
are in league with each other, fling off its grasp as the
impalpable night-air flings off an evil smoke, escape its
venom as the voyaging wind purges itself of a graveyard
smell.

Walt Whitman's grand "triad"—perhaps it was his Welsh
blood that taught him the art of such uttermost fusions—is
always the same: "love, death, the soul"; "death, the soul,
love"; "the soul, love, death."

These three incomprehensibles lie, according to him, at
the bottom of life, and each of the three has something
of beyond-life in it; each of the three can hold life in its
hand "as a very little thing."

*Death is without emergencies here, but life is perpetual emergencies
here,*
*Are your body, days, manners, superb? after death you shall be
superb,*
Justice, health, self-esteem, clear the way with irresistible power;

How dare you place any thing before a man?
Fall behind me States!
A man before all—myself, typical, before all.
Give me the pay I have served for;

. . . . . .

I have loved the earth, sun, animals, I have despised riches,
I have given alms to every one that asked, stood up for the stupid
and crazy . . .
Claimed nothing for myself which I have not carefully claimed
for others on the same terms.

Has it occurred to any reader of this essay to note what a triumphant contempt for "psychology" and "pathology" Walt Whitman's poetry indicates?

How wise he was to cover his own psychological and pathological tracks so well, that to this day no one really knows what the actual sex-peculiarities were of this sublime supersexualist!

He is a reversion to Homer and the Old Testament in this; and I think his primordial, physiognomic, unanalytical carnality—the healthy body quite as mysterious as the twisted mind or the damned nerves—would have pleased Goethe. It would certainly have pleased Rabelais.

If he is anything in politics he is an anarchist; and it is hard not to wonder whether any young syndicalist of Barcelona to-day, fighting for a free Spain, recalls these words, entitled "Spain 1873-74":

Out of the murk of heaviest clouds
Out of the feudal wrecks and heaped-up skeletons of kings.

. . . . .

Ruined cathedrals, crumble of palaces, tombs of priests,
Lo, Freedom's features fresh undimmed look forth—the same
immortal face looks forth,

. . . . .

Thou waitest there as everywhere thy time.

Some have objected to his extraordinary use of foreign words—mostly French—and indeed one does begin to wonder sometimes among what circles, in the Philadelphia of the "seventies" and "eighties," these singular expressions circulated. Or did he pick them up from the woman he loved in New Orleans?

But personally I feel as if this curious Frenchified lingo has a lively charm and a secret power all its own, initiating us into some occult confraternity of libertarian free spirits, "citizens of the world" who use French very much as ecclesiastics use their Latin or thieves their argot, to indicate a certain sly solidarity, a certain emancipated roguery that treats with a mocking and sentimental cynicism both the pious gravities of virtue and the tender prejudices of "belles lettres."

It is natural enough that his pathetic boast that his poetry "went well with simple uneducated persons" should be the exact opposite of the truth. What it were best to assume he meant was that he himself went well with such people; which undoubtedly *was* the case.

Of course, there have been plenty of tiresome individuals of both sexes who have used his unexcluding embrace, I speak metaphorically, as an encouragement to an irritating expansiveness far more unpleasant than the most archaic conventionality; but the honest truth is that his most passionate and devoted lovers are self-centred intellectuals, while the sort of young men who were his principal inspiration, if they read poetry at all, read a very different kind from his.

But all that is as it should be. It is more than doubtful if Wordsworth's leech-gatherer could have enjoyed the poem written in his praise. That heroic old wayfarer got his leeches and his chimney-corner, while we, through the mediumship of Wordsworth, have our nerves fortified and our imagination quickened by the poem to which *they both* contributed. And if it seems ironical that he who felt himself to be—and who actually was—the medium through whom the self-reliant, kindly, profane, cynical-sentimental, average "Americano" took his place among our national types, should become the favourite of a nervous and sophisticated *intelligentsia*, rather than of those whose "free and flowing" aplomb was his inspiration, we must remember that just as it is always the dumbness, the inarticulateness, the withdrawnness of Nature's secrets that rouses to reciprocity the mediumship of genius, so the deeper significance of the average man is revealed rather to the prophet than to himself.

What undoubtedly is hardest for the normal human conscience to swallow in Walt Whitman's soothsaying, and I confess hardest for my own, is his telluric "celebration" of the evil along with the good.

I am not the poet of goodness only, I do not decline to be the poet of wickedness also.
What blurt is this about virtue and about vice?
Evil propels me and reform of evil propels me, I stand indifferent,
I moisten the roots of all that has grown.

Now, of course it is possible to take this sentence in a large, easy, careless way, and not try to press the logic of it too far; and one must remember that in any country where the puritan conscience—a thoroughly diseased conscience—has been long rampant, a good deal of "wickedness" is virtue, and plenty of "virtue" is evil in the deepest sense.

With any great writer, too, it is often advisable to go behind the superficial meaning of any particular words while we follow the general tidal stream of his habitual feeling. But one cannot help, I think, even so, recognizing in Walt Whitman a mood that crops up now and again, which, if you were Attila or Genghis Khan or even the Emperor Nero, would be the reverse of any austere check upon your orgies. It is true he is not always consistent in this beyond-good-and-evil vein. So human is it to have *some* values and discriminations that he often permits himself this privilege, however contrary to his antinomian theory. And we are only taking him at his own word when we refrain from demanding consistency at every point of the emotional compass. Identifying ourselves, all the same, with the main drift of the mystical gulf-stream of his passion, we come, I think, to feel in his refusal to play the reformer, in his refusal to reject anything that life has tossed up, in his refusal to be negative *even for the noblest reasons*, something that seems almost to belong to the great pulse-beat of being itself.

For, as Hegel explains, the antagonist and opposite of being—what Hegel would call its "other"—is not wickedness but nothingness, not strife but inertness, not violence but futility.

I speak with some hesitation here, for I suppose it is possible that while the path for most of us is to try to follow what Matthew Arnold calls the "stream of tendency that makes for righteousness," there *may* be such a thing as a cosmic quietism so abysmal that it can even include the opposite of being in its embrace!

But one must realize all that this would mean; and it would mean the inclusion not only of the deepest depths of futility but of a deep below even that.

In his imaginative heroism over the sharing of extreme pain he was on a path sufficiently hard for most of us, as when he declared, in his mood of reincarnating exultation, that "agonies were his changes of garments"; but I confess, if he did really feel at moments that he could "accept" all the cruelties that are done under the sun from the point of view of the cruel as well as the victims, and "moisten *their* roots" equally with their victims', I can only say, humbly and blindly, that as far as my own conscience goes I must part company at that point.

It may be the highest path never to resist evil; but to "stand indifferent" where cruelty is concerned is surely another matter. I prefer the cry of the old Gothic king when he heard of the Crucifixion: "Would I had been there with my Franks!"

But to return to the sex-question. In spite of the fact that Walt Whitman's passionate and romantic vein is excited more strongly by men than women it would be a great mistake to regard him as anything but an absolute "egalitarian" in regard to the two sexes. In his cosmogonic celebration of women he starts at the opposite pole from Goethe's. To Goethe her chief value was her power of luring the soul of man "forward and upward"; whereas Walt Whitman, beginning at the other end, treats the Feminine Principle, just as the ancient Taoist sages did, as *prior* to the masculine, and as *including* the masculine.

> *Unfolded out of the sympathy of the woman is all sympathy;*
> *A man is a great thing upon the earth and through eternity*
> *but every jot of the greatness of man is unfolded out of woman;*
> *First the man is shaped in the woman, he can then be shaped*
> *in himself.*

Perhaps it is not remarkable that this despiser of "embroideries and embroiderers" should be of all poets except Shakespeare the most original in moulding words and fusing words and transmuting words and snatching words from anywhere to serve his turn. It is this that gives his mysticism such sap and salt, makes it so sticky and adhesive, so full of stinging, caressing, biting, bubbling, spitting, splashing, sucking, lapping, bleaching, wetting, soaking, slithering, drenching *reality*.

How one comes to welcome all those curiously characteristic expressions of his that are so often recurring, such as "tally" and "promulge" and "filaments" and "prismatic" and "float" and "drift" and "electric" and "libertad" and "fluid" and "résumé" and "finale" and "absorb" and "exhibit" and "husky" and "cohering" and "effuse" and "efflux" and "ecstatic" and "sagging" and "adhesiveness" and "en-masse"!

And doesn't it almost seem as if there were some curious *chemical* quality in the larger number of these words, "indicating" (as he would himself put it) the flux and the surge and the merge and the recession of the huge masses of our astronomical elements till they touch something else, till the substance of matter itself *is transmuted into another dimension*, or at least trembles and shivers on its edge?

Certainly we come to feel as we read him as if the old Empedoclean notion of the love and war of the elements is not far wrong, and that earth and water and fire and air are attracted and repelled by the same love-hate as attracts and repels ourselves!

It is in things of this kind that the wise Goethean heathenness of Walt Whitman so beautifully shows itself. And how refreshing after the narrow tyranny of orthodox theology and orthodox science to return to the natural magic of the real elements of our life!

It is one of those silly unimaginative mistakes, like the one that turns Nietzsche into an advocate of bullying and brutality, to regard Walt Whitman as if he were "the great boaster" in *Hiawatha*. Walt Whitman's arrogance is indeed as much of a spiritual cult as the humility of the author of the *Imitation*. It is a deliberate personal cult and it is also a representative cult, made on behalf of the souls of all. He is arrogant for living beings, simply *as* living beings, including the lowest and most contemptible. And he is arrogant for them *as against God*, arrogant for the filthiest and vilest and meanest of them, as against God's favoured great ones, and as against the world's favoured great ones!

In all this he is the true pluralistic anarchist. All souls are equal and every soul is a disguised god.

The pert apparel, the deform'd attitude, drunkenness, greed,
*   premature death, all these I part aside.*

·   ·   ·   ·   ·

These shows of the East and West are tame compared to you,
These immense meadows, these interminable rivers, you are
*   immense and interminable as they,*

·   ·   ·   ·   ·

Master or mistress in your own right over nature, elements,
*   pain, passion, dissolution——*

·   ·   ·   ·   ·

Through birth, life, death, burial, the means are provided,
*   nothing is scanted,*
Through angers, losses, ambition, ignorance, ennui, what
*   you are picks its way.*

How easy it would be to pile up on the soul of Walt Whitman, as it "picks its way" still among us, every single one of the "complexes" that the new pathology reveals! The "Messiah-complex," for instance—wouldn't those syllables be illuminating and confounding? Illuminating with regard to the person who used them, but certainly not confounding to Walt Whitman.

As long as the hearts of men and women wrestle with matter and the void, as long as they struggle to get a little happiness before they die, this great life-heightener will be reborn, and his anarchism and his mysticism will be reborn! You can mould into conformity nations and states and empires; you can call prophecy a "complex," and immortality an illusion; but one thing you cannot do. You cannot make a man say "yes" when the soul within him, from a dimension beyond both life and death, says "no."

We have reached the moment in human history when

mass-movements made possible by mechanical science are moulding the nations into integrated hostile groups. There is certainly more justice between rich and poor than there formerly was and less chance for the minority to enjoy their parasitic leisure and quiet and culture in unperturbed complacency.

And just because of these things there never was a moment in the evolution of humanity when the mental attitude of the average person was so important. Is his type of intelligence going to become more and more slavish, submissive, drilled, mechanical; or is he going to insist on enjoying to the full the spiritual intellectual inheritance that has come into his hands from the lucky ones whose leisure to attain it was made possible by his labour? Doctrinaire communists murmur, and perhaps with some measure of truth, of the *bourgeois mentality* that must be destroyed before justice between man and man can cover the earth.

All right then! Let *us* destroy our own "bourgeois" mentality, and substitute for it mentality of a nobler, larger, more magnanimous, more sensitive, more subtle kind. One cannot but agree that a great deal of the printed matter in our bourgeois shelves is poor enough stuff, paltry and uninspired, mere selfish cringing before God and great men, reeking of moralistic hypocrisy.

But it certainly will be an evil day for the human race when some modern morale of tyrannical mass-movement grows able, by the diabolical aid of a conscienceless science, to do what the Inquisition couldn't do, and the puritans couldn't do, and the old oppressors couldn't do; that is to say, really and truly crush down and obliterate the free thoughts of individual men and women. We shall be arrested and imprisoned perhaps in this mass-psychologized and science-enslaved age for possessing a copy of *Leaves of Grass*. It'll have become like a translation of the Gospels in Catholic days, or like a translation of Rabelais in Protestant days.

The new blood-and-iron State, with its armies of bureaucrats riding about in armoured cars, will be as nervous of this great anarchist's talk of the souls of independent people as the old aristocracy used to be of the promulgations of Tom Paine.

And then—who knows?—some miraculous renaissance of the average human soul may suddenly—

> *Camerado, this is no book,*
> *Who touched this touches a man,*
> *(Is it night? are we here together alone?)*
> *It is I you hold and who holds you,*
> *I spring from the pages into your arms—decease calls me forth.*
>
> . . . . .
>
> *Dear friend whoever you are take this kiss,*
> *I give it especially to you, do not forget me,*
> *I feel like one who has done work for the day to retire awhile,*
> *I receive now again of my many translations, from my avataras*
> *ascending, while others doubtless await me,*
> *An unknown sphere more real than I dream'd, more direct, darts*
> *awakening rays about me, So long!*
> *Remember my words, I may again return,*
> *I love you, I depart from materials,*
> *I am as one disembodied, triumphant, dead.*

FEODOR MIKHAILOVICH DOSTOIEVSKY

Dostoievsky

To my mind Dostoievsky is as much greater than all other novelists as Homer and Shakespeare than all other poets. For he is superior to the rest in all the main essentials of fiction. He is a greater artist; a greater psychologist; a greater prophet; and a greater thinker.

By the "art" of Dostoievsky I mean, first of all, his power of communicating an irresistible sense of reality. He creates a world of his own; but the Dostoievsky world is not only one degree, but several degrees nearer our common impression of the world we live in than is the work of others.

As a realist in this sense he is unapproachable. Once led into his world, the convincing verisimilitude of it all is overpowering. It is for this reason that so many find it hard to read him. The terribleness of the things we all have to bear, the pity and frightfulness of so much in life, returns upon us with too deadly an impact from his pages. Compared with his penetration into the startling, corrosive, explosive stuff of our universal experience other realism, composed of the mere piling up of physical details, seems not only gross, heavy, and unillumined, but false to our natural human experience.

And the extraordinary thing is that he arrives at this startling closeness to the actuality of our impressions by following a method that leaves out the one aspect of our common human life that fills the largest space of all. I refer to our *work*.

All the accompaniments of the various jobs that occupy so great a part of our time are absent. Peasants come in and out; but there is no description of the way they till the soil or gather its produce. The whole subject-matter of Hardy's novels, for instance, is simply non-existent here.

Tradesmen, artisans, labourers, craftsmen, merchants, shopkeepers, factory hands, bakers, butchers, tinkers, tailors, apothecaries, masons, cobblers, brewers, tanners, printers, along with all the economic paraphernalia of their occupations, scarcely appear, even as a vague background, in this overpoweringly real world!

All that huge mass of economic complication of which Balzac, for example, makes so much, and of which we are all so vividly conscious, has melted into thin air! Nobody has a job—nobody works, either with hand or brain. Many of his people are rich. Many are very poor. Some of them *must* have had to work in their time, but we hear nothing of it.

All we know of them is their passion and their pain, their spiritual sufferings and their spiritual ecstasies, their loves and their hates, their faith and their un-faith, their obsessions, their crimes, their intrigues, their illuminations, their devotions, their vices, their pride, their cruelty, their pity, their humility.

It cannot be repeated too often that every great writer creates his own world, but a world, all the same, drenched and saturated in the crude elements of the chaotic reality around us.

It is impossible to imagine a world more different from Homer's, for example, than the world of Dostoievsky. Both are real; both are crowded and vital, both of huge epic proportions, both of oceanic grandeur and turbulence and mass.

But between Homer and Dostoievsky Christianity has appeared, forcing the great flood of human feeling inwards, thrusting the whole stage of the human tragedy, together with its background, upon an interior plane.

In reading Dostoievsky we get a prophetic sensation that some vast spiritual change is coming over human life. It is like reading the Book of Revelation. Its interest is apocalyptic, charged with startling premonitions of mystical events. This must be one of the reasons why there is such an amazing neglect of the materials, appurtenances, experiences, of ordinary human labour.

There is exactly the same sort of spiritual tension in the books of the New Testament, the profound psychology of which Dostoievsky exploited to such an extreme point that it would be possible to call the whole mass of his writings "the Fifth Gospel"—the Gospel according to the soul of Russia! Christ in his parables refers, it is true, more frequently than does his strange Russian disciple to the ordinary labours of humanity; but on the other hand he is for ever calling people away from these things, "for the end of this world is at hand."

It is this tremulous and vibrant anticipation of some kind of "second coming," when, as the apostle says, and as Kirilov in *The Possessed* says, "We shall all be changed," that renders the psychological atmosphere of Dostoievsky's books so singularly like the atmosphere of those early turbulent communal churches, with whose erratic motions from mystical ecstasy to sensual excess St. Paul is for ever contending.

No real lover of the imaginative rendering of human life in books can miss the stupendous contrast between what Spengler would call the new "Magian Culture" in Dostoievsky and the old springtime "Classic Culture" in Homer.

To see the spiritual ecstasies and the emotional lacerations of the great Russian in their true world-setting, consider one of the desperate soul-rending talks between Kirilov and Shatov, or between Prince Mishkin and Rogozin, over their samovars, and compare it with this not less tremendous crisis in the Odyssey. I quote from A. T. Murray's translation. "And for them the strong and mighty Alcinoüs sacrificed a bull to Zeus, son of Chronos, god of the dark clouds, who is lord of all. Then, when they had burned the thigh-pieces, they feasted a glorious feast, and made merry, and among them the divine minstrel Demodocus, held in honour by the people, sang to the lyre.

"But Odysseus would ever turn his head towards the blazing sun, eager to see it set, for verily he was eager to return home.

"And as a man longs for supper, for whom all day long a yoke of wine-dark oxen has drawn the jointed plough through fallow land, and gladly for him does the light of the sun sink that he may busy himself with his supper, and his knees grow weary as he goes; even so gladly for Odysseus did the light of the sun sink."

Human life upon earth was the same in essentials then as in the middle of last century when Dostoievsky's desperadoes of the spirit met over their samovars; but what a change in the imaginative perspective!

And since Dostoievsky the outward wheel has turned again, and once more, though with steel engines in place of wine-dark oxen, the labour of men's hands, along with their physical relief when the sun descends upon it, becomes the modern stimulus to powerful writing.

But Dostoievsky would not be the greatest of novelists if he were not, beneath his "Magian" visions and his "Fifth Gospel" illuminations, an inspired artist.

To find a parallel for his grandest effects in imaginative realism we have to leave prose literature altogether and turn to Shakespeare. There is the same use of small, homely, insignificant things, endowed at a crisis with an atrocious and frightful livingness. There is the same indescribable concentration upon some single fatal gesture, isolating it under a blood-red search-light and causing the rest of the visible world to vanish into black annihilation, as if what took place were projected on a flame-lit promontory washed by a gulf of timelessness.

There is the same appalling sense of the monstrously grotesque—Stavrogin's putting soap on his death-rope—those jars of disinfectant that the murderer arranges round the body of Nastasia, Father Karamazov's preparations for Grushenka—and the same pitifully humorous repetition of some particular phrase or image that plays the part of those pregnant refrains of the old tragical ballads.

And in spite of the huge life-gap left unfilled, by the absence of all ordinary scenes of diurnal human labour, so that one almost comes to feel as if everyone in these books were either rich, idle, irresponsible magnates, or priests, beggars, hangers-on, courtesans, mystics, intellectuals, pensioners, policemen, officials, visionaries, tramps and paupers, there are such rapid, vivid, unforgettable vignettes of natural background, sketched in to give perspective and weight to the mighty tide of the plot, that we are continually being reminded of those tremendous vistas of natural surroundings, across which such sudden and magical lights are thrown in crisis after crisis in Shakespeare's plays. Palpable and breathing effects of dawn and noon and twilight and thick darkness catch us suddenly, as if by the hair of the head, forcing upon us the very smell of the damp, of the dust, of the mud, of the rain, of the low-hung clouds travelling across the horizons of desolation.

Like Dickens, only with less detail, he can conjure up the magical effects of life in a great city, endowing the inanimate with a brooding identity of its own, which acts and reacts upon the moods of the characters.

How overwhelming is his unearthly, phantasmal handling of metropolitan reality, by which the effect upon the mind of city life, its streets, its squares, its slums, grows so portentous, and hangs heavily over us with a dim, rich, thick-smouldering Gothic gloom!

How we are made to feel the towering-dusky porticoes and all the intricate masonry, arches and windows and stairways and attics, of the famous Nevski Prospect, for instance, with the rain and the snow and the biting winds and the faint spring airs and the dark water!

And what deep holes, as one might say, into the underworld, and *through that* into dim eternities of occult desperation, open as we read him, under our feet! Spiritual mineshafts they are, sinking down into mysteries just as impalpable and insubstantial—only of a darker significance —as the airy gulfs and spacious horizons of the most magical rural scene. I am, all the same, inclined to feel that it is not in his Moscow or Petersburg, but rather in his smaller provincial towns, left purposely nameless, that the purest Dostoievskian essence is distilled. Think how, in *The Possessed* and *The Brothers Karamazov*, he accentuates, with an overpowering weight of piled-up suggestion, what you might call "neighbourhood reality," till the whole place becomes a living entity!

In this massed, entangled, and intricately rooted effect he can rival Balzac; for he has that same rare gift, granted to so few novelists, of conveying the full cubic sense of a community's life, the sense of the gathered-up weight of a human group, as it acts and reacts on itself within a given circle, and is swept to and fro by the mysterious currents and eddies and backwashes of popular prejudice and opinion.

And the astonishing thing is that he can accomplish this miracle, perhaps the hardest thing of all to a writer, without having recourse to the ordinary details of our daily work! Those unlucky factory hands in *The Possessed*, for instance, living an isolated slum-life in a particular quarter of "our town," down there by the river, whose boarded foot-paths, muddy banks, and melancholy wooden hovels suggest similar districts in America, who knows what their daily labour is? And yet in some subtle, unaccountable way the psychic "aura" of their condition surges up at the chief crisis of the story, and becomes an important, almost a predominant element in the final catastrophe. And what a startling Shakespearean gift he has for suggesting, as it were sideways, and by the most casual and haphazard indirections, the natural backgrounds of his dramatic scenes!

Those desolate Dostoievsky roads stretching out into the unending plains around these straggling towns—roads that remind us so often—save for the new concrete and the automobiles!—of the spacious American scene, how wonderfully, as in his great master Gogol, is their infinite melancholy suggested!

And the muddy foot-paths between wooden fences leading from house to house in these old-fashioned provincial places, how they lend themselves to sinister encounters! And how well, too, we come to know these old Russian gardens, so many of them, like the one in which Smerdiakov's idiot-mother was seduced and where he himself, in his ghastly dandified way would, between his fits, solace himself with music, dedicated to assignations and murderous conspiracies. And though the labour on which all this weird intellectual and spiritual and vicious life must have depended, like leprous fungoid growths upon the roots of a tree, is kept out of sight, the everlasting tragedy of absolute penury, the existence of the tramp, the beggar, the desperate wayfarer, is never long allowed to be forgotten.

Dostoievsky's imaginative awareness of the feelings of these wanderers, as the worm i' the bud of all our well-being, is as Shakespearean as it is Homeric and Biblical, and brings us down, as Lear was brought down, to the basic level:

> *Poor naked wretches, wheresoe'er you are,*
> *That bide the pelting of this pitiless storm,*
> *How shall your houseless heads and unfed sides,*
> *Your loop'd and window'd raggedness defend you*
> *From season such as these? O! I have ta'en*
> *Too little care of this.*

Or as the disguised Odysseus tells the friendly swineherd: "Than roaming naught else is more evil for mortals; yet for their cursed belly's sake men endure evil woes, when wandering and sorrow and pain come upon them."

There are moments in reading Dostoievsky when he seems to become a veritable medium through whom all the wild froth of the Russian soul and the Russian nerves—and a bloody spume from the heart's abyss it often is rather than froth—spills over, and wastes itself in a mad frenzy of words.

Again and again in listening to the desperate talk of these people—and it is by no means only his chief characters who become as voluble as tipsy demons—I find myself reminded, for they are all obsessed by religious revelations, of that warning given by St. Paul, who himself, as a thaumaturgic pathologist, had so much in common with it, against the excess of speaking in "strange tongues," lest this thing prove a stumbling-block to certain sturdy heathen among us!

"If therefore the whole church"—as seems not unfrequently to occur in our author's stories!—"be come together into one place, and all speak with tongues, and there come in those that are unlearned or unbelievers, will they not say that ye are mad?"

The truth is, Dostoievsky carried the whole massive art of novel-writing into a new dimension—*the dimension of the nerves*.

And he carried it there without abating a jot of its weighty circumstantial realism. His nervous explosions would not be what they are if they did not burst forth like waterspouts from a swelling ocean of human drama.

Nor do these prophetic utterances, that diversify the tension of his emotional plots, *idealize away* the convincing power of his tremendous realism. They emerge from the realistic tide and they return to it. They are the spume of the voyaging whales, they are the leaps of the flying fish, of these terrific navigations. The ship of reality goes on her path undeterred by them; but not without an abiding sense of an unearthly touch upon the rudder! The most comprehensive of all human arts, the art of the novel, must now of necessity be divided into two great historic epochs; the novel *before* Dostoievsky and the novel *after* Dostoievsky.

It is extraordinary how as we read him we are convinced of the reality of these strange beings and of the reality of their backgrounds. So many modern writers, who here and there catch something of his demonic psychology, fail entirely in the creation of living characters. How he does what he does is one of the insoluble secrets of the art of writing; and it is the more impressive to us because of the absence of those devices of obscurity and fantasy and preciousness and premeditated roughness which in our day have established themselves as the hall-marks of genius. As far as a reader ignorant of Russian can judge, neither Balzac nor Scott is freer from stylistic mannerism.

But after all, what makes Dostoievsky so much greater than other novelists is that this superb and mysterious art of his, an art that like Shakespeare's cracks and breaks beneath the dark thunder of the tragedy of the soul, is, all the way through, the vehicle of a disturbing and *prophetic* philosophy.

When Spengler, whose own greatness is rather that of a poet than a logical thinker, looks about him to-day for any sign of the birth of a new spiritual "culture" among the nations, it is in Dostoievsky alone that he finds anything approaching such a thing. Nietzsche too, as he steered the lightning-struck barque of his desperate sailing past the flickering light-ships of man's forlorn coasts, crossed more than once the bows of Dostoievsky's phantom ship and lowered with awe his pirate flag.

It would be making as great a mistake as so many have made in Nietzsche's own case to try and deduce a clear and definite system of thought from the trail of this portentous comet as it falls from the zenith into the bottomless sea.

Nietzsche learned much from him of the infernal thaumaturgy of weakness, of the potency of those tears of self-laceration that are, as William Blake would say, "intellectual things." But this terrible secret of the ecstasy of yielding to the limit, of distilling a strange dark magic dew out of such tears, Dostoievsky derived, not only from the deep wells of his own nature, but from that limbec of siren treacheries, the New Testament of Christ, the mere inclusion of which, in the same volume as the virile Hebrew Scriptures, was to Nietzsche the supreme betrayal of the human spirit.

Contemplating the death-masks of these two great seers, the tragic Lucifer and this still more mysterious Demogorgon of our Faustian decadence, it is hard not to feel that the Russian was the stronger and more formidable personality. There is a rugged force in Dostoievsky's countenance, to which the only parallel I know is in the portrait busts of the old Greek dramatists, notably in that of Euripides.

Among the Greeks it is perhaps Euripides whose tone comes nearest to Dostoievsky's; though in other respects those "psychological mole-runs" of his cast up an earth-mould whose taste is sometimes singularly reminiscent of Paul of Tarsus. Some of us have a foolish tendency to heap praise on certain modern writers—Nietzsche started this unenlightened simplicity—on the ground that they keep themselves unspotted from the "unclean spirit" of Christian consciousness. We even praise Goethe for being such an imperturbable heathen, forgetting that his own words run to a quite different tune, and that *Faust* is anything but a wholesome pagan production!

As a matter of fact, it is hard to see how a deep and formidable artist can remain indifferent to the thickening and subtilizing of the human situation brought in by the phenomenon of Christianity.

To accept these "secrets of God" in an orthodox sense is one thing: to make use of them to intensify and deepen our natural vision is another; and, as Spengler hints, the better way is to regard the Christian element in Dostoievsky simply as the richest and subtlest of his "organs of research," research into the mystery that baffled and disturbed him to the end.

I have found myself wishing that Dostoievsky had written a commentary upon that strangest book in the Bible, the Book of Revelation. That this most weird and magical *finale* to the Scriptures did arrest his interest is proved by his putting into the mouth of one of the least engaging characters in *The Idiot* that curious passage about "the star called Wormwood."

I cannot find myself in agreement with Spengler and others in their emphasis upon the character of Alyosha Karamazov as the final embodiment of Dostoievsky's spiritual philosophy. Certain aspects of his vision of human goodness undoubtedly reach their climax in this engaging character. But I feel as if the same startling insight into the mysteries of the human soul which culminates in the creation of Alyosha is at work through book after book, on parallel though opposite lines, in the case of his most characteristic wicked characters.

What interests him, like a divine-demonic obsession, is first and last the ultimate depths in the soul of spiritual

good and spiritual evil. And the thing that startles us most
as we read him is a dawning suspicion that these two
underground channels, both thaumaturgic, both tapping
fathomless reservoirs of magical power, come, in those subterranean regions of the spirit, into astonishing proximity!
One feels this in the case of Raskolnikov in *Crime and
Punishment*, and even—though more faintly—in that of the
terrible Svidrigilaiov in the same story. In Ragozin in *The
Idiot* you feel it, and much more in the enigmatic Stavrogin
in *The Possessed*. In Ivan Karamazov these thaumaturgical,
half-supernatural currents of good and evil drift alarmingly
close to each other, at times almost coalescing.

Both Kirilov and Shatov in *The Possessed* and the hero's
father in *The Raw Youth* are borne along on the double
streams, that, like a fresh and a salt current running side
by side, flow tortuously through the lake of the soul.
Alyosha makes me think of Walter Pater's "Diapheneité"
and of those strangely guileless and spiritually incorruptible
figures of Raphael who look, in their inherent purity, so
immune to all obsessions from the underworld of our
nerves! The Idiot himself is quite different from this; and
to me he always seems a much subtler and deeper creation.

Quite as untouched by the wickedness round him as the
other, he yet—as though his very physical infirmity and
mental danger made his imaginative sympathy more clairvoyant—seems able to enter much further than Alyosha
into the mystery of the evil he rejects.

Just as Dostoievsky disregards as of minor importance
the burden and heat of our daily struggle for bread, that
struggle which he himself found so bitter, so he carries us
into a stratum of life, into a dimension of good and evil,
barely hinted at in other novelists.

And who can help noticing that the appalling mental
drama, continuous throughout his books, depends upon
one terrible and fatal reality—the reality of free will?

In no writer does the mysterious arbitrariness of our insane and monstrous power of will play such a part.

Did Dostoievsky believe in God? Like one of his own characters when driven to the wall on this crucial point he would refuse, I think, a categorical affirmative to that question. And yet his answer would certainly not have been a negative one. The truth seems to be that like Jacob with the angel he wrestled all his life with a great Darkness, with Something that was and yet was not, holding that Nameless Thing by the hair of its head with all the fury of his demonic will, never quite believing in it, but always feeling the *alternative* to it to be so horrible as to be unthinkable! Then a second question. Did he believe in Christ? His silence this time would I think be of a more intimate nature, more committed, more explosive, more tragic and involved, more emotionally reckless of reason.

The truth is that whatever these traditional expressions "God" and "Immortality" really meant to his deep and dark soul, they served, as did the sign of the Earth-Spirit, with Faust, to conjure up, against all logical evidence, an inner reality before which he reeled and staggered, exultant, triumphant, dead to all that intervened!

There is no doubt that into this wrestling with what sometimes seemed a cloud, sometimes a fire, sometimes a bottomless void, he threw both the spiritual good in him and the spiritual evil. In reading him you feel over and over again that other divers into the desperate Tyche of our doom have no notion what the words "good" and "evil" mean.

A man on the edge of despair and suicide could read Dostoievsky, when all other books would be to him a mockery and an aggravation.

When he uses the traditional religious expressions they take on a different aspect, a different colour. They seem to burn with a black interior flame that trembles under the breath of the eternal.

Turgeniev called him "sadist"; but that terrible word only proves how spiritually deep his insight into evil was. Dostoievsky never plays *for its own sake*, as certain modern writers do, upon that fatal nerve. His allusions to it are always allusions to the past, to a past repented of in the flame of the abyss. They are the confessions of lost souls, or of redeemed souls, never indulgences in a present excitement, never the gloating relish of a literary "voyeur's" lust.

When Ivan Karamazov, who accepts God but cannot accept His world, "returns" Him "the ticket," it is of sadistic cruelty to the helpless in His intolerable performance that he is especially thinking.

The most significant passage in all Dostoievsky, except perhaps the tormented outcries wrung from Shatov and Kirilov in *The Possessed*, is the passage in which in *The Underground Spirit* he speaks of man's *will* to self-abasement and self-destruction, and of his divine-demonic yearning that "two and two" should make "five" instead of "four"!

It would be silly to claim for him anything approaching the humour of his master Gogol, a humour that is *sui generis* and without parallel; but there is no doubt that the chemical constituents of that ghastly and appalling humour, which one might almost call the grimace of reality upon the earth, are diffused from beginning to end of his work.

It is indeed with the word "reality" that we begin and end in thinking of him; but *his* reality is only in part the reality which is here and now. Another reality, that of the thing which is not yet but *will* be, gathers weight and substance as we saturate ourselves with his work. For he stands between the living and the dead. He is the medium of the spirit of man, changing as it evolves, but changing into something compared with which all the outward mutations of mechanical science are as the rising and setting of the star Wormwood!

Melville and Poe

Poetry can round off a subject better than prose, so I will break the natural chronological order and begin with Herman Melville. It is hard for me to understand any reader selecting as his favourite work of this great genius any book but *Moby Dick or The White Whale.*

Compared with *Moby Dick*, both *Typee: Narrative of a Four Months' Residence among the Natives of a Valley of the Marquesas Islands* and *Omoo: Narrative of Adventures in the South Seas* are characteristic and original productions; but hardly "immortal works of art."

But an "immortal work of art" in the purest sense is *Moby Dick.* In fact I regard it as the greatest book about the sea ever written; and it interests me to note how our best present-day sea-writer, James Hanley, in every new sea-tale he writes, approximates more and more closely to the particular category of human imagination represented by Melville, and less and less to that represented by Joseph Conrad. Though few writers could be more of a land-lubber than I, I am inclined to claim certain advantages in analysing Melville's genius not permitted to all. Criticism, as Goethe says, ought to be positive. Carping, captious, academic stricture is totally devoid of value; though it is true that sometimes an inspired distaste, a devastating personal revulsion, like Nietzsche's against Wagner, is more illuminating than any but the profoundest and subtlest love.

But frequently one experiences an indignant longing to

379

compel a critic to give, so to speak, his *credentials*, his licence from the muses to take upon himself so daring and drastic a task. The most effective form of criticism, second to killing your author, is what we call "the conspiracy of neglect."

The first of these methods was the one applied by the Bacchanalian pietists—who still feel the same urge to censorship—to the poet Orpheus and in a certain round-about way to Edgar Allan Poe, whom no nymphs of the purer element were able to save.

> *Ay me, I fondly dream*
> *Had ye been there—for what could that have done?*
> *What could the Muse herself that Orpheus bore,*
> *The Muse herself for her enchanting son*
> *Whom Universal Nature did lament,*
> *When by the rout that made the hideous roar*
> *His gory visage down the stream was sent,*
> *Down the swift Hebrus to the Lesbian shore.*

But it was not by rolling his head down the Hudson, or even by burning all the volumes that could be procured of *Pierre, or the Ambiguities* in a bonfire in the town of Pittsfield, that the America, of the fifties and sixties, punished Herman Melville. It was by giving him what I understand is technically known as "the fade-out"; and I have lived long enough in his native Manhattan, and long enough in those "up-state" regions he writes of in *Pierre*, to see exactly how this less violent method of dealing with a genius of his type can be successively applied.

Yes, few great men have been as neglected as Herman Melville. The later years of his life were allowed to fall into a sort of ghostly posthumousness; but the wheel has turned at last and by steady degrees he is coming into his own.

Were the muse to demand my own credentials for writing on this man, who takes, along with Emerson and Whitman

HERMAN MELVILLE

and Henry James, the front row in American letters, I could only say that though my knowledge of cetology is limited to a sight of the living spoutings of these creatures in the Atlantic and a sight of the memorials of their destruction in the town of New Bedford, I *can* claim to be a congenital disciple of the particular kind of imagination, both mystic and realistic, both monstrous and grotesque, that was so natural to Melville.

I follow him in my attraction to those "ambiguities" in our mad life at which both the public and the coteries instinctively boggle. And before the tremendous artistry of *Moby Dick* I cannot but feel a thrill of pride to think that I have entered myself as a pupil in this sea-bottom school of sub-human intimations!

The imagination displayed in *Moby Dick* is indeed a model for all time of the most penetrating form that this great faculty can take. It does not show itself, as in Homer, in happily chosen similes that become, as you might say, poems within the poem, nor does it display itself in far-fetched flights of fancy as in so many poetical novelists. It makes use of that deepest of all kinds of metaphor, the kind that sinks down into the very substance, essence, and occult life of the thing described, indicating its inmost esoteric affinity, nay! its spiritual identity, with some kindred emanation from the world-reservoir, whose external appearance is different, but whose root in the great underlying Noumenon is the same.

If, as Goethe says at the end of *Faust*, everything in our transitory experience is a symbol of the underlying unknown, imagination of this sort looks down into the depths of the thing upon which it is concentrating until the thing's outer semblance yields, melts, dissolves, only to gather again its dispersed lineaments, like the fragments of a broken reflection in water, into a larger, grander, more diffused image, and one that carries with it hints, glimpses, memories, revelations, that have hitherto floated in and out of our human consciousness without leaving any definite or lasting impression upon the retina of the mind.

Perhaps it was this same deep Imagination that in itself led to the gross neglect from which Melville suffered; this, combined with his proud, lonely, Diogenes-like philosophy, which treated all competition, all rivalry, all ambition, all that is implied in the lively expression "making good," with transcendental contempt.

But I think it was also his peculiar brand of humour. Melville's humour is of the kind more adapted to alienate than attract. To the average mind it is not humour at all; but on the contrary comes near to showing itself in the light of a malicious wilful rejection of what ordinary humanity means by humour. Indeed, in this whole matter of Melville's *humour-that-is-no-humour* may be found the secret of his character, of his philosophy, and of his genius!

What *is* ordinary humour? Well! that is a question curiously difficult to answer, for different human races have a different "ordinary humour." If you take Mark Twain, who is a master of ordinary American humour, and compare him with Dickens, who is a master of ordinary English humour, or if you take, in more recent times, our English humourist Neil Lyons and compare him with the American Ring Lardner, you will find yourself confronted by two distinct forms of "ordinary humour." Both kinds are appreciated, and deeply so, in *both countries*, but their origin, their method, the particular nerve to which they appeal, is totally different.

The examples I have given represent, of course, the humour of the ludicrous and the absurd; a thing that of necessity exaggerates our national differences; but, apart from this, the average American and the average Englishman have a sense of what I might call the universal *tragic-comic*, a sense that they share equally between them, and share too, as is proved by the popularity of *Don Quixote* and Charlie Chaplin, with the whole Western world.

But the peculiar "humour-that-is-no-humour" of the author of *Moby Dick* and *Pierre* is neither the brilliant sense of the ludicrous of the writers I have named nor is it the eternally human farce, so close to tragedy, of *Don Quixote* and Chaplin. It is indeed a thing *sui generis*, this peculiar Melville tone, and one of its hall-marks is a fierce malicious urge to lead this whole business of "being funny" such a dance that it will hardly be able to recognize its own features in the circus-mirror.

That I really do know what I am talking about here is proved as I say, by my having taken out my own apprentice papers in this sub-oceanic, Hermanic, cetological School of humour that is not comical.

One grand aspect of this peculiar Melvillean humour is its huge and unashamed *naïveté*, a tremendous simplicity of buffoonery that is as imperturbable to the harpoons of facetious cleverness as the featureless forehead of Moby Dick himself.

Another aspect of it, if so it may be called, which is rather its seaweed root in the dim *morbidezza*, of the man's marine soul, is Melville's abysmal pessimism. Here I am of opinion he is as profoundly American as Walt Whitman is American in his optimism. These two are indeed the grandest products of American genius, with Emerson standing like a canny Arctic explorer between a Leviathan spouting sub-human joy and a kraken wallowing in the sea-ooze of sub-human spleen.

The truth is the pessimism of Melville actually does resemble what we may well suppose to be the attitude to life of the Father of all Devil-Fish as it lies at the bottom of the bottomless sea. It is an inarticulate pessimism, enormous, sluggish, titanic, such as the first children of

Uranus and Gaia may well have had as they pondered on the gulfs of existence.

It is closely linked with the peculiar sadness of the more *continuous* elements; of the desert where there is only sand, of the sea where there is only water, of the poles where there is only snow: and it is linked too with certain uncanny phenomena in nature which are weird rather than beautiful, such as the extraordinary yellow substance known as *brit* upon which the Greenland or "right Whale" feeds, and such as this monstrous sea-bottom *squid*.

> Slowly wading through the meadows of brit, the *Pequod* still held on her way north-eastward towards the island of Java, a gentle air impelling her keel . . . but in this profound hush of the visible sphere a strange spectre was seen by Daggoo from the mainmast head. In the distance a great white mass lazily rose, and rising higher and higher and disentangling itself from the azure, at last gleamed before our prow like a snow-slide, new slid from the hills. Thus glistening for a moment as slowly it subsided and sank. Then once more arose and silently gleamed. . . . Almost forgetting for the moment all thoughts of Moby Dick we now gazed at the most wondrous phenomenon that the secret seas have hitherto revealed to mankind . . . furlongs in length and breadth . . . long arms curling and twisting . . . no perceptible face or front did it have; no conceivable token of either sensation or instinct; but undulated there on the billows, an unearthly, formless, chance-like apparition of life. As with a low sucking sound it slowly disappeared again, Starbuck, still gazing at the agitated waters where it had sunk, with a wild voice exclaimed, "Almost rather had I seen Moby Dick and fought him than to have seen thee, thou white ghost!"
>
> "What was it, sir?" said Flash.
>
> "The great live squid which they say few whale ships ever beheld and returned to their ports to tell of it. . . . They fancy that the monster to which these arms belonged ordinarily clings by them to the bed of the ocean; and that the Sperm

whale, unlike other species, is supplied with teeth in order to attack and tear it."

It is, in fact—as one follows Melville's imagination plunging into the heart of this Scylla, of this Briareus of fabulous legend; and what would one not give for a scientific and historical work by him on the sea-serpent?—it is, I say, exactly the sort of pessimism that the Titans must have had, and that an incredibly vast sea-monster in its dumb, blind way might be conceived as possessing, that is darkly intimated in *Moby Dick*.

Melville was too kraken-like a man even to *want* to be redeemed by Jesus Christ, too deeply acquainted with the appalling cannibalism of life to be able to feel anything towards the Absolute but the deep, dark discomfort and sullen suspicion of primeval matter made conscious of itself through pain. Sorrow and pain to this man's mind were certainly more characteristic of the nature of the universe than joy and well-being. In this, as in almost everything else, he is the extreme opposite of Emerson, who like Goethe made a cult of turning away from the mad and the sick and the monstrous.

But the curious thing about the pessimism of Melville is that it is a *mystical pessimism*. Almost all mystics are by nature happy. Like Blake—perhaps the only perfectly happy prophet—they find in the mystical world their grand escape from the miseries of the actual.

But the mysticism of Melville is a dark satanic mysticism. He seems to detect in the First Cause himself an element of mysterious evil. It is clear he is a reader of Rabelais; but Rabelais gives him no comfort. The man who knows the truth, he says, the man who *is* the truth, is the Man of Sorrows.

With a wise knowledge of his own limitations, Melville differentiates very little between the tone and accent and peculiar lingo of his Cape Cod mate, his Martha's Vineyard mate, and his Nantucket mate. None of them utter their sentiments in a style that differs very much, save in degrees of passionate intensity, from the style of Ahab, the *Pequod*'s captain. They all use the "thou" and "thee" of the Quakers; but beyond this they all speak in Melville's own huge, imagistic, occult manner.

It is true they are all constantly indulging in saturnine jesting, that curious jesting of Melville that resembles the jests that might be made by some monstrous nodding mask among the freaks in a circus-parade; but just as the *Pequod* itself seems like a phantom ship upon a fabulous cruise, so the talk of these men is so heightened by the mystic quest they are following as to resemble anything rather than the real talk of real whale-fishers upon a real sea.

The three harpooners however—Queequeg, the kindly Caliban from the South Seas, Tashtego the pure-bred Indian from "Gay's Head," Cape Cod, and Daggoo, the majestic Negro—are sometimes permitted, but even in their case rarely, to use a speech other than the grandiose language of their author. The old Manx sailor, with his Druidic predictions, and Fedallah, the mysterious Parsee, whose fate is so closely linked with that of Ahab, never utter a word that isn't in the dark, brooding Titan-speech of Melville. The real exception is Pip, the Negro boy, who in a fit of panic jumps out of the boat and goes insane from being left in the sea so long. *His* mad words are wonderfully dramatic and natural; and indeed, in everything relating to Pip, Melville introduces a more humanly poignant note.

But the symbolic grandeur of this brooding and sombre masterpiece, in which the fathomless American reserve, and the fathomless American pessimism, and the fathomless American occultism are all embodied, finds its consummation in the figure of the White Whale himself.

"The White Whale swam before him as the monomaniac incarnation of all those malicious agencies"—and how well one knows these half-mystic half-material "agencies" against which such "Black Rocks" as Dreiser and Masters have to petrify their promontories!—"which some deep men feel eating in them, till they are left living on with half a heart and half a lung. That intangible malignity that has been from the beginning; which the ancient Ophites of the East reverence in their statute devil . . . all that most maddens and torments, all that stirs up the lees of things; all truth with malice in it; all that cracks the sinews and cakes the brain; all the subtle demonisms of life and thought. . . .

"Here then was this grey-headed, ungodly old man . . . at the head of a crew made up of mongrel renegades and castaways and cannibals . . . and how it was that they aboundingly responded . . . what the White Whale was to them . . . or how in some dim unsuspected way he might have seemed the gliding great demon of the seas of life—all this to explain would be to dive deeper than Ishmael can go. The subterranean miner that works in us all, how can one tell whither he leads his shaft by the ever shifting, muffled sound of his pick?"

I am continually being made aware, as I too—a timid and awe-struck bookworm—follow in the wake of the *Pequod*, in the wake of Queequeg and Tashtego and Daggoo and Pip, of rhythms and lilts and cadences and diapasons, which in the heave of their vessel, a vessel rigged with the hemp of our deepest nerves and figure-headed with the phallic coulter of our most dangerous defiance, make me think of the resonant prose-music of Sir Thomas Browne.

And in spite of Melville's cetological substitute for what our facetious sun-fishes call "a sense of humour," there come passages sometimes, as for instance where white Ahab and black Pip play priest and acolyte as he nails the doubloon to the mast, that mount up to the *tossing bells* and *streaming beard* of a frenzy not unknown to us:

EDGAR: Look where he stands and glares! Wantest thou eyes
at trial, madam?
Come o'er the bourn, Bessy to me—
FOOL: Her boat hath a leak
And she must not speak
Why she dares not come over to thee.

The old prophetic Manxman is now staring at the
doubloon—and I do not know a grander example of the
mystic identity between the souls of things and the souls
of events than the part played by this doubloon:

"I've studied signs and know their marks . . . the old witch
in Copenhagen taught me . . . and now in what sign will the
sun then be? The horseshoe sign; for there it is, right opposite
the gold. . . ."

"Here comes that ghost-devil Fedallah . . . ah! only makes
a sign to the sign and bows himself . . . there's a sun on the
coin . . . a fire-worshipper . . . this way comes Pip . . . would
he had died or I. . . . Stand away and hear him."

"I look, you look, he looks; we look, ye look, they look. . . .
Caw! Caw! Caw! Caw! Caw! . . ."

"I can stand the rest; for they have plain wits; but he's too
crazy-wittin for my sanity. . . . Here's the ship's navel, this
doubloon here, and they are all on fire to unscrew it . . . when
aught's nailed to the mast its a sign that things grow desperate . . . Ha! Ha! old Ahab! the White Whale; he'll nail ye!
This is a pine tree. My father, in old Tolland county, cut
down a pine tree once, and found a silver ring grown over
in it . . . and so they'll say one day . . . Oh, the gold! the
precious, precious gold! the green miser'll hoard ye soon!"

But of the concluding passages of this book, unequalled
for imaginative grandeur save in the great poets, I will only
as a *finale* quote one minor passage:

The ship? . . . Soon they, through dim bewildering
mediums, saw her sidelong fading phantom as in the gaseous
Fata Morgana; only the uppermost masts out of water, while

fixed by infatuation or fidelity or fate to their once lofty perches, the pagan harpooners still maintained their sinking lookouts on the sea.

But as good an example as could possibly be found of the mystical fusing power possessed by Melville is the manner in which he speaks of the *Pequod*, as she sank, dragging down with her the sky hawk caught against the masttop by the harpooner's hammer, and thus, like Satan, refusing to sink to hell "till she had dragged a living part of heaven along with her, and helmeted herself with it."

And if Melville's imagination is an immortal triumph of the peculiar American genius, like no other in the world, so also, though in a very different sense is the imagination of Edgar Allan Poe.

The best spiritual bridge that I can find, to lead us backward in an inevitable reversion to this great poet, is a line or two from Melville's extraordinary chapter in praise of the supernatural element of terror that is the inverse side of the traditional holiness which our race attributes to the Gargantuan mystery of *whiteness*.

All lovers of Poe will recognize, I think, in this analysis of the shudder that comes over us in the presence of certain aspects of *whiteness* a mood akin to Poe's genius; and it must be remembered that *Moby Dick* was not written till just about one year after the death of Poe.

Melville has been speaking of a New England colt, terrified by the shaking in the air behind him of a buffalo-skin:

> Though neither knows where lie the nameless things of which the mystic sign gives forth such hints; yet with me, as with the colt somewhere those things must exist. Though in many of its aspects this visible world seems formed in love, the invisible spheres were formed in fright . . . and pondering all this the palsied universe lies before us like a leper. . . .

Now if Melville was underrated by the nineteenth century, Poe, just as unfairly, is underrated in the twentieth; and yet it is this very same supernatural shiver—as if in the presence of "invisible spheres formed in fright"—that he, of all men, is the hierophant.

How are we to account for the downward trend at this particular hour, especially in England, of this great poet's reputation?

I think there are many causes. For one thing, all human ideas move in spiral circles as evolution proceeds. Behind the philosophy, the science, the amusements, the con- science, the psychology, the religion, of each age moves some fatal destiny.

Now this destiny is like a tide sweeping round the feet of the individuals who have the power to make what we call world-literature, and all these, as Goethe so profoundly says, are linked to their age *by their weakness*. Their strength and their greatness, however, consist in their ability to resist this tide, for the highest and deepest things are the things least affected by this spiral flow. Homer would understand Shakespeare, and Aeschylus Hardy; whereas the minor men of talent of such different epochs would patronize each other with supercilious contempt.

Nothing reveals the real stature of a modern mind more effectively than its attitude to the great figures of the past. When you hear a clever modern roundly disparaging some tremendous figure of the past, it is a proof that he himself is of so moderate a stature that the tide of evolution has carried him off his feet. His voice is the voice of a straw on the swift current, whose chief service is to indicate what is not very obscure, the direction in which the stream is flowing.

What those of us mean by *poetry*, who are transported with pleasure by the poetry of Homer and Shakespeare and Milton and Keats and Blake and all the anonymous ballads, is a certain very definite blend of emotion and magic and music. As Milton says it is something that is "simple, sensuous, and passionate," but as Milton also says it is something that doesn't depend on rhyme; something therefore that *can* certainly include the "free verse" of volumes like *Leaves of Grass* and *Spoon River Anthology*.

But it is something, as those of us who love it most and are most steeped in its subtle laws know to our cost, that does *not* include the witty, clever, startling, epigrammatic, social-philosophic verse that is the top-crest to-day of the literary fashion.

I would be a fool to disparage the value of this phenomenon as a new and remarkable *aesthetic medium*; but it is only a clouding of issues to confuse the purely mental and virtuoso-artistic pleasure which we derive from the work of those who use this new medium, a medium which is neither "simple nor sensuous nor passionate" but on the contrary is obscure, intellectual, and dispassionate, with the emotional, magical, and musical pleasure we derive from what for more than two thousand years we have learnt to call *poetry*.

But there is I think another reason why, at least among English critics, there is so marked a tendency to disparage Edgar Allan Poe. He is in a very peculiar sense an *un-English* poet. Of Northern Irish parentage, riddled through and through with the *genius loci* of the most English of the American colonies, educated at a boarding-school in England during his most impressionable years, he is, in his dominant mental tendency, as remote from the English as was Oscar Wilde or Benjamin Disraeli, or, in spite of the cult they made of these islands, Conrad or Henry James; while the literature upon which his genius exercised its chief influence when he was dead was not ours but that of France.

And not only is our English spirit peculiarly liable to be

unfair to Poe, who had, from our point of view, no "sense of humour," and whose "art for art's sake" strikes us as a teasing affectation, and his mania for analysis as a knife in the morgue, both the two chief modern schools of poetry in England, the one I might call the "Curfew and Cowslip" school and the one I might call the "Barbed Wireless" school, are at the opposite pole from his erotic fantasias and sepulchral bizarreries. The one lives sensibly and genially on ale in the tavern, the other sensibly and angrily on whisky in the gas-house: while the least drop of that nepenthe which Helen of Troy brought from Egypt was enough to turn Edgar Allan Poe's wits.

Many of the circumstances of Poe's life had no small resemblance to those of the life of Coleridge; and I confess I find it hard to see how lovers of the subtly-imaginative, subtly-musical, and subtly-terrifying Coleridgean effects, can refuse their impassioned adherence to the almost precisely similar note in Poe.

It is of Poe as one of our major poets that I want to speak, not of Poe as a prose-writer, else it would be possible to extract from his *Tales of Mystery* specimens of a power of conjuring up what Melville might call the fear-spasms of God which would make many moderns, who have forgotten to what terrors he can steel himself, wish they had let him alone! The dark engine he employs to evoke these horrors might be called *the imagination of the nerves*. Pain plays little part in it. It is rather the quivering of the antennae of the pain-nerves before the actual shock comes which concerns him.

And I suspect no one but a professional psychologist knows the amount of steely will, of adamantine will, of aboriginal Red-Indian will, that was required when he allowed his trembling soul to be hunted, as slave-dealers hunt slaves, or harriers hares, till, turning at bay at the black-ice-wall of the last barrier, he defied "those spiritual spheres which were created in fright."

It would almost seem as if Poe were the most entirely *non-moral* poet who ever lived! Unlike Shelley and Byron he is completely devoid of any social or revolutionary enthusiasm. He is equally devoid of any philosophic or, in the ordinary sense of the word, any spiritual doctrine.

Like Keats he reverences nothing in heaven or earth save "the Principle of Beauty and the memory of Great Men"; but unlike Keats there is nothing in him of that Shakespearean humanity, that Homeric sense of the pathos and tragedy of normal human life, which is perhaps a richer poetic inspiration than any spiritual or metaphysical message. His life-illusion is subjective and egocentric to a degree such as only a nature of hard and crystalline detachment could sustain without going mad. But so intense and so concentrated was his genius that he has done what few merely artistic poets can do, he has created, or perhaps it would be better to say he has discovered, a world of romantic and morbid loveliness, into which, now that he has pointed the way, lovers of his poetry can pass at will. It hangs suspended in the middle air, this region, like an enchanted sky-pillared mirage, like the mysterious and magic *Caer Sidi* of the old Welsh bards. It is the impalpable city, built upon the waters, "out of Space, out of Time," wherein all the wild self-centred erotic cravings, such as philosophy destroys and morality condemns, may take refuge. It was of this unearthly but yet distinctly un-celestial region that he wrote in his second published volume, his *Endymion* as it were, and called it by the Arabian name, *Al Aaraaf*. But the appearance of this book, early in 1830, excited, so one of his biographers assures us, "more merriment than interest" among its readers.

It was this same *Al Aaraaf* that he "palmed off," as my biographer of the early nineties says, fifteen years later,

"before a disappointed audience at the Boston Lyceum."
Well! this queer poem excites in the present writer other
emotions than those of "merriment."

To my mind, youthful though it is, it is a much more
significant and interesting production than the more popular *Bells* which he finished only a few months before his
death. To me it contains, indeed, many premonitory hints
and embryo suggestions of some of his grandest and most
inspired effects.

The Paolos and Francescas who select *Al Aaraaf* as their
refuge after death are doomed, the youthful Poe informs
us in his notes, to eventual annihilation; but they regard
their experiences in this region as worth even that price.

Their fate is suggested in the final lines of this curious
poem:

> *Thus, in discourse, the lovers whil'd away*
> *The night that waned and waned and brought no day.*
> *They fell: for Heaven to them no hope imparts*
> *Who hear not for the beating of their hearts.*

Well! it appears that the partisans of the schools of
English poetry to which I have referred are as unsympa-
thetic to-day as "Heaven" was then to the denizens of *Al
Aaraaf*.

Let them be so! We must console ourselves by the
thought that the two greatest living poets in these Islands,
the poets who follow the poetic tradition of twenty centuries,
W. B. Yeats and Walter de la Mare, display in their different ways a closer resemblance to Poe than to any other poet
in our tongue except William Blake.

What floating fragments of his enchanted city "far down
within the dim West" did this American poet gather as a
child from the high-walled ancient parks of the landscape
adjoining his English school?

For myself I have caught again and again, among the

ghostly backwaters and "melancholy seignorial woods" of
Maryland and Virginia, glimpses of "alleys Titanic of
cypress" and of lonely swamps "where the toad and newt
encamp," and of "time-eaten towers that tremble not,"
where—

> *Travellers, now within that valley*
> *Through the red-litten windows see*
> *Vast forms, that move fantastically*
> *To a discordant melody.*

But it was in my own youth long before I had seen
Virginia that none other than Thomas Hardy pointed out
to me, with more passionate appreciation than I ever heard
him display *for any other author*, the power and beauty of
Poe's *Ulalume*, that weird poem that represents the inmost
essence of his genius; and indeed any one who has ever
visited the enclosed recesses and leafy watercourses of
Bindon Abbey, not many miles from the mounded sepul-
chres Hardy used to watch in his lifetime, might well cry
aloud:

> *Ah what demon has tempted me here?*
> *Well I know now this dim lake of Auber,—*
> *This misty mid-region of Weir,—*
> *Well I know now this dank tarn of Auber,—*
> *This ghoul-haunted woodland of Weir.*

Yes, literary fashions may change as they will, and light
tide-borne intelligencies may follow them as they will: but
the figures whose stature permits them to keep their feet
on the river-bed will be always able to recognize one
another.

Edgar Allan Poe is certainly a unique figure among
poets! Compared with his unearthly non-moral *ego-
centrism*, creating its vistas and avenues of eternally-receding
romantic escape from everything normal and mellow and

human, Oscar Wilde seems a genial wit, Baudelaire a bourgeois *bonhomme*, and Verlaine an honest Pantagruelian tosspot.

One suspects that the *amount* of his drinking has been viciously exaggerated. Probably the least drop of alcohol flung that arctic-cold, insanely analytical brain into a hectic fever. The man was the purest cerebralist who has ever written poetry; and what is more he carried with him his cold sardonic American grimness into that "luminous void"; till like a steel-white engine among "azure towers" and "winged odors," his infernal logic ticked out its frozen commentary beneath the moonlit battlements of the empyrean.

The natural result of clamping down such steely scale-armour upon normal human sympathies was that his intense ego shot like a luminous projectile towards whatever dark moon of Venus it may be that contains the deepest and the *deadest* seas of erotic desire!

And thus it comes about that the erotic element in Poe is less spiritual than with Emily Brontë, less poignant than with Hardy, less passionate than with Keats, but has a neurotic intensity of its own beyond all these.

Eroticism of this intense kind is naturally obsessed by the "whiteness" of death; for the dead alone cannot escape from it. And thus with the *tick, tick, tick* of the terrible logic-machine *which is its heart*, it circles for ever over that sepulchre by the sea, that "tomb by the sounding sea."

It was a romantic and ideal lust this maniacal Eros, whose inhuman desire inevitably "killed," in Wilde's phrase, "the thing it loved"; for an embalmed immortality in a "leg-ended tomb," reached by a "route obscure and lonely," could alone satisfy a possessiveness that was jealous of every breath of air its poor Ulalume drew.

The scurviest trick by which our cowslip-ball school of poetry seeks to disparage this unique genius is the old

EDGAR ALLAN POE

pedantic device of dragging in poor patient Mrs. Radcliffe
and her obedient partner "Monk" Lewis whenever our
immortal *Eros Necrophilios* drives a poet among the tombs!
But to explain the mania for sepulchred loveliness which is
so dominant a note in Poe by any lugubrious literary fashion
among New York and Baltimore ladies is as unfair as to
explain the fairylike wit of Shakespeare by the fact that the
jargon of the court in his time was riddled with fantastical
Euphuism.

One marked characteristic of Poe's most formidable
poetry, which our recent arbiters, drunk on their "cowslip-
tea" or deafened by their "barbed wireless," find I suppose
simply cheap and vulgar, is the sardonic playfulness with
which he deliberately introduces what in his own analysis
of *The Raven* he calls "an air of the fantastic, approaching as
nearly to the ludicrous as is admissible."

As a matter of fact, if the ghost of this great poet will
permit us to carry his researches a little further still, this
"air of the fantastic approaching the ludicrous" sublimates
itself when he is at his very greatest, which of course is not
in *The Raven*, into something that might be called a Vir-
ginian counterpart of the sardonic tone we know so well
in both Hamlet and Hardy.

Modern critics of Poe seem sometimes to play Rosencrantz and Guilderstein to these airs of the fantastic!

> *See! it flickers up the sky through the night!*
> *Ah, we safely may trust to its gleaming.*
> *And be sure it will lead us aright.*
> *We safely may trust to a gleaming*
> *That cannot but guide us aright,*
> *Since it flickers up to Heaven through the night.*

ROSENCRANTZ: I understand you not, my lord.
HAMLET: I am glad of it: a knavish speech sleeps in a foolish
ear.

ROSENCRANTZ: My lord, you must tell me where the body is
and go with us to the king.
HAMLET: The body is with the king, but the king is not with
the body. The king is a thing—
GUILDERSTEIN: A thing, my lord!
HAMLET: Of nothing: bring me to him. Hide fox, and all
after.

Is it not proper and right in this chaotic world that there
should be one unique poet—call him a demented "escapist"
if you will—who turns away in Luciferan indifference from
both the good and the true and builds up for himself his
solitary "cave of ice" out of those quarries on the other
side of the moon that beauty still keeps for herself alone?

Few things are more painful, more jarring and disconcerting, than the perusal of almost any ordinary "Life of
Edgar Allan Poe"; and I suspect the cause of this is that
the average biographer is more concerned with his own
delight or his own indignation over the startling queerness
of the outward events that occur than with the more subtle
problem of the relation between these weird happenings
and the provocations and frustrations they work, in the
occult Al Aaraaf of Poe's unique imagination. Lively psy-
choanalytical speculations are naturally roused in us by
the erotic element in Poe's life; but nothing is more treacherous than to apply such a detailed psychological science
to the creative imagination. Much safer is it, it seems to
me, to treat these intimations as if they were an inspiration
from some Platonic over-world, peopled by the imaginative
"escapes" of all the successive generations, and already
there, pre-existent and imperishable, in a planetary super-
consciousness.

Perhaps, as Goethe seems to hint, there are revelations
from what we call "beauty" that are in direct and independent contact with the creative energy that builds the

world, and are totally beyond the reach of analysis, even
of such analysis as this extraordinary poet loved to practise.

Such is at any rate what Melville would teach us; and if
we were content to regard Poe's *City in the Sea*—

> *Where the good and the bad and the worst and the best*
> *Have gone to their eternal rest,*

—as a symbol resembling the White Whale, we should be in
a position to reply to Poe's disparagers that this crazed lust
for the "whiteness of death" is only another aspect of
Faust's craving to reach the secret of the cosmos.

It avails nothing to bring against this great poet the
charge of futility. Poe's hit-back at the Divine Comedy,
indicated with such ghastly power in *The Conqueror Worm*,
is no reasoned philosophy of universal disillusionment nor
is it an artistic affectation. It is a voice proceeding from
Satan, as he stands in the presence of the "Ancient of
Days." In other words, it is a voice from one of the Janus-
faces of the "Ancient of Days" himself.

> *Out—out are the lights—out all!*
> *And over each quivering form*
> *The curtain, a funeral pall,*
> *Comes down with the rush of a storm,*
> *And the angels, all pallid and wan,*
> *Uprising, unveiling, affirm*
> *That the play is in tragedy "Man"*
> *And its hero the Conqueror Worm.*

Great creative nature, in league with that daughter of
hers, who is also, some think, her sister—Tychē Sotēr,
Chance the Saviour—was kinder to Poe than his fellow-men.

Nature and chance together aided him in his life-and-
death struggle with the horrible society and the monstrous
morality into which he had been born. Culture may have

been more lively in "our Boston," as Poe calls it, than in New York, Philadelphia, Baltimore, and Richmond; but one does have a feeling that morals were a trifle more lax in those sunnier places.

At any rate, no poet has ever been luckier than Poe was in that extraordinary pair of intimates, his aunt and his aunt's child. Respectable and normal human relationships were, I suspect, completely disregarded in that fortunate ménage—a ménage after all that could hardly have existed anywhere but in those southern states. Poe's feeling for that mother and child must have been of a most curious kind. Both of them seem to have been devoted to him, and the girl was like a Paracelsian elemental created by himself out of air and water.

However unlucky he may have been in his other, later loves, it is impossible not to feel that in spite of all the miserable poverty he endured with those two he was incredibly lucky in that "more than mother" and in that little-girl-wife who seems to us still as if she were only *half-incarnated* and for that very reason could no more die than a spirit could die! His romantic cerebral nympholeptism was spared the danger by this good luck of dissipating itself in casual encounters and in hopeless obsessions, and he could make of its fortunate fulfilment and too brief duration an ideal that transcended all mortal bounds.

Alive or dead this child-wife's frail and evasive identity could now fuse itself with all those weird unearthly regions of the imagination through which he moved with a clarity of vision beyond the reach of any other poet.

But what things, what things went on in the reality behind these "ultimate dim Thules" of his creation! For instance, how like a passage out of Dostoievsky is this pitiful scene as described by my present authority, when the girl lay dying in that cottage on Fordham Hill, near New York!

Once when Mrs. Mary Gove, whom Poe called a mesmerist, a Swedenborgian, a phrenologist, a homoeopathist, and a disciple of Priessnitz, went to call upon them, she found Mrs. Poe suffering from "the dreadful chills that accompany the hectic fever of consumption." Wrapped in her husband's military overcoat, she lay on a straw bed with a snowwhite counterpane and sheets for its only clothing. A large tortoise-shell cat snuggled to her bosom to keep her warm, while Poe held her hands and Mrs. Clemm her feet.

How many different accents of subtle disparagement have to be swept away before justice can be done to this rare poet! I think the tone of half-moralistic, half-facetious commiseration is the most blighting of these; although the most unintelligent is the one that refuses to take his romantic subjectivity seriously, but insists on treating it as an artistic affectation and cold-blooded charlatan-trick.

But the most *malicious* of these lines of attack is undoubtedly the one that finds in him not only charlatanism but a theatrical insincerity, corroding his nature to the very depths of his soul. Well! the only answer that is finally confounding to all these temperamental hostilities is the one he would give himself—the incomparable *beauty* of his best work!

But unfortunately the best poetry is precisely the thing which you can least defend; *for it is an absolute*, and like all "absolutes" it is accepted in an act of faith, an act that fuses reason and logic and analysis and appreciation in one single intuitive assent. Where Poe is at a disadvantage compared with Shelley, in the hearts of the "loving" and the "noble," is the fact that his mania for beauty, as a facet of the absolute, allows no room for either social or pantheistic idealism.

Where he is at a disadvantage compared with Keats is that his *particular kind of beauty* excludes those magical interpretations of real and breathing nature which have so much more of a general and popular appeal. Keats, like Shakespeare, merges the narrower subjectivity of his personal emotion in the universal feelings of our race; and *his* landscapes are the familiar foregrounds of our earthly experience, felt through a sensibility a thousand times richer than our own and expressed in a language that "resolves itself into the thing it contemplates."

Poe also is a great poet, but his poetic realm, like that of Coleridge, narrows itself down to a certain romantic and unearthly mood, to a certain romantic and unearthly *milieu*, which, though they are shared, heaven knows, and shared only too fully, by natures akin to his own, can never be as *influential* in our mystical culture as, for instance, the more universal spiritual world of William Blake.

But on the other hand no malicious moralistic attempts to bring down the reputation of Edgar Allan Poe can be for long successful; for his poetry, narrow though its scope undoubtedly is, remains the only flawless representation in rhythm and rhyme of a particular individual mood that can only perish with our race; a mood that gathers into itself, from a dim margin of tribal memories, the lonely feelings of millions of isolated souls, whom public virtue could not heal nor public piety cure of the "deep scars of thunder" of our original fall from heaven.

When we are tempted, as camp-followers of the Cowslip Club or paying guests of the Barbed Wireless Club, to regard Poe as the circus-Petrushka of a theatric dance of death, we must remember that both the great universalists, Shakespeare and Homer, "find room for this also."

Here is what that Poe-like visionary, Theoclymenus in the *Odyssey*, saw, as he contemplated one laughing assembly:

"Ah, wretched men, what evil is this that you suffer?
Shrouded in night are your heads and your faces and your
knees beneath you; kindled is the sound of wailing, bathed

in tears are your cheeks, and sprinkled with blood are the walls and the fair rafters. And full of ghosts is the porch and full the court, of ghosts that hasten down to Erebus beneath the darkness, and the sun has perished out of heaven and an evil mist hovers over all." So he spoke, but they all laughed merrily at him.

And there are cheerful souls who "laugh merrily" still, though let us hope to a happier issue, when Poe writes:

> *By a route obscure and lonely*
> *Haunted by ill angels only,*
> *Where an Eidolon, named Night,*
> *On a black throne reigns upright,*
> *I have wandered home but newly*
> *From this ultimate dim Thule.*

It is because our critical approach to Poe's poetry has been from the wrong direction that we have laid him open to these disparagements. In place of trying to explain what psychological perversions in his character and what unhappy accidents in his life moulded his genius, we ought to accept his genius—for all his own mania for analysing it—as the pure inspiration it was, and then, occupying ourselves with the *nature of this inspiration* rather than with the pathological weaknesses of its mortal medium, to seek to follow him into those particular purlieus of our race-consciousness whither his intense and abnormal subjectivity carried him.

And the interesting thing to notice here is, as I have already hinted, that there should be so little that we can *localize*, or trace the *origin* of, in the actual New York or Maryland or Virginia of this poet's sojournings.

For myself, as a traveller for a score of years between all of Edgar Allan Poe's particular cities, and knowing the country round them a good deal better than I know my native Derbyshire, I confess—though it may be because of a kindred sensibility towards the ghostly, the weird, and the horror-hinting—I *have* found even in those districts, though of course far more in the "deeper" South, elements here and there that corresponded with disturbing closeness to the frightening things in his imaginary landscapes.

But it is not from those haunted pine-woods and those livid morasses and those treacherous estuaries and those weedy Lethean wharfs that the darker vistas and more troubling visions of Poe's inspirations come.

They are conjured up from the occult symbols of pre-incarnate tremblings that we all find written on the nerves of our race, though only a few abnormal individuals can render articulate these hieroglyphs of "holy terror."

And it is as if by turning this burden of ancestral "night-thoughts" into the loveliness of perfect rhyme he was able to bestow an enchanted peace—the peace and fulfilment of beauty—upon the "perturbed spirits" of this "ghoul-haunted" region of the human brain.

A traveller along strange roads is the soul of man; and there come to us all, along with the undying life-seed of the generations, hints and glimpses of dark moods and occult experiences, that only a few individuals, down the long line of our dead, have been destined really to know.

Poetry as beautiful and strange as this could only have been written by a proud and lonely spirit whose intense subjectivity tapped some abiding reservoir of these de-bouchings from the normal path of the pilgrim soul.

Yes, it is not he alone—"ah, bear in mind this garden is enchanted"—who has crossed those "ramparts plumed and pallid" of Porphyrogene! It is not only he who has learnt that "no more—

> (*Such language holds the solemn sea*
> *To the sands upon the shore*)
> *Shall bloom the thunder-blasted tree*
> *Or the stricken eagle soar!*

It is still *there*, in the long deep memory of the Mnemos-
yne of our race, that "City of the Sea," where gleams the
light that is older than the light of the sun; and when we
hear people making so much of the "crass casuality" of
this proud poet's end, and of the brutal and ghastly chance
that bore him down, let us think of that other great poet,
sepulchre-obsessed, who, lost *his* Ulalume in hell. In no very
different barbarous dissonance he too perished, and he had
gods, not human rivals, for *his* detractors; but their common
cry into the great darkness—"Eurydice! Eurydice!"—is not
to be stifled by any "hideous roar," whether of the one or
the other.

> *And all my days are trances*
> *And all my nightly dreams*
> *Are where thy dark eye glances*
> *And where thy footstep gleams,*
> *In what ethereal dances,*
> *By what eternal streams. . . .*

17

Arnold

THE peculiar advantage, or some would say disadvantage, that comes to a poet when, as in Milton's case, his poetry is only one aspect of a life devoted to political reform, or as in Goethe's to a life of intellectual curiosity, places Matthew Arnold in a totally different category from that of his more narrowly poetic contemporaries.

What a heavy burden of *premeditated originality* a poet has to carry when his own proud life-illusion and the imperative demands of a vast reading public call upon him to become a "professional," that is to say to make poetry-writing his sole and lifelong occupation!

This was the case with both Tennyson and Browning; and the harm done to the level of their work is distressingly obvious as you extricate their more inspired productions from their exhausted and exhausting "surplusage."

But with the possible exception of *Merope*, Matthew Arnold's poetry—this one not very thick volume as compared with his rivals' shelves—is arresting from cover to cover.

And what a comfort to the poetry-lover it is when he is spared by the author himself the task of skipping and selecting! He is spared then in the only way that is really satisfactory to the insatiable reader; for no bookworm can quite reconcile himself to *another* bookworm's selections!

And how few "Complete Poetical Works" are contained

in one not very big large-printed volume saving us from our usual toil through thickly crowded pages *with a line down the middle,* as we search for some new discovery!

I don't say that all Matthew Arnold's verses can be called poetry; but, and even where they can't, they do not fill us with that angry disgust at the puerility, egoism, and loquacity of famous men, which it is hard not to feel at the mere *look* of so many of these Standard Authors. The whole atmosphere, tone, and temper of Matthew Arnold's volume is the atmosphere, tone, and temper of an easy-going amateur, who only writes when he is inspired to write, and entirely avoids—as Goethe told Eckermann to avoid— "great works."

If what you want in your poet is either a laborious and concentrated artistry, growing more elaborate, more mannered, more idiosyncratic as the poet's years increase, or the sort of popular sentiment and prolific invention that becomes more lax, more voluble, more facile as the poet's pontifical prestige gathers weight, you will never be an adherent of Matthew Arnold.

Not only was his prose, which was all "occasional," and composed as the chances of the time urged, more like that of a lecturer than an artist; but his poetry never reached his public—it has not yet reached it!—with the portentous professional prestige of Tennyson, Browning, or Swinburne.

And yet how completely it has outlived the delicate artistry of the first, the convoluted psychologizing of the second, and the rhythmic rhetoric of the third!

It is the old law—true in things aesthetic as in things spiritual—that by taking yourself with a certain careless lightness you are more likely to float down the stream to posterity than by carrying too much proud ballast on board. Students of professional poetry will I suppose always be more interested in Tennyson, Browning, and Swinburne: for these voluminous writers are preoccupied with all the technical problems of their difficult art. But those among us who are struggling to keep our minds calm and sane in this confused modern arena, "where ignorant armies clash by night," will still turn with relief to this less *poetized* intellect who confronts the human situation as the clear-eyed sages of antiquity confronted it.

Yes, Matthew Arnold is the great amateur of English poetry; seeking not so much to add "immortal contributions to our National Literature" as to express his angers and contempts, his loves and his admirations, as the occasion drove. It is this very freedom from what might be called the *professional responsibility* of a recognized poet that gives such a fresh, free, spontaneous charm to his work.

He is so much franker too in his personal poetry than his famous contemporaries, "giving himself away" without a scruple.

Can any one conceive of Tennyson or Browning publishing such touching and betraying and extremely natural love-poems to a young lady across the water as the passionate verses to "Marguerite"? And his propaganda for that completely un-Christian stoicism, by which he endured her loss and the other trials of his life, how free and open and unashamed it is!

It must be confessed that like many an ancient Greek philosopher this inspector of British schools did thoroughly *enjoy* his witty disturbing of credulous minds and his railings at pontiffs. But why not? He certainly had something to say that his fellow-countrymen needed, that indeed they need still; and why should he confine himself to indicating it indirectly, in "objective art"? He was a pedagogic soothsayer, just as Socrates was; and while he preached for the love of preaching, the wayward Muse he treated so cavalierly rewarded him by touching his airy discourses with a magic far more lovely than he could ever have attained by "taking thought."

A great deal too much has been made of Matthew Arnold's "pathetic wistfulness," as he noted the collapse of the Christian faith. He wrote of this event with sympathy and tenderness; but it is surely clear that it gave him profound philosophic satisfaction and now and then I even detect a touch of heathen glee.

That abysmal respect for Christianity, that infinite terror of giving offence to "believers," which Tennyson and Browning displayed and which I am sure led in Swinburne's case to that exaggerated orgy of cerebral Priapism that to-day affects us no more than the old faded amorous vignettes in the bawdy chap-books of the eighteenth century, didn't touch Matthew Arnold at all. We need no psychologist to tell us that Swinburne's "pale Galilean" so pitifully outraged by the biting and foaming raptures of Faustinian lust, is in reality as much a product of the poet's awareness of *horrified Christian feelings* as any discretion practised by Tennyson or Browning.

But Matthew Arnold simply *does not care*. He teases his bishops as lightly as he would have teased his "dear Dr. Arnold" of Rugby. He is mildly astonished when it distresses the friends of the great philanthropist, Lord Shaftesbury, to see that noble name applied to the three Persons of the Trinity; but between proselytizing scientists and panic-stricken pietists Matthew Arnold's attitude is really the attitude of Socrates. He derives—as no doubt Socrates did—a mischievous satisfaction in teasing the orthodox, but this extremely mild roguery never leads him into scribbling phallic insults upon the gates of the temple.

Swinburne's taunt that Matthew Arnold was an "elegant Isaiah" hits the nail admirably; and properly considered it is praise not blame. "Elegant" can only refer to the discreet cloth, rather than camel's hair, in which this devoted advocate of secondary education travelled about from school to school; and if it be the role of a prophet to coin with an inspired genius phrases that illumine the whole mystery of life, I think that such things as his "Eternal not ourselves that makes for Righteousness," and his "Secret" compared with his "Method" of Jesus, entirely justify us in regarding him in this light.

The fact that his passionate advocacy of self-culture, his Goethean desire to live "according to the best that has been thought and said," is a different thing from the heroism and devotion of a social reformer doesn't detract from the value of his criticism of life: and although Goethe's dictim: "To act is easy: to think is hard" cannot be said to hold good with everyone, it is surely true that the part played by critical onlookers in the evolutionary struggle is no negligible one. By such detached criticism, as a matter of fact, the practical activities of whole revolutions have been swerved to the left or the right.

Matthew Arnold's peculiar kind of humour is the clue to his prevailing temper. Too proud as well as too kind to be anything but humble in his relations with simple people, he enjoyed to the full the play of his persiflage when dealing with scientists and clergymen and with the limitations of public opinion.

He had the advantage over his intellectual contemporaries in the fact that his indefatigable *literary culture*, his custom of daily pondering over the old poets and philosophers, kept his intelligence malleable and fluid, kept it entirely uncommitted to the transitory fashions of the hour. He is the supreme example of what a persistent reading of the classical writers can do for a modern man's character and brain, making it mellow, sceptical, ironical, while at the same time it gives it a massive stoical power to bear up under the tribulations of life. It is this lucky accident that his culture was literary rather than metaphysical that makes him so completely *utrumque paratus*, so "prepared for either event," and frees him from the dogmatism of both scientists and religionists.

Like Socrates, beyond the conviction that it is important to be good, he has no convictions; and beyond the principle that it is best to be reasonable, he has no principle! And it is this literary fluidity in him, this intellectual *amateurishness*, that proved as annoying to his contemporaries, as it is still annoying to the theologians and the scientists of to-day.

Professionals have always a hatred for amateurs and a humorous amateur who keeps repeating the same hit in the same weak spot rouses them to fury.

Matthew Arnold's mischievous and illuminating phrases are the creation of a man following a trained literary instinct—but a man devoid of dogmatic convictions *on any subject*, except perhaps his conviction that orthodox Christianity is untrue, and that this country ought to have a sound system of education.

I confess I think his instinct led him wrong in one important point. I refer to his reiterated affirmation in *Literature and Dogma* that the most remarkable thing about Jesus Christ was his sweet reasonableness or *epieikeia*.

In this dangerous and risky matter—full of blind alleys for the most clairvoyant—I confess to a preference for the formidable Jesus of William Blake, and even for the psychological Jesus of St. Paul, over this rational and amiable figure conjured up by Matthew Arnold. Of all noble qualities that of "reasonableness"—sweet or otherwise—seems to me the very last that I would attribute to this mysterious overturner of normal human values, this bewildering enchanter, whose paradoxical wrath

> *His seventy disciples sent*
> *Against Religion and Government!*

He goes wrong again, it seems to me, in his famous definition of religion itself as "morality touched by emotion";

and I think this error came about by the curious absence from his own nature of what, remembering his own expression "natural magic," might be called "magical awe" or "divine idolatry," the thrilling pleasure, namely, so many people feel in the mere gesture of bowing down before some tremendous mystery, even if such a mystery be no more than the sun or the moon, or the indwelling "genius" of some consecrated spot, some spot made holy by the natural piety of traditional reverence.

There is surely no tinge of "morality" in *this* religious feeling. The most unrepentent of scoundrels could experience it, as he moved from one crime to another; and I am tempted to attribute its absence from the prevailing temper of this enlightened moralist to an overrational stoicism, wherein Epictetus leads him away from the Socrates of Plato.

As a critic of poetry Matthew Arnold reveals sometimes an inspired penetration, a penetration that is rendered the more convincing by the way he concentrates on particular passages, using as his divining-rod that literary instinct for the essence of style which is only very imperfectly suggested by his rational quest for what he calls "the highest truth and the highest seriousness." Compared with his *artistically masked* poetic contemporaries the honest light of a free, frank, universal intelligence shone through him, as it shone through Goethe and Emerson. No smouldering manias, no distorted moral prejudices, no fuliginous obsessions, no sulky egotism clouded the integrity of his vision.

Writing thus, freely and easily, of the real actual sights and sounds and smells as he comes bolt upon them from his books and his desk, he has no psychological burden of self-conscious "artistic vision" to separate from the simplest, most obvious, most universal reactions of our normal senses.

There is therefore something in his descriptions of nature

MATTHEW ARNOLD

that comes *several degrees nearer* to her real life than anything in Tennyson or Browning or Swinburne. What this "something" is it is very hard to define. He gets it sometimes by deliberately disregarding the melody of the verse. But whatever it is, it is nature with her blurred, littered, frayed edges unpolished, and the bloom of her atmospheric magic unimpaired.

The ancient poetic tradition of our Western world— now some two thousand years old—is always reverting to Homer; and it is Homer who not only supplies Matthew Arnold with a background of classical charm; but who, like a perpetually rising and sinking tide, washes even the foreground of his mind clean of the confused rubble of modern aesthetic problems. The concentration of his whole character being fixed, not on the struggle to be, or to be regarded as, a great poet, but on the struggle to live according to "the best that has been thought and said" he can afford to forget to be an artist. He can afford to become a reed, waving aloof by the grey waters of our northern seas, a reed through which the divine wind can blow as it will, blowing Homeric imagery, blowing Celtic romance, blowing the secrets of the English pastures, till he becomes, except for Keats and Shakespeare, the most magical of all our poets.

Wordsworth can capture—and in yet simpler language— the vaguer impressions, the subtler presences and half-presences of dawn and twilight, of day and night; but there are certain *less usual* natural occurrences—but yet phenomena we have all seen without seeing, heard without hearing, felt without feeling, that Keats and Shakespeare and Matthew Arnold alone have the power to convey.

And Matthew Arnold works this miracle by the use of the same device as Shakespeare and Keats, the simple, obvious device—but none of the rest are bold enough to dare it—of using extremely realistic, and, from any artistic or picturesque standpoint, extremely startling and even *unpoetical* expressions.

Where he falls short of these masters is in his singular lack not only of melody, which is pardonable, but of harmony too, which is a more serious lapse.

Shakespeare and Keats can capture this "natural magic" and yet keep—in fact *enhance*—the music of their verse.

Matthew Arnold again and again will be found sacrificing melody, found sacrificing even harmony to the evocation, at all costs, of this magical touch. Indeed I would go so far as to call this union of discordant sound with magical imagery his chief characteristic as a poet.

It cannot be denied that the *purely aesthetic* motive for writing poetry is present only very faintly in Matthew Arnold's work. The larger portion of what he wrote in poetic form is what we call "occasional," written that is to say under the urge of some particular event or situation or passing train of thought.

This alone gives his verse a certain airiness and ease, a certain playfulness even; and it endows it, too, with that fresh spontaneity, which often catches, much more realistically and vividly than any artistic premeditation could do, the direct impact, with its taste and tang and escaping overtones, of the thing he is describing.

And his poetry springs naturally from his character. It conveys, even in its most casual and least premeditated outbursts, the high and luminous vision of things which was the essence of his life. To open his volume almost at random is to experience something of that heightening of our feeling for planetary existence that we get from the essays of Emerson.

And the secret of his power as a poet lies in his inartistic sincerity, in his unaffected effort to keep his mind fixed steadily upon the riddle of existence and its ultimate *alterna-*

tives as far as human destiny is concerned. Unlike our other English poets he follows Goethe in linking up the moral situation with the cosmic one. His personal bias is towards a clarified and monumental stoicism; but a certain lightness of touch, a certain easy playfulness of tone, combined with his genius for the evocation of "natural magic," prevents this stoicism from growing dogmatic or harsh or austere.

Modern sophistication tends to revolt against the simple and transparent efforts Matthew Arnold makes to live, like Emerson, in a large and luminous atmosphere of philosophical detachment; but to my mind there is something disarming and touching about the majestic simplicity with which he struggles to attune his temper to "the best that has been thought and said" in the long history of our race.

To our younger generation, who lack both the vitality and the tenacity of purpose to remain steadily in this serene mountain air, there must often seem too much of the preacher in his work, and far too little rebellious devilry or Satanic malice against the system of things.

Nor does the loftier and more tragic reaction to the bitter ironies of life that we get so much of in Shakespeare and Hardy enter into his tone. Its place is taken by a certain airy philosophical detachment, a detachment archly playful and even supercilious, which just avoids the danger of sinking into the priggish.

What concerned him most was the daily struggle to keep his normal mood upon the high level of the sages' thoughts upon which he was always pondering, and it was the tragic gulf between this rarefied air and the hullabaloo about him that provoked his outbursts of supercilious and not always considerate humour.

He was a great generalizer, and his avoidance of metaphysical and scientific logic gives to his generalizations a swift human point and a weighty cogency. He was in his

best vein, for instance, when he generalized about the contribution to the imagination of our race of its Celtic element, and indeed all through his poetry the glamour of
race contrast is a recurrent spring of romantic interest.

This passion of his for the poetry of race was made more
effective and circumstantial by his inspired use of geo-
graphical proper names, the value of which, as in Homer
and Milton, lies in the way it universalizes—even to the
ends of the earth—that romantic continuity of the human
drama, to appreciate which is the chief glory of poetic
scholarship.

It is just this element of magical geography that one feels
so lacking in the great cosmic poets like Wordsworth and
Shelley, and naturally in our modern interpreters of the
heroism of the industrial struggle the long drama of the
planet is narrowed down to the tragedy at our doors.

There are many occult hints of Pythagorean ideas in
Matthew Arnold. It is hard to read his poetry for long
without feeling steal over you that strange presence of many
invisible generations, that seems so personal and yet so
impersonal, as if we had all passed through cycles upon
cycles of incarnations.

> *The Guide of our dark steps a triple veil*
> *Betwixt our senses and our sorrow keeps;*
> *Hath sown with cloudless passages the tale*
> *Of grief, and eased us with a thousand sleeps.*

And without being dogmatic about it, holding it not as
a metaphysical conclusion but as a natural possibility,
there runs through his verse an unmistakable hint of the
Goethean idea that it is only by our own exertions that
we mount—"and that hardly"—to eternal life. It cannot
be denied that when his feelings in this ambiguous matter
really escape him they betray an intellectual pride a good
deal more heathen-stoical than Christian.

Thin, thin the pleasant human noises grow,
And faint the city gleams;
Rare the lone pastoral huts—marvel not thou!
The solemn peaks but to the stars are known,
But to the stars, and the cold lunar beams;
Alone the sun arises, and alone
Spring the great streams.

A poet's attitude to poetry in general, whether it be detached and half-humorous as Shakespeare's, or proud and
grave as Dante's, is always a matter of curious interest; but
a poet's own work reveals much more than this. It reveals
not only in definite statements, but in what you might call
its diffused atmospheric pressure, the most hidden and
secret life-longings, life-frustrations, life-suppressions of the
poet's identity.

Some poets, Browning for instance, betray, in this diffused atmospheric revelation of themselves, a warm, glowing, almost sexual attraction to the human spectacle.
Others, and Matthew Arnold is an extreme example of
this, betray a cold and weary distaste, a fastidious shrinking,
a magnetic *repulsion* from the rough-and-tumble of human
intercourse.

Almost every one of Matthew Arnold's most characteristic gestures in poetry is a gesture of *differentiating himself*
from the passions, ambitions, superstitions, illusions of the
mass of his fellow-men. To shake off the too hot, the too
dusty, the too familiar pressure of life, to *thin life out*, and
to sever himself from this or that in a cold passion for more
air, more space, more solitude seems to be the recurrent
effort he is always making.

He seems to derive a certain intimate satisfaction even
from the very tragedy of such separation, such severance,
such estrangement!

The greatness of Matthew Arnold as a poet lies in the

fact that he combines the rare emotional appeal of thaumaturgic place-names, dependent upon books, with the fresh-
est and most naturalistic impressions of nature. He is a true
scholar, who, just because he emerges dazed and entranced
from his books, responds with a special childlike naïveté to
what he encounters in the open air. Just because he has
been so stirred by old geography, old romance, old chronicles, and is so steeped in Homeric tags and Miltonic echoes,
the mere sight of "an unskilful gardener" mowing the grass
and cutting by mischance some fragrant hyacinth near the
lawn's edge will strike him, as he comes back to the real
world, with a startling vividness.

And Matthew Arnold's *Sohrab and Rustum* is a poem of
precisely this nature. It is a poem Coleridge would have
loved; and yet, in its firm, clear, circumstantial "architectonics," it is less fragmentary than most of the projec-
tions of that great and disordered imagination. Its material
comes obviously from a scholar's shelves, but from those
of a scholar, as I suggest, whose senses when he goes out
at last into the air, respond with a buoyant and elemental
freshness to what he sees and feels.

What a heavenly thing indeed is this multitude of old
books! Not "vain," as the Preacher murmured, but pregnant unto immortal thoughts and imperishable longings.
It was from an imagination quickened by "much study"
that Matthew Arnold summed up so well the life of all of
us upon earth, putting his conclusion into his young
Sohrab's mouth when, not knowing what he did, the boy
lifted up his spear against his father.

> *For we are all, like swimmers in the sea,*
> *Poised on the top of a huge wave of fate.*
> *Which hangs uncertain to which side to fall,*
> *And whether it will heave us up to land,*
> *Or whether it will roll us out to sea,*

> *Back out to sea, to the deep waves of death,*
> *We know not, and no search will make us know;*
> *Only the event will teach us in its hour.*

But it is the closing pages of this great poem that move me as few other lines in literature have ever done. What an inspiration it was—and yet he learnt it all from books!—to leave the dead boy, with the father who had killed him crouching over him there in the sand, while he makes us follow the course of the great Oxus stream till it reaches *its* resting-place!

> *But the majestic river floated on,*
> *Out of the mist and hum of that low land,*
> *Into the frosty starlight, and there mov'd*
> *Rejoicing, through the hush'd Chorasmian waste,*
> *Under the solitary moon: he flowed*
> *Right for the polar star, past Orgunjè,*
> *Brimming, and bright, and large: then sands begin*
> *To hem his watery march, and dam his streams,*
>   *And split his currents; that for many a league*
> *The shorn and parcell'd Oxus strains along*
> *Through beds of sand and matted rushy isles—*
> *Oxus, forgetting the bright speed he had*
> *In his high mountain-cradle in Pamere,*
> *A foil'd circuitous wanderer:—till at last*
> *The long'd-for dash of waves is heard, and wide*
> *His luminous home of waters opens, bright*
> *And tranquil, from whose floor the new-bath'd stars*
>   *Emerge, and shine upon the Aral Sea.*

Thus in true Homeric style does this supercilious scourge of the bishops sink his teasing controversies, forget his lost Marguerite, let the *epieikeia* of Jesus go, to lose himself in the calm eternal peace of those godlike elements, that are at once subhuman and superhuman.

But if he shows in *Sohrab and Rustum* to what good purpose—not merely copying the similes of the ancient Muse
but catching her very accent—he has read Homer, in
Tristram and Iseult he achieves an even greater miracle.
How superior to all the laboured and artistic attempts of
Tennyson and Swinburne—and of so many others down to
this present hour!—to catch what is really the most evasive
secret in the whole overworld of inspiration, is this casual,
easy, careless unfinished fragment!

Here we find him—always the arch-amateur—launching
forth upon Welsh matters; and I have a dim conviction
that, outside the Welsh *mabinogi* themselves, never has this
peculiar enchantment—an enchantment that, for all his
rush of eloquence, completely escaped Swinburne, and was
only touched at rare intervals by Tennyson—been so
miraculously captured.

I have no hesitation in declaring that Matthew Arnold
is alone, with Shakespeare, among our great English poets
in doing justice to the Welsh genius; and he had I suspect
less opportunities than Shakespeare in this direction. It was
pure clairvoyance influenced to some extent, I fancy by
his passion for Homer, but also, no doubt, by some kindred
strain in his own childlike, subtle nature.

In reading any great poet's work there is a curious
interest, if you possess a certain grim realistic humour, in
noting the contrast between what we all see of the author,
as he goes about among us in his "usual attire," and the
wild imaginary situations *into which*—as he projects what
might be called the underconsciousness of his soul—*he thinks
himself.*

In some cases, in the case of Shelley and Keats, for instance, there seems no shock of incongruity between the
poet as he was in his daily life and this imaginary projection
of himself, "ceasing upon the midnight with no pain" as
he listens to the nightingale, or dissolving his body into a

melting cloud or a leaf-scattering wind. But when one thinks of Matthew Arnold's patient educational labours, when one thinks of his conscientious if not always considerate anticlerical propaganda, above all when one thinks of his stiffly conventional *appearance*, there comes a singular twinge of human poignance in following his purer soul into these unearthly metamorphoses.

But in *The Forsaken Merman* this supercilious amateur of "the best that has been thought and said" showed how it was possible to use the inspiration he fished up from the books he loved, till, setting free the soul within him from the life he had to lead, and from the bodily vesture he had to carry, it evoked something that approached in beauty the immortal sea-sorcery of Shakespeare himself.

> Sand-strewn caverns, cool and deep,
> Where the winds are all asleep;
> Where the spent lights quiver and gleam,
> Where the salt weed sways in the stream,
> Where the sea-beasts, ranged all round,
> Feed in the ooze of their pasture-ground;
> Where the sea-snakes coil and twine,
> Dry their mail and bask in the brine;
> Where great whales come sailing by,
> Sail and sail, with unshut eye
> Round the world for ever and aye.

But among his more casually and airily written poems the one perhaps that conveys most persuasively his peculiar genius is *The Strayed Reveller*.

Here again we get that rare device of lifting us up to the top of a planetary watch-tower, from which the inhabitants of our round globe can be caught in the historic and geographic glamour of their immemorial occupations; and from which, as from the deck of some philosophic airship, the past and the present betray their basic and poetic continuity.

In this poem with its short easily flowing unrhymed lines —a form of verse by which his not very musical ear was spared the labour of more artful versification—he reiterates his large, free, luminous, unpsychological theory of the nature of the poet's vision. It is a vision by no means free from pain, but pain mellowed to a stoical lucidity and attuned to a calm disillusioned peace.

> *They see the Heroes*
> *Sitting in the dark ship*
> *On the foamless, long-heaving*
> *Violet sea,*
> *At sunset nearing*
> *The Happy Islands.*
>
> .   .   .   .   .
>
> *They see the Heroes*
> *Near harbour;—but they share*
> *Their lives, and former violent toil in Thebes,*
> *Seven-gated Thebes, or Troy;*
> *Or where the echoing oars*
> *Of Argo first*
> *Startled the unknown sea.*

It must be admitted that an amateur in poetry whose life-purpose is not the "contribution to our Literature of immortal works," but the struggle to live—and help his fellow countrymen to live—"in the best that has been thought and said" from the beginning of time, will sometimes be found sacrificing beauty, and even dignity, to *preaching*.

When this occurs however in Matthew Arnold it is a very different thing from the unredeemed dulness in Wordsworth at his worst, or the tediousness and infinitely commonplace cheapness of Byron at his second-best.

It *is* preaching, it *is* moralizing; sometimes it is priggish and supercilious moralizing to a point that becomes absurd, but it is never boastful in the intolerable manner of Browning, and it never comes as near to a Sunday-school lesson as Tennyson is capable of doing.

In a vein quite contrary to the *epieikeia* of Jesus, our planetary inspector—and I like to fancy he composed it while he was actually crossing the deep grave of that lost Atlantis—writes a poem to advise us to stick to our predestined job and not worry about the wickedness or madness or ignorance of our less lucky neighbours in the tellurian trenches.

I often repeat the lines to myself when I am tempted to some human weakness; and although they don't jump with my conscience they are marvellously comforting to my egoism.

In the way we know so well—in what some of us would call his grand "pathetic fallacy"—he thus, in true Empedoclean style, calls upon us to imitate the elements. "Would'st thou *be* as these are? *Live* as they." So far so good; but once having let himself go, as his transatlantic liner carries him over the watery grave of *one* human civilization, the secret of his heart escapes, and he reveals what Nietzsche would call the "great loathing."

> *Unaffrighted by the silence round them,*
> *Undistracted by the sights they see,*
> *These demand not that the things without them*
> *Yield them love, amusement, sympathy.*
>
> *And with joy the stars perform their shining*
> *And the sea its long moon-silver'd roll;*
> *For self-poised they live, nor pine with noting*
> *All the fever of some differing soul.*

Bounded by themselves and unregardful
In what state God's other works may be,
In their own tasks all their powers pouring,
These attain the mighty life you see.

The conventional expression "God's other works" does not, I think, conceal from us the inhumanity of this doctrine: but after all—un-Christian as it is—it does have behind it a considerable weight of mystical tradition; and no doubt many of the ancient hermits were elementalists in this sense.

But it is *The Scholar-Gipsy* and *Thyrsis* that will always remain, for the casual and incurious reader, Matthew Arnold's masterpieces; and indeed there are few lovelier poems in our language.

Just as Milton flung into *Lycidas* so much more than an elegiac dirge over the loss of young King, so Matthew Arnold seized the opportunity offered by the death of Clough to compose, in his airiest, and most archly amateur fashion, a couple of poems that reveal the overtones and undertones, the moral values and intellectual conclusions of his youth, his culture, his experience. What days these young men must have passed together, in a youth as guarded, as privileged, as favoured, as that of any young Mariuses or Florians or Gastons of Walter Pater's invention!

As I have hinted, the mere *realism* of these pastoral vignettes of the scenery round Oxford surpasses all nature poetry in our language save certain passages in Shakespeare and Keats. The fact that the *kind* of landscape described is not grand or stupendous or awe-inspiring—no mountains like those in Wordsworth, no seas like those in Homer, no wide salt-marshes or vast horizons like those in Walt Whitman—does not lessen its value. It is *foreground* scenery, it is simple, pastoral scenery, just as we have it in Keats and Shakespeare; but unassuming and ordinary as it is, I confess I look in vain for anything to equal it in what has been written before or since of what most Englishmen mean when they talk of the *country*.

And just because of this intimate quality I think it takes a native-born critic to give these poems their true place. Their peculiar tone, conveying something of the familiar classical playfulness that is such a pretty thing when the great Milton unbends, adds to the spontaneity—I refuse to call it affected spontaneity—with which the impressions are recorded. And the point is these are *honest* impressions! They are not the impressions of a poet pretending to be a farmer, but those of a bookish student following the familiar track of generations of bookish students.

But how English they are! Even the odes of Keats are more adaptable to other, alien landscapes, less soaked in English dew, less drenched by English rain, less "cool-rooted" in English earth!

For all his secret aloofness from human warmth Matthew Arnold must have displayed plenty of *epieikeia* in his domestic life.

Like Cowper he had a "penchant" for pets, a significant psychological indication, I suspect, if all were known; and he doesn't boggle at slipping into his "Poetical Works" a courtly apology to his dying canary, for—

> *Troubling with our chatter vain*
> *Ebb of life and mortal pain*

and one can't help asking oneself whether as he wrote down the words,

> *Us, unable to divine*
> *Our companion's dying sign*
> *Or o'erpass the severing sea*
> *Set betwixt ourselves and thee,*

any trace of a flicker of Heine-like mischief crossed his face

as he remembered that this was not the first time he had
used in his poetry the words, sever, severing, *severance?*

> *Who renders vain their deep desire?*
> *A God, a God their severance ruled!*
> *And bade betwixt their shores to be*
> *The unplumb'd, salt, estranging sea.*

But he dismisses this other *animula vagula* in the tone of
a classic tenderness older than the Christian hope.

> *Fare thee well, companion dear!*
> *Fare for ever well, nor fear,*
> *Tiny though thou art, to stray*
> *Down the uncompanion'd way!*

No, there is a residue of a curious kind of poignance in the
contrast between his patient, conventional, kindly life and
the far-off incarnations of his wandering spirit.

From which of the sages of the *logoi* he was always reading
did he learn the secret of adjusting his amiable-sociable
outer life with the cold, aloof, "soulless" *inner* life, this queer
Neckan-life of his, this life of an unconverted merman who
couldn't keep grave when he heard how much the bishops
of Winchester and Gloucester "wanted to do something for
the honour of Our Lord's godhead"?

The particular influence he exerted all his days must
have been of a piece with this queer double life—of kindly
rectitude and infinite disillusionment. How he must have
been hated in certain quarters! None knew in what curious
and new direction he would make his next attack, but it
would be sure to be against something profoundly respected
by the moral instincts of every class in the country.

And if his poetry was amateurish compared with all the
volumes of Browning and Swinburne, how amateurish were
his onslaughts on theology! They resembled Goethe's attacks on Sir Isaac Newton. Indeed, like Goethe he held the

view that there was a "penetrable" and an "impenetrable" in nature and that the Christian revelation belonged to the sphere of the impenetrable.

Like Goethe's in *his* day Matthew Arnold's aphorisms and generalizations go far deeper than appears on the surface. They have a certain challenging airiness of tone, but like transparent water they reflect the very abysses of the far-off sky. That "Eternal not ourselves which makes for righteousness" does remain—say what you will—the obstinate and incredible miracle in this careless cosmos.

But how appropriate, how singularly suitable for one who was always something of a male Undine under his inspector's umbrella, that the most definite statement of his secret thoughts should be put into the mouth of Empedocles, the philosopher par excellence of the non-human elements!

Empedocles on Etna is one of the most curious and interesting poems in our language. It is a poem for lonely people; for recluses and hermits, for misfits and misanthropes, for all those who underneath their patient toil and amiable chatter have a longing, figuratively speaking, to throw themselves into a fiery crater or into the path of an avalanche.

Not for nothing did Matthew Arnold select the old Empedocles as his mouthpiece. There is I fancy among poets and mystics a long, long occult tradition, reverting to the megalithic age, of this worship of the most inhuman of all the elements, the worship of stones and water.

Even in our own time that proud antisocial poet of the Pacific Coast, the American Jeffers, promulges some such reversion to the most primeval of all animisms—if it be animism! For the chemistry of our bodies will always draw some among us, and the nostalgia of our souls will always draw some among us, away from the warm securities of flesh-and-blood to that prehistoric remoteness and unapproachableness, that final escape of hunter and hunted, the elements from which we came.

In speaking of the old Welsh tales that we now call *The Mabinogion*, Matthew Arnold, with one of those subtle inklings of pure genius that he sometimes displayed, makes use of the following significant words:

> The mediaeval story-teller is pillaging an antiquity of which he does not fully possess the secret; he is like a peasant building his hut on the site of Halicarnassus or Ephesus; he builds, but what he builds of is full of materials of which he knows not the history, or knows by a glimmering tradition merely: stones "not of this building," but of an older architecture, greater, cunninger, more majestical.

Ha, master! was it then to this "older architecture," to these stones "not of this building," that you secretly responded all your life? Responded even while you were tormenting the bishops of Winchester and Gloucester? Responded even while you were explaining that the word God only meant "shining," and that the word religion only meant "morality touched with emotion"? Responded while you were listening to the "grating roar of pebbles" on Dover Beach, like Sophocles on *his* beach, and were "finding in that sound," what in your quaint pedagogic way you called "a thought," but which really was a cry to your lost love—

> . . . *for the world which seems*
> *To lie before us like a land of dreams,*
> *So various, so beautiful, so new,*
> *Hath really neither joy, nor love, nor light,*
> *Nor certitude, nor peace, nor help for pain;*
> *And we are here as on a darkling plain*
> *Swept with confused alarms of struggle and flight,*
> *Where ignorant armies clash by night?*

Responded even while you were listening to that *other* cry, the cry of the "armies of the homeless and unfed"?

And was this response to an architecture "cunninger and more majestical" nothing less than a response to that "house not made with hands" whose builder and ruler is Death?

We have overheard in recent years various hints and rumours telling of an unconscious yearning within us—there is no need to give it a more technical name; but it is some kind of navel-string nostalgia—a yearning to revert to our prenatal condition within the body of our mother. And if the maternal womb of us all—as the drift of speculation seems to point—was nothing less than the shell-strewn *wind-row* between sea and shore, may we not regard this worship of water and stone, this atavistic "religion" *un*touched by morality, as a longing for that untroubled *bios-akinesis*, that blessed existence without motion or thought, which was interrupted when we were born?

But agnostic still as to the fate of the soul at this critical juncture, our author's Empedocles fears that even after death the terrible *thinking power* may be our bane.

> . . . *thought and mind*
> *Will hurry us with them on their homeless march,*
> *Over the unallied unopening earth,*
> *Over the unrecognising sea; while air*
> *Will blow us fiercely back to sea and earth,*
> *And fire repel us from its living waves.*
>> *And then we shall unwillingly return*
>> *Back to this meadow of calamity,*
> *This uncongenial place, this human life;*
> *And in our individual human state*
> *Go through the sad probation all again,*
> *To see if we will now at last be true*
> *To our own only true, deep-buried selves,*
> *Being one with which we are one with the whole world.*

Sometimes when one thinks of that mid-Victorian era and compares it with our own it seems like an epoch of giants! Think of the men who were contemporaries of Matthew Arnold! The roll of their tremendous names is overpowering; nor do I think, if it were a simple question of outstanding originality, we should dare to rank him among the first of these titans. Curiously enough, however, as Oscar Wilde so admirably hints, great critics of life and literature are really much rarer than these vital geniuses.

And consider how blind, how absurdly prejudiced, how ignorant and childish, these original ones are in regard to each other's work!

The number of really great *critics* in the historic roll of English letters is indeed strikingly small compared with the crowd of eccentric creators; while I suppose—Matthew Arnold would certainly say so—it is the other way round across the Channel!

Holding a natural brief for his own detached on-looker's point of view, which he quite properly praises as a "Hellenic" one, Matthew Arnold was tempted to deplore the absence from England of any concentrated body of intelligent criticism parallel with what exists in Paris.

Personally I hesitate to follow him here. Well-balanced criticism can, of course, be a help in keeping erratic geniuses to their proper predestined path, but when you consider the predestined path of our whole Anglo-Celtic imagination, its chaotic, meteoric, dark-star orbits, its terrific individualism, its heroic provincialism, it seems a question whether in the long run it doesn't fare better and achieve more natural and autochthonous results by being spared the assistance of such highly trained critical aid!

The present work is a book upon books, and in such a survey to omit Matthew Arnold would be like dropping our best pilot when our small craft is in the middle of the reefs and shoals. Our present-day critics have either so violent a social *parti pris*, or they are themselves, in their charming gossiping manner, so extravagantly personal, that a true literary criticism, going, as his did, to the root of the matter, and using for his criterion not so much personal whims and caprices as a detailed comparison with "the best that has been thought and said," is no less rare and precious in our era of mass movements than it was among the self-absorbed giants of his time. He is a light weight, we must admit, compared with his master Goethe, but like Goethe—and of how many others can *that* be said?— the method he reiterates is the old Socratic one of patient self-culture based upon the great works of the past but accompanied by a purgative and wholesome scepticism of *all* the dogmas of the past!

This method of self-culture has the supreme advantage of detaching us from the catchwords of the hour and of fixing our minds upon what is abiding; and the grand example of his own application of it is his treatment of the Bible.

He may have made mistakes in this Biblical exegesis. He was always a careless amateur. But when one encounters in so many quarters the same neglect—I speak of pure cultural neglect, for indifference to dogma is another matter—of the Bible as of Homer or Rabelais, it does seem, considering what he called the instinct of self-preservation in the soul, it does seem as if we would be wise to accept his "method," though his Empedoclean "secret" may not be for us.

But perhaps we say even this too quickly! At any rate let the Power we still call Nature, that great non-human Power he worshipped in preference to the Second Person of the Trinity, have the last word *here* . . .

Race after race, man after man,
Have thought that my secret was theirs,
Have dreamed that I lived but for them,
That they were my glory and joy.
. . . They are dust, they are changed, they are gone!
I remain.

18

Hardy

How long it seems since in my early twenties, some forty years ago, I first saw Thomas Hardy!

I had addressed some boyish verses to him in my first printed book; the opening lines of which ran as follows,

> *Master of human smiles and human moan,*
> *Of strange soul-searchings, raptures, agonies,*
> *Passions that ask for bread and find a stone,*
> *Hopes hungered into madness, like the seas,*
> *And Pity dumb and pleading, like the wind;*

and he had asked me to visit him at Max Gate, and in return had come by train to Montacute, just over the Somerset border, to spend the day at my father's vicarage, bringing with him the first Mrs. Hardy.

And now with more recent memories of one of the best friends my brother Theodore and I have ever had or are likely to have—I speak of the late Mrs. Hardy, his second wife—I still find that my deepest impression of this great man's genius has to do with his pity—"Promethean" I called it in my youth and it seems to me not less than that still—for the frustrated loves of simple hearts, thwarted by the "crass casualities" of a blighted planet. Matthew Arnold speaks of "the something that infects the world" and it was with this primeval "something" that Hardy was concerned, however its origin may be explained.

433

The number of thorough-going pessimists in English Literature is singularly small, considering the "vapours" and the "spleen" of which our neighbours across the Channel used to accuse us; and even in Burton's *Anatomy* Hardy's cause for melancholy finds no mention.

His cause for rising up "in the fertile pastures of Wessex" and cursing the "President of the Immortals" was not a political or an economic one, was not even the moral one of the cruelty of man to man. It went deeper than that. It went to the bitter root of the whole matter. There are no Iagos in the Wessex novels, and hardly any thoroughly wicked people. The evil-doers are only a little less pitiable than the righteous. All are victims together of *the nature of the universe*.

Yes, I would be tempted to call Hardy the only great pessimist in our literature—for certain terrifying moods in Swift and an isolated challenge here and there, like that of *The City of Dreadful Night*, can hardly be said to represent an undeviating philosophical vision of life—were it not for Shakespeare. Save for an occasional indulgent and careless obeisance to the faith of his fathers, it is hard to see—in spite of the familiar academic view of him in which most of us have been brought up—how the general drift of his plays can be called anything but deeply pessimistic. I would go so far as to say that in pure pessimistic feeling Shakespeare is the only Hardyesque writer we have. The outcries to this effect—to this indictment of the nature-of-things as being responsible for our pain rather than any particular wrong-doing—follow one another throughout his tragic plays like straws and feathers on a wind that for ever reverts to the same quarter. "Still through the hawthorn" blows this cold wind of Shakespeare's anticipation of Hardy; and what it amounts to psychologically is surely nothing less than that these two poets were at once more sensitized to the sufferings of our race—especially to those that spring from

wounded hearts—and less padded with comfortable pallia-
tives, less sprinkled with the holy water of forgetting, than
the other men of genius in our list.

"As flies to wanton boys are we to the gods. They kill us
for their sport." This is the unadulterated Hardy note in
Shakespeare; and we get it repeated with the very accent
of one after another of the Hardy women, in Lady Mac-
duff's words before they kill her.

> *Whither should I fly?*
> *I have done no harm. But I remember now*
> *I am in this earthly world, where, to do harm*
> *Is often laudable, to do good sometime*
> *Accounted dangerous folly; why then alas!*
> *Do I put up that womanly defence,*
> *To say I have done no harm?*

But I must lay no undue stress on these Hardyesque
passages, for from every birthday-book in the kingdom tags
could be shuffled together that would be glib to the opposite
tune. The point I want to make is that in the spiritual
essence of the plays—never mind where he picked up the
plots—and in the handling of the characters and in the
particular kind of poetical atmosphere he throws round
them his mood comes nearer to the Hardy mood than to
any other temper—moral or immoral—to which you could
point. Shakespeare's poetic magic, that unequalled magic
that throws its own wistful and tender charm over the
crazy cruelties of life, is steeped in simple, unsophisticated
ballad pessimism, which is the most unadulterated pessimism
in the world, and our immorally cheerful propagandists can
pile up their consolatory tags from his plays, beginning
with "there's a divinity that shapes our ends" and ending
with "flights of angels" as high as they please, without
being able to change the fact that the ballad beauty that

dominates his work is the beauty of tragedy, not of redemption.

But though the old ballad touch, with its wild sad tenderness and homely realism, often enters into Hardy's work, the main driving-force of his genius is a philosophical arraignment of the ways of God to Man.

When Wordsworth looked at any landscape with its woods and fields he drew something from its "colours and forms," and divined something in its "language of the sense" that charged with a mystical hope the "still sad music of humanity" even if it didn't change its key.

But Hardy when he looked at a similar landscape was aware of the cruel drama that is being played below this apparent calm. He saw the ivy killing the tree, he saw the weasel killing the rabbit, he saw the trees strangling each other as they contended for light and air, he saw the sportsman wounding the pheasant and the collector bringing down the rare migratory bird. And he saw the cruelties that are an essential part of nature's life and have nothing to do with man. He saw all the children of the earth feeding upon each other. He saw the dark unseen tragedies that go on all the while in these peaceful places. Instead of a "Presence that disturbs us with the joy of elevated thoughts" he felt a blind irrational "Immanent Will" driving vegetation to strangle vegetation, beast to destroy beast, bird to prey upon bird, insect to torture insect. And as he brooded upon all this, the mindless and meaningless Chance that governs the destiny of living things took to itself demonic lineaments and became something much more sinister than mere "crass casualty," became, in fact, the dominant pressure of a supermundane Mischief, that with an ironic and goblinish malice persecutes the luckless children of its wanton creation.

Hardy is perfectly honest in the way he makes no tricky attempt to bridge the logical gulf between this dumb, blind, irrational "Immanent Will," working through all the meaningless accidents and chances of life, and this deliberately personified "President of the Immortals" who is so mischief-loving. Nor is there any need that he should make such an attempt. He accepts in himself on behalf of us all the inevitable human tendency to *anthropomorphize* the inscrutable Power behind the universe; and in place of estimating its characteristics in terms of the presence of a Wordsworthian Over-Soul, felt in our rare moments of ecstasy, he estimates them in terms of those wanton and wayward "ironies" that require no rare moments of sensuous well-being for their disclosing.

What makes Hardy—with Shakespeare—the greatest of our pessimists is that his pessimism isn't a matter of personal nerves or personal misfortune but a matter of indignant sympathy with a suffering world; but it is significant—as with Shakespeare, too—that the kind of suffering on which he concentrates, is not, though the physical enters also, the misery of hardship and destitution so much as the emotional tragedies of the heart.

A great writer reveals himself in his ideas of good and evil as much as in anything; and it is most interesting to note the difference between a Hardy "good man" and a Dostoievsky "good man." Hardy's good men are above all else what we call strong characters. They invariably display a mixture of simplicity and sagacity, and they seldom, if ever, surprise us by explosions of morbid nerves or of imaginative weakness. Even Henchard, the ill-starr'd Mayor of Casterbridge, is passionate rather than imaginative or subtle; and it was much more by the force of his character and by the strength of his passionate will that tragedy came upon him than by any neurotic infirmity. Loyalty, fidelity, simplicity, sagacity, disinterestedness, are the marks of a "good" Hardy character; and these would scarcely be the characteristics that would first leap into our minds in thinking of the "good" Dostoievsky characters! It is true that both the Idiot and Alyosha Karamazov are "simple" in a certain sense; but it is an enigmatic simplicity, a mysterious spiritual simplicity; anything but the downright stoical goodness, earthy and unself-conscious, of Giles Winterbourne and Gabriel Oak and The Reddleman.

And it is the same with Hardy's good women. Tess is certainly "a good woman," if ever there was one; and what a comfort to feel how the moral sense of the age has advanced since such a "wounded name" as Tess's needed the bosom of a great and daring genius to house it!

But fidelity, simplicity, loyalty, are Tess's virtues, just as they are Giles's and Gabriel's. Indeed I suspect there are few of our younger generation who as they read her story don't find themselves actually indignant with her for her extravagant docility. "*Too* good!" is what some of these youngsters must feel about her; but no one would call Raskolnikov's sweetheart with her heroic "yellow ticket" *too* good; and it would be hard to apply this word at all to such proud and wayward creatures as Lisa and Nastasia and Aglaia and Grushenka!

Tess is like the patient Griselda of the old story; and she is still more like those unprotesting Margrets and Maisies and Annies of the ballads. In spite of all ill-usage from men, and from a Providence who behaves to her like a man, she still would reply, as Burd Ellen did to the cruel Childe Waters:

> *O I will drink of the wan water,*
> *And eat of the bread of bran*
> *And aye will I bless the happy hour*
> *That ever I loved a man.*

I have an inkling that the author himself set a higher value upon his poetry than upon his prose. I can only say that for myself I would put certain great descriptive pas-

sages—like the one about Egdon Heath at the beginning
of *The Return of the Native*, and the one about Stonehenge
in *Tess* and about Tess's crossing the farm garden in early
dawn, and the one about the approach of the storm in *Far
from the Madding Crowd*—above any verses he wrote; but on
the other hand I feel as if the "Collected Poems" make up
a volume of such absorbing interest and of such uninter-
rupted value that in comparison with it *half the contents* of
the "Complete Works" of Byron or even Shelley are un-
arresting and unrewarding.

And why should this be? Surely because what thrills us
beyond everything else is a story when it is told by a master
story-teller. And who can touch Hardy in dramatic intensity? With the exception of the Elizabethans and the old
anonymous ballads Hardy's poetry is the most intensely
dramatic that we possess. Short poems of dramatic narrative—which are really nothing less than little Odysseys in
realistic miniature—are the hardest of all poetry to write;
and apart from the ballads there are few of such poems
that hold us spellbound till we've finished them. But this
is what Hardy's poems do; and they do it by means of
intensity, of concentration, of a laconic and sardonic power
of biting into the subject till the teeth touch the bone.

Like certain other very great writers, though not like all,
Hardy created a style for himself which is recognizable at
a glance. In this he resembles Dante; and not only in this.
There is indeed a particular kind of intensity that Dante
and Hardy possess in common and that no other writers
possess; and the expression of this, in a certain stripped
abandonment of the syllabic sound to the very body of the
thing described, carries what we call "realism" to a point
beyond which it could not go, to the point in fact where
between the words and the matter of the words there is as
little space as between the flow of drapery in a Pheidian
figure and the form it follows.

Hardy's Promethean championship of thwarted and frustrated mortality against the malefic element in life, whether he chooses to hypostasize this element as Demiurgic Malice, or to let it go as blind and purposeless chance, was met, when it culminated in the premeditated protest of *Jude the Obscure*, by that evil insensitivity, masquerading as cheerful piety and humorous commonsense, which plays the Herod to all such inopportune voices, whether they rise from beyond the Jordan or from beyond the Frome. But the critical reception of one of the bitterest *hit-backs* at providential malignity that this country has produced, only set him the more resolutely upon preparing his brief for the Pot *versus* the Potter in the higher court of poetry.

A poet he always was, first and last; and in poetry he could not only mould his style to his design in a bolder, more drastic, more personal way than in his prose, but he could express the burden of his appeal for a more magnanimous attitude towards the victims of the "Immanent Will" more directly, free from the restraints of the less subjective form of art.

Seeing him at intervals during a period of more than thirty years the mortal lineaments of the man have come to brand themselves on my consciousness as few other human countenances. There was much of the falcon about his aquiline nose and his hovering and "pouncing" eyeglances, an intensity of regard that was accentuated by the slightness of his figure, by the curiously elfin tilt of his eyebrows, and by his trick of holding his head a little on one side, as though the frailty of his form were constantly deprecating the terrible and august passion of his thought.

His apprenticeship to the art of the architect fell upon something eminently congenial in his temper; and it is hard not to link the monumental building-up of his sentences, their words of Saxon origin so deftly balanced against the sonorities and plangencies of a Latinity that showed the influence of Sir Thomas Browne, with the handicrafts that are akin to architecture, the tools of the sculptor in stone, and the carver in wood.

His landscapes are the landscapes rather of a draughtsman than of a colourist; and it might be said that his supreme power as an artist lay in his genius for reproducing in words what you might call the *tactile values* of the things he looked at.

Dorset scenery, and especially the scenery round Dorchester, lends itself to this manner of treatment; for the bare open spaces of that part of Wessex, culminating in the uplands of the chalk downs, have a way of throwing into clear relief every tree and gate, every tumulus and ridge, every quarry and telegraph post, every thorn-bush and haystack, every sea-gull that follows the plough, every raven that flies croaking across the welkin.

Like Wordsworth—and I well recall my pride when this particular point, made in my first encounter with him, was accepted with approval, though it led to a characteristic animadversion upon Wordsworth's obstinate piety—he has an extraordinary power of making you feel the palpable presence of those half-abstract, half-concrete entities; the processes of dawn and twilight for instance, as they move in their mystic visitations over foreground and background, making the familiar unfamiliar, the accustomed phantasmal, and the reassuring ghostly and strange.

Few lovers of Wessex can keep the thought of Hardy, and his far-swooping hawk's eye, out of their minds when they see the shafts of a deserted plough protruding from a bare hill-top, or the outline of a solitary human form silhouetted against a pale sky, or a horse and wagon following the dwindling perspective of some distant white road.

Yes, he saw most things—from a tuft of wind-swept grass to the swinging tail of a stalled ox, from the crumpled wrinkles of a bed-ridden woman's cheek to the crater ridges in the voyaging moon, from the grinning skull of a dead rabbit to the quivering snout of a living hedgehog—under what might be called their *lineal absoluteness*, the imprint that they make ere the universal flux carries them away upon the "camera obscura" of the timeless.

He was one to notice everything that moved over the face of that curved segment of the planetary rondure that we call Dorset. With the eye of a kestrel he noted all that scurried, crawled, waded, swam or flew! He knew how to track the burrowings of the mole, the skulkings of the fox, the noon-sleep of the adder.

I recollect well how on that day—so memorable for me and my brothers—when I decoyed him to Montacute, I saw him stand staring, like one in a trance, at a certain spot in the road, a spot where his eyes had marked down—as if he'd been some wayfaring elf, and no preoccupied biped—the microscopic rufflings upon an infinitesimal puddle that betokened the approach of frost.

He knew every tellurian hieroglyph in the wanton script of the heedless Master of Life, that kept its aeonian secret on our Dorset cliffs; and the majestic cadences of his intense sentences, "tuned to other notes than to the Orphean lyre," seem to throb to far-off cataclysmic upheavals in the scoriac evolution of the globe. He dropped the architecture of bricks and mortar only to build into the "ferro-concrete" of his pages both the hugest megaliths and the tiniest snail-shells of the dark track of the Immanent Will.

It gives me a peculiar satisfaction to think how much he appreciated my architect-brother, the late A. R. Powys, and it pleases me to think that it was from the sale of one of his manuscripts that the ancient shrine was restored which the restorer selected for his own burial.

There is no doubt that there is an element in Hardy's genius, just as there was in the genius of the Elizabethan

Webster, that, like the hands of King Lear, must needs be "wiped" by the overparticular lest they "smell mortality."

He it was, the very first time I saw him—more than forty years ago now—who introduced me to that most startling and characteristic of all Poe's poems, the one called *Ulalume*.

Of late I regret to say there have been attempts in one or other of our modern schools of verse to disparage the genius of Edgar Allan Poe. These posthumous disparagements are inevitable. They have occurred in all ages. And they are, of course, balanced by exaggerated fashions of revival, which are often just as unbalanced.

Take the recent "boom"—if I may use so gross a word— of my own "forefather," as Cowper called him, the fantastical John Donne. Donne was a rare and exceptional genius; but when groups of modern writers are prepared to *put him up* against Milton I feel as if the critics of poetry were madder than the poets themselves.

Or consider the modern "furore" for Dryden. I protest I appreciate as much as any the brave swing of such a sentence as,

> *Old as I am, for ladies' love unfit,*
> *The power of beauty I remember yet,*
> *Which once inflamed my heart, and still inspires my wit,*

but when I think of what a simple-minded lover of *poetry* must feel when he hears of such hectic maladjustments and wilful confusions of values I should be bitter at heart if it weren't that I remember how Shakespeare had *his* hour of such clever seesaw aspersions, and that from this new point of view not only *Lycidas* but *Thyrsis* and *The Scholar-Gypsy* must seem the most frivolous and affected of airy trifles.

Can't they see that a certain rich vein of the romantic-sardonic that Poe—alone among poets, for Baudelaire is "literary" in comparison—quarried with success, has been unearthed again by an equally goblinish and much more realistic mattock in Hardy's poetry?

Might it not be called a subtle and laudable retort to the irony of the Immanent Will to make use of the same kind of sardonic humour, *only on the other side?*

I sometimes find myself wondering whether the architectural element in Hardy's genius didn't lead him in some of his stories to design the plot in too premeditated and too rigid outlines. But he was a great reader of Greek tragedy; and it may well be that it was his long brooding on the sculptured processions of doom followed by the unhappy ones of the houses of Atreus and Oedipus that led him to force the gargoylish inspirations of his Gothic muse into these austere classic moulds.

As with Shakespeare's clowns Hardy's comic supernumeraries, his Christopher Cantles and William Worms, utter their irrelevant commentaries upon the course of events in whimsical contrast to those events' importance.

The part of the Greek chorus—the voices of the "ironies" and the "pities"—is taken by the author himself and is often implicit rather than explicit; and this method gains in grandeur and emphasis by the classical simplicity of the psychological element in the novels.

Much here is deliberately sacrificed to the exigencies of the rigidly planned plot, much to the absorbing interest of the narrative, and the dialogues are frequently marked, I would hesitate to say marred, for it is all part of his rather formal method, by a certain old-fashioned stiffness, too simple to be called stilted, wherein the tragic intensity of the march of fate forbids the fluttering and wayward debouchings of more natural conversation between men and women.

This intentional formality of dialogue wherein the caprices and spontaneous surprises of human intercourse are sacrificed to the pity and terror of the situation is broken

Underwood & Underwood

THOMAS HARDY

as soon as dialect is used. But Hardy employs dialect very sparingly, making much less use of it, for instance, than my brother Theodore does in *his* pictures of the same region.

But it is always in what might be called the *humours of Providence*, especially when these assume a poignant and picturesque outrageousness, as when one pair of rivals for a woman's love gamble by the light of glowworms, or another pair travel to find their girl while her coffin journeys by the same train, or a maiden saves a man's life by making a rope of her underclothes, or Tess is caught by her pursuers asleep upon the altar-stone of Stonehenge, or her seducer paints blood-red "Damnations" upon the bars of gates, or Arabella flings at Jude a gobbet of the raw flesh of the pig she is slaughtering, that the "miching-mallecho" of Hardy's retort reaches its culmination.

Like Shakespeare, and unlike the Greeks, he takes a grim satisfaction in making the supreme crises in his tales turn upon some trifling occurrence that is entirely due to chance.

Tess's letter to Angel Clare, for instance, confessing to him about her seduction, goes by pure accident, when she pushes it under his door, *under the carpet*, so that the man never receives it; while the trifling fact that Yeobright's furze-cutting hook has been propped against the entrance to Eustacia's house is enough to make his mother certain that he is within; enough to drive her forth in desperation to the sun-scorched Heath and the adder's bite.

King Lear was evidently—as well indeed it might be!—Hardy's favourite among Shakespeare's plays. It pleased him to think that his native Egdon was the actual site of those "sulphurous and thought-executing fires, vaunt-couriers to the oak-cleaving thunderbolt" that "singed" that white head; and with one of the grandest and most beautiful plagiarisms in literature—for to plagiarize from the great is always a sign of greatness—he makes Mrs.

Yeobright use words from her wounded heart almost identical with Lear's "mine enemy's dog—"

Sophocles and Shakespeare were Hardy's models, and his deliberate echoes of them are to me only another convincing proof that there is in literature an undying underground stream of tradition as to the kind of subject and even as to the kind of treatment of that subject which strikes deepest into the universal and unchanging such as binds all the really great writers together and leaves outside in each successive generation the clever "originals" of the passing cults.

In the case of *Jude the Obscure*, one of the most poignant tales in English fiction and a tale he wrote in the full plenitude of his mental power, the bulk of the criticism brought against him was of the pious "cheerful" type; but it was also delicately deplored that he must needs put into the mouths of Jude and Sue such a lot of *university-extension chatter*.

This is the old story. It is Ben Jonson's aspersion upon Shakespeare! No doubt the whole of Shakespeare's classical equipment was "university-extension chatter," what he picked up, in other words, from the "university wits" of his time, with perhaps a little help from Montaigne when he, in *his* turn, was engaged in cribbing with disconcerting gravity, from Plutarch's *Lives*.

The truth of the matter is that Hardy had presumed to handle in *Jude the Obscure* subjects for which our conventional and academic exponents have invented a particular tone, a *social* tone, a tone of discreet House-of-Commons badinage, and a tone that is careful to avoid taking too seriously the explosive and troublesome Thomas Hardys of the classical past!

The more I think of it the more significant does it seem that his philosophy of defiance and pity—defiance of the cruelty of the First Cause and pity for the wounded hearts of its creatures—should have won the hearing in his poetry that was refused to *Jude the Obscure*.

What has given the monumental syllables "Thomas Hardy" such a carved and graven niche in the minds of so many is the "mortised and tenon'd" simplicity of what it represents. To have made his own a whole segment of the globe from zenith to nadir has a peculiar congruity with the single chord—deep as life and inevitable as breath— upon which, all through both his prose and his verse, he was for ever harping—I mean the passion of love.

Think of the complications that go to make up the rich interwoven tapestry of any novel of Henry James! Think of the innumerable facets of social and mental life that are crowded into any page of George Meredith! But from first to last with Hardy, save for that terrific "tour de force," *The Dynasts*, it is the heart, with its wounds and its bruises, that fills the entire scene. Swooping down like a hawk upon our human panorama, he sweeps aside all the modern tangle of social and pathological riddles, and concentrates upon the ancient undying tragedy of the love-hate between men and women, as its obsessing drama, criss-crossed by all the malignities of chance, plays itself out between earth and sky.

"How little," said Henry James once to Robert Louis Stevenson, "how little does Hardy know about sex!" And when one considers the bewitched forest into which our younger generation—led by what Rabelais might call the "dark lanterns" of psychoanalysis—have carried their smoky catchwords, and when one considers how the loves of men and women are daily offered up, as so many specimens for dissection, upon the operating-tables of an inhuman and bestializing science, it comes to us as the renaissance of a lost miracle to look into the hearts of Hardy's simple lovers.

In our owlish search through the fascinating morgue of

lust-drowned complexes, in our Iagoish treatment of romantic love as "an itch of the blood and a permission of the will" the more formidable of our writers seem to have left the emotions that absorbed Shakespeare, intrigued Jane Austen, and dominated the Brontës, to the faithful adherents of honeysuckle novelettes.

They say that over the grave of old ironist Anatole France, the new school of authors, like the ghost-demons in a Mexican-Indian orgy, danced for joy. We are more restrained, or less concerned over aesthetic matters; but I dare say many of us in our scientific hearts turn from these love-tragedies of Wessex and their Promethean apologist as only one more old-fashioned *escape* from the pressing problems of the day.

Escape? Escapist? Ah! In the long history of our hunted and enduring human species how much more do we owe to those who have made us forget, than to those—with the noble exception of a few Lord Shaftesburys—who in the process of relieving our troubles have plunged us into worse!

From Homer to Hardy all the great story-tellers of our race are "escapists." Escape we must, or we perish. The opposite road to the road of escape is the road to madness. To follow reason to the limit in *any* direction, whatever your "problems," is insanity. Madmen are people who never can escape. They are compelled *sans cesse* to use their undistracted reason. That is why an absent-minded novel-reading public prefer to have them shut up.

What illogical nonsense this is to blame a great story-teller like Hardy for making his imaginary love-affairs so vivid, so moving, so enthralling, so heart-breaking, that many of us even go so far as to skip some of the finest descriptions of nature ever set down in prose just to see *what happens next* to these Marties and Graces, these Thomasines and Elizabeth-Janes, these Bathshebas and Susans!

For that is the whole point. Hardy's enormous superiority over Meredith, which all people who read for the pleasure of vicarious pity and terror must surely feel, is due to the fact that from Homer down to our own day what thrills the average reader beyond all else, what helps him to escape from himself most completely, is a love-story. To our puritanical "intelligentsia" who call Hardy an "escapist" because his novels are domestic rather than social the best retort is to appeal to Homer. The scene, for instance, between Odysseus and Penelope over their nuptial bed—the bed for whose posts he had used a living tree—is full of the poignant *heightened domesticity* that is at once pure "escapism" and pure "Thomas Hardy."

All life is an escape. All time is an escape. All space is an escape. The great Macrocosm itself, so the astronomers say, is in a process of escaping; and escaping too, as we poor microcosms would be wise to do, eternally from itself.

No, the classic greatness of Hardy's writings is that they are concerned first and last with the human heart. Is it not a singular thing that it should be precisely "the human heart" that we clever writers of to-day with our fantastical inventions, dodge, sheer off from, and avoid like the plague? The heart *hath* its authors, of course, and their readers far outnumber ours; but they are not authors who, like Hardy, write with the eye of a hawk. They are writers who write with the eyes of sparrows.

Hardy is much more of a *stylist* than many great novelists, more than Balzac, for instance, or Scott or Dostoievsky, and one can recognize any sentence of his, at least any descriptive sentence; but his purpose is so obviously to mould and hammer and carve and plane his syllables so as to compel them to follow every convexity and concavity of the object that one never feels conscious of that kind of atmospheric mannerism cultivated by Henry James or of any witchery of premeditated seduction such as one enjoys in Walter Pater.

But a true craftsman he was; and I can remember well when he showed me the manuscript of *Tess*, how surprised and even perhaps a little shocked I was while he spoke of an earlier epoch when he was *"feeling about for a method."* With Keats' words in my head about inspiration coming like growing leaves, or Goethe's about it coming like happy children and crying "here we are!" there was something disturbing in the idea of a great genius searching for a "method."

But, after all, what matters it whether the effects produced by a supreme artist come consciously or unconsciously, deliberately or at random, as long as they come? It remains that in the midst of those who aim at creating a glow of sensuous well-being in their readers and of those who aim at disturbing their readers with frightfulness and disgust, the figure of Thomas Hardy stands out clear and distinct—*monumentum aere perennius*—as one whose purpose was to capture the simple truth; and to present it, whatever the effect on his readers might be, with the patient taciturnity of the monotones of nature as they refuse to change one note of their grey neutrality under the prayers and imprecations of our troubled race.

19

Nietzsche

WHEN you examine closely—I do not mean with any particular pathological clairvoyance, such as he himself possessed, but with ordinary critical commonsense—what might be called the Nietzschean antithesis or spiritual see-saw, it seems to me that it is not so much a case of Dionysus *versus* Christ, as he says at the end of *Ecce Homo*, as a case of Nietzsche *contra* humanity; for both the spiritual dynamite with which he destroyed what he hated and the spiritual energy with which he created what he loved were used with the deliberate intention of substituting something else—a new being—for the creature hitherto known upon this earth as Homo Sapiens.

The human race, its ways, its values, its virtues, its religions, its rationalisms, were all repugnant to Nietzsche. They excited disgust in him. They nauseated him.

At the supreme crisis of his spiritual life in his desire to go to the uttermost tragic limit of that "love of fate" which was his ideal, he conceived as the worst possible of all issues, and therefore as the thing he *wanted* to be true, the doctrine of *eternal recurrence*.

And he tells us how *Zarathustra*, pondering on this truth, was so overpowered by disgust when he thought of an eternal repetition of us "petty souls," that from the pit of his stomach there was torn forth the frantic cry: "Loathing! Loathing! Loathing! Loathing!" and he fell into a swoon that lasted for seven days.

451

Now Nietzsche was not the first to feel this loathing for our "baffled, thwarted, and much-enduring humanity," as Hardy calls it. All the way down the long history of our bewildered race certain lonely "great" ones have felt it, and God alone knows how many lonely "little" ones!

Many before and since Heraclitus, many before and since Swift, have groaned under the weight of this "great despising" but none save Nietzsche has dared to make it the foundation of his message to the world. His whole philosophy is to be found in *Thus Spake Zarathustra*; and as he tells us in *Ecce Homo* he expressed himself here in oracular and dithyrambic poetry, so as to *catch the ear of humanity* and compel it to hear him.

Well! he certainly has compelled humanity to hear him, at least the Western portion of it, as no other destroyer of human values has ever done, and what we have to do with his writings is first to extricate from them as clearly as we can what his actual doctrines are, then to criticize and appreciate these doctrines, and finally to indicate as well as we can—and this is by far the most difficult, as it is by far the most important aspect of our labour—what particular spiritual temper and mood and tone and atmosphere are communicated to us by his books quite apart from their proveable or unproveable "truth."

The personal and psychological basis of Nietzsche's work —what "set him off," so to speak, steering his vessel *north-northeast*, was undoubtedly this neurotic disgust in the presence of average flesh and blood. This loathing for average humanity and for average humanity's moral values will be found to have a very close connection if not an actual identity with the sadistic nerve.

Now I cannot regard this sadistic urge, which I am sure is an element in his whole attitude to the human race, as ever having the remotest connection with his attitude to individuals. The mere fact of his putting into the mouth of the old woman, who gave her advice to *Zarathustra*, those famous words about women and the whip, is for any pathologist who has learnt his art from Dostoievsky sufficient proof that Nietzsche's sadism was no ordinary itch of the blood *but entirely of the spirit*. Sadism as a nervous vice was not a temptation to Nietzsche, *as it undoubtedly was*— although he succeeded in doing what people now-a-days call "sublimate" it—to Dostoievsky.

But "once a sadist always a sadist," and Dostoievsky's sublimation never conceals from a reader, who has learnt psychology at the fountain-source, the fact that this particular nerve-quiver was always, in a personal sense, his grand temptation.

This however is not the case with Nietzsche. Never for one single flickering second do the writings of Nietzsche reveal *anything else* than the translunar vein of purely spiritual sadism, a vein that seems much more like the mood of one of Dante's angels of the revolving spheres than like the mood of Dante himself.

Criticizing Darwin for his idea that the struggle for existence implied the will to live, Nietzsche declares that all living entities, whose perpetual battle with one another is the basic fact of life, want something much more exciting than just merely to remain alive, something much more active than the seeking of nourishment and the propagation of their species. They want, all these living things, to assert themselves, to exhibit themselves, to attack, to dominate! Not the "will to live" but *the will to power* is the moving force of the world.

Being in his inmost nature and through his whole soul a passionate idealist—"Thou too art pious," says the "old Pope" to Zarathustra—it was absolutely essential to his spirit to give life a meaning and a goal. Struggling against illness, struggling against what he calls his own "decadence," he sought through health, through the overbrimming pride and strength and harmony that come with health, and above all through *courage*, to move towards this purpose.

Thus he is the enemy of pessimists, of defeatists, of all who poison the wells of life by their murmurs about the "ultimate futility."

His final argument against the existence of God is really Walt Whitman's. "How can I, in my overbrimming ecstasy of life, feel and act like a god if *God* exists?"

But if the only true road to the purpose of life is the road suggested by the earth herself, and by the healthy ways of living things, and by the natural *will to power* of living things, how can he find—this naturally religious, naturally pious, naturally idealistic soul—a purpose for our earth-life in harmony with strength and health and beauty and courage? How can he find a purpose for life that shall at once satisfy his passion for a spiritual ideal, leave unrebuked his mania for beauty and strength and pride, and give scope to his translunar sadism?

And there is yet another *desideratum* to be won before Nietzsche can feel that he *has the right*, as he would put it, in his haughty chivalrous manner, to satisfy his strange "piety." The natural healthiness of a strong, brave, fighting spirit demands an element of the pure joy of destroying, of *the will to destruction*.

But the ideal of our Western humanity under the influence of Christianity has corrupted this healthy belligerency. A set of unnatural values has appeared, begotten upon the sick, perverse, morbid instinct of the enslaved masses by crafty priests and nature-hating prophets, values that place the human ideal in "another," a "better" world, values that treat as "evil" the three most beautiful things in life—voluptuousness, passion-for-power, and courageous selfishness.

"Good," according to this "slave-morality," is to be loving to one's neighbour *so that he shall love us in return*; to repress sexual voluptuousness so as to poison the natural happiness of the beautiful and the brave; and to despise the body for the sake of the "spirit," so that our weakness and "unselfishness" shall perpetuate humanity *as it is*.

In Homer, Nietzsche would remind us, the word *kakos*, "bad," means the base and cowardly, and the word *agathos*, "good," means the beautiful and the valiant; whereas Christianity, by its implication that sex-pleasure and honest selfishness are wrong, has poisoned the wells of life.

But while engaged upon his task of dynamiting these false values, Nietzsche was slowly building up in his mind an ideal worthy of that saturation with "piety" which the "old Pope" detected in *Zarathustra*.

We have seen how that new "religion" of his implies a wholesome satisfaction for his translunar sadism, by the blowing sky-high with voluptuous sexual excitement of all these morbid asylums for the weak and the cowardly that we call "God," a "Better World," "Immortality," "Purity," "Love," and, above all, "Pity." What we have not yet arrived at in our summary of his doctrines is the Ideal *for the sake of which* this "old artillery-man," as he loves to call himself has *transvalued* all our "human too-human" values.

Voluptuous quiverings of sadistic pleasure accompanied the explosion of each charge of his dynamite, and this he freely confesses, for he is far too honest and too subtle to pretend, as our scientists do with their poison-gases and their vivisection, that his cruelty is "for humanity" or "for the Truth."

To strip "God," "Immortality," and "Free-Will" from the trembling shoulders of cowering idealists gave him what he would describe as an "innocent-wicked" delight. For him, as for Heraclitus, life and war were synonymous terms. "A good war," he says, "justifies *any* cause."

But the spirit of the great Nietzschean "war" looked forward over uncounted generations to a future harder, stranger than itself. Here indeed he found a "cause" more exciting to the nerves of a cosmic sadist than the dynamite-shock of any "transvaluation of values."

For the purpose of life, what we must, according to this man's doctrine, call the ideal of all true "higher men" is nothing less than the substitution of a being *different from man* for the familiar humanity to which we now belong.

Now there is a distinct suggestion of something of this sort in the words of Kirilov to Peter Stepanovitch in Dostoievsky's *Possessed*. But there is no hint that the godlike beings predicted by Kirilov would like Nietzsche's "Overmen" force the masses of humanity to play the part of "helots," that is to say, of protected and well-nourished slaves to their radiant selves.

Under our Nietzschean rulers we should have, it is true, certain important privileges. We should be permitted to retain our "slave-morality" and possibly even to wrap ourselves up in whatever shreds may have been left clinging to the parched bushes when the "Great Noon" was over of such ragged old clouts as "God," "Immortality," and "Free-will."

And let us now examine a little more closely the nature of the beings who will in future rule our earth, exulting in their proud and beautiful life, and for whose sake our "higher men" have to cultivate "hardness" and "innocent wickedness" and loneliness and courage and the dancing feet of those who have conquered remorse.

Well, I do not think we can blame Nietzsche for not defining in very exact terms what these *Overmen* are to be; for since they are to be as different from human beings *as human beings are different from animals* it is clear that even a

"Higher Man" like Zarathustra himself can only visualize them, and their manners and their ways, very dimly.

Their nature is expressed symbolically, however, so that we can in a measure guess roughly at it, in the great yellow lion who appears at the mouth of the cave at the close of *Zarathustra*. The word "Superman" seems to be a somewhat inadequate rendering of this leonine symbol of the Nietzschean Overman, since what it suggests, owing to the infirmity of our language, is nothing better than the excess of such qualities as Herculean muscles, satanic wisdom, and godlike beauty, all of which, if not normal human characteristics, are certainly normal story-book characteristics; and represent what the more childlike and unphilosophic among us have from paleolithic days regarded with excitement and awe.

There must be indeed, I think, to the mind of any of the *old* races of the world, like the Chinese, or the Egyptian, or the Welsh, or the Basque, or the Jewish, or the Arabian, something singularly childlike and fairy-story-like about Nietzsche's *Beyond-Man*; and I have a suspicion that *all women of every race*, would prefer to continue being the companions of the gullible and easy-going humanity dispossessed by these austere warriors.

But the great yellow lion at the end of *Thus Spake Zarathustra* is perhaps rather a sign that the "Overmen" are at hand than a complete symbol of their nature. Seduced by the old "Soothsayer," who may be regarded as an incarnation of Schopenhauer, Zarathustra, contrary to the "hardness" he has assumed for the sake of the future, that is to say for the sake of his "children," the "Overmen," has followed a pitiful "Cry of Distress" and has collected in his cave all the "Higher Men" of existing humanity. Here is the "Magician," representing art in the person of Wagner. Here is the "last Pope," representing the best in the old religion. Here is "the Conscientious One of the Spirit," representing science; and here, along with the "Ugliest Man," the atheistic God-Murderer, is the "Voluntary Beggar" who may be regarded as a symbol of the Buddha.

All these various "Higher Men" in Zarathustra's absence have been seduced into worshipping an ass; but the Master has been playfully indulgent to this lapse from the austerity of his teaching, treating it as a humorous sign of convalescence.

> "Forget not this night and this ass-festival, ye higher men! . . . And should ye celebrate it again, this ass-festival, do it from love to yourselves, do it also from love to me! And in remembrance of *me*!"
> Thus spake Zarathustra.

But before *the Great Noon* in the revolving of the eternal circle of all things, when the clock of the cosmos strikes twelve, Zarathustra teaches these poor ass-worshippers his mystic song, "the name of which is 'Once more,' and the significance of which is 'Unto all eternity!' "

> *O man! Take heed!*
> *What saith deep midnight's voice indeed?*
> *I slept my sleep—*
> *From deepest dream I've woke, and plead;*
> *The world is deep,*
> *And deeper than the day could read.*
> *Deep is its woe—*
> *Joy—deeper still than grief can be:*
> *Woe saith; Hence! Go!*
> *But joys all want eternity—*
> *—Want deep, profound eternity!*

And the reader of *Thus Spake Zarathustra*, waiting with his spirit strung like a bow for the loosening of the arrow, will perhaps recall at this crucial moment that other strange Litany of the Absolute at the end of the third part, whereof the rhythmic refrain repeats itself thus:

Oh, how could I not be ardent for Eternity, and for the marriage-ring of rings—the ring of the return?

Never yet have I found the woman by whom I should like to have children, unless it be this woman whom I love: for I love thee, O Eternity!

For I love thee, O Eternity!

But at this moment, as he sits on a big stone at the exit from his cave, along with his "pet animals," the eagle and the serpent, drawing the fresh, deep, lonely air into his soul, he is aware of the sign.

"What happeneth unto me," thought Zarathustra in his astonished heart . . . and while he grasped about with his hands . . . behold there then happened to him something still stranger; for he grasped thereby unawares into a mass of thick, warm, shaggy hair; at the same time, however, there sounded before him a roar,—a long soft lion-roar.

"The sign cometh," said Zarathustra and a change came over his heart.

By degrees, as he caressed the Lion and allowed a crowd of doves that had come with this beast to perch on his shoulders and on his white hair, he realized that the hour of his "Overmen" had come, *that future* for the sake of which he had rejected pity and had transvalued all values.

When all this went on Zarathustra spake only a word: "My children are nigh, my children—"

But at this moment the assembly of "Higher Men" came out of the cave; and the Lion, leaving Zarathustra, sprang towards them roaring so that they cried all aloud as with one voice and fled back and vanished in an instant.

This was the second time that he had heard the "cry of distress" from the "Higher Men"; but this time, for the sake of the *Great Noon* that was approaching, for the sake of "his children," for the sake of *Those* who were to be as different from Man as Man was from the Beasts, he hardened his heart.

Suddenly he sprang up—"*Fellow-suffering!* Fellow-suffering

with the higher men!" he cried out, and his countenance changed into brass. "Well! *that*—hath had its time!

"My suffering and my fellow-suffering—what matter about them! Do I then strive after *happiness*? I strive after my *work*!

"Well! The lion hath come, my children are nigh, Zarathustra hath grown ripe, mine hour hath come:—

"This is *my* morning, *my* day beginneth: *arise now, arise, thou great noontide!*—"

Thus spake Zarathustra and left his cave, glowing and strong, like a morning sun coming out of gloomy mountains.

An alert reader will have noted in the Clock-striking Song, Zarathustra's "roundelay," the reference to joy and grief, and how grief cried out for the end of all, but how joy "wanted eternity"; and how joy was "deeper than grief."

And it is impossible not to ask oneself the question: what was the main urge—for we have learnt from St. Paul and from Dostoievsky that in psychology and not in metaphysic lies the secret of life—that drove Nietzsche to round off his revelation with the doctrine of *eternal recurrence*.

Consider for a while, reader, this sublime and appalling fancy; for one can hardly regard it as either a metaphysical or a scientific "truth." Well, according to this wild doctrine, every single event, person, character, scene, every single moment of what, as it streams past us we call the Present, is eternally recurring in a vast, never-ceasing infinite circle! Does it seem to you that this idea came to Nietzsche as a scientific conclusion drawn from the scientific assurance that while *energy* was limited and for ever taking new forms, time was unlimited; and that therefore in the circle of infinite time and after infinite other forms have appeared, *the same forms* are bound to come round again, and to come round not only once again or even a million times again, *but eternally again*?

Or does it seem to you that it was from pondering on the

Brown Bros.

FRIEDRICH WILHELM NIETZSCHE

mystery of pleasure and pain in their psychological essence, that he was driven to this thought?

Or finally—and this is my own explanation—does it seem to you that the same vein of what might be called *cosmic sadism* in him that drove him to the idea of sacrificing Man to "Overman," drove him also upon this horrible closed circle?

Surely it is not impossible to imagine the very stages— *psychological* in the most appalling sense!—by which he arrived at this frightful conclusion.

Let us attempt to reconstruct them.

In the first place, we must remember that for seven years he taught Greek and studied classical culture in that school at Basle. It was during this epoch that he used his *psychological imagination*, that mental weapon in the use of which no great genius except Dostoievsky has ever equalled him, upon two things—the philosophy of music and the secret of Greek tragedy. His professional subject as a German scholar was *philology* but there seems little doubt that he might in addition to this have become a formidable composer. Thus at the back of all his work—and one sees how, in this way, he became the greatest prose-stylist in the German language—lay the science of words and mystery of rhythm.

In those seven years of scholastic work at Basle he fathomed Greek tragedy to its depths; and it was here he not only conceived his illuminating aesthetic antithesis, "Apollonian art" *versus* "Dionysian art" but found in the birth of tragedy out of music the clue to the yet greater antithesis, Dionysus *versus* Christ—that resounding chord upon which he was playing in his favourite Italian city when his brain but not his spirit broke.

The philosophy of Schopenhauer and the music of Wagner were together—the "Soothsayer" and the "Magician" —the *point d'appui* from which he leapt into the arena; but it was from the Greek conception of tragedy, which implied to his mind an exuberance and overbrimmingness of life, and *not* any essential despair, that he derived what might be called the *aesthetic formula* for his optimism in the midst of torture.

Thus we reach what might be called the "jumping-off-point" for the Nietzschean doctrines, a reaction against three things—against Wagner, against Schopenhauer, and against what he calls the corrupting "Nihilism" of socialists, anarchists, philanthropists, and Christians.

But the tidal wave of his "yea-saying" to both the pain and the pleasure of life mounts steadily higher and higher, till its terrible exultation, after one final fanfare of sea-trumpets in *Ecce Homo*, breaks its sea-wall and floods everything!

But meanwhile his conception of the *eternal recurrence* shows itself in its true light as the only logical terminus to which this optimism-under-torture could drive him. He had taken the phrase *amor fati* as his motto, and he now forced himself to exult in fate, to *love it backwards and forwards*, so that to everything that has ever happened and to everything that ever *will* happen, including the most horrible frightfulnesses, he sets his ecstatic seal.

And thus finally he was driven by the urge of his trans-lunar sadism to take the one last step; namely, to make this rapturous love of everything that has ever happened or *will* ever happen, good and evil alike, pain and pleasure alike, into an eternal and for ever-recurrent circle!

What he calls "the Great Noontide," therefore, is the dramatic point on the curve of this circle when *Man*, that living bridge between beast and *Overman*, that weak, cowardly, neighbour-fearing, neighbour-envying, neighbour-loving creature who *must be surpassed*, evolves into "Overman"! He does not tell us what ultimate fatality it is that befalls *Overman*; but this very likely may be the destruction of his planet or of his whole solar system.

At any rate, it is something that means that the portentous process of evolution has to begin all over again. It is when Zarathustra realizes what to him would be *the worst thing that could happen*, namely that man *as he is now*, with all his cowardice and "lovingness" and faith in a "better world" should *return again exactly as he is*, and that the actual moment through which we are now passing, down to its most infinitesimal detail and gesture, should return exactly as it is, and has indeed so returned an infinite number of times, that he decides that this *must* be how things are.

The doctrine of *the eternal recurrence* was in fact to Nietzsche the most frightful test to which it was possible to put his *amor fati*. If his *amor fati* could swallow *this*—loathing! loathing! loathing!—and still cry its "yes" to life, why then it was indeed the great "noontide philosophy" of the eternal circle!

And thus we arrive at the real reason for Nietzsche's announcement of the *eternal recurrence*. Being by nature full of pity, being by nature akin to a medieval saint, the worst possible world would be a world in which all the unspeakable frightfulnesses of life repeated themselves *sans cesse*. *Therefore this was the truth*.

Covering, as it were, these bare nerves of the Nietzschean system with a little real flesh, we must note that the man's cosmic sadism began with himself. It was autosadism here, and yet always connected with the entire system-of-things. Beginning with the long illness from the conquest of which all his "hardness," all his "flair" for decadent spiritual smells, all his "healthiness," all his "dancing" thoughts, arose, what we contemplate in Nietzsche's life is the metamorphosis, through autovivisection, of a natural saint into a *tour-de-force* Dionysus.

How different this cruel process was, in its furious

Euclidian artificiality, from the really healthy, really normal, really human *theatricality* of his friend-enemy Wagner!
There is no one in the remotest degree like Nietzsche, as far
as I know, in the whole history of literature.

It is ironic that he, the great champion of the body
against the soul, and of life against "beyond-life," should
have been the most purely *spiritual* of all great writers.
Shelley perhaps was more ethereal, and Shelley's *nerves* were
less involved in his work, but how vague and wordy is
Shelley's eloquence compared with the forked lightning and
crashing thunderbolts of Nietzsche!

When one thinks of the part played by the bodily constitution and the bodily senses in the work of most talented
men, it seems as if the genius of Nietzsche was made of pure
intellect, pure nerves, and pure spirit. As he says himself
in *Ecce Homo*, he is completely impersonal in his attacks;
and yet we follow his sword-thrusts with a delicious, dizzy
sense of becoming the very blade and point as they strike
home! He denounces alcohol and was a hermit in his
tastes but his work goes to the head like vodka or potheen.
Is it the absence from his style of everything belonging to
the body *except the nerves* that makes his thoughts affect us
as if they were the burning tunes for which armies have
perished and cities been sacked?

Benjamin de Casseres, who, like the impassioned "Strayed
Reveller" in Matthew Arnold's poem, has picked up the
thyrsus dropped by some "bright procession of eddying
forms" in this "Dance of Siva," is profoundly right in calling to our notice the *musical* element in Nietzsche's hypnotic
thought.

No wonder the serpent and the eagle and the lion and
the doves all clung to Zarathustra! 'Tis as though Lucifer
himself has turned snake-charmer; and we can imagine the
glittering scales of the great Norse world-snake rising gleam-

ing and coiling to the surface under his spell—"superficial out of profundity"!

Come let us imitate "Heedless Blurter" in the wayward philosophy of Kwang-Tse, and whisper the truth.

It is *not* essential that we should accept his frightful dogma of the *eternal recurrence*. It is not essential that we should harden our hearts against pity for the poor "Higher Men," or against pity for ourselves in the process of being "surpassed."

It is not essential that we should accept the "pathos of distance," that pretty euphemism for the selfishness of man to man, or that we should treat ourselves to the "golden-brown drops of perfect happiness" squeezed from the ripe round fruit of the eternal circle, while the "petty souls" of the commonalty drug themselves with neighbour-love.

It is not essential that we should accept a single one of all the Nietzschean *doctrines*. What *is* essential, if we are not, in the fatal consistency of our prejudice, to stop our ears to the most prophetic voice since Blake, is that we should apply to the spiritual drama of our own life the searching psychology Nietzsche applied to his, and let the arctic wind of his relentless purification blow free upon us.

For, like the old Greek philosophers, Nietzsche has a way of making us feel our own personal mental drama as no modern thinker can make us feel it. If we were a *pariah*, or a *chandala*, or the most shame-faced "untouchable,". who can only read his own "surpassing" as the "Great Noon" draws nearer, we still could derive from this arrowy eloquence that heightening of the pulse which even the cruellest logic gives when its deadly edge flashes with gleaming rainbows.

Even if we were stirred to that malicious "resentment," which Nietzsche detects in the virtue of the weak, it would be a different emotion from the feeling that all was vanity and futility. At least the sun-sparkles would gleam for us on the sea-horses of chance, and upon the blind forehead of the "Moby Dick" of our fate the moonbeams would glitter, and galley-slaves to the future though we were, we should gain a fierce purchase for the pull of our oars and catch a suicidal beauty in the lift of our keel.

The glory of reading Nietzsche is that it *forces the issue*, that terrible issue between the "haves" and the "have-nots" which *ought* to be forced.

For myself I have learnt from St. Paul and Dostoievsky a certain curious delight in yielding to the strong and the well-constituted, which I sometimes fancy goes deeper than the "resentment" unearthed by Nietzsche. Indeed it goes so deep—or I think it goes so deep—that sometimes it seems to me "stronger," if I may say so, than the triumph to which it yields! These are deep secrets; but I would like to suggest just here that there *may* be in that "low" life-love, whose method the proud and aristocratic would describe as, "Kick me, but let me live!"—a mood that descends as far down into the life-force as any heroic and honourable belligerency.

But one thing is certain. What we get from Nietzsche's book is the greatest of all gifts that any writer can give us— namely a heightening of our dramatic *interest* in life.

As I have hinted before, when people say, "I couldn't stand it if it weren't for my sense of humour," they don't mean that their troubles seem comic to them, or that dull and annoying and stupid people make them hilarious.

They mean that life *as* life, on the most annoying and dis- tressing terms, is *an exciting drama*. They mean: "I couldn't stand it if it weren't such an interesting show and if the *dénouement* weren't so uncertain!"

But wherein lies this redeeming interest? Surely it lies in two things: in the excitement of our contact with alien selves; subhuman selves if we are hermits, the Cosmic Self if we are religious, and all other human beings if we are normal.

And it lies in our complete ignorance of the future. Now Nietzsche shows us how we can so pierce down into the depths of human psychology and so grasp the dramatic issues of human life that everything dull and monotonous and commonplace, everything "taken for granted" simply ceases to exist. Whether death ends us or not, whether we are moralists or immoralists, whether space is infinite or not, whether God is dead or not, in the mere fact that we are now alive and must shortly die, in the mere fact that we are wickedly dominating others or voluptuously yielding to others, in the mere fact that we are eternally ignorant about *tomorrow*, whether it will bring unthinkable frightfulness or unthinkable delight, in the mere fact that good and evil can be reversed if we set ourselves *to will their reversion*, in other words in the mere fact that we can be hard or soft to life itself just as if life were a woman, *there* lies sufficient cause to cry, "Yes!" instead of "No!" to existence!

And bodiless though Nietzsche's thoughts are, and fantastical though his conclusions may be, there is that in his tone, in his mood, in his spirit, which, just because it is so bodiless, just because it quivers with such a white heat of psychological inspiration, seems much nearer to the heart of our ego, even if we are *not* "higher men," than all the cumbrous paraphernalia of the best metaphysical system.

A first encounter with Nietzsche must be always an event in a person's life, the sort of event wherein you recall the place and the occasion. But the curious thing is that the same stir of excitement is repeated after a lapse of years.

For myself though I *can* recall where I first struggled with Hegel and the occasion when I first held in my hands Haldane's translation of Schopenhauer's *The World As Will and Idea*, I have never opened those volumes again, and never shall!

But I cannot see a volume of Nietzsche in any shelf without opening it, and it is like the Tree of Knowledge of Good and Evil; you cannot open it without feeling, just as you did at first, the old fatal intoxication.

This is because Nietzsche, though a philosopher, resembles those prophetic soothsayers of the ancient world who use a language that is sometimes dramatic and poetic and sometimes gnomic and oracular. He draws his bow with his brain, but the arrows of his thought are feathered with his imagination, spliced with his nerves, dipped in his blood.

And how meet, right, and salutary it is that the foundation-values of our "good" and our "evil" *should* be challenged! Things as important as our basic notion of right and wrong *ought* to be challenged. That is what philosophers, what prophets, what poets *are for*.

Let the constituted authorities, the vested interests, the indignant tyrants of Church and State, bar and ban and confiscate and burn; let the self-preservative instincts of the masses disparage and deride: the lonely soul of man will always turn to spiritual explosives and mental gunpowder, to the dynamite of Lucifer and to the deadly flame, driving the holy hyaenas away, that Prometheus carried in his fennel-stalk!

This artillery-fire from the batteries of "Anti-God" and "Anti-Man" is precisely what our deepest human values *need* to drive them to salutary desperation!

This is the sort of onslaught that keeps our "kindness," and our "pity," and our "patience," sound and formidable and sweet. Rotten and smelling of corruption grows our Christian virtue when it grows *safe*; when, like a golden cross on a "capon-lined" belly, it no longer tosses in the wind, tattered and bloody, against the fury of the heathen.

Our Christian virtue, as Blake taught, must bear up under devilish persecution or it ceases to be itself. "In the world ye shall have tribulation. But be of good comfort. *I* have overcome the world!"

And what a mischievous Satanic humour there is in the fact that still to-day, just as it was in Dostoievsky's tale of the Grand Inquisitor, this crafty world continues outwitting its divine Enemy by melodiously intoning every morning and every evening in its sly episcopal throat, "Lo! I *am* overcome!"

No, no! The persecution of Christians is the best thing that can happen to Christianity. If it survives, it means that that shrewd "Higher Man," the Grand Inquisitor, has not yet been able to "square" his troublesome Prisoner.

Nietzsche informs us most significantly in *Ecce Homo* that he always got on very happily with real Christians; and one can understand this well, for his secret soul was riddled with religion. He speaks quite frankly of his admiration for Pascal, calling him a kindred spirit; and *so he was*, a Nietzschean self-sadist the other way round, with his sprinklings of holy water and his deliberate *bêtise*! *Ecce Homo*, even more than *Zarathustra*, is the book to read to understand Nietzsche; for his brain when he wrote it was exactly like what Dostoievsky describes in the case of Prince Mishkin before one of his fits.

It was abnormally clairvoyant, abnormally lucid, and with all its mental powers at their best. It is in *Ecce Homo* that he declares that he only attacks strong opponents and opponents worthy of his most tempered steel. Such a strong opponent is, he feels—but in reality it is perhaps rather *big* than strong—this Minotaur-monster, born of the incestuous marriage of Christ and the Pharisees, that we call *official* Christianity; and certainly, as far as most book-lovers are concerned, the fiercer he can make the fight with this worldly beast the better for all our souls!

But it is quite right also that those *really* powerful things, those "invisible" things as St. Paul would say, those things that are the opposite of "big and strong," those things which the churches theoretically exploit and practically oppose, should be subjected to the Nietzschean cannon-shot.

It is perfectly right that our most sanctified and most malicious humility, our profoundest Pauline *agapé*, yes! and such kindred human aberrations as Shakespearean indulgence, Socratic irony, Rabelaisian evangelicalism, and Dostoievsky white magic, should be dragged into concentration camps and driven into the firing-line. If the blows and the bullets kill them; if Christ finds he *can't* forgive, Shakespeare he *can't* be indulgent, Socrates that his irony loses its bite, Rabelais that the heart is taken out of his cosmic aplomb, well then, so much the worse for them! But if they survive and "overcome the world" so much the better for us all, and the worse for Nietzsche's diagnosis!

Nietzsche would say, if he were alive to-day, that the persecution of Jews is not only a sign of our own weakness but a sign of our helpless anger in the presence of something too subtle for us.

But I think that Nietzsche, with the help of Dostoievsky, made one of the profoundest psychological discoveries ever made when he declared that there is a cunning layer of malicious poison in almost all forgiveness. And how grandly he defends "hitting back," on the ground of our delicacy of feeling towards our opponent, and our desire to spare him from being "abashed"!

When, however, ye have an enemy, then return him not good for evil: for that would abash him. But prove that he has done something good to you. And rather be angry than abash anyone! And, when ye are cursed, it pleaseth me not that ye should then desire to bless. Rather curse a little also! And should a great injustice befall you, then do quickly five small ones besides. Hideous to behold is he on whom injustice presseth alone.

Did ye ever know this? Shared injustice is half justice. And he who can bear it, shall take the injustice upon himself!

A small revenge is humaner than no revenge at all. And if the punishment be not also a right and an honour to the transgressor I do not like your punishing. Nobler is it to own oneself in the wrong than to establish one's right, especially if one be in the right. Only one must be rich enough to do so.

I do not like your cold justice; out of the eye of your judges there always glanceth the executioner and his cold steel.

It seems that Nietzsche did not always conceal his indignation when mean and unpleasant people excused their brutalities on the ground that when pursuing without shame or remorse their own satisfaction they were good Nietzscheans.

And yet this attitude in such people was natural enough, considering the mischievous delight Nietzsche took in making god-fearing men open their eyes by his praise of a daredevil like Cesare Borgia as a commendable link in the bridge from animal to Overman!

The mistake our modern Borgias make lies in thinking they are *wicked*, when all they are is childishly greedy. Any well-trained priest would know more about the silly conceit of these baby Satans, whose "sin," as Father Zosima would tell them, is not really, as they would have us think, "voluptuousness" or "passion for power," but simply an incurable self-deception, an everlasting tendency *to act lies*!

After all, when one thinks of the protected life Nietzsche lived, though he *was* so ill and so neglected, compared with the wild chaotic extremities of terror and pity that made up the existence of Dostoievsky, it is clear he never had the opportunity to drop his plummet into the deeper seas of evil. And yet who can say? Had he *had* the experiences of Dostoievsky it would probably have been just the same.

For let me whisper the truth. The mere fact that he selected a murdering, intriguing, light-weight rogue like the young Borgia as his symbol of "evil," whether we admire his choice or the reverse, is proof that, compared with the evil hinted at by Dostoievsky and incarnated in a character like Stavrogin, Nietzsche had a most simple conception as to what wickedness was. His innocent-wicked "evil" is simply insensitive and bloody rascality.

Even Goethe's Mephistopheles could have given Zarathustra enlightenment in the metaphysics of such matters; and so, too, could Shakespeare's Iago.

However! Nietzsche would no doubt maintain that when to our Christian mood, or to our Diogenes-in-his-tub mood, the power-lust of even such great men as Alexander and Caesar and Napoleon appears childish, it is because an element of human envy and secret malice enters into our spiritual superiority.

I find myself wishing that that classic heathen, Walter Savage Landor, were alive to-day, so that we could persuade him to compose an "Imaginary Conversation" between Marcel Proust and James Joyce on the subject of Nietzsche. I confess it seems to me that the history of Joyce's greatness among the intellectuals of to-day and the history of his influence upon the literature of to-day beautifully illustrate the Nietzschean conception of the "Higher Men" among us, who are to evoke with so much labour and pain the electric clouds out of which the Overman will finally burst, and burst with anything but a "still small voice."

Does it not seem as though the power of Joyce's brain, his astounding erudition, his contempt for all the old-fashioned literary values upon which we've been brought up, the sense we have, when attempting to read him, of something absolutely new in the sphere of lexicons, grammars, syntaxes, dictionaries, prosodies, rhythms—though one catches faintly now and again stray lilts from Rabelais and Shakespeare—together with something absolutely new in the sphere of realistic "streams of consciousness," have exactly that effect upon us of troubled and puzzled awe that one would expect when in some weird leap forward of evolution our old human ideas of what is excellent in literature are in the process of being "surpassed."

For what would we expect from a new Nietzschean "Higher Man," following Zarathustra's "Ugliest Man" of "the Great Despising," and his "Soothsayer" and his "Magician" and his "Conscientious One of the Spirit"?

Would we not expect him to be like a Gulliver among Lilliputians? Would we not expect him to parody our pathetic human ideals, sentiments, illusions, idioms, accents, gestures, moralities, immoralities, our monkey-ways and our monkish ways? Would we not expect him to be only interested in us as subjects for artistic experiments, experiments that will be as much beyond our comprehension as this new type of brain exceeds our brain?

The difficulty that we, "the Many, too Many," experience in reading Joyce, does indeed become, when linked up with Nietzsche's prophesyings, a most fascinating problem.

One begins to ask: "How far were Homer and Rabelais and *Don Quixote* and Shakespeare and even the anonymous ballads and the Gothic cathedrals and the Old Masters in painting, appreciated by the commonalty in *their* time? Is this great gulf that has begun to yawn between the "intelligentsia" and the people a completely new phenomenon, or has it, in reality, always existed?

In the medieval Scholastic days, by reason of the scarcity of books and the absence of the art of printing, *learning* anyway was confined to the few. Was this case also with regard to the appreciation of poetry and music?

This is a question to be asked. And another follows from it. Are we to rejoice, in a proud, lonely, Nietzschean spirit, at the very difficulty that most of us feel as we confront this Irish titan, whose astounding philological experiments, whose amazing mythological learning, whose seductive syllabic rhythms, whose sardonic realism, are used to parody with remorseless ease all our old human ideals and sentiments? Or are we to wait in sulky expectation some inspired popular voice, some *new* Shakespeare, some *new* Dickens?

All that an open-minded Lollard of literature can do, it seems to me—in the absence of a Landorian "Conversation" between Marcel Proust and James Joyce—is to apply to *literary* values what we have learnt from Nietzsche to apply to moral values and then decide, according as *our attitude may be* to this great "despising" and "surpassing," whether the old "simplicity," and the old "being-understood by the masses" which we have been brought up to assume was the lot of books like Homer and Shakespeare and the Bible and *Pilgrim's Progress* and *Don Quixote* and Rabelais and Dickens and St. Paul and Dostoievsky, is or is not destined to yield to a completely different standard of excellence, and excellence whose virtue is not, as hitherto, an inspired and imaginative criticism of life for the Many, but an inspired and imaginative criticism of life for the Few, leading up perhaps to a yet further narrowing down, when the great men of letters write only for the *Very* Few; until at last—

But I am beginning to assume the rôle of "the Ugliest Man" in *Thus Spake Zarathustra*, who permitted himself to speak as follows of the simple admirers of the spirit of Jesus and Don Quixote and Dickens as he strained forward in his self-despising towards Man's surpassing:

"Beyond all these do I look, as a dog looketh over the backs of thronging flocks of sheep. They are petty, good-wooled, good-willed, grey people.

"As the heron looketh contemptuously at shallow pools, with backward-bent head, so do I look at the throng of grey little waves and Wills and souls.

"Too long have we acknowledged them to be right, those petty people: *so* we have at last given them power as well;—and now do they teach that good is only what petty people call good.

"And 'truth' is at present what the preacher spake, who himself sprang from them, that singular saint and advocate of the petty people, who testified of himself: 'I—am the truth.'

"That immodest one hath long made the petty people greatly puffed up,—he who taught no small error when he taught: 'I—am the truth.' "

But we have followed this line of thought far enough if we have succeeded in suggesting that the creation, by the efforts of lonely "Higher Men," of the same sort of trans-valuation of values *in literature and art* as Nietzsche struggled to suggest in *morals* is a natural implication of this evolutionary leap forward towards the "Great Noontide." Some readers of Nietzsche will naturally be tempted to go further afield still and to drag his formidable name into our present-day racial and ideological contentions; but it is very hard to hazard a guess upon what side he would range himself were he alive to-day.

He certainly would be opposed to the mass-spirit and the nationalistic spirit of the totalitarian states. But on the other hand, I cannot see him as very sympathetic to our capitalistic, parliamentary democracies. I have a faint inkling that something about our English aristocracy would appeal to him; but at the same time I cannot see him "taking refuge" in England! Were one to select for him a spot upon the surface of the earth from which he could survey the "good wars that justify any cause" one would, I think, hesitate between Switzerland and Tibet; for the truth is—and we may as well out with it—that this great champion of "frightfulness" and "hardness" and swords and guns not only "fought shy," as we say, of those "dangerous play-things" with small waists and soft bosoms that are the perplexity of "Higher Men," but had in his own life little experience, till his brain broke down, of what human beings *can* suffer—things a good deal worse than the physical weakness and the mental neglect which he shared with so many.

But the Nietzschean battle-field is, after all, the *mind of man*; and heaven knows there is enough "war" and "frightfulness" *there* to try the spirit of the most heroic. And one feels that there must have been many mothers of our much-enduring race tempted to retort, in the words of Euripides' Medea, that the travail of child-birth is as much a test of courage as swords and bullets.

All the same, I am ready to confess it does rouse my anger to hear some clever smug rogue who knows nothing of what our old Puritans used to call "wrestling with the Lord" make vulgar sport of Nietzsche's desperate spiritual paradoxes. At the worst they are *splendid lies*; and a person who isn't stirred to the depths by their heroic challenge is a "petty soul" in a more serious than a Nietzschean sense! How fundamental are the problems into which he flashes his dagger! Is that queer urge, for instance, to repress sex-pleasure, which goes back to immemorial antiquity, to be regarded as an evolutionary instinct in Nature herself, or to be held as a perversion of Nature, arbitrarily thrust upon us by the will to power of sick souls?

And suppose, reader, that you were a Catalan anarchist fighting inch by inch for the ideal of personal liberty against politicians, generals, bishops, landowners, capitalists, and dictators, couldn't you snatch a fine weapon from Zarathustra's sayings and turn it against himself, declaring that you also had an iron determination to *create the future*, and to create it on behalf of *humanity*?

Yes, I am sure the thing to do is to accept Nietzsche as we accept the Aurora Borealis; not to try to light the coals on our hearth by it, but coals in our heart! I cannot for a moment believe that there is any justification, either from the science of his day or of ours for the notion that the spatial-temporal, psycho-physical content of our astronomical world recurs eternally in vast periodic cycles; nor can I believe that Nietzsche or any other scientific prophet has the right to assume that the mystery of life, which Zarathustra himself declares to be so *deep*, excludes the possibility of dimensions of existence totally outside the astronomical universe.

Nothing is more interesting to me than to study the death-masks of Dostoievsky and Nietzsche. And what a much more formidable, what a much more *deep* countenance the former has than the latter!

Dostoievsky's face has the raw, rugged, scoriac look of a volcanic crevasse, out of which at any moment a fire might break forth—black or white—from the *other side* of "the thick rotundity of the world"; and compared with *this* look the sword-dance duellist-stare of the proud Transvaluer shows brittle in its tense beauty.

In his extraordinary book *Ecce Homo* Nietzsche sets himself actually to describe the *phenomena of inspiration*; and none has done it so well:

> If one had the smallest vestige of superstition left in one, it would be hardly possible to set aside the idea that one is the mere incarnation, mouth-piece, or medium of an almighty power. . . . One hears—one does not seek; one takes—one does not ask who gives; a thought suddenly flashes up like lightning, it comes with necessity, without faltering—I have never had any choice in the matter. . . . Everything happens quite involuntarily, as if in a tempestuous outburst of freedom, of absoluteness, of power and divinity. The involuntary nature of the figures and similes is the most remarkable thing; one loses all perception of what is imaginary and metaphor—

These proud words are I confess a great comfort to me

when I find it hard to bear the thought of the death-in-life that, even while he wrote them, hung over his head. If any great writer got ecstatic happiness from the process of writing, that writer was Nietzsche.

The translation of *Zarathustra* that I am now using is Thomas Common's, with notes by Anthony M. Ludovici, and it must be remarked how easily and naturally Nietzsche's German passes into our own Biblical tongue. Lines like these, for instance, hardly seem a translation at all:

> False shores and false securities did the good teach you. In the lies of the good were ye born and bred. Everything hath been radically contorted and distorted by the good. . . .
>
> Keep yourselves up betimes, my brethren, learn to keep yourselves up! The sea stormeth: all is in the sea. Well! Cheer up! Ye old seamen-hearts!
>
> What of fatherland! *Thither* striveth our helm where our *children's land* is! Thitherwards, stormier than the sea, stormeth our great longing!—

But it is as the poet of a rapturous happiness in the midst of suffering that Nietzsche is at his greatest, and let us boldly say of this "happiness of Zarathustra" that it does not matter what strange theories of the logical brain lie behind it, because *in itself*, apart from our treacherous reason, it holds the mystery of life!

We all of us have these moments of strange causeless happiness, when the atrocities of existence are forgotten. I do not say they are solved or absorbed; for even while we are happy something in us, aware of the individual nature of our luck, is ashamed of being "squared" while others perish in torment. But at least we have touched the fringe of a feeling of universal redemption; and here again, as Goethe says, "Feeling is all in all," and the reasons we give for the feeling, all these logical "surpassings" and "recurrences," are of little moment.

Hush! Hush! Hath not the world now become perfect? What hath happened unto me?

As a delicate wind danceth invisibly upon parqueted seas, light, feather-light, so—danceth sleep upon me.

No eye doth it close to me, it leaveth my soul awake. Light is it, verily, feather-light. . . .

How long and weary it becometh my strange soul! Hath a seventh-day evening come to it precisely at noon-tide? Hath it already wandered too long, blissfully, among good and ripe things? . . .

O happiness! O happiness! Wilt thou perhaps sing, O my soul? Thou liest in the grass. But this is the secret, solemn hour, when no shepherd playeth his pipe.

Take care! Hot noon-tide sleepeth on the fields.

Do not sing! Hush! The world is perfect. Do not sing, thou prairie-bird, my soul! Do not even whisper! No—hush! The old noon-tide sleepeth, it moveth its mouth: doth it not just now drink a drop of happiness—

An old brown drop of golden happiness, golden wine? Something whisketh over it, its happiness laugheth. Thus—laugheth a God. Hush!—

The least thing precisely the gentlest thing, the lightest thing, a lizard's rustling, a breath, a whisk, an eye-glance—*little* maketh up the *best* happiness. Hush! . . . What? Hath not the world just now become perfect? Round and ripe?

Thus spake Zarathustra—to himself.

20

Proust

LIKE the masterpieces of all great novelists Marcel Proust's *A la Recherche du temps perdu* is a whole world in itself, a world into which you can pass, in which you can dwell, in which you can continually be discovering new avenues, new vistas, new horizons.

This is true in a measure of every great novel but I think it is for many reasons especially true of *A la Recherche*. The book, with its shelf of volumes, covers not only the physical impressions and the mental development of its hero, but reduplicates its theme in the secondary *motif* of Swann, whose jealousy over Odette anticipates the hero's imprisonment of Albertine, and who enters the circle of the odious Mme. Verdurin—by far the most unpleasant and by far the most savagely handled person in the book—while the hero was still a child.

When one thinks of the work of James Joyce, our *other* famous modern, and considers what enormous erudition, philological experimentation, and symbolic architecture he labours under, one feels as if Proust's great shelf of volumes were created by the easiest method of all possible literary methods—the *rambling autobiographical essay*!

Having once "established" his characters, he seems only, without bothering about plot, to let them live and love and hate and die at the uninterfered-with pleasure of chance and fate; and this appears to make his job so easy that one almost begrudges him his success.

It must have been so easy to do, one tells oneself. And yet one would have to take a considerable slice—though not quite the whole!—of the *Comédie humaine*, wherein the same characters appear, to match the richness, thickness, solidity, and orbital independence of this Proustian world!

As we contemplate it lying here before us in all its plenitude, with the titles, so familiar to us now, of its various parts—but I can well recall how strange they looked to my eyes in one of those crowded Chicago streets, "off Michigan," when I was first introduced to them by my fellow-Celt Llewellyn Jones!—the merest glance at those gnomic inscriptions, *Swann's Way*, *The Guermantes Way*, and *A l'Ombre des jeunes filles en fleurs*, carries for us, at least for bookworms of my years, the same sort of enchanted escape from the flowing of time that the hero of the tale himself enjoyed, when he lingered for hours in his great-aunt's enclosed garden on the Rue de Saint-Esprit in Combray, unearthing the buried treasures of his favourite Bergotte.

And our escape from the importunity of time and the desecration of time is thickened out for us as we catch those magic syllables "Swann," or "Guermantes," or "*A l'Ombre*" by a rich, dim cloud of half-realized impressions, "borne aloft or sinking as the light wind lives or dies," that reach us not only from the scenes of Proust's great invention but also from the vague memories that the mere thought of Proust's evocations calls up out of the long-forgotten tracts of our own experience.

For the beauty of Proust's masterpiece is that while it hits off with such exquisite malice all the fine shades of middle-class snobbishness and upper-class arrogance, and discloses with such subtle sympathy all the humorous refinements of old family-retainers, its *real theme*, its inmost essence, has to do with the most evasive element in our secret personal life, namely with those obscure feelings of delicious ecstasy which are as hard to arrest or analyse in their swift passage as it is hard to explain why such small, slight, trivial, and casual chances are the cause of their rising up out of the depths.

These rare individual ecstasies are to Proust—or at least to that prophetic soul in Proust embodied in his hero— precisely what the same experiences were to Wordsworth, that is to say, authentic "intimations of immortality"; and it is impossible to think of any great novel that proves this daring proposition, and this very definite proposition, so effectively as Proust does. Neither Goethe in *Wilhelm Meister* nor Romain Rolland in *Jean Christophe* conveys to us such a clear-cut unmistakable "message" as to the nature of the human soul and its relation to the Eternal as Proust does in *A la Recherche du temps perdu*.

In other words while catching so vividly one after another the insect-flights, the plant-loves, the aquarium-gestures of human society's snobbishness and perversity, the book begins and ends with those "obstinate questionings," so congenital with the Hebrew spirit, as to the relation between the individual soul, incarnated in time, and *that* which lies beyond time.

Whatever we forget in the criss-cross interplay of these swirling crowds of delicately delineated figures, one recurrent *motif* it is impossible to get out of our heads, the effect upon the hero's mind, as it reaches him through his senses and as he struggles so intensely to catch its philosophic significance, of that memorable incident—so trivial and yet so world-deep—of the *petite madeleine* dipped in lime-flower tea—the phenomenon recurs once or twice again; but its culminating occurrence is at the end of the book, when the hero is middle-aged and the generation before him have become old men and old women, and he is on the point of entering the great reception-rooms of the final gathering of all the "dramatis personae" of the tale, where to our fairy-story satisfaction as well as to our metaphysical content the picture sinks away into its predestined perspective.

And soon mechanically [thus is the first occurrence of this revelation described], weary after a dull day with the prospect of a depressing morrow, I raised to my lips a spoonful of the tea in which I had soaked a morsel of the cake.

No sooner had the warm liquid, and the crumbs with it, touched my palate than a shudder ran through my whole body, and I stopped, intent on the extraordinary changes that were taking place. An exquisite pleasure had invaded my senses, but individual, detached, with no suggestion of its origin.

At once the vicissitudes of life had become indifferent to me, its disasters innocuous, its brevity illusory—this new sensation having had on me the effect, which love has of filling me with a precious essence; or rather this essence was not in me, it was myself. I had ceased now to feel mediocre, accidental, mortal.

The curious thing about these sensuous "intimations of immortality" in Proust is that *they come by chance* and that they are connected with irrelevant and perfectly trivial occasions. Here, as in other things, we note in our author a complete lack—as if he were colour-blind or had no ear for music—of that particular nerve in the human soul which is the cause of so much nobility of character as well as of so much sickening hypocrisy, and which we name by the ambiguous word "spirituality."

There is nothing "spiritual" in Proust; and this it is that gives such formidable authority to his aesthetic and philosophic generalizations. What indeed we have come to feel, and not without justice, is that an "intimation of immortality" based upon the effect on our soul of a *petite madeleine* dipped in lime-petal tea is of more actual and living weight than all the mental arguments of the Platonic Socrates!

The second dominant *motif* of a book that is surely the

most important work of fiction of our time is the gradual clarification and definition of the hero's first principles of art. These are also summed up in the final volume of *Le Temps retrouvé*, and they condense themselves into a convincing proof of the *subjectivity* of all great art as against the noisy and aggressive heresy, so tempting, so plausible, so obvious, that beauty, like truth, has an objective reality in the cosmos, before which the business of each artist is to reduce his personal imagination to a blank.

Thus we find this great work of Proust, as it takes its place beside all these other masterpieces of human genius, reaffirming the doctrine implicit in Homer and the Hebrew Prophets as well as in Rabelais and Shakespeare and Goethe that man's redemption lies in the character of the individual and not in mechanized efficiency.

What might be called the third *motif* of the work is the problem of erotic jealousy. To emphasize this particular theme Proust has recourse to the inspired device of projecting into the first place in the book two protagonists who hold much the same symbolic relation to each other as do Daedalus and Bloom in Joyce's *Ulysses*.

But Proust's young man has a more personal resemblance to his friend Swann than Daedalus ever had to Bloom; and it is wonderful to note—considering the complicated "streams" of so many different "consciousnesses," for which, as his tale moves forward, he has to dig channels and lead them like currents of various temperature and density round and about each other in the sub-aqueous world of his own mind—how free from any *real* obscurity Proust's art is.

It has many resemblances to the art of Henry James; but I think it can be said—certainly as far as individual paragraphs are concerned, and even in some cases, remembering *The Sacred Fount*, in the final disentangling—to be clearer than that great master's method!

Some of our modern geniuses make deliberate use of obscurity, at least of something that is obscure to ardent but not abnormally clever readers like myself, an obscurity that seems to utter a pontifical challenge—"Who are you to understand *me?*"—as if from the hanging folds of some dark magisterial tapestry to all who presume to enter so recondite a temple. And I do think there *is* a certain aesthetic value in obscurity *just for its own sake alone*, as there is a peculiar beauty in twilight; a beauty that satisfies a profound and mystical love of "abracadabra" in all our hearts, a beauty that at once rouses the imagination and troubles the reason. But at the same time—in spite of Spinoza's saying that the best things are difficult—I think that all the supreme literary works in the world—for we are talking of literature not metaphysics—are free from obscurity; for though obscurity is the cause of one of the most delicious of human feelings, intellectual superiority to others, it does undoubtedly interfere with the work's universal appeal.

I admit, however, that ever since the days of the old "mysteries" there has been an exciting *religious* titillation in thaumaturgical nebulosity, and this undoubtedly does have, as the god of the *orgia* hints in the *Bacchanals*, a definite aesthetic repercussion.

But there is absolutely nothing of this kind of thing in Proust. If he is difficult to read it is for just the opposite reason. It is because he throws a too exhausting searchlight upon too many riddles in too quick succession!

Proust's enormous work is in fact as artful and simple in its story-book complications and unravellings as *Tom Jones*. We soon discover if we presume to skip a page that we have lost some important clue; and as so rarely happens with even the finest novels there goes on here, side by side with the analysis of the characters *in statu quo*, a constant and often surprising development, sometimes a startling transformation, in the said characters.

Charles Swann is, as I have hinted, a sort of *alter ego* to the young hero, reproducing some of the latter's strongest emotions on a different and wider plane. Thus the "little phrase" from Vinteuil's sonata which becomes such a symbolic accompaniment to the elder man's passion for Odette, and which was composed by the unhappy musician as an outlet to his feelings about his daughter's Lesbianism, strikes a chord of tragic beauty which is destined to repeat itself in the hero's own alternations of frantic faith and desperate doubt over the same vice in Albertine.

A reader would have to have suffered from feverish possessiveness, and also to have been tormented by an insatiable suspicion as to the ubiquity of this second "City of the Plain," to enter with full sympathy into the torturing jealousies of Swann and the young Marcel. Love to Proust means frantic jealousy; and jealousy to Proust means an inquisitorial desire to know *everything* about the least butterfly-stirring of the "prisoner," her faintest gesture in the direction of any lure, whether innocent or guilty, that is not connected directly with ourselves!

So vibrant are these chords of jealousy throughout this book and so furiously, one might almost say from an Anglo-Celtic point of view so comically devoid of all impulses of magnanimity towards the objects of their desire, that one begins to sigh for that more indulgent, more generous, less analytical touch of—well! say of the sonnets of Shakespeare, a touch which can still be found in the poetry of as young a poet as our Dorsetshire Kenneth Hopkins:

> *Describe each patterned circumstance of love!—*
> *As well coerce and govern the grey rain,*
> *With easy arrogance, whose vapours move*
> *And quench the light from the uneasy grain,*

Whose golden gratitude to the kind sun
Fades in the dusk to unripe green again:
As well persuade the noon that night is come
Or bid the tide run out before his time.

And our mind turns, too, towards the devoted lovers in Hardy, and towards the self-restrained generosity, so heroic and long-enduring, of the unexacting amorists from the New World in Henry James.

Is it untrue to experience, is it false to nature, this estimate of what the old ballads call "true love" in Hardy and James?

But Proust's microscopic analysis of "each patterned circumstance of love" is only equalled by the devastating realism with which he traces, step by step, its pitiful disillusionment and final perishing; for Proustian love certainly *does* "alter when it alteration finds."

Here again, in this universal dissolution under the sliding away of the golden sands, one pauses to ask oneself whether time, even time itself, cannot sometimes be tricked?

But one thing is certain, the whole subject of Proust's great book is the battle of man's soul with what Hardy calls the "delving imps" of time.

Time is the antagonist of this book; and the timeless— revealed in art and revealed in these rare outbursts of the self that is eternal—is the protagonist. But this deeper theme in the book is half-concealed by the wavering consistence of the element that embodies it, just as the vital centre of a jelly-fish is surrounded by the floating substance of its transparent body.

And this gelatinous element that rises and falls with the fitful undulations of the tide of our life is the element of our secret sense of superiority to one another—in other words, the element of snobbishness.

Now in Proust's book this snobbishness is primarily

social, and only secondarily intellectual and aesthetic; whereas in the psychic chemistry of many impassioned readers of Proust the social variety of this universal ingredient plays a subordinate part, while its kindred emotions, such as cultural, moral, and even professional snobbishness, are revealed to the most cursory introspection. For it must be remembered that the most devoted lovers of *A la Recherche*, are not the sort of persons, whether they be men or women, to become *social climbers* in the sense in which the good Dr. Cottard and his simple lady can be counted in this category, or even to possess any very sensitive divining-rod in its baleful presence.

Doubtless most Proust-lovers *have* met in the course of their experience intriguing wretches like the appalling Madame Verdurin, the most repulsive figure in the book, and hypocritical fools like M. Legrandin; but these are extreme examples of snobbishness, and I believe our Proustian initiates would have to admit that in their own experience they have encountered many more types like the hero's grandmother, or the pure-minded Vinteuil, or that patient, unworldly gentleman, Saniette, than they have seen specimens of these glittering society-fish, whose shining tails and gleaming fins are always beating against the glass of the great Proustian aquarium!

But just as Walt Whitman is always "celebrating" the one type of person of all others least likely to read his poems, so we may be sure that few Mme. Verdurins or Legrandins among us will have the discomfort of recognizing themselves in Proust's pages, or, I suspect, few Orianes de Guermantes either!

But the truth is there are uncommonly few great writers, though there must have been many portrait-painters, who have had the privilege of living cheek-by-jowl with the beau monde as Proust did; and we may note that among the novelists who *have* described such circles, such as Thack-

eray, Disraeli, and Henry James, and some would add
Balzac and Tolstoy, there is nothing to approach the
microscopic analysis—at once aesthetic and scientific—of
Proust's investigations in these glass houses of his botanical
garden.

And if, as seems likely enough, these particular breeds of
human orchids are, as our revolutionaries would say,
"liquidated" out of existence, together with the particular
kind of snobbishness that their presence implies, we may
be perfectly sure, human nature being what it is, that some
other form of coveted "distinction," very likely a good deal
less harmless than that which made an ideal of Oriane's
receptions, will take its place, implying in *its* turn a new
form of our ancient vice and, let us hope, a new Proust, not
to moralize or sentimentalize over it *à la* Thackeray, not
to bewitch us and drug us with its charm in the manner
of Henry James, but to do what the author of *A la Recherche*
alone has done—date, collate, and isolate its flowerings,
from the pollen of its least pistil to the curve of its least
calyx!

Proust is surely right in his emphasis on the enormous
part played in our daily life—in England and America as
well as on the continent of Europe—by the estimation in
which we think we are held, or fear to be held, *by our
neighbours*.

It is, I think, this less active aspect of snobbishness which
is really universal; for this is shared by the least ambitious
among us, while the exhausting process of "social climb-
ing," entailing so many rebuffs and such heart-rending
frustrations, even though it *may* lead to a Guermantes salon
in the end, must be the lot of few. It is, however, as absurd
to quarrel with Proust—as he makes point after point as
to wherein consist the real degrees of social distinction—
on the ground of his being snobbish as it would be to quarrel

with a collector of butterflies on the ground of his carrying a butterfly-net.

And, after all, what we call "fashion," with all its subtle psychological and aesthetic implications, is something that must exist as long as our race exists, though the particular set of people at any given epoch favoured by being the ideal repository of this cult must always be changing.

It is perfectly right that this *fashion-phenomenon* should be of great interest to novelists, since so many human values, not always as superficial as cynics suppose, can be tracked down in these *mores* of sophisticated tribal custom.

Proust is always reverting in his own mind to certain famous social *memoirs* of the past, and he is careful to inform us that his own Mme. Villeparisis, Oriane de Guermantes' old-fashioned aunt, was engaged upon the compilation of *her* memoirs.

Over the most frivolous memoirs floated, according to him, the purest perfumes of history, and what those unearthed ashes of Urn-Burial, "cooled a long age in the deep-delvèd earth," were to Sir Thomas Browne, these tricky mementos of the paper-chase of time were to Proust.

Lovers of Walter Pater will remember those unequalled passages in which that great virtuoso analyses the work of Watteau. Well! the work of Proust was, if I may say so, the work of a *Watteau reversed*; for with a tragic intensity in frivolity he seeks to retrace what Lord Chesterfield would call *des graces* of the fleeting present, till they sink back and away into the immortal shadow-shapes of a mythological *temps retrouvé*.

His hero, for instance, is always catching, in the most fleeting expression of his Gilberte or his Albertine, those looks on a girl's face that revert to the legendary women of the past; and his *alter ego* Swann does the same with Odette. It is, in fact, the "eternal recurrence" of the imperishable secret of feminine beauty as it can be caught on the profile

of the most casually-met *grisette* that these Proustian lovers
are always seeking—

> *Like those Nicaéan barks of yore*
> *That gently o'er the perfumed sea*
> *The weary, way-worn wanderer bore*
> *To his own native shore;*
> *On desperate seas long wont to roam—*

Few Proust-lovers will disagree with me when I maintain
that as a painter of the Great World's dependents, or perhaps I should rather use the heraldic word and say "sup-
porters," he is unsurpassed, except—and with what a
difference of emphasis!—by our own Sir Walter Scott.

Proust's Françoise is indeed one of those characters whose
existence is a better excuse for the presence of "gentlefolk"
in the world than "gentlefolk" always offer for themselves;
and in regard to Françoise any upper-middle-class person in England, that is to say of the class in which Proust
places his hero's parents, will of necessity conjure up from
his own childhood some old servant—whether she be a
"Nanny" or otherwise—whose peculiarities are vividly
recalled by this unequalled old woman.

If there are certain scenes in Proust where we are reminded of Disraeli's novels, the moment Françoise comes
on the scene, we reach an atmosphere of such touching
subtleties of loyalty that Disraeli is forgotten, and we think
of the feudal retainers in Scott's books.

Proust's way of analysing all that St. Paul declares to be
"a shame so much as to speak of" strikes my mind as the
best possible way in which a writer *can* deal with these
things, unless of course, either for his own pleasure, or the
pleasure of temperaments akin to his own, he wants to be
provocative.

I would say myself that Proust is never provocative; but
since there seems to be no limit to what certain natures

can find disturbing to their peace of mind it is better not to be dogmatic about this.

The truth is that directly you touch any human sex-nerve, whether it be normal or abnormal, and both are in nature, you touch a nerve *that can only be understood from inside.*

Take the case of what we have come to call "sadism." Now there are obvious infinite varieties of this vicious emotion, all of which may be roughly defined as sexual excitement produced by cruelty.

The most harmless of these varieties of sadism is the pretence of cruelty in a sadist towards a masochist, when each of them is equally guilty of perverse excitement. Less harmless than this is the half-conscious sadism of audiences at cruel performances.

Much more serious is the sadistic pleasure of writers—a pleasure instantaneously recognized by persons of the same kidney—in inventing cruel scenes.

Now I think it may be laid down as an absolute psychological law that unless a particular sadistic impulse is a temptation to oneself, and the cause of sexual agitation to oneself, it is impossible to be convincing in describing it.

Now my own humble contribution just here to a critical analysis of the sadistic element in Proust is that he is totally unconvincing in his description of the wicked emotion enjoyed by M. Vinteuil's daughter, who, in the process of being made love to, encourages her friend to spit, or at least to talk of spitting on the portrait of her father which she has deliberately placed near them.

Now that this perverse, but inherently good girl, should derive sadistic pleasure from being caressed under the picture of the dead parent is quite credible to me; but this spitting in the face of the picture strikes me as totally incredible.

I do not mean that it is incredible for a heartless child to spit into the face of a dead parent's picture. I mean that the introduction of this spitting in M. Vinteuil's face into a scene where the inhumanity is purely sadistic and consists in being caressed in his presence is an irrelevance.

It is a brutality that has nothing to do with the sadistic nerve. You must remember that we have been especially told that the musician's daughter was not in any sense a bad, or a brutal, or a malicious, or even a spiteful girl.

In a word, while it is natural enough that she should get pleasure by being caressed before the photograph, the idea of spitting on it is unnatural. It was in fact a spiteful, not a sadistic action. It is as though Dostoievsky, in his "Confession of Stavrogin," had made the unhappy man admit that in the midst of his sadistic sensuality he had perpetrated some act of vulgar brutality, the crudity of which sprang from a callousness in his nature that had no connexion at all with his perverted feelings.

But if I find lapses in Proust's handling of "the most dangerous of human nerves," I am reduced to astonished awe at his perfect insight into the heart of a selfish aristocrat. We need never, I think, have known such persons ourselves to feel the delicious shock of absolute truth in what he reveals about them.

Psychological reality of this sort carries its own conviction; just as we need never have known a murderer or a murderer's accomplice to accept every Shakespearean revelation as to the feelings of Macbeth and Lady Macbeth.

And thus while to our astonishment it seems quite natural for the inherited good breeding of M. de Guermantes to leave his young visitor—who cannot at that epoch have been more than seventeen—for three-quarters of an hour to enjoy his picture-gallery in peace, while he keeps a large company of guests awaiting the signal to move into the dining-room, it seems also the pure essence of truth about this man that when he condescends to present himself in the Proust flat to inquire about the dying grand-mother he should be so absorbed in the immense honour he is doing them as to be totally oblivious of the human tragedy going on under his nose.

At moments like this—and let readers who upbraid Proust for his snobbishness ponder on this—the indelible "Indian ink" at the point of his sharp pen takes on a satiric bite worthy of Jane Austen.

> At this point my mother, who was waiting impatiently for some cylinders of oxygen which would help my grandmother to breathe more easily, came out herself to the hall where she little expected to find M. de Guermantes. I should have liked to conceal him, had that been possible. But convinced in his own mind that nothing was more essential, could be more gratifying to her or more indispensable to the maintenance of his reputation as a perfect gentleman he seized me vio-lently by the arm and although I defended myself as against an assault with repeated protestations of "Sir, Sir, Sir," dragged me across to Mamma, saying: "Will you do me the great honour of presenting me to your mother?"
>
> And it was so plain to him that the honour was hers that he could not help smiling at her even while he was composing a grave face. He apparently proposed to enter into conversa-tion, but my mother overwhelmed by her grief told me to come at once and did not reply to the speeches of M. de Guermantes—

A similar obtuseness in this perfect gentleman manifests itself when Charles Swann, a much closer intimate than our hero could ever hope to be, had the temerity to hint to Oriane de Guermantes, as she and the Duke were hurry-ing off to a party, that his, Swann's, days upon earth were numbered; but he might just as well have informed the lady's red shoes or the man's opera-hat of this irrelevant fact.

> "I don't know why I am telling you this; I have never said

a word to you before about my illness. But as you asked me, and as now I may die at any moment . . . But whatever I do, I mustn't make you late; you're dining out remember," he added, because he knew that for other people their own social obligations took precedence of the death of a friend, and could put himself in her place by dint of his instinctive politeness. But that of the Duchess enabled her also to perceive in a vague way that the dinner to which she was going must count for less to Swann than his own death. . . .

Mme. de Guermantes advanced resolutely towards the carriage and uttered a last farewell to Swann. . . . "I expect they gave you a dreadful fright, come to luncheon whatever day you like" (with Mme. de Guermantes things always resolved themselves into luncheons), "you will let me know your day and time," and, lifting her red skirt, she set her foot on the step. She was just getting into the carriage when, seeing this foot exposed, the Duke cried in a terrifying voice: "Oriane, what have you been thinking of, you wretch? You've kept on your black shoes! With a red dress! Go upstairs quick and . . . " "But, my dear," replied the Duchess gently, annoyed to see that Swann, who was leaving the house with me but had stood back to allow the carriage to pass out in front of us, could hear, "since we are late."

"No, no, we have plenty of time. It's only ten to; it won't take us ten minutes . . . and after all if we turn up at half-past eight they'ld have to wait for us, but you can't possibly go there in a red dress and black shoes. . . . "

The Duchess went up to her room.

"It's not unbecoming," said Swann. "I noticed the black shoes and they didn't offend me in the least. . . . "

"Good-bye, my children," said M. de Guermantes thrusting us gently from the door. "Get away before Oriane comes down again. . . . "

And so it was simply from good breeding and good fellowship that, after politely showing us out, he cried "from off stage" in a stentorian voice from the porch to Swann who was already in the courtyard: "You, now, don't let yourself

be taken in by doctors' nonsense, damn them. They're don-
keys. You're as strong as the Pont Neuf. You'll live to bury
us all!"

In regard to Proust's *method* of writing, his most remarkable device, or perhaps we should say discovery, is the
imaginative bringing together of ideas, or essences, or
images that in objective reality are scattered through many
various levels and dimensions, but can be fused together
by our power of feeling things, not in their isolation, like
instruments of torture in a museum, or like nectarines in
cotton-wool, but in their living, breathing, fluctuating environment, permeated by the airs and sounds and smells
about them, and by our own complicated feelings with
regard to them.

But the art of fusing together these scattered essences,
moral, emotional, psychological, sensual, and all treated,
for the whole process implies both sensibility and analysis,
with what might be called *aesthetic science*, is no easy achievement. It entails, if the style is to represent the dissolving
horizons into which the ripples of these psychic-sensuous
"events" vanish, a certain stretching out of sentences and
paragraphs, yes! and even of pages, to a length before
which all but inveterate Proustians are forced to cry,
"Hold, enough!"

The truth is there are two urges in this great writer; and
not all of us can sympathize equally with both. Thorough-
going Proustians, like thorough-going Wordsworthians, are
rare birds.

In one of these urges the scientific element predominates
—though the science is Proustian science—while in the
other the aesthetic element, which lies closer to the author's
private philosophy, leaps up to monopolize the field.

In certain illuminating passages we encounter a definite
and conscious clash between these two, though no doubt

it is a more *serious* clash to the young hero of the book than to his scientific creator.

For instance, after devoting the best part of an entire volume to the by no means inspiring chatter at a De Guermantes dinner-party, the author permits his young man to utter a heart-felt sigh of disappointment and to prop up his tottering illusion by a shaky hope that when these people are *by themselves* they are less fatuous.

> I barely listened to these stories, stories of the kind that M. de Norpois used to tell my father; they supplied no food for my favourite train of thought; and besides, even had they possessed the elements which they lacked, they would have had to be of a very exciting quality for my inner life to awaken during those hours in which I dwelt in my skin, my well-brushed hair, my starched shirt-front, in which, that is to say, I could feel nothing of what constituted for me the pleasure of life. . . . Was it really for the sake of dinners such as this that all these people dressed themselves up and refused to allow the penetration of middle-class women into their so exclusive drawing-rooms—for dinners such as this?

And if Proust permits his youthful hero to sigh like this over the inability of the fashionable world to supply grist for his mill, may we not ourselves be allowed to express a wish that in this huge mass of "herbarium" or "aquarium" investigations—they are his own comparisons—there had been a little more of the *madeleine motif*, a little more of those "ways" that would have interested Walter Pater more than Saint-Simon?

It is interesting in any case to note how in the vast canvas of *A la Recherche du temps perdu* the Proustian "science" often gives the Proustian "aesthetic" a little more than it can carry off. This is curious, considering his steady faith in subjective as against objective methods of art.

In the hands of Dorothy M. Richardson and in those of James Joyce the art of the novel makes use of what I believe

May Sinclair was the first to call the "stream of consciousness." Now strictly speaking, this is *not* the method of Proust; for while we are told what the hero thinks or what Swann thinks we are told this rather by the author than either by the "I" of the story or by Charles Swann.

In fact, Proust permits himself to do to the limit the very thing that is anathema to the artist-type of author; that is, to intersperse his fiction with what is not so much a "stream of consciousness" as a stream of Proustian commentaries upon consciousness!

Let us for a moment compare these "streams of consciousness" as we receive them from Dublin, London, and Paris. Let us listen to Joyce, to Dorothy Richardson, and to Marcel Proust; as each of them soliloquizes in these cities through the lips of their protagonists.

Let us begin with Joyce:

> Stephen closed his eyes to hear his boots crush crackling wrack and shells. You are walking through it howsomever. I am, a stride at a time. A very short space of time through very short times of space. Five, six: the *nacheinander*. Exactly: and that is the ineluctable modality of the audible. Open your eyes. No. Jesus! If I fell over a cliff that beetles o'er his base, fell through the *nebeneinander* ineluctably. I am getting on nicely in the dark. My ash sword hangs at my side. Tap with it: they do. My two feet in his boots are at the end of his legs, *nebeneinander*. Sounds solid: made by the mallet of *Los Demiurgos*.
>
> Am I walking into eternity along Sandymount strand? Crush, crack, crick, crick. Wild sea money. Dominic Deasy kens them a'.

> *Won't you come to Sandymount,*
> *Madeline the mare?*

Rhythm begins, you see. I hear. A catalectic tetrameter of iambs march ing. No, agallop: *deline the mare*.

Now whether we can follow or not the meaning of
nebeneinander, or can say what a "tetrameter of iambs" is,
or what is conveyed by the words "deline the mare," most
of us, less erudite readers, can I think catch in all this the
sad, bitter, satirical-scholastical, metaphysical-circus tone
of a modern Hamlet fooled to the top of his bent. But whatever we catch or whatever, by reason of our imperfect education, we fail to catch, here undoubtedly our Dubliner
passes completely into the person of Stephen; and it is
Stephen's "stream of consciousness," however obscure to
the unsophisticated, that we are being obsessed by and
absorbed in.

Now let us leave Dublin and Stephen's bitter Hamlet-
metaphysics, and plunge into a London "stream of consciousness," the impressions, namely, of Miriam Henderson,
Miss Richardson's heroine.

> Sitting exempted, sipping her milk while the others talked,
> lounging, in smooth gentle tones, three forces . . . curbed to
> gentleness . . . she felt the room about her change from gloom
> to a strange blurred brightness, as if she were seeing it through
> frosted glass. . . . A party of young men were getting up to
> go, stamping their feet and jostling each other as they shook
> themselves to rights, letting their jeering, jesting voices reach
> street level before they got to the door. They filed past, their
> faces, browless under evilly flattened cloth caps, or too large
> under horrible shallow bowlers set too far back, were all the
> same, set towards the street with the look, even while they
> jested, of empty finality; choiceless dead faces. They were
> not really gay. They had not been gay as they sat. Only
> defiantly noisy, collected together to banish, with their awful
> ritual of jeers and jests, the closed-in view that was always
> before their eyes; giving them, even while they were at their
> rowdiest, that look of lonely awareness of something that
> would never change. That was *why* they jeered? Why their
> voices were always defensive and defiant? What else could
> they do when they could alter nothing and never get away?

Now in this little segment of the "stream of consciousness," as it passes through the mind of Miss Richardson's Miriam, we may note that, as in the case of Joyce's priest-educated Stephen, the author identifies himself completely with the character's thoughts.

But although there are passages in Proust where the author, like a cloudy deity hovering over the head of the "I" of the story, *does* almost attain a similar identification, his more usual way is to let this secondary "I" bustle into the situation, and then to take the matter out of his hands, and to deliver, as it might be out of the air, an all-knowing generalization upon the situation in question, a generalization that might, or might not be, *over the "I" 's head*.

It is for this reason that the whole of *A la Recherche* comes to resemble one long subtle and serpentine *essay*, a soliloquy not of the little "I" of the plot but of the ubiquitous "I" of the inventor of the plot.

For instance, when the little "I" comes for the first time to Balbec, the big invisible "I" in the background allows its inexhaustible soliloquy, which is the salt tide of the whole book and which is now dealing with the magic of place-names and to what false conclusions they often lead us, to be interrupted, as if by a stream of fresh water coming suddenly to the surface, by the physical proceedings of the little "I," who, plunging into the town from the station, is horrified to find its precious church, with the name that had swallowed up everything in its Persian syllables and its suggestion of the mystery of the sea, situated close to a café with the word "Billiards," an omnibus-office, a tramway, and a bank.

And again, in connexion with the silly stories related by the clever, good-natured, but not over-sensitive Bloch, whose humour it is, sometimes in season but much more often out of season, to parody Homer, we find the little

"I"'s impulsive admiration severely corrected by the big
"I" seated in the clouds above his head, who—and the
passage has much significance in regard to Proust's whole
method—refers to the flatness and dulness of certain
aspects of Saint-Simon's historic gossip.

> Saint-Simon's portraits composed by himself (and very
> likely without his admiring them himself) are admirable,
> whereas what he cites as the charming wit of his clever friends
> is frankly dull where it has not become meaningless. He
> would have scorned to invent what he reports as so pointed
> or so coloured when said by Mme. Cornuel or Louis XIV.

And the ubiquitous *essayist*, whose vivid soliloquy upon
contemporary life contains all the characters of *A la
Recherche* like flies in amber, proceeds to add, in connexion
with his admired Saint-Simon, that "in the state of mind
in which we 'observe' we are a long way below the level
to which we rise when we create."

Alas! there is a good deal in these wonderful volumes
where Proust himself is "observing"; that is to say is making
his portraits say things more worthy of Mme. Cornuel and
Louis XIV than of their chronicler.

Dyed-in-the-grain Proustians will defend this on the
ground of "truth to nature"; but others among us know
too well their own weakness for this treacherous "truth to
nature" to be led astray by such talk.

No, it isn't on the ground of "truth to nature" that I
would defend as essential to his main design the duller
pages in Proust. I don't enjoy them. I have been guilty of
wishing they weren't there. Many passages would be far
pleasanter to read without them. But the book as a whole
would not be so great or so convincing a work.

The pleasures of reading are not confined to the immediate excitement of reading. There are also after-thoughts;
and when an exciting book leaves no after-thoughts we

know well what has been wrong. *The author has been afraid of being dull.*

But the grand secret of Proust, that sacred "message," which I as a good Lollard of literature so obstinately seek for, has to do with that *madeleine* dipped in tea and with the two or three other occasions of the same revelation, until the culminating one at the end rounds off the book?

And to what does this really amount? Surely to the conclusion, daring and startling as it is, that the mood in which we arrive at the kind of ecstasy described by Proust and without which, he admits, many people go through their entire life, is not a mood connected with what we call "beauty," nor with what we call "truth," nor with what we call "love." It is a mood, or let me say *a moment*, when we are made rapturously happy by what Wordsworth calls "the pleasure which there is in life itself."

Now "beauty" does not have this effect; and in any case "beauty" is something that a really lofty and magnanimous spirit finds it *must do without*; not because it isn't inspiring in itself but because its cult makes us unsympathetic and inhuman.

"Truth" again, by its inherent nature, cannot reconcile us to life. The more "truly" we face life, the more seriously, as our oft-quoted Russian says, we return our Creator His ticket.

Nor when you consider the nature of what the great ascetics and the great founders of religion have taught about spiritual love and the sacrifice of the self to other selves, can it be said that Proust's *madeleine* has anything in common with the "highest" of all historic ideals.

Nor has this *madeleine* feeling anything to do with the reason, or the intellect, or metaphysics, or science. *It is a sensation;* but a very rare and a very singular sensation.

Speaking with respectful nicety, it might justly be called the Miracle of the Mass in the natural world. It is something that *happens by chance*; and could occur to a selfish person, a criminal person, to a devilish person, just as easily as to a saint.

What therefore are we to think? Shall we say it seems exactly the sort of ironic *trick* that a Janus-faced First Cause might play upon its creatures? or shall we say that it goes deeper even than that? Shall we say that the *madeleine* sensation of immortality and of universal reconciliation is a momentary consciousness, levelling every mortal living thing to the same level and proving the wisdom of evangelical humility, of being one with the First Cause?

This is certainly what Miss Richardson's Miriam implies in the sweet blasphemy of her "profane" secret. "She thought of the autumn sunlight, held it in her mind, thought of it as existing in their minds and in the minds of everyone in London to-day; the hint of an answer, the moment one paused to look at it, to every problem in the world."

For the point is—according to these "streams of consciousness" in Paris and London, growing as they both do, Miss Richardson in her *Pilgrimage*, Proust in his *A la Recherche*, into an impersonal secular protest against our modern futility and our modern brutality—the point is that this *madeleine* feeling does go beyond death. It resembles the strange and unexpected emotion produced in the mind by the way the best short story ever written, "The Great-Coat," by Nikolai Gogol, "goes beyond death."

Philosophy can help us to bear up under life and even to be cheerful, but to be able to do more than that, death must be *brought into it*; and brought into it in some other way than as a ghastly Cimmerian epilogue or a "blackening-out" of the whole business.

Proust's *A la Recherche du temps perdu* is like a dance of the glittering mackerel of the sea, which, as they dart and gleam in the element of time, are unaware that all the while their dorsal fins are not in the sea at all, but in the timeless air above.

Thus if we regard Marcel Proust and James Joyce as the two most formidable writers of the present epoch, it is interesting to note that while the Irishman treats all his characters except Stephen as a titanic Gulliver of satire and parody who is enjoying a burlesque show of Lilliputians with a mixture of disgusted relish and relishing disgust, Proust keeps up his serpentine progress through the hearts, nerves, and brains of all his people with an intensity of analysis so exquisite, so fine-spun, so *levelling*, that instead of feeling the mixture of puzzled and respectful awe that we feel in the presence of Joyce and even of his *alter ego* Stephen, we are prepared to argue with him in our own minds, so real have his people become to us, and expostulate with him as to his treatment of them, as if all he had done was just to introduce us to them, and that formality once safely over we could take our own view of their proceedings and their fate.

But so frightening, so disturbing, so difficult, to an old-fashioned sentimental-romantic mind is the style of Joyce, that many of us feel as "rattled" in reading him as Panurge felt when the Pantagruelian ship happened "in Landloper's phrase to be temporising it," and they were hailed across the water by Harry Cottiral with a strange crew "*qui tenoient de la Quinte.*"

It is Proust's secondary hero, however, our good Swann, who in his fits and his furies about Odette is brought nearer to the entelechy of humanity's *bon espoir* than the bitterest throb of poor Stephen's "agenbite of the inwit" could make *him* come; for the "little phrase" of old Vinteuil's sonata, while it takes upon itself the infirmity of our mortality, brings to us something of its own pre-existent immortality.

Its destiny was linked, for the future, with that of the human soul . . . perhaps it is not-being that is our true state; but if so we feel that it must be that these phrases of music, these conceptions which exist in relation to our dream are nothing either. We shall perish, but we have for our hostages these divine capture who shall follow and share our fate. And death in their company is something less bitter, less inglorious, perhaps even less certain.

In this passage one cannot help catching, as if on the "wireless" of a special Proustian "announcement" for modern ears, our age's inherent scepticism, scepticism of every kind of wisdom that cannot be "checked-up" by chemical or electrical or mathematical support.

The feeling that the "little phrase" in its mysterious perfection comes down to us from the realm of Platonic Ideas, and that in what we call "beauty" we can get support for our hope of surviving death, does not weigh one quarter as an argument compared with the *madeleine*.

And why is that? Simply because at every single point this *madeleine* phenomenon can be verified by sensible evidence. Proust in fact *plays* with Plato; but in the matter of memory in relation to the timeless he is as serious and scrupulous as a literary Einstein.

Our present generation in the literature of Europe and America have no men of genius that even approach Proust and Joyce. I am old enough now to have lived through three great literary dictatorships. When I was at college Dostoievsky and Nietzsche were the rulers of our spirit. When I first visited America Anatole France and Thomas Hardy were our masters. But all the way through the decade that is now closing the more serious book-lovers among us, I mean those who are concerned with real original genius and not with mere skilful craftsmanship, have turned perforce, whether we go deeply into their work or not, to Proust and Joyce.

Joyce is the most difficult great writer we have ever had, and Proust is the most non-moral; so that those of us who have been caught by our less initiated friends chewing the sweet cud of snobbish satisfaction that we can enjoy what is "caviare" to others will do well to remember that neither a gnomic style throwing alluring and tantalizing stumbling-blocks before unerudite and unphilological minds, rousing snobbish satisfaction in some and infuriated facetiousness in others, nor long-winded struggles to find the secret of the eternal in our memory are absolutes in the art of writing.

Neither literature nor philosophy began with these discoveries; nor will they end with them. Hear the words of Rabelais upon this point:

> Pray, why is it that People say that Men are not such Sots now-a-days as they were in the days of Yore? Sot is an old word that signifies a Dunce, Dullard, Jolthead, Gull, Wittal, or Noddy, one without Guts in his Brains, whose cock loft is unfurnished, and in short a fool. Now would I know, whether you would have us understand by this same Saying, as indeed you logically may, that formerly Men were fools, and this generation has grown Wise?
>
> How many and what Dispositions made them Fools? How many and what Dispositions are waiting to make 'em Wise? . . . Pray, how came you to know that Men were formerly Fools? How did you find out that they are now Wise? Who the Devil made 'em Fools? Who a God's name made 'em Wise? . . . Why did the old Folly end now, and no later? Why did the Modern Wisdom begin now and no sooner? What were we the worse for the former Folly? What the better for the succeeding Wisdom?

Well, for myself, for these things are always personal, I can only say that I have been "the better" for Proust's "modern wisdom" in the sense that I have learnt from him a certain trick of taking the unpoetic details of daily life as if they were just as extraordinary, and just as significant of the "Méséglise way" of our soul's planetary sojourn, as any Venetian palaces or Alpine peaks.

But poetic or unpoetic, they are as they are because *we* are as *we* are.

She thought of the Autumn sunlight, held it in her mind, thought of it as existing in their minds and in the minds of everyone in London to-day; the hint of an answer, the moment one paused to look at it, to every problem in the world.

Conclusion

D O LOVERS of books overestimate the influence of literature upon the world? I fancy it depends upon what particular race and epoch you have in your mind. The Chinese must have been more influenced by books than by anything else except sex and starvation. Our old English Puritans must have been more influenced by the Bible than by all the heredity and environment you could name. Homer, whether read or recited, must have permeated the ancient Greek mind; so must the Koran, the Mohammedan, and as for the Jews, from the days when Moses flung down his tables of stone to the days when Heine mocked at omnipotence, books have moulded their thoughts, their character, their feelings, their whole attitude to life.

It is true that except for Homer these are all religious books; but when you put Shakespeare aside, who is, I suppose, the only thoroughly secular genius of all great writers, the problem of religion, that is to say, the problem of good and evil in connexion with the supernatural, enters into all the books by which men have lived, whether mystically as in *Faust*, humorously as in Rabelais, critically as in Lucretius, or with esoteric universality as in Walt Whitman.

In the stirring-up of social revolutions it must be allowed that books have had serious rivals in those terrible concretions we so smoothly and glibly call "economic forces."

508

And religion itself, quite apart from books, along with anti-religion apart from books, has played a formidable part in most bloody upheavals; for though both sides are always appealing to books, the real urge, for or against the religious instinct, comes much nearer to sexual emotion than to anything intellectual or aesthetic.

And the personal genius of individual revolutionaries and individual reactionaries is something else that is independent of books. Indeed, one sometimes feels as if the American, the French, the Russian, and certainly the Spanish revolution could be explained without introducing Rousseau or Tom Paine or even Marx or Bakunin.

I speak of the fact that these things happened at all; but, of course once started, books *are* brought upon the scene. Hunger and oppression, assisted by the magnetic hypnosis of eloquent leaders, would probably have produced *some* sort of violent change in all these cases; but it is still possible to doubt if they would have taken the particular form with which we are familiar had it not been for literary articulation.

And one can say the same of all the convulsions and reactions, the stiffenings and the weakenings, the new lives and the incredible conversions, that occur in individual human souls.

Our personal character—in its impact with chance and circumstance—is no doubt our fate; but I fancy there are many among us who if they were brought to the confessional would be compelled to admit that the deciding influence in the crises of this fate was the effect of certain books.

And this leads to another question. Is it in our youth or in our maturity that books affect us the more? Some would say at once that as year follows year in our normal lives and we continue in pain and disillusion and weariness and disgust to harden our hearts, we grow less and less responsive to books and more and more cynical as to the effect of books upon society.

But I confess I am myself inclined to take a different view. It is true that youth of both sexes is always ready—as its elders know to their cost—to appeal, with more or less passion and prejudice, to the authority of the written word; and it is true that in its idealism and its arrogance youth tends to repeat what it has picked up from books rather than, as its elders are never tired of reminding it, what it has "thought out" for itself. I suspect, moreover, that it rarely fails to present itself to youth under these strictures, that what its elders call their "experience" and their "practical commonsense" is in reality nothing but a narrow and unenlightened selfishness, due to anything rather than a rich and varied response to a fuller life, due very often to mere frustration and the drying-up of the sacred fount.

All this may be perfectly true, and yet I would be tempted to retort that the argument about selfishness is neither here nor there, for every pleasure can be "selfish" and it is an open question whether to be "taken out of oneself" by the movies or the radio is the nobler pastime than to "find yourself" in a powerful novel, or to bank yourself up, with all your whims and caprices, in some philosophical work that suits your taste and can buttress you against the catapults of chance.

I certainly think that youth is more addicted than maturity to depend on the passing fashion in its reading, and much more inclined, in its craving for topical subjects, to dodge the *effort of detachment* which is necessary if we are to enjoy, deliberately and quietly, any of the great books of the past. This has been a book about the works that have already received the verdict of posterity; and the fact remains that such works must be judged rather by their power over the lives of individuals than by their power to produce social upheavals.

We all have to live; we all have to snatch at *some* margin of pleasure as we scramble through life; and while there are plenty of influences, within us and without us, that determine our political and economic convictions, there are only a limited number of books that can permanently increase our happiness, deepen our power of endurance, and touch the whole spectacle with a magic that not only heightens the larger outlines but makes it possible to get extraordinary satisfaction out of all manner of little primitive and elementary things.

But there it is! We cannot *like* to the same degree all the books that have received the "imprimatur" of the generations; and indeed we are perfectly justified in picking and choosing as we go along.

But there is, I think, a natural comprehensiveness of taste in ordinary intelligent readers that ought to be deliberately cultivated as we get older, so that we should not miss, by reason of a little superficial laziness or some trifling and accidental prejudice, any book that might really change our whole life, lifting some unspeakable mental load off our brains or nerves or consciences, and giving us deep draughts of the water of life from one of its original fountain-heads.

The books I have tried to appreciate in this volume are certainly very different from one another; but I have offered them to my readers as the ones from which in my own life I have got the most lasting satisfaction. Had space permitted I would have added Walter Scott and Hugo—the latter in translation—and Sir Thomas Browne and Bunyan to this brief list, and I would probably have added the poet Virgil too and Walter Pater; but undoubtedly for the actual struggle of day-by-day life I have got more out of the books already included than out of any of these others, and the point I want to make now at the end has to do with the possibility of using in our daily life *and with equal thoroughness* such very different writings as Homer's *Odyssey* and St. Luke's Gospel.

How well I know the peculiar aggravation that my particular way of treating these terrific works will excite in certain minds! But a critic with any spirit at all is bound to evoke contempt and distaste in temperaments antipathetic to his own.

I expect the truth is there's a sort of *odium literarum* that exactly corresponds to the *odium theologicum*; for the teasing, tickling, itching irritation which one type of book-lover feels when he comes in contact with another type is much more acute, I fancy, than what either of us feels towards a person insensitive to the whole business. I could describe eloquently, and in both Rabelaisian and Pauline terms, my own particular antithesis among bookworms; and no doubt he could, and probably will, describe me, in a style drawn partly from the airier manner of So-and-So, my *bête noire* among geniuses, and partly from the obscurer manner of So-and-So my *bête noire* among critics; but I think what really annoys him is that any simple and unscholarly heretic should take a gnomic and oracular tone in place of trying to be ingratiating, whimsical, and entertaining. My seriousness must annoy this type of authority exactly as the peculiar seriousness of an old-fashioned Nonconformist would annoy a disillusioned and witty prelate. It affects him as if a guest at his table should not only commit the impropriety of smoking a cigarette with his port, but of referring in passionate earnestness to the blood of Jesus. He smells the rhetoric of an extension lecturer, "throwing his weight about" at a party of college Fellows.

Well! It can't be helped. I am writing for book-lovers of my own kidney, and what we Lollards of literature want is the direct application of our scriptures to the smallest detail of our domestic lives. We want, as Walt Whitman says, to decoy the Muse to our hearth, till we get her installed "amid the kitchen-ware."

Why shouldn't the most unathletic of men enjoy his

emergence from sleep and his morning ablution in the very spirit of the sedate Telemachus in the golden palace of the fair-haired Menelaus?

Why shouldn't our first thought be to worship the four elements, even if all we see of them be a patch of blue, a smoke-blackened common, a wind-blown water-butt, and a smoking fire?

And because we have allowed ourselves such high and heathen prerogatives, is that any reason why, when we encounter our spiteful or overloving relatives, we shouldn't practise on them the supernatural malice of St. Paul, and even something of his abysmal and treacherous charity?

And who, I ask you, will be able to protest—for who indeed will know anything about it?—if when you arrive at the scene of your diurnal labour you allow yourself the abandoned and spiritually sexual pleasure of *feeling yourself*, to the most extreme and shameless limit, *into* the jumpy nerves of your companions, both masculine and feminine; drinking in their unspoken confessions—and all in the deepest secret—and sharing their suppressed reactions to one another?

And who is to prevent you, as you pursue your abstracted path homeward, from debouching a trifle out of the rush of the traffic, and from sending Dostoievsky and his psychological mole-runs "to the Devil," while you share, this time, the patient endurance of a certain familar thorn-stump by the way-side, or of some seaweed-covered post by the water, or catch from the long perspective of a remote white road crossing an unknown hill-top a sudden intimation of immortal race-memories that lie dormant within us all?

And who again is to discover, behind your cautious and propitiatory greetings, as you enter a public house or plunge into a circle of broad-mouthed cronies, whence it is that you draw your unfastidious appreciations, your immunity to midden-smells, your toleration of the most monstrous sex-lapses, and your gift for catching the huge and royal unction—as if of pantheistic giants—of some profane group of poor jolt-headed loblollies and pitiable scrubs?

Nor, when night descends on your dwelling and your obstreperous family are safe in bed, will any one be the wiser if, as you rub your shins before the red coals and say to yourself, "So much for *this* day!" and "Sufficient for to-morrow be the worries thereof!" you let "the measureless float" of time's river bring a more muted and more mystic mood; a mood in which as the night deepens about you you feel the released and Lethe-purged souls of all the sleepers in your quarter of the globe flowing into the great sea of escape in which the chemistry of the darkness antici-pates the chemistry of death and the invigoration of death.

Your family will not know, and your neighbours will not know, when the lively dust of to-morrow's "rich-running" life glitters once more in the sun, what it was that you said to the darkness and said to death as those coals faded.

I too pass from the night,
I stay a while away O night, but I return to you again and love you.
Why should I be afraid to trust myself to you?
I love the rich-running day but I do not desert her in whom I lay
*   so long,*
I know not how I came of you and I know not where I go with
*   you but I know I came well and shall go well.*

Different as human temperaments are, I cannot help thinking that there are many people, who if they made a definite vow, as Goethe did, to read a passage every day out of some old great book that suits their nature—and I can only pray, that your choice, reader, may prove even more effective for your purpose than Homer and St. Paul and Rabelais have proved for mine—would soon begin to tap an unfathomable reservoir of strength and endurance. It strikes me as being the one essential thing in our reading to be absolutely independent of the fashion of the hour, both at its cleverest and at its stupidest.

And we must be good Lollards and Anabaptists of literature, shameless Nonconformists, content in our pursuit of salvation to appear naïve and solemn and innocent and priggish, devoid of all sense of proportion, devoid, if you like, even of what you call a sense of humour. We must, in fact, be content to take as guides to our real, actual, rough-and-tumble existence, many curious ancient works that our clever young writers "have no use for" and that our witty scholars regard as recondite "matters of breviary," not in any way conceivable as "human nature's daily food."

Oh! how strongly I am persuaded that in our choice of books we should be both eclectic and pragmatic; humble, as Keats says, before the "eternal spirit" that inspires them all, but bold and unscrupulous in giving their most sacred and exclusive eloquence a shrewd twist to suit our present-day hand-to-mouth occasions!

Passing into the souls of those that feed upon them, books are likely enough to outlive all other products of time. Sharing the immortality of their readers—if Sir Thomas Browne, the greatest of all our stylists, is justified in the orchestral conclusion to his "Hydriotaphia"—they will survive the maggots of the earthliest corruptions as well as the "funeral blazes" of the grandest cremations.

To subsist in lasting monuments, to live in their productions, to exist in their names and predicament of chimeras, was large satisfaction unto old expectations and made one part of their Elysiums. But all this is nothing in the metaphysics of true belief. To live indeed, is to be again ourselves, which being not only a hope, but an evidence in noble believers, 'tis all one to lie in St. Innocent's churchyard as in the sands of Egypt. Ready to be anything, in the ecstacy of being ever, and as content with six foot as with the *moles* of Adrianus.

Such high assurances may be vain, vain for all Pantagruel's mighty words and the certainties of Walt Whitman, but, even if they are, those who steer their path through life by the gleam of such majestic "lanterns" will have had many intimations before they perish of what in the depths of being, remains imperishable, though this be neither they themselves as individual persons, nor the books they have loved as individual books.

For it may well be that what gives us the deepest happiness we know is merely to touch, though we ourselves and the books that inspire us must sink into oblivion, that level, that dimension, that plane of existence, from which proceeds the inexplicable imperative to follow goodness and mercy in a world built upon a different plan.

Index